SKB
LIBRARY
St Helens
College
Library

109044

KU-537-385

Networking:
A Beginner's Guide

Third Edition

Bruce A. Hallberg

McGraw-Hill/Osborne

New York   Chicago   San Francisco
Lisbon   London   Madrid   Mexico City
Milan   New Delhi   San Juan
Seoul   Singapore   Sydney   Toronto

The **McGraw·Hill** *Companies*

McGraw-Hill/Osborne
2600 Tenth Street
Berkeley, California 94710
U.S.A.

To arrange bulk purchase discounts for sales promotions, premiums, or fund-raisers, please contact **McGraw-Hill**/Osborne at the above address. For information on translations or book distributors outside the U.S.A., please see the International Contact Information page immediately following the index of this book.

Networking: A Beginner's Guide, Third Edition

Copyright © 2003 by The McGraw-Hill Companies. All rights reserved. Printed in the United States of America. Except as permitted under the Copyright Act of 1976, no part of this publication may be reproduced or distributed in any form or by any means, or stored in a database or retrieval system, without the prior written permission of publisher, with the exception that the program listings may be entered, stored, and executed in a computer system, but they may not be reproduced for publication.

1234567890 FGR FGR 0198765432

ISBN 0-07-222563-7

ST. HELENS
COLLEGE

004.6
HAL

109044

NOV 2003

LIBRARY

Publisher   Brandon A. Nordin
Vice President & Associate Publisher   Scott Rogers
Acquisitions Editor   Francis Kelly
Project Editor   LeeAnn Pickrell
Acquisitions Coordinator   Martin Przybyla
Technical Editor   Tony Ryan
Copy Editor   Laura Ryan
Proofreader   Susie Elkind
Indexer   Rebecca Plunkett
Computer Designers   Tabitha M. Cagan, Tara A. Davis
Illustrators   Melinda Moore Lytle, Michael Mueller, Lyssa Wald
Series Design   Jean Butterfield
Cover Series Design   Sarah F. Hinks

This book was composed with Corel VENTURA™ Publisher.

Information has been obtained by **McGraw-Hill**/Osborne from sources believed to be reliable. However, because of the possibility of human or mechanical error by our sources, **McGraw-Hill**/Osborne, or others, **McGraw-Hill**/Osborne does not guarantee the accuracy, adequacy, or completeness of any information and is not responsible for any errors or omissions or the results obtained from the use of such information.

*For my lovely wife, Christy, who enriches
my life every day in more ways than I can count.*

About the Author

Bruce Hallberg has consulted on many network system and software implementations for Fortune 1000 companies and presently works as an IT director in the biopharmaceutical industry. He is the author of more than 20 computer books on Windows NT, NetWare, Exchange Server, and other networking and computer technologies.

Contents

Acknowledgments

Francis "Franny" Kelly reprised his role as the acquisitions editor for this third edition of *Networking: A Beginner's Guide,* and was a joy to work with. Franny kept me on schedule, but was also very understanding and kind in relaxing the schedule somewhat because of some minor surgery I needed during the writing of the third edition. His concern and generosity allowed me to get through that period with substantially less stress than I otherwise would have felt. Thanks, Franny!

Franny was assisted by Martin Przybyla, who coordinated the process of moving the various modules through to all of the different people who needed to work on them, and always kept track of what was where.

LeeAnn Pickrell was the chief project editor on this third edition. Apparently, I didn't do a good enough job of scaring her away after the second edition, for which she performed the same role. LeeAnn, aside from making sure that all of the chapters came together in a high-quality fashion, also did a yeoman's job in dealing with my impression of a *prima donna* author, which I have to admit appeared a couple of times during the project. LeeAnn's tops in my book (or any book!).

Jenn Tust also helped in doing the project editing for the third edition. I haven't worked with Jenn before, but after seeing her competent and adroit work, I hope I again have the opportunity to do so. Thank you, Jenn!

Laura Ryan did most of the copy editing on the third edition, and also jumped in and helped develop some of the mastery check questions in various parts of the book. Laura was a very consistent copy editor, and one with a very nice touch.

Tony Ryan (no relation to Laura) was the technical editor on the third edition, and was extremely helpful in making sure that the book is as accurate as possible, and also in suggesting various topics or additions throughout the text. The book is a much better book because of Tony's input and expertise.

Finally, I would be seriously remiss if I failed to thank my family for putting up with my being unavailable for the better part of three months. Most particularly, I would like to thank my wife, Christy. Her support truly made my work on the book possible.

Introduction

I've run into many people over the years who have gained good—even impressive—working knowledge of PCs, their operating systems, applications, and common problems and solutions. Many of these people are wizards with desktop computers. Quite a few of them have been unable to make the transition into working with networks, however, and they have had trouble gaining the requisite knowledge to conceptualize, understand, install, administer, and troubleshoot networks. In many cases, this inability limits their career growth because most companies believe networking experience is fundamental to holding higher-level MIS positions. And, in fact, networking experience *is* very important.

Certainly, networks can be complicated beasts to learn about. To add to the difficulty, most companies aren't willing to let people unskilled with networks experiment and learn about them using the company's production network! This leaves the networking beginner in the difficult position of having to learn about networks by:

- Reading an endless number of books and articles

- Attending classes

- Building small experimental networks at home, using cobbled-together and/or borrowed parts and software

This book is designed for people who understand computers and the rudiments of computer science, but who want to begin an education about networks and networking. I assume you understand and are comfortable with the following topics:

- How bits and bytes work.

- The notion of binary, octal, decimal, and hexadecimal notation.

- How basic PC hardware works, and how to install and replace PC peripheral components. You should know what IRQs, DMAs, and memory addresses are.

- Two or three desktop operating systems in detail, such as Windows 9x, Macintosh, OS/2, Windows NT, and maybe even DOS.

- Detailed knowledge of a wide variety of application software.

The purpose of this book is both to educate and familiarize. The first part of the book discusses basic networking technology and hardware. Its purpose is to help you understand the basic components of networking, so you can build a conceptual framework into which you can fit knowledge that is more detailed in your chosen area of expertise. The second part of the book is concerned with familiarizing you with three important network operating systems: Windows 2000, Windows .NET Server, and Linux. In the second part, you learn the basics of setting up and administering these network operating systems and about additional networking services available for Windows 2000.

This book is meant to be a springboard from which you can start pursuing more detailed knowledge in the areas that interest you. Following are some ideas about areas that you may wish to continue exploring, depending on your career goals:

- **Small-to-medium network administrator**   If you plan on building and administering networks with 200 or fewer users, you should extend your knowledge by studying the network operating systems you intend to use, server hardware, client PC administration, and network management. You may find more detailed knowledge of network hardware, like routers, bridges, gateways, switches, and the like useful, but these may not be an important focus for you.

- **Large network administrator**   If you plan on working with networks with more than 200 users, then you need to pursue detailed knowledge about TCP/IP addressing and routing, and network hardware, including routers, bridges, gateways, switches, and firewalls. Also, in large networks, administrators tend to specialize in certain areas, so you should consider several areas of particular specialization, such as e-mail servers like Lotus Notes or Microsoft Exchange, or database servers like Oracle or SQL Server.

- **Internet administrator**   Many people these days are pursuing specialization in Internet-based technologies. Depending on what area you want to work in, you should learn more about web and FTP servers, HTTP and other application-level Internet protocols, CGI and other web scripting technologies, HTML design, and SMTP mail connections. You may also want to become an expert in TCP/IP and all its related protocols, addressing rules, and routing techniques.

TIP

If you're working toward getting a job in the field of networking, find job postings on the Internet and carefully study the job requirements. This can be a useful technique to direct your studies appropriately. When you do this, you will notice that for their most important jobs most employers ask for people who are certified by Microsoft, Cisco, Novell, or other companies. You should seriously consider pursuing an appropriate certification. While certifications can never replace experience, they are one way that a person can demonstrate a needed level of knowledge and expertise in a particular area, and this difference may be key in getting the best possible job offers, and in being able to gain more experience. Often, an appropriate certification can be worth several years experience in terms of compensation and job responsibilities, so it's an investment in yourself that will usually pay for itself over a fairly short period of time.

Part I

Networking Ins and Outs

Module 1

The Business
of Networking

3

This book is a soup-to-nuts beginner's guide to networking. Before delving into the bits and bytes of networking, which are covered in the rest of the book, you should start by understanding the whys and wherefores of networking. This module discusses networking from a business perspective. You'll learn about the benefits that networking brings a company and the different types of networking jobs available. You'll also discover how networks are supported from the business perspective, and how you can begin a career in networking.

CRITICAL SKILL

· 1.1 Investigate the Corporate Perspective Regarding Networking

To be truly effective in the field of networking, you need to start by understanding networking from the corporate perspective. Why are networks important to companies? What do they accomplish for the company? How can networking professionals more clearly match the needs of the company with the networks that they build and maintain? It's important to realize that there are no single correct answers to these questions. Every company will have different needs and expectations with regard to their network. What is important is that you learn the relevant questions to ask about networking for your company, and arrive at the best possible answers to these questions for your particular company. Doing so will ensure that the company's network best meets its needs.

What Does the Company Need?

There are many possible reasons that a company might need or benefit from a network. In order to understand your particular company, you should start by exploring the following questions. You might need to ask a variety of different people in the company their perspective on these questions. Some of the officials whom you might need to interview include the chief executive officer or owner, the chief financial officer, and the heads of the various key departments within the company, such as manufacturing, sales and marketing, accounting, purchasing and materials, retail operations, and so forth. The range of officials that you interview will depend on the type of business in which the company is engaged.

It's important that you first start by understanding the business and the business-oriented perspectives of these different individuals. Consider the following questions for each of these key areas:

- What is their function for the company?

- How do their objectives tie into the companywide objectives?

- What are the key goals for their function in the coming year? How about in the coming five years?

● What do they see as the chief challenges to overcome in achieving their objectives?

● What sorts of automation do they think might help them accomplish their objectives?

● How is the work in their area accomplished? For instance, do most of the employees do mechanical work, like on a production line, or are most so-called "knowledge workers" who generate documents, analyze information, and so forth?

Your objective in asking these questions, and others that might occur to you, is to get a good understanding of each functional area: what it does and how it does it, as well as what it wants to be able to do in the future. With those understandings in hand, you can then start to analyze the impact that the network—or improvements to the existing network—might have in those various areas.

Beginning from a business perspective is absolutely essential. Networks are not built and improved "just because." Instead, any particular network or network upgrade needs to be driven by the needs of the business. Justifications for networks or improvements to existing networks should clearly show how they are necessary to the proper functioning of the business, or how they will play an important role in the company achieving its objectives, consistent with the cost and effort involved.

After getting a good understanding of the company, its objectives, and how it accomplishes its work, you can then analyze different ideas that you might have for the network, and how those ideas will benefit some or all parts of the business. In doing so, you need to consider at least the following areas:

● Are there any areas in which the lack of a network, or some failing of the existing network, is inhibiting the company from realizing its goals or accomplishing its work? For example, if an existing network is undersized and this causes people to waste too much time on routine tasks (such as saving or sending files, or compiling programs), what improvements might address those shortcomings?

● Are there capabilities that you could add to the network that would provide benefits to the business? For example, if many people in the company are constantly sending faxes (for instance, salespeople sending quotations to customers), would adding a network-based fax system produce significant productivity benefits? What about other network-based applications? (Module 3 lists some common network features that you might want to review to help in answering this question.)

● What other automation plans exist that will require the support of the network? For example, say you're the network administrator in a company. What new applications or features will be added to the network that you need to support? Is the company planning on installing some kind of video-conferencing system, for instance? If so, do you know what changes you will need to make to the network to support the system?

● What needs to be done to the network simply to maintain it? In most companies, file space requirements grow rapidly, even if the business itself isn't expanding. How much additional storage space does the network need to keep going forward? How many additional servers and what other things are going to be needed to keep the network working smoothly?

Obviously a list such as the preceding one can't be exhaustive. The important point is that you need to approach the job of networking first from the perspective of the company and its needs. Within that framework, use your creativity, knowledge, experience, and acumen to propose and execute a plan for the network. The remainder of this book discusses the information you need to start learning about this important part of any company's infrastructure.

CRITICAL SKILL

1.2 Explore Networking Jobs

If you're planning on entering the field of networking (and if you're reading this book, you presumably are), it's important to have some understanding of the various networking jobs that you're likely to encounter and what they typically require. Of course, actual job requirements will vary widely between different companies and for different established networks. Also, different companies might have different entry-level opportunities through which you can enter a networking career. That said, the following descriptions are broad overviews of some key jobs.

Network Administrator

Network administrators are responsible for the operations of a network or, in larger companies, of key parts of the network. In a smaller company that has only one network administrator, duties include the following:

● Creating, maintaining, and removing users

● Ensuring that necessary backups are made on a regular basis

● Managing the "keys" to the network, such as the administrative accounts and their passwords

● Adding new networking equipment, such as servers, routers, hubs, and switches, and managing that equipment

● Monitoring the network, its hardware, and its software for potential problems and for utilization levels for planning network upgrades

● Troubleshooting network problems (usually quickly!)

Network administrators might also be called system administrators, LAN administrators, and other variations on that theme.

Typically, you should have several years' experience performing network-related duties with a similar network for this job. Certifications such as the Microsoft Certified Systems Engineer (MCSE) for Windows NT/2000 networks or Novell's Certified NetWare Engineer (CNE) for NetWare networks can reduce the amount of experience that an employer will require. Employers usually consider these certifications important, because they clearly establish that a candidate meets minimum requirements for the networking system in question.

Network Engineer

Network engineers are more deeply involved in the bits and bytes of a network. They typically hold a degree in electrical engineering, and are expected to be expert in the network operating systems with which they work, and especially expert in the network's key hardware, such as its hubs, routers, switches, and so forth. Network engineers are also usually the troubleshooters of last resort, who are brought in to diagnose and fix the most vexing problems that surpass the ability of the network administrator to resolve.

Aside from usually holding a degree in electrical engineering, network engineers typically have at least five years' experience running and troubleshooting complex networks. Also, network engineers typically carry certifications from networking equipment companies, such as Cisco's well-regarded certification program.

Network Architect/Designer

Network architects (sometimes also called network designers) usually work for companies that sell and support networks or for large companies that have large networks that are constantly changing and expanding. Network architects design networks, essentially. They need to combine important qualities to be successful. They need to understand the business needs that the network needs to meet, and they need to understand thoroughly all of the networking products available, as well as how those products interact. Network architects are also important when growing a sophisticated network and helping to ensure that new additions to the network don't cause problems elsewhere in the network.

Other Network-Related Jobs

There are a wide variety of other network-related jobs, including some that aren't directly related to the network, such as the job of database administrator. Others include e-mail administrator, webmaster, web designer, network support technician, and others. In fact, a dizzying number of different jobs are available in the networking field.

If you've chosen to enter the field of networking, it would make sense to spend time browsing job ads for different types of networking jobs and to get a sense of what these different types of jobs require. Once you find one that reflects your interests, you can then analyze what additional skills, classes, or certifications you might need to enter one of those jobs. There are many opportunities. The important thing is to get started and pursue your objectives.

Module Summary

Many people I've met who work in some area of Information Technology, such as networking, don't consider the business reasons for the network when they go about their day-to-day jobs, or when they propose improvements to the network. This certainly isn't limited to the field of networking; many people who work in all areas of a company sometimes forget that the reason their function exists is to support the objectives of the company in which they work. The most successful employees of any company keep firmly in mind why they do what they do, before they consider how best to do it. Some of the suggestions in this module should help you to approach managing and improving a network successfully, by keeping in mind the benefits the network brings to the company. Once you know what the company needs, you can then propose the best solutions to problems that arise, or improvements that need to be made.

This module also discussed several broad areas you might consider pursuing in the field of networking, should you decide to do so. Demand for trained, capable networking people is extremely high, salaries are top-notch, and people working in the networking field have jobs that are—more than most—fun, stimulating, and rewarding in many ways.

The next module starts exploring the technical details of networking by briefly discussing some basic computer science concepts that you need to understand. If you already know about different numbering systems and about how data rates are measured, you can probably skip the next module and move on to the networking topics that follow, although be warned that you need a strong grasp of how binary numbers work to understand some of the discussion surrounding network protocols in Module 7.

Module 2

Laying the Foundation

You don't need to have a Ph.D. in computer science to be an effective networking person, but you do need to understand some rudiments of the subject. This module discusses basic computer terminology and knowledge that you should possess to make the information in the rest of the book more useful and understandable.

If you've been working with computers for a while, and especially if you have training or experience as a computer programmer, you might not need to read this module in detail. However, it is a good idea to at least skim it unless you are certain that you already understand these subjects thoroughly.

**CRITICAL SKILL
2.1**

Explore Numbering Systems: Bits, Nibbles, and Bytes

Most people know that computers, at their most fundamental level, work entirely using only 1's and 0's for numbers. Each one of these numbers (whether it be a 0 or 1) is called a *bit*, which is short for *binary digit*. String eight bits together and you have a byte, string about 1,000 bits together and you have a *kilobit*, or you can string about 1,000 bytes together for a *kilobyte*. (A rarely used unit is composed of four bits strung together and is called a *nibble*. Remember this for when you play *Jeopardy!*).

Understanding Binary Numbers

Before you learn about binary numbers, it's useful first to recall a few things about the numbering system that people use on a daily basis, called the *decimal numbering system* or, alternatively, the *base-10 numbering system*. The decimal numbering system is built using ten different symbols, each of which represents a quantity from zero to nine. Therefore, ten possible digits can be used, 0 through 9 (thus the base-10 numbering system gets its name from the fact that only ten digits are possible in the system).

An important part of any numbering system is the use of *positions* in which the numerical symbols can be placed. Each position confers a different quantity to the number being represented in that position. Therefore, the number 10 in the decimal system represents the quantity ten. There is a 1 in the *tens position* and a 0 in the *ones position*. This can also be represented as $(1\times10) + (0\times1)$. Or, consider the number 541. This number uses the *hundreds position* as well as the tens and ones positions. It can be represented as $(5\times100) + (4\times10) + (1\times1)$. Or, in English, you could state this number as five hundred plus forty plus one.

Every written number has a *least-significant digit* and a *most-significant digit*. The least significant digit is the one farthest to the right, while the most significant digit is the one farthest to the left. For binary numbers, people also talk about the least- and most-significant bits, but they amount to the same things.

So far, this section has simply reviewed basic number knowledge that you learned in grade school. What grade school didn't cover is the fact that basing a numbering system on ten is completely arbitrary; there's no mathematical reason to favor a base-10 system over any other. You can create numbering systems for any base you like. You can have a base-3 numbering system, a base-11 numbering system, or whatever else you want or need to create. Humans have come to favor the base-10 system, probably because we have ten fingers and thus tend to think in tens. Computers, on the other hand, have only two digits with which they can work, 1 and 0, so they need to use a different numbering system. The natural numbering system for a computer to use would therefore be the base-2 numbering system, and, in fact, that's what they do use. This system is called the *binary numbering system*. Computers use only 1's and 0's at their most basic level because they understand only two states: on and off. In the binary numbering system, a 1 represents on, while a 0 represents off.

Recall that in the decimal numbering system, the position of each number is important. It is the same in the binary numbering system, only each position doesn't correspond to powers of 10, but instead to powers of 2. Here are the values of the lowest eight positions used in the binary numbering system:

128	64	32	16	8	4	2	1

So, suppose that you encounter the following binary number:

1	0	1	0	1	1	0	1

You would follow the same steps that you use to understand a decimal numbering system number. In this example, the binary number represents 128+32+8+4+1, or 173 in the decimal system. You can also write (or calculate) this number as follows:

$(128 \times 1) + (64 \times 0) + (32 \times 1) + (16 \times 0) + (8 \times 1) + (4 \times 1) + (2 \times 0) + (1 \times 1).$

So, two main things separate the decimal numbering system from the binary numbering system: The binary system uses only 1's and 0's to represent every value, and the value of numerals in the different positions varies.

You might be wondering how you can tell whether you're reading a binary number or a decimal number. For instance, if you're reading a book about computers and you see the number 10101, how do you know whether it's supposed to represent ten thousand one hundred and one, or twenty-one? There are a couple of different ways that you can tell. First, usually binary numbers are always shown with at least eight positions (a full byte), even if the leading digits are 0's. Second, if you're looking at a bunch of numbers and only 1's and 0's are showing,

Ask the Expert

Q: What's the easiest way to quickly convert binary, octal, hexadecimal, and decimal numbers?

A: The Windows Calculator that comes with all versions of Windows allows you to convert values quickly between decimal, binary, octal, and hexadecimal. With the calculator open, place it into Scientific mode (open the View menu and choose Scientific). This mode reveals a lot of advanced features in the calculator. In the upper-left area of the calculator, you can now see four option buttons labeled Hex, Dec, Oct, and Bin. These correspond to the hexadecimal, decimal, octal, and binary numbering systems. Just choose which system you want to use to enter a number, and then click on any of the other options to convert the number instantly. For instance, suppose that you click the Bin option button and enter the number 110100100110111010. If you then click the Dec button, the calculator reveals that the number you just entered is 215,482 in the decimal system. Or, if you click the Hex button, you find that the binary number that you entered is 349BA in the hexadecimal numbering system. Likewise, if you click the Oct button, you discover that the number is 644672 in the octal numbering system. You can also go in the other direction: Choose the Dec button, enter some number, and then click on the other option buttons to see how the number looks in those other numbering systems. (You'll learn more about the hexadecimal and octal numbering systems later in this module.)

it's a pretty good bet that you're seeing binary numbers. Third, binary numbers don't use the decimal point to represent fractional values; 10100.01 should be assumed to be a decimal system number. Fourth, decimal numbers should use commas as you were taught in school. So, the number *10,100* should be read as ten thousand one hundred whereas the number 10100 should be read as the binary number for the quantity twenty. Fifth, sometimes people put the letter *b* at the end of a binary number, although this convention isn't widely followed. Put all these things together, plus a little common sense and you'll usually have no doubt whether you're reading a binary or decimal value.

Other Important Numbering Systems

There are two other important numbering systems that you encounter in the world of networking: octal and hexadecimal. Hexadecimal is far more prevalent than octal, but you should understand both.

The octal number system is also called the base-8 numbering system. In this scheme, each position in a number can hold only the numerals 0 to 7. The number 010 in the octal numbering system corresponds to 8 in the decimal numbering system. Octal numbers can be indicated with a leading zero, a leading percent symbol (%), or a trailing capital letter O.

The hexadecimal numbering system is pretty common in networking, and is often used to represent network addresses, memory addresses, and the like. The hexadecimal system (also called the base-16 numbering system) can use 15 different numerals in each of its positions. Since we have written numerals for only 0 to 9, the hexadecimal system uses the letters A through F to represent the extra numerals.

Hexadecimal numbers are usually preceded with a leading zero followed by the letter x, and then the hexadecimal number. The letter x can be either lower or upper case, so both 0x11AB and 0X11AB are correct. Hexadecimal numbers may also be shown with a trailing letter h, which also can be lower or upper case. Rarely, they may be preceded with the dollar sign ($) (for example, $11AB). Often, you can easily recognize hexadecimal numbers simply by the fact that usually the values include some letters (A to F). For hexadecimal numbers, A equals 10 in the decimal system, B equals 11, C equals 12, D equals 13, E equals 14, and F equals 15.

You can determine the decimal value for a hexadecimal value manually using the same method as shown earlier in this module for decimal and binary numbers. The hexadecimal position values for the first four digits are

4096	256	16	1

So, the number 0x11AB can be converted to decimal with the formula $(1\times4096)+(1\times256)+(10\times16)+(11\times1)$, or 4,523 in decimal.

Progress Check

1. Identify whether the following numbers are decimal, octal, hexadecimal, or binary:

   A. 00110110

   B. $15A9

   C. %123

   D. 12,345

   E. 0x1053

2. Convert all the numbers above to their decimal values. (Hint: It's OK to use the Windows calculator to do this, but if you want a bigger challenge, then use the multiplication method discussed in the preceding section.)

Use Basic Terminology to Describe Networking Speeds

The business of networking is entirely about moving data from one point to another. Accordingly, one of the most important things that you need to understand about any network connection is how much data it can carry. Broadly, this capacity is called *bandwidth,* which is measured by the amount of data that a connection can carry in a given period of time.

The most common measurement of bandwidth is *bits per second*, abbreviated as *bps*. Bandwidth is, simply, how many bits the connection can carry within a second. More commonly used are various multiples of this measurement, including thousands of bits per second (Kbps), millions of bits per second (Mbps), or billions of bits per second (Gbps).

TIP

Remember that bits per second is *not* bytes per second. To arrive at the bytes per second when you know the bits per second (approximately), divide the bps number by 8. In this book, *bits per second* always uses a lower-case letter b, while *bytes per second* always uses a upper-case B (for example, 56Kbps is 56 thousand bits per second, while 56KBps is 56 thousand bytes per second).

A closely related measurement that you will also see bandied about is Hertz, which is the number of cycles being carried per second. Hertz is abbreviated as *Hz*. Just like with *bps*, it is the multiples of Hertz that are talked about the most, including thousands of Hertz (KHz, or kilohertz), and millions of Hertz (MHz, or megahertz). A microprocessor running at 100MHz, for instance, is running at 100 million cycles per second. The electricity in the United States runs at 60Hz. Hertz and bits per second are essentially the same, and are sometimes intermixed. For example, thin Ethernet cable is said to run at 10Mhz, and also is said to carry 10Mbps of information.

---

1. A. Binary; B. Hexadecimal; C. Octal; D. Decimal; E. Hexadecimal
2. A. 54; B. 5,545; C. 83; D. 12,345; E. 4,179

TIP

While this is a beginner's book about networking, the book would have to double in size if it had to explain every networking term every time it was used. Instead, the rest of the book assumes that you understand the basic concepts presented in this module, as well as the information found in the glossary near the end of the book. Most people leave glossaries unread until they come across a term they don't know. I would instead recommend that you first spend a few minutes reviewing this book's glossary before you read the following modules, to make sure that you don't miss any terms that are used. Terms such as *node, host, broadband, baseband, workstation, client,* and *server* are examples of terms that you should be familiar with, and which the rest of the book assumes that you understand. The glossary covers these terms and many others.

✓ Module 2 Mastery Check

1. Hexadecimal refers to the base-___ numbering system.

2. Octal refers to the base-___ numbering system.

3. In the binary system, a single digit is called a _____. Eight of these strung together is called a _____.

4. What is the value of a number written as 1010 in each of the following numbering systems (express the answers in decimal):

   A. Decimal _____

   B. Binary _____

   C. Octal _____

   D. Hexadecimal _____

5. What does the abbreviation Mbps mean? How is that different from MBps?

6. Which is faster, 100 KHz or 0.1 Mbps?

7. Each position in the base-10 numbering system is a power of 10. What does each position in the hexadecimal numbering system represent?

8. If you needed to transfer 562,000 bytes over a connection running at 56Kbps, how long would the transfer take?

9. True or false? Numbering systems can be created using any base that one wishes.

10. Four bits together is called a _____.

Module 3

Understanding Networking

Networking can be a complex subject, but you'll find that you can be an extremely effective networking professional without having a Ph.D. in computer science. However, there are *a lot* of aspects to networking, and this tends to make the subject seem more complex than it really is. In this module, you learn about the fundamental aspects of networking, laying the groundwork for the more detailed modules to follow. This module discusses some basic and key networking concepts and gives an overview of some of the more detailed networking information in the remainder of the book.

If you're new to networking, getting a good fundamental understanding of the subjects in this module will enable you to build a mental framework into which you can fit more detailed knowledge, as it is presented later in the book. In addition, the rest of this book assumes you're comfortable with all the concepts presented in this module.

CRITICAL SKILL
3.1 Explain Network Relationship Types

The term *network relationships* refers to two different concepts about how one computer makes use of another computer's resources over the network.

Two fundamental types of network relationships exist: Peer-to-peer and client/server. These two types of network relationships (in fact, you could even refer to them as *network philosophies*) define the very structure of a network. To understand them better, you might compare them to different business management philosophies. A *peer-to-peer network* is much like a company run by a decentralized management philosophy, where decisions are made locally and resources are managed according to the most immediate needs. A client/server network is more like a company that works on centralized management, where decisions are made in a central location by a relatively small group of people. Circumstances exist where both peer-to-peer and client/server relationships are appropriate and many networks have aspects of both types within them.

Both peer-to-peer and client/server networks require that certain network *layers* be common. Both types require a physical network connection between the computers and the same network protocols be used, and so forth. In this respect, no difference exists between the two types of network relationships. The difference comes in whether you spread the shared network resources around to all the computers on the network or use centralized network servers.

NOTE

The mechanics of how a network actually functions are broken down into *layers*. The concept of layers and what goes into each layer is described in more detail later in this module.

Peer-to-Peer Network Relationships

A *peer-to-peer network relationship* defines one in which computers on the network communicate with each other as equals. Each computer is responsible for making its own resources available to other computers on the network. These resources might be files, directories, application programs, or devices such as printers, modems, or fax cards, or any combination thereof. Each computer is also responsible for setting up and maintaining its own security for those resources. Finally, each computer is responsible for accessing the network resources it needs from other peer-to-peer computers and for knowing where those resources are and what security is required to access them. Figure 3-1 illustrates how this works.

NOTE

Even in a pure peer-to-peer network, using a dedicated computer for certain frequently accessed resources is possible. For example, you might host the application and data files for an accounting system on a single workstation and not use that computer for typical workstation tasks, such as word processing, so that all of the computer's performance is available for the accounting system. The computer is still working in a peer-to-peer fashion, it's just not used for any other purposes.

Client/Server Network Relationships

A *client/server network relationship* is one in which a distinction exists between the computers that make available network resources (the *servers*) and the computers that use the resources (the *clients*, or *workstations*). A pure client/server network is one in which *all* available

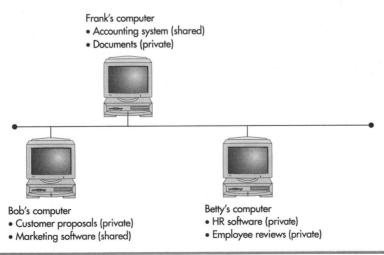

Frank's computer
• Accounting system (shared)
• Documents (private)

Bob's computer
• Customer proposals (private)
• Marketing software (shared)

Betty's computer
• HR software (private)
• Employee reviews (private)

Figure 3-1 A peer-to-peer network with resources spread across the computers

network resources—such as files, directories, applications, and shared devices—are centrally managed and hosted, and then are accessed by the client computers. No client computers share their resources with other client computers or with the servers. Instead, the client computers are pure consumers of these resources.

NOTE

Don't confuse client/server networks with client/server database systems. While the two mean essentially the same thing (conceptually), a client/server database is one where the processing of the database application is divided between the database server and the database clients. The server is responsible for responding to data requests from the clients and supplying them with the appropriate data, while the clients are responsible for formatting, displaying, and printing that data for the user. For instance, Novell NetWare or Windows 2000 Server are both client/server network operating systems, while Oracle's database or Microsoft's SQL Server are client/server database systems.

The server computers in a client/server network are responsible for making available and managing appropriate shared resources, and for administering the security of those resources. Figure 3-2 shows how resources would be located in such a network.

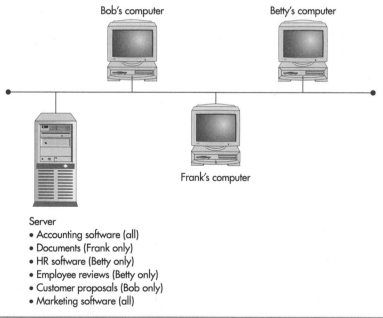

Figure 3-2 A client/server network keeps resources centralized

Comparing Peer-to-Peer and Client/Server Networks

As mentioned earlier, most networks have aspects of both peer-to-peer and client/server relationships. While it is certainly possible—and even sometimes desirable—to have just one type of relationship or another, the fact is both relationships have their place. Before deciding on setting up a network using one or both types of relationships, you have to examine the pros and cons of each and determine how each meets your needs and the needs of your company. Consider the following pros and cons for exclusively using a peer-to-peer network.

Pros for Peer-to-Peer Networks

There are a number of advantages to peer-to-peer networks, particularly for smaller firms, as follows:

- **Use less expensive computer hardware**   Peer-to-peer networks are the least hardware-intensive. In a pure peer-to-peer network, the resources are distributed over many computers, so there is no need for a high-end server computer. The impact on each workstation is usually (but not always) relatively minor.

- **Easy to administer**   Peer-to-peer networks are, overall, easiest to set up and administer. Because each machine performs its own administration—usually for certain limited resources—the effort of administering the network is widely distributed to many different people.

- **No NOS required**   Peer-to-peer networks do not require a network operating system (NOS). You can build a peer-to-peer network just using Windows 98, Windows 2000, or Windows XP on all the workstations, or all Macintosh computers for that matter. All of these workstation operating systems include all the features necessary to do this. Similarly, you can do this with all UNIX-based computers (although this is admittedly much more complex to set up and maintain, just because UNIX is very powerful and complex).

- **More built-in redundancy**   If you have a small network, with 10-20 workstations and each one with some important data on it, and one fails, you still have most of your shared resources available. A peer-to-peer network design can offer more redundancy than a client/server network because fewer single points of failure can affect the entire network and everyone who uses it.

Cons for Peer-to-Peer Networks

There are also various drawbacks to peer-to-peer networks, particularly for larger networks, or for networks that have more complex or sophisticated requirements, such as the following:

- **Might hurt user's performance**   If some workstations have frequently used resources on them, the use of these resources across the network might adversely affect the person using the workstation.

- **Not very secure**   Peer-to-peer networks are not nearly as secure as client/server networks because you cannot guarantee—no matter how good the users of the network are—that they will appropriately administer their machines. In fact, in a network of any size (say, more than 10 people) you can almost guarantee at least a few people will not follow good administration practices on their own machines. Moreover, the most common desktop operating systems on which one runs a peer-to-peer network, like Windows ME or the Macintosh, are not built to be secure operating systems.

- **Hard to back up**   Reliably backing up all the data scattered over many workstations is difficult, and it is not wise to leave this job up to the user of each machine. Experience has shown that leaving this vital task up to users means it will not get done.

- **Hard to maintain version control**   In a peer-to-peer network, with files potentially stored on a number of different machines, it can become extremely difficult to manage different document versions.

Pros for Client/Server Networks

Client/server networks, on the other hand, offer the opportunity for centralized administration, using equipment better suited to managing and offering each resource. Client/server networks are the type that you almost always see for networks larger than about 10 users, and there are quite a few good reasons for this, as follows:

- **Very secure**   A client/server network's security comes from several things. First, because the shared resources are located in a centralized area, they can be administered at that point. Managing a number of resources is much easier if those resources are all located on one or two server computers, as opposed to having to administer resources across tens or hundreds of computers. Second, usually the servers are physically in a secure location, such as a lockable server closet. Physical security is an important aspect of network security and it cannot be achieved with a peer-to-peer network. Third, the operating systems on which one runs a client/server network are designed to be secure. Provided that good security and administration practices are in place, the servers cannot be easily "hacked."

- **Better performance**   While dedicated server computers are more expensive than standard computer workstations, they also offer considerably better performance and they are optimized to handle the needs of many users simultaneously.

- **Centralized backup**   Backing up a company's critical data is much easier when it is located on a centralized server. Often, such backup jobs can even be run overnight when the server is not being used and the data is static. Aside from being easier, centralized backups are also much faster than decentralized backups.

- **Very reliable**   While it is true more built-in redundancy exists with a peer-to-peer network, it is also true a good client/server network can be more reliable, overall. Dedicated servers often have much more built-in redundancy than standard workstations. They can handle the failure of a disk drive, power supply, or processor, and continue to operate until the failed component can be replaced. Also, because a dedicated server has only one relatively simple job to do, its complexity is reduced and its reliability increased. Contrast this with a peer-to-peer network where actions on the part of the users can drastically reduce each workstation's reliability. For example, having to restart a PC with Windows 98 or a Macintosh every few days is not uncommon, whereas dedicated servers often run for months without requiring a restart or crashing.

Cons for Client/server Networks

Balancing the pros of client/server networks, you also need to realize that there are drawbacks, particularly for companies that don't have their own in-house network administration, or who want to minimize the expense of the network as much as possible, as follows:

- **Require professional administration**   Client/server networks usually need some level of professional administration, even for small networks. You can hire a network administrator or you can use a company that provides professional network administration services, but it's important to remember that professional administration is usually required. Knowing the ins and outs of a network operating system is important and requires experience and training.

- **More hardware-intensive**   In addition to the client computers, you also need a server computer; this usually needs to be a pretty "beefy" computer with lots of memory and disk space. Plus, you need a network operating system and an appropriate number of client licenses, which adds at least several thousand dollars to the cost of the server. For large networks, it adds tens of thousands of dollars.

In a nutshell, choose a peer-to-peer network for smaller networks with fewer than 10–15 users, and choose a client/server network for anything larger. Because most networks are built on a client/server concept, most of this book assumes such a network.

Progress Check

1. Suppose you are being hired as a network consultant to set up a network for a new company, or a new office of a larger company. What factors would you consider to decide whether to pursue a peer-to-peer or a client/server network?

2. What do you think are the most compelling reasons to decide on a client/server network for a new network that will eventually support around 50 people?

---

1. Some of the primary considerations will include: Number of expected users; growth rate and eventual size; budget considerations; types of applications being used and their performance requirements; administrative resources for the network; data backup requirements and capabilities.

2. A peer-to-peer network supporting 50 users would be extremely difficult to manage, back up, and support. Additionally, if you spread the cost of a dedicated server among the 50 users, the incremental cost for a client/server network is relatively small.

3.2 Learn Network Features

Now that you understand the two basic ways computers on a network can interact with each other, understanding the types of things you can do with a network is important. The following sections discuss common network features and capabilities.

File Sharing

Originally, file sharing was the primary reason to have a network. In fact, small and mid-size companies in the mid-1980s usually installed networks just so they could perform this function. Often, this was driven by the need to computerize their accounting systems. Of course, once the networks were in place, sharing other types of files becomes easier as well, such as word processing files, spreadsheets, or other types of files to which many people need regular access.

File sharing requires a shared directory or disk drive to which many users can access over the network, along with the logic needed to make sure more than one person doesn't make different conflicting changes to a file at the same time (called *file locking*). The reason you don't want more than one person making changes to a file at the same time is that they might both be making *conflicting* changes simultaneously, without either person realizing the problem. Most software programs don't have the ability to allow multiple changes to a single file at the same time and to resolve problems that might arise. (The exception to this rule is that most database programs allow multiple users to access a database simultaneously.)

Additionally, network operating systems that perform file sharing (basically, all of them) also administer the security for these shared files. This security can control, with a fine level of detail, who has access to which files and what kinds of access they have. For example, some users might have permission to view only certain shared files, while others have permission to edit or even delete certain shared files.

Printer Sharing

A close runner-up in importance to file sharing is printer sharing. While it is true that laser printers are currently so inexpensive you can afford to put one in every office, if you wish, sharing laser printers among the users on the network is still more economical overall. Printer sharing enables you to reduce the number of printers you need and also enables you to offer much higher-quality printers. For example, a high-end color laser printers costs about $5,000. Newer digital copiers that can handle large printouts at more than 60 pages per minute can cost more than $30,000. Sharing such printers among many users makes sense.

Printer sharing can be done in several different ways on a network. The most common way is to use *printer queues* on a server. A printer queue holds print jobs until any currently running print jobs are finished and then automatically send the waiting jobs to the printer. Using a printer queue is efficient for the workstations because they can quickly print to the printer queue without having to wait for the printer to process their job. Another way to share printers on a network is to let each workstation access the printer directly (most printers can be configured so they are connected to the network just like a network workstation), but each must wait its turn if many users are vying for the printer at once.

Networked printers that use printer queues always have a *print server* that handles the job of sending each print job to the printer in turn. The print server function can be filled in a number of ways:

- By a fileserver with the printer connected directly to it (this option is not usually recommended because it can adversely affect the fileserver's performance).

- By a computer connected to the network, with the printer connected to that computer. The computer runs special print server software to perform this job.

- Through the use of a built-in print server on a printer's network interface card (NIC). For example, nearly all Hewlett-Packard LaserJets offer an option to include a network card in the printer. This card also contains the computer necessary to act as a print server. This is far less expensive than the previous option.

- Through the use of a dedicated network print server, which is a box about the size of a deck of cards that connects to the printer's parallel or USB port (or even a wireless 802.11a or 802.11b connection) on one end and the network on the other end. Dedicated print servers also contain the computer necessary to act as a print server.

Application Services

Just as you can share files on a network, you can often also share applications on a network. For example, you can have a shared copy of Microsoft Office, or some other application, and keep it on the network server, from where it is also run. When a workstation wants to run the program, it loads the files from the network into its own memory, just like it would from a local disk drive, and runs the program normally. Keeping applications centralized reduces the amount of disk space needed on each workstation and makes it easier to administer the application (for instance, with some applications you have to upgrade only the network copy; with others you also must perform a brief installation for each client).

Another application service you can host on the network is a shared installation point for applications. Instead of having to load a CD-ROM onto each workstation, you can usually copy the contents of the CD-ROM to the server, then have the installation program run from the server for each workstation. This makes installing the applications much faster and more convenient.

CAUTION

Make sure any applications you host on a network server are licensed appropriately. Most software licenses do NOT let you run an application on multiple computers. Even if you need only one copy of the application to set up the files on the server, you still need a license for every user. Different applications have different fine print regarding licensing this (some require one license per user, some require one license per computer, some allow your network users to use a copy at home freely, and so forth). Make sure to carefully read the license agreements for your business software and adhere to their terms and conditions.

E-Mail

An extremely valuable and important network resource these days is e-mail. Not only can it be helpful for communications within a company, but also it is also fast becoming a preferred vehicle to communicate with people outside a company.

E-mail systems are roughly divided into two different types: file-based and client/server. A file-based e-mail system is one that consists of a set of files kept in a shared location on a server. The server doesn't actually do anything beyond providing access to the files. Connections required from a file-based e-mail system and the outside (say, to the Internet) are usually accomplished with a stand-alone computer—called a *gateway server*—that handles the e-mail interface between the two systems using gateway software that is part of the file-based e-mail system.

A client/server e-mail system is one where an e-mail server contains the messages and handles all the e-mail interconnections, both inside the company and to places outside the company. Client/server e-mail systems, such as Microsoft Exchange or Lotus Notes, are more secure and far more powerful than their file-based counterparts. They often offer additional features that enable you to use the e-mail system to automate different business processes, such as invoicing or purchasing.

Unless a company has at least 50 employees, though, e-mail servers or dedicated e-mail systems are usually overkill and are too costly to purchase and maintain. For these smaller companies, e-mail is still just as important, but there are other strategies to provide e-mail these days that do not require that you run your own internal e-mail system (whether it be file-based or client/server). For instance, many small companies instead simply set up a shared connection to the Internet that all of their computers can access, and then set up e-mail accounts either through their Internet service provider (ISP) or through a free e-mail service such as Yahoo! Mail or Hotmail.

Remote Access

Another important service for most networks is remote access to the network resources. Users use this feature to access their files and e-mail when they're traveling or working from a remote location, such as their homes. Remote access systems come in many different flavors. Some of the methods used to provide remote access include

- Setting up a simple remote access service (RAS) connection on a Windows 2000 Server, which can range from using a single modem to a bank of modems.

- Using a dedicated remote access system, which handles many modems and usually includes many computers, each one on its own stand-alone card.

- Employing a workstation on the network and having users dial in using a remote control program like PC Anywhere.

- Setting up a virtual private network (VPN) connection to the Internet, through which users can access resources on the company network in a secure fashion through the Internet.

- Installing Windows Terminal Services (on Windows 2000) or Citrix MetaFrame, both of which allow a single Windows 2000 Server to host multiple client sessions, each one appearing to the end user as a stand-alone computer.

As you can see, there are many ways to offer remote access services to users of the network. The right solution depends on what the users need to do remotely, how many users exist (both in total and at any given time), and how much you want to spend. See Module 9 for more information on remote access.

Wide Area Networks

You should think of a wide area network (WAN) as a sort of "metanetwork." A WAN is simply the connection of multiple local area networks (LANs) together. This can be accomplished in many different ways, depending on how often the LANs need to be connected to one another, how much data capacity (bandwidth) is required, and how great the distance is between the LANs. Solutions range from using full-time leased telephone lines that can carry 56Kbps of data, to dedicated DS1 (T-1) lines carrying 1.544Mbps to DS3 lines carrying 44.736Mbps to other solutions (like private satellites) carrying even higher bandwidths. You can also create a WAN using VPNs over the Internet (although this method usually offers inconsistent bandwidth, it's often the least expensive).

WANs are created when the users of one LAN need frequent access to the resources on another LAN. For instance, a company's enterprise resource planning (ERP) system might be running at the headquarters' location, but the warehouse location needs access to it to use its inventory and shipping functions.

Ask the Expert

Q: What are all these terms ending in *AN?*

A: There is a myriad of terms that refer to what are essentially wide area networks (WANs), all with variations on the xAN acronym scheme. Some examples of these variations include metropolitan area network (MAN), distance area network (DAN), campus area network (CAN), and even—I am not making this up—personal area network (PAN), which was an IBM demonstration technology where two people shaking hands could exchange data through electrical signals carried on the surface of their skin. All of these different names, and others that I haven't listed here, are a bit silly. I suggest you just stick with the two core terms, LAN and WAN.

TIP

As a general rule, if you can design and build a system that doesn't require a WAN, you're usually better off because WAN links are often expensive to maintain. However, the geographic and management structure of a particular company can dictate the use of a WAN.

Internet and Intranet

There's no way around it these days: The Internet has become vital to the productivity of most businesses, and handling Internet connectivity on a network is often an important network service. Many different types of services are available over the Internet, including e-mail, the Web, and Usenet newsgroups.

An Internet connection for a network consists of a telecommunications network connection to an ISP, using a connection such as a leased 56KB line, an ISDN line, or a fractional or full DS1 (T-1) connection. This line comes into the building and connects to a box called a CSU/DSU (channel service unit/data service unit), which converts the data from the form carried by the local telephone company to one usable on the LAN. The CSU/DSU is, in turn, connected to a router that routes data packets between the local network. Internet security is provided either by filtering the packets going through the router or by adding a firewall system. A firewall system runs on a computer (or has a computer built into it if it's an appliance device) and offers the highest level of security and administration features.

An *intranet*, as its name suggests, is an internally focused network that mimics the Internet itself. For example, a company might deploy an intranet that hosts a web server, and on that web server, the company might place documents such as employee handbooks, purchasing forms, or other information that the company publishes for internal use. Intranets can also host other Internet-type services, such as FTP servers or Usenet servers, or these services can be provided by other tools that offer the same functionality. Intranets are usually not accessible from outside the LAN (although they can be) and are just a much smaller version of the Internet that a company maintains for its own use.

Understanding the technologies, services, and features of the Internet is complex. You can learn much more about some of the hardware that makes the Internet work in Module 7.

Network Security

Any time you share important and confidential information on a network, you have to carefully consider the security of those resources. Users and management must help set the level of security needed for the network and the different information it stores and they need to participate in deciding who has access to which resources.

Network security is provided by a combination of factors, including features of the NOS, the physical cabling plant, how the network is connected to other networks, the features of the client workstations, the actions of the users, the security policies of management, and how well the security features are implemented and administered. All these things come together into a chain and any single weak link in the chain can cause it to fail. Depending on the company, any failures of network security can have severe consequences, so network security is usually an extremely important part of any network. For a more detailed discussion of network security, see Module 10.

Progress Check

1. For which type of service do most businesses set up their first network?

2. What is needed to connect a company network to the Internet?

CRITICAL SKILL
3.3 Understand the OSI Networking Model

The Open Systems Interconnection (OSI) Model defines all the methods and protocols needed to connect one computer to any other over a network. The OSI Model is a conceptual model, used most often in network design and in engineering network solutions. Generally, real-world

---

1. Most businesses originally set up early networks for file and print sharing. While this is still the most important underlying service, these days Web and e-mail access to the outside world is also a critical network service.

2. Minimally, a router between the LAN and the ISP connection is needed, plus a device to translate the network's signals into the medium used for the ISP connection, such as an ISDN "modem" or a CSU/DSU for frame relay service. Also, of course, an ISP is needed.

networks conform to the OSI Model, although differences exist between the theory of the OSI Model and actual practice in most networks. Still, the OSI Model offers an excellent way to understand and visualize how computers network to each other, and it is required knowledge for anyone active in the field of networking. Just about all employers expect networking professionals to be knowledgeable about the OSI Model, which defines a basic framework for how modern networks operate. The model also forms a key part of most networking certification tests. Dry the model might be, but it's important to learn it!

The OSI model separates the methods and protocols needed for a network connection into seven different *layers*. Each higher layer relies on services provided by a lower-level layer. As an illustration, if you were to think about a desktop computer in this way, its hardware would be the lowest layer and the operating system drivers—the next-higher layer—would rely on the lowest layer to do their job. The operating system itself, the next-higher layer, would rely on both of the lower layers working properly. This continues all the way up to the point at which an application presents data to you on the computer screen. Figure 3-3 shows the seven layers of the OSI model.

NOTE

The OSI model is sometimes called "the seven-layer model." It was developed by the International Standards Organization (ISO) in 1983 and is documented as standard 7498.

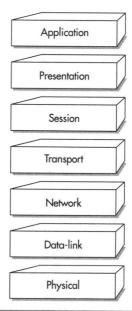

Figure 3-3 The seven layers of the OSI Model

For a complete network connection, data flows from the top layer on one computer, down through all the lower layers, across the wire, and back up the seven layers on the other computer. The following sections discuss each layer in turn, making comparisons to real networking systems as appropriate.

Physical Layer

The first layer, *the physical layer,* defines the properties of the physical medium used to make a network connection. The physical layer specifications result in a physical medium—a network cable—that can transmit a stream of bits between nodes on the physical network. The physical connection can be either point-to-point (between two points) or multipoint (between many points, such as from one point to many others), and it can consist of either *half-duplex* (one direction at a time) or *full-duplex* (both directions simultaneously) transmissions. Moreover, the bits can be transmitted either in series or in parallel (most networks use a serial stream of bits, but the standard allows for both serial and parallel transmission). The specification for the physical layer also defines the cable used, the voltages carried on the cable, the timing of the electrical signals, the distance that can be run, and so on. A NIC, for example, is part of the physical layer.

Data-Link Layer

The data-link layer, Layer 2, defines standards that assign meaning to the bits carried by the physical layer. It establishes a reliable protocol through the physical layer so the network layer (Layer 3) can transmit its data. The data-link layer typically includes error detection and correction to ensure a reliable data stream. The data elements carried by the data-link layer are called *frames*. Examples of frame types include X.25 and 802.x (802.x includes both Ethernet and Token Ring networks).

The data-link layer is usually subdivided into two sublayers, called the logical link control (LLC) and media access control (MAC) sublayers. If used, the LLC sublayer performs tasks such as call setup and termination (the OSI Model can be applied to telecommunications networks as well as LANs) and data transfer. The MAC sublayer handles frame assembly and disassembly, error detection and correction, and addressing. The two most common MAC protocols are 802.3 Ethernet and 802.5 Token Ring. Other MAC protocols include 802.12 100BaseVBG, 802.11 Wireless, and 802.7 Broadband.

On most systems, drivers for the NIC perform the work done at the data-link layer.

Network Layer

The *network layer,* Layer 3, is where a lot of action goes on for most networks. The network layer defines how data *packets* get from one point to another on a network and what goes into each packet. The network layer defines different packet protocols, such as Internet Protocol (IP) and Internet Protocol Exchange (IPX). These packet protocols include source and destination routing information. The routing information in each packet tells the network where to send the packet to reach its destination and tells the receiving computer from where the packet originated.

The network layer is most important when the network connection passes through one or more *routers*, which are hardware devices that examine each packet and, from their source and destination addresses, send the packets to their proper destination. Over a complex network, such as the Internet, a packet might go through 10 or more routers before it reaches its destination. On a LAN, a packet might not go through any routers to get to its destination or it might go through one or more.

Note that breaking the network layer (also known as the *packet layer*) into a separate layer from the physical and data-link layers means the protocols defined in this layer can be carried over any variations of the lower layers. So, to put this into real-world terms, an IP packet can be sent over an Ethernet network, a Token Ring network, or even a serial cable connecting two computers to one another. The same would hold true for an IPX packet: If both computers can handle IPX, and they share the lower-level layers (whatever they might be), then the network connection can be made.

Transport Layer

The transport layer, Layer 4, manages the flow of information from one network node to another. It ensures that the packets are decoded in the proper sequence and that all packets are received. It also identifies each computer or node on a network uniquely. Different networking systems (such as Microsoft's, or Novell's) implement the transport layer differently, and, in fact, the transport layer is the first layer where this occurs. Unique at this layer are Windows NT networks, Novell NetWare networks, or any other networking system. Examples of transport layer protocols include Transmission Control Protocol (TCP) and Sequenced Packet Exchange (SPX). Each is used in concert with IP and IPX, respectively.

Session Layer

The session layer, Layer 5, defines the connection from a user to a network server, or from a peer on a network to another peer. These virtual connections are referred to as *sessions*. They include negotiation between the client and host, or peer and peer, on matters of flow control, transaction processing, transfer of user information, and authentication to the network.

Presentation Layer

The presentation layer, Layer 6, takes the data supplied by the lower-level layers and transforms it so it can be presented to the system (as opposed to presenting the data to the user, which is handled well outside of the OSI Model). The functions that take place at the presentation layer can include data compression and decompression, as well as data encryption and decryption.

Application Layer

The application layer, Layer 7, controls how the operating system and its applications interact with the network. The applications you use, such as Microsoft Word or Lotus 1-2-3, aren't a part of the application layer, but they certainly benefit from the work that goes on there. An example of software at the application layer is the network client you use, such as the Windows Client for Microsoft Networks, the Windows Client for Novell Networks, or Novell's Client32 software. It also controls how the operating system and applications interact with those clients.

Understanding How Data Travels Through the OSI Layers

As mentioned earlier in this section, data flows from an application program or the operating system, and then goes through the protocols and devices that make up the seven layers of the OSI Model, one by one, until the data arrives at the physical layer and is transmitted over the network connection. The computer at the receiving end reverses this process, with the data coming in at the physical layer, traveling up through all the layers until it emerges from the application layer and is made use of by the operating system and any application programs.

At each stage of the OSI Model, the data is "wrapped" with new control information related to the work done at that particular layer, leaving the previous layers' information intact and wrapped within the new control information. This control information is different for each layer, but it includes *headers*, *trailers*, *preambles*, and *postambles*.

So, for example, when data goes into the networking software and components making up the OSI Model, it starts at the application layer and includes an application header and application data (the real data being sent). Next, at the presentation layer, a presentation header is wrapped around the data and it is passed to the component at the session layer, where a session header is wrapped around all of the data, and so on, until it reaches the physical layer. At the receiving computer, this process is reversed, with each layer unwrapping its appropriate control information, performing whatever work is indicated by that control information, and passing the data onto the next higher layer. It all sounds rather complex, but it works very well in practice.

Progress Check

1. How does data travel through the seven OSI layers on the sending machine? The receiving machine?

2. What are the names of the bottom and top layers of the OSI model, and what does each do?

CRITICAL SKILL
3.4 # Discuss Network Hardware Components

This module is really about understanding networks, with a "view from 30,000 feet." Following this module, much more detailed modules further explore most of the concepts presented in this module. However, before jumping off into the more detailed modules to follow, it's important to complete this discussion by overviewing specific hardware that makes networks operate. Understanding the general types of devices you typically encounter in a network is important, not only for planning a network but also for troubleshooting and maintenance.

Servers

A *server* is any computer that performs network functions for other computers. These functions fall into several categories, including

- File and print servers, which provide file sharing and services to share network-based printers.

- Application servers, which provide specific application services to an application. An example is a server that runs a database that a distributed application uses.

- E-mail servers, which provide e-mail storage and interconnection services to client computers.

- Networking servers, which can provide a host of different network services. Examples of these services include the automatic assignment of TCP/IP addresses (DHCP servers), routing of packets from one network to another (routing servers), encryption/decryption and other security services, VPN servers, and so forth.

- Internet servers, which provide Web, Usenet News (NNTP), and Internet e-mail services.

- Remote access servers, which provide access to a local network for remote users.

---

1. Data starts at Layer 7 on the transmitting machine, travels down through all seven layers to the physical layer, where it actually makes its way to the receiving machine. On the receiving machine, data is received at Layer 1, and then travels up through all seven layers until it emerges at the application layer.

2. Layer 1, the physical layer, is considered the "bottom" layer, while Layer 7, the application layer, is considered the "top" layer. The physical layer actually transmits data over the physical medium, while the application layer accepts interfaces with the device's operating system.

Servers typically run some sort of NOS, such as Windows 2000 Server, Novell NetWare, or UNIX. Depending on the NOS chosen, all the functions previously listed might all be performed on one server or distributed to many servers. Also, not all networks need all the previously services listed.

NOTE

You can learn more about servers in Module 12. Server computers can be nearly any type of computer but, today, they are mostly comprised of high-end PCs using the Intel architecture. You might also see certain types of servers that use a different platform. For instance, many dedicated web servers run on UNIX-based computers, such as those from Sun Microsystems, IBM, Hewlett-Packard, and others.

A number of things distinguish a true server-class computer from a more pedestrian client computer. These things include built-in redundancy with multiple power supplies and fans (for instance) to keep the server running if something breaks. They also include special high-performance designs for disk subsystems, memory, and network subsystems to optimize the movement of data to and from the server, the network, and the client computers. Finally, they usually include special monitoring software and hardware that keeps a close eye on the health of the server, warning of failures before they occur. For example, most servers have temperature monitors in them; if the temperature starts getting too high, a warning is issued so the problem can be resolved before it causes failure of any of the hardware components in the server.

Hubs, Routers, and Switches

Hubs, routers, and switches are the most commonly seen "pure" networking hardware. (They're "pure" in the sense that they exist only for networking and for no other purpose.) Many people refer to this class of equipment as "internetworking devices" because that's what they're for. These are the devices to which all the cables of the network are connected and that pass the data along at the physical, data-link, or network layers of the OSI Model.

NOTE

Hubs, routers, and switches are discussed in more detail—along with other networking hardware—in Module 5.

A *hub*, sometimes called a *concentrator*, is a device that connects a number of network cables coming from client computers to a network. Hubs come in many different sizes, supporting from as few as two computers, up to large hubs that can support 60 computers or more. (The most common hub size supports 24 network connections.) All the network connections on a hub share a single *collision domain*, which is a fancy way of saying all the connections to a hub "talk" over a single logical wire and are subject to interference from other computers connected to the same hub. Figure 3-4 shows an example hub and how it is logically wired.

A *switch* is wired very similarly to a hub, and actually looks just like a hub. However, on a switch all of the network connections are on their own collision domain. The switch makes each network connection a private one, and then collects the data from each of the connections and forwards it to a network backbone, which usually runs at a much higher speed than the individual switch connections. Often, switches will be used to connect many hubs to a single network backbone. Figure 3-5 shows a typical switch and hub wiring arrangement.

A *router* routes data packets from one network to another. The two networks connect to the router using their own wiring type and connection type. For example, a router that connected a 10Base-T network to an ISDN telephone line would have two connections: one leading to the 10Base-T network and one leading to the ISDN line provided by the phone company. Routers also usually have an additional connection that a terminal can be connected to; this connection is just used to program and maintain the router.

Cabling and Cable Plants

Many types of network cable exist, but you need to be concerned with only a few of the more common ones. The most common network cable for LANs is Category 3 (Cat-3) twisted-pair cable. This cable carries the network signal to each point through four wires (two twisted-pairs). Cat-3 cable is used to support 10Base-T Ethernet networks.

NOTE

The twisting of each pair in the cable jacket reduces the chances of the cable picking up electrical interference.

Higher in quality and capability than Cat-3 cable is Category 5 (Cat-5) cable. This is similar cable, made up of sets of twisted-pairs, but it contains twice as many pairs as Cat-3

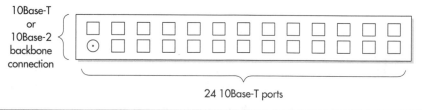

10Base-T
or
10Base-2
backbone
connection

24 10Base-T ports

Figure 3-4 A typical network hub

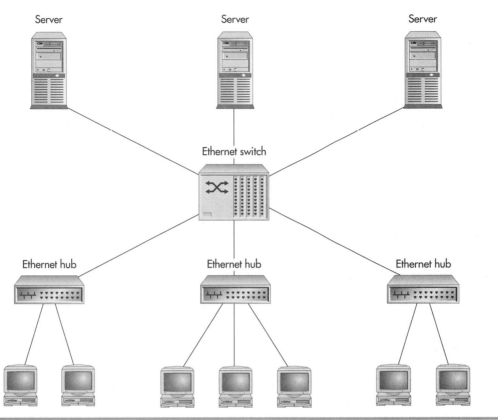

Figure 3-5 Using switches and hubs in concert

cable. Cat-5 cable is required for 100Base-T networks. You can also use Cat-5 cable to carry two simultaneous Cat-3 network connections.

Coaxial cable (called *coax*) is not currently used for new cable installations, but you might still come across it in older buildings. Coax cable has a center core of copper (called the *conductor*) surrounded by a plastic wrapper, which is in turn wrapped with braided metal, called the *shield,* and then finally an outer plastic coating. For instance, the cable that you use to connect a television to a cable TV network is a type of coax cable (the same coax is used for cable modems, by the way). Most coax cable used for networks is a type called RG-58, which is used for 10Base-2 (thin Ethernet) networks. Another is RG-56, used for ARCnet networks. The different types of coax cable refer to the specifications of the cable, which determines whether a particular network type can make use of the cable. You cannot mix different types of coax cable in a single network, and you must use the correct type for the network you are building.

NOTE

Read Module 4 for more information on network cabling.

The term *cable plant* refers to the entire installation of all your network cable. It includes not only the cable run throughout a building, but also the connectors, wall plates, patch panels, and so forth. It's extremely important that a new installation of a cable plant be performed by a qualified contractor trained to install that type of cable. Despite the apparent simplicity of cable, it is actually quite complex and its installation is also complex.

Workstation Hardware

Any computer on a network that is used by people is usually referred to as a *network workstation*. Sometimes such workstations are also called *network clients*. Usually, a network client is an Intel-based PC running some version of Windows, which has an NIC installed into it along with network client software, all of which allow the workstation to participate on the network. Network workstations can also be any other type of computer that includes the necessary network hardware and software, such as an Apple Macintosh or some form of UNIX-based computer.

TIP

Don't confuse a network workstation (a generic term) with workstation-class computers. Workstation-class computers are high-end computers used for computer-aided design, engineering, and graphics work.

Module 3 Mastery Check

1. The lowest level of the OSI Model is called the _____ layer. It describes how which of the following things work:

   A. Keyboards and mice

   B. Disk drives

   C. Network cable

   D. Network routers

2. The two main types of relationships between computers on a network are called _____ and _____.

3. The OSI Model is divided into _____ layers. It was developed by the _____ in 1983.

4. Which of the following are advantages of client/server network systems relative to peer-to-peer network systems?

    A. They are more secure.

    B. They cost less.

    C. It is harder to back up the stored data.

    D. They provide centralized management of a network's resources.

5. Which of the following distinguishes a server-class computer from a standard desktop computer:

    A. Faster processor

    B. Faster graphics rendering

    C. Faster disk drives

    D. Redundancy, such as in the power supplies or cooling fans

6. Client/server network systems should not be confused with client/server _____ systems.

7. A connection between a LAN and the Internet *requires* which of the following hardware:

    A. Firewall

    B. Router

    C. CSU/DSU

    D. Server computer

8. Cat-3 network cable supports __Base-T networks, while Cat5 network cable supports ___Base-T networks.

9. What is the main difference between a hub and a switch?

10. True or false. One can change the technology at any particular OSI network layer without affecting the higher layers in any way.

Module 4

Understanding Network Cabling

I f you were to compare a computer network to the human body, the network cabling system would be the nerves that make up the physical manifestation of the nervous system. The network cabling system is what actually carries all the data from one point to another and determines how the network works. How a network is cabled is of supreme importance to how the network functions, how fast it functions, how reliable the network will be as a whole, and how easy it will be to expand and change the network. With any new network, the first thing you do after assessing the needs for the network is to determine how the network should be wired; all the other components of the network are then built on that foundation.

Many people think that network cabling is relatively simple. After all, what could be simpler than running a wire between a number of points? As you will see, though, the topic of network cabling encompasses more than meets the eye, and it's an extremely important area to get right. If you make mistakes selecting or installing network cable, your network will likely be unreliable, and may perform poorly. Because of the labor costs involved in wiring a network, the best time to fix any potential problems in this area is well *before* they occur.

CRITICAL SKILL

4.1 Compare Cable Topologies

Because the word *topology* basically means *shape,* the term *network topology* refers to the shape of a network—how all of the nodes (points) of a network are wired together. There are several different topologies in which networks are wired, and the choice of a topology is often your most important choice when you plan a network. The different topologies have different costs (both to install and maintain), different levels of performance, and different levels of reliability. In the next several sections, you learn about the main topologies in use today.

Bus Topology

A *bus topology*, more completely called a *Common Bus Multipoint Topology*, is a network where, basically, one single network cable is used from one end of the network to the other, with different network devices (called *nodes*) connected to the cable at different locations. Figure 4-1 illustrates a simple bus topology network.

Different types of bus networks have different specifications, which include the following factors:

- How many nodes can be in a single segment
- How many segments can be used through the use of repeaters
- How close nodes can be to each other
- The total length of a segment
- Which coax cable type is required
- How the ends of the bus must be terminated

Ask the Expert

Q: What is a network segment?

A: A *network segment* can mean somewhat different things depending on the topology of the network, but the concept is simplest with bus networks and is essentially the same for any topology. A *segment* is a single length of cable to which all the nodes in that segment are connected. In truth, a segment is not a single strand of cable because it is broken at each computer connection point with a connector that lets the node connect to the network cable, but the cable is electrically one single length. In any given segment, all the network traffic is "seen" by all the nodes on that segment. You need to take this into account when planning how many nodes you will connect to any given segment. If you have 20 computers all fully using that segment at the same time, each computer will only achieve approximately $1/20^{th}$ of the available maximum bandwidth. This is simplified; you learn more about how this works later in this module and in following modules.

New network wiring installations these days rarely use bus topologies, although many older networks do still use them. Bus topology networks use coaxial cable, described in the previous module. Each end of each segment of the network has a special cable terminator on it, without which the network will not function. Bus topology networks use BNC connectors to tie all the individual pieces of cable together. Each computer is connected to the network through the use of a BNC *T-connector* (called that because it's shaped like the letter *T*) that allows the network to continue its bus and lets the computer connect to it. Figure 4-2 shows several different BNC connectors.

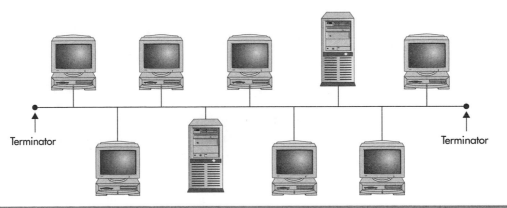

Figure 4-1 A simple bus topology network

Ask the Expert

Q: What does BNC stand for?

A: Depending on whom you ask, BNC stands for Bayonet Nut Connector, British Naval Connector, or Bayonet Neill-Concelman (with the latter two words standing for its inventor, Mr. Neill-Concelman). BNC is a bayonet-style connector that quickly attaches and detaches with a quarter turn. A variety of different parts—T-connectors, barrel connectors, elbow connectors, cable ends that splice onto appropriate cable, and so forth—use BNC connectors, so you can achieve nearly any type of connection needed. The BNC connector is extremely easy to use and makes a secure connection.

Bus network topologies are by far the least expensive to install because they use much less cable than the other two topologies and, accordingly, they use less material and need less installation labor.

But bus networks have some big drawbacks. Because all the subcables that make up the segment and run from node-to-node must be connected at all times, and because a failure in any part of the segment will cause the entire segment to fail, bus networks are prone to trouble. And even more important, that trouble can take a long time to track down because you must work your way through all the cable connections until you find the one causing the problem. Because of the tendency of bus networks to be unreliable, they aren't installed much for new networks any more.

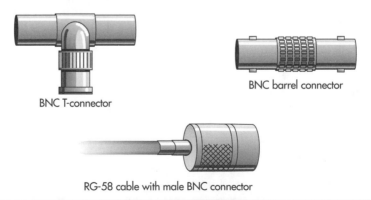

BNC T-connector

BNC barrel connector

RG-58 cable with male BNC connector

Figure 4-2 BNC connectors used in a coax-based bus topology

By far the most prevalent bus network in existence today is one called 10Base-2 Ethernet, or more commonly, Thin Ethernet. This network type has the following characteristics:

- Has a rated maximum speed of 10Mbps.

- Uses RG-58/AU or RG-58/CU coaxial cable and BNC connectors.

- Requires a 50 ohm terminating connector at each end of each segment to function.

- Can handle a maximum of 30 nodes per segment.

- Can be run up to a maximum segment length of 185 meters (607 feet).

- Can use extended segments through the use of repeaters. If repeaters are used, you can connect a maximum of three segments together, and each segment may have up to 30 nodes (with the repeater counting as a node). You can also have two additional segments (a total of five) if those extra two segments are used for distance only and have no nodes on them. An entire repeated segment must never exceed a total of 925 meters (3,035 feet). Remember the 5-4-3 rule: five segments, four repeaters, three populated segments.

- Requires each node to be at least 1.5 feet (cable distance) from any other node.

NOTE

Repeaters are hardware devices that electrically boost the signal on a cable so it can be extended further; they do not route any of the data. In fact, a repeater is "ignorant" of any of the data that it carries. Repeaters are inexpensive and reliable. Remember, however, a cable extended with a repeater means that all the network traffic on one side of the repeater is echoed to the cable on the other side of the repeater, regardless of whether that traffic needs to go on that other cable.

Star Topology

A *star topology* is one in which a central unit, called a *hub* or *concentrator*, hosts a set of network cables that radiate out to each node on the network. Technically, the hub is referred to as a Multi-station Access Unit (MAU), but that particular terminology tends only to be used with Token Ring networks, which use a ring topology (see the following section). Each hub usually hosts about 24 nodes, although hubs exist that range in size from two nodes up to 96 nodes. Regardless of the hub size, you can connect multiple hubs together to grow the network in any way that makes sense. See Module 6 for more on connecting hubs together in different configurations. Figure 4-3 shows a simple star topology network.

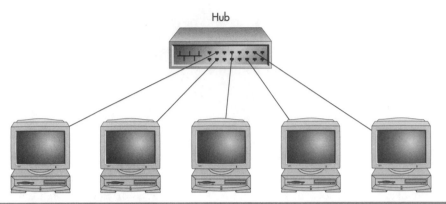

Figure 4-3 A star topology network

All the network traffic used on any of the network connections to the hub is echoed to all the other connected nodes on that particular hub. Because of this, all the bandwidth of any single node connection is shared with all other node connections. For example, if one of the nodes connected to the hub is using half the available bandwidth, all the other nodes must contend with that use for their own. In other words, if you're using a network type with a capacity of 10Mbps, that's the total amount of bandwidth available to all nodes connected to the hub in aggregate.

Ask the Expert

Q: What's the difference between physical wiring and logical wiring?

A: You'll often hear the terms "physical" and "logical" bandied about when discussing networks. These terms are used for quite a few different things. *Physical,* used in the context of networking, means the actual, physical thing; what you can see and feel. *Logical* means how something works, despite its appearance. For example, a Token Ring network is physically wired in a star; each cable radiates out from the MAU to each node. Logically, though, it's a ring, in which the signals travel from node to node in a circular fashion. The fact that the signals physically travel from the node to the MAU and back to the next node is usually unimportant when thinking about the logical circular arrangement of the Token Ring.

NOTE

Networks that are physically wired in a star topology are logically either a bus or a ring. This means, despite what the network looks like, it still "behaves" as either a bus or a ring. Ethernet networks wired in a star fashion are logically a bus, while Token Ring networks wired in a star fashion are logically a ring.

Star topology networks can use one of several forms of Ethernet. The most common in existence is 10Base-T Ethernet, which provides 10Mpbs of bandwidth. Used for the majority of new networks is 100Base-T Ethernet, which provides 100Mpbs of bandwidth. A newer standard called Gigabit Ethernet (1000Base-T) offers 1Gbps of bandwidth. Most recently, a new standard has been approved, called 10 Gigabit Ethernet (or alternately 10GBase-X), which can run at 10Gbps over fiber-optic cable.

10Base-T requires a type of twisted-pair cable called Category 3 (Cat 3) cable, while 100Base-T requires Category 5 (Cat 5) cable (10Base-T can also use Cat 5, but 100Base-T cannot use Cat 3; these days one should always use the most recent Cat 5 cable—called Cat5E—even if it's only intended for a 10Base-T network).

10Base-T networks share the following wiring characteristics:

- Require four actual wires (two twisted pairs in a single sheath); can be either unshielded twisted pair (UTP) or shielded twisted pair (STP).

- Can be run on either Cat 3 or Cat 5 cable (Cat 5 cable provides eight wires—four twisted pairs—and so can carry two node connections in each cable if desired).

- Are limited to a length of 100 meters (328 feet) for each node connection.

- Are not limited in the number of nodes in a single logical segment.

- Use RJ-45 connectors for all connections (this type of connector is similar to a modular telephone connector, but the RJ-45 is larger).

100Base-T networks are similar to 10Base-T networks and have these characteristics:

- Require four actual wires (two twisted pairs in a single sheath).

- Must use Cat5 cable or better (Some vendors are supplying cable called Cat6 and Cat7. While these cables may be of higher grade than Cat5 [or equivalent to Cat5e], the standards are not yet finalized and these cable categories do not yet officially exist.).

- Are limited to a length of 100 meters (328 feet) for each node connection.

- Are not limited in the number of nodes in a single logical segment.

- Use RJ-45 connectors for all connections.

1000Base-T networks are notable in that they can run over existing Cat 5 cable but at 10 times the speed of 100Base-T networks. Running over Cat 5 cable is a significant advantage for 1000Base-T, because around 75 percent of installed network cabling today is Cat 5, and rewiring an entire building for a new networking standard is an extremely expensive proposition. 1000Base-T over Cat 5 has these characteristics:

● Require eight actual wires (four twisted pairs in a single sheath).

● Must use Cat 5 cable or better.

● Are limited to a length of 100 meters (328 feet) for each node connection.

● Are not limited in the number of nodes in a single logical segment.

● Use RJ-45 connectors for all connections.

Two tradeoffs are involved with star topology networks as compared to bus networks. First, star topology networks cost more. Much more actual wire is required, the labor to install that wire is much greater, and an additional cost exists for the needed hubs. To offset these costs, however, star topologies are far more reliable than bus topologies. With a star topology, if any single network connection goes bad (is cut or damaged in some way) only that one connection is affected. While it is true that hubs echo all the network signals for the connected nodes to all other nodes on the hub, they also have the capability to *partition*, or cut off, any misbehaving node connections automatically—one bad apple won't spoil the whole bunch. In addition, because each cable is run directly from the hub to the node, it is extremely easy to troubleshoot; you don't have to go traipsing over an entire building trying to find the problem.

Ring Topology

A ring topology is actually not a physical arrangement of a network cable as you might guess. Instead, rings are a logical arrangement; the actual cables are wired in a star, with each node connected on its own cable to the MAU. However, electrically the network behaves like a ring, where the network signals travel around the ring to each node in turn. Figure 4-4 shows a sample ring topology network.

Ring topology LANs are based on Token Ring instead of Ethernet. Some may also run Fiber Distributed Data Interface (FDDI)—a 100Mbps fiber-optic network—instead of copper-based cable. Rings are also used for some larger telecommunications networks like Synchronous Optical Network (SONET), as well as in Storage Area Networks and some other applications.

Compare Rings to Stars and Buses

To understand how rings compare to stars and buses, you first need to understand a basic concept of how original Ethernet networks worked. These Ethernet networks managed all the

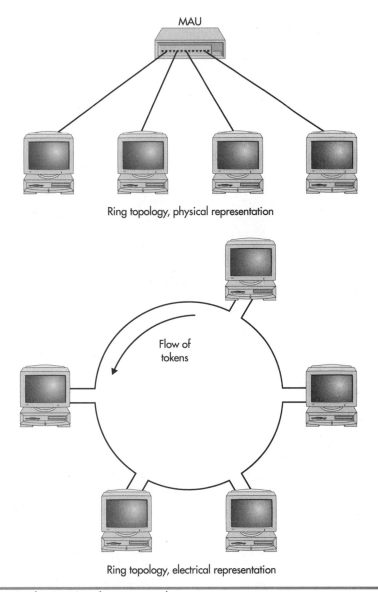

Figure 4-4 A sample ring topology network

needed signals on the network using a technique called CSMA/CD, which stands for Carrier Sense Multiple Access with Collision Detection. CSMA/CD allows each node on a segment to transmit data whenever it likes. If, by chance, two nodes try to transmit at the same time, they each detect this occurrence with their collision detection, and then both nodes wait a random amount of time (counted in milliseconds) to retry their transmission.

NOTE

All half-duplex Ethernet networks (e.g., 10Base-T and most 100Base-T implementations) use CSMA/CD except for a defunct standard proposed by Hewlett-Packard called 100-BaseVG, which used a hybrid of Ethernet and Token Ring collision management techniques.

If you think about how data packets flow on a network using CSMA/CD, you'd probably think that it could quickly become a confusing mess with data and collision retries causing more collisions. And you'd probably think the potential exists for the network to reach a saturation point where virtually nothing gets transmitted because of excessive collisions. You'd be right. For 10Base-T networks, this point occurs somewhere around 3.5Mbps (about a third of the 10Mbps theoretical maximum that one node could achieve sending a stream of data to one other node). However, the reality is that excessive collisions don't pose much of a problem on most networks for two reasons. First, most network traffic is *bursty*, and network nodes rarely consume all the bandwidth on a particular network for any significant length of time. Second, even on a network where excessive collisions are hampering performance, breaking the network segment into smaller pieces and reducing the chances of collisions proportionately is relatively easy. In the real world, CSMA/CD works well and Ethernet is the predominant network standard in the world because it works so well and it is so flexible.

Token Ring networks operate on a different principle than CSMA/CD. Token Ring networks manage their bandwidth with a technique called *token passing*. Electrically, a data entity called a *token* circulates around the logical network ring. The token has two states: free and busy. When a node wants to transmit some data, it waits until the token coming into it is in a free state, and then the node marks the token as busy. Next, after adding to the token packet the data to be sent and the destination address, the node sends the packet on to the next node. The next node, finding the token set to its busy state, examines the destination address and passes the token on unchanged toward the destination. Once the destination node receives the token, it gets its data, marks the token as free, and sends it along to the next workstation. If the token somehow becomes "lost," then a workstation generates a new, free token automatically after a set period of time passes.

The beauty of Token Ring networks is that they behave predictably as the bandwidth needs of the nodes increase. Also, Token Ring networks are never bogged down by collisions, which are impossible in such a network. However, these benefits of Token Ring networks are offset somewhat by the greater overhead and processing needs to handle the tokens. Overall, Token Ring networks perform about as fast as Ethernet networks with similar bandwidth.

IBM invented the Token Ring network technology in the late 1960s, and the first Token Ring networks started appearing in 1986. While quite a few Token Ring LANs are installed (running at either 4Mbps or 16Mbps), you tend to see them predominantly in companies that have a strong IBM relationship and, perhaps, also use an IBM mainframe or minicomputer.

If you're designing a new LAN, generally your best bet is to use Ethernet in a star topology. You'll find network equipment for this choice is readily available, inexpensive, and many qualified installers are available for 10Base-T, 100Base-T, or 1000Base-T. For new networks, always choose Cat5e cable, even if you're only going to initially use 10Base-T, so that you have a ready upgrade path to the faster standards.

Choose Token Ring if some external need is driving this, such as connectivity needs to an old IBM mainframe that doesn't support Ethernet.

Progress Check

1. How do Ethernet networks manage simultaneous signals on the cable from multiple nodes?

2. What is the difference between the physical and logical arrangement of a 100Base-T network?

3. For a new network being built from the ground up, what cable topology should you choose, and what networking standard should you run over that topology, given no underlying requirements (like an old IBM mainframe that only interfaces to Token Ring) to choose one standard over another?

CRITICAL SKILL
4.2 Demystify Network Cabling

Network cabling can be incredibly confusing. Not only do lots of different types of network cables exist, all with their own names and properties, but often you can select different types of cables for a single type of network. For example, Ethernet networks can use an astonishing number of cables, ranging from coaxial cable, to unshielded or shielded twisted-pair cable, to thick coaxial cable, to fiber-optic cable. To design or support any given network, you need to know what your cable choices are and how to maintain that particular type of cable.

---

1. Carrier Sense Multiple Access with Collision Detection (CSMA/CD)

2. The physical arrangement is what you actually see, and is in the shape of a star. The logical arrangement is how it works, and in the case of 100Base-T, the logical arrangement is that of a bus.

3. The best current choice is to wire the building with at least Cat5e cable, running 100Base-T over that cable.

The focus in this section is to demystify cabling systems for you. You learn primarily about the most common types of network cable, the kinds that you'll find in 99 percent of the networks in existence and that you'll use for 99 percent of any new networks. When appropriate, this section will make passing reference to other cable types so that you know what they are, but you should focus your attention on only a few ubiquitous cable types—the ones primarily discussed here.

Learn Basic Cable Types

There are many different basic cable types. The most common are unshielded twisted-pair (UTP) and coaxial, with UTP being by far the most common today. Other common types of network cabling are shielded twisted-pair (STP) and fiber-optic cable.

Unshielded twisted-pair cable consists of two or more pairs of plastic-insulated conductors inside a cable sheath (made from either vinyl or Teflon). For each pair, the two conductors are twisted within the cable, helping the cable resist outside electrical interference. Rigid standards exist for how this cable is made, including the proper distance between each twist of the pair. Figure 4-5 shows an example of UTP cable.

STP is similar to UTP, but STP has a braided metal shield surrounding the twisted pairs to reduce further the chance of interference from electrical sources outside the cable.

Coaxial cable consists of a central copper conductor wrapped in a plastic insulation material, which is, in turn, surrounded by a braided wire shield and, finally, wrapped in a plastic cable sheath. (The coaxial cable used for televisions is similar in design.) Two main types are used for networks. Thin Ethernet (10Base-2) uses RG-58/AU or RG-58/CU cable, while Thick Ethernet (10Base-5) uses—you guessed it—a much thicker coaxial cable called RG-8. Figure 4-6 shows an example of coaxial cable.

Fiber-optic cable uses a glass strand and carries the data signals as light instead of electricity. It used to be that fiber-optic cable was used for higher-speed networks, but this is changing. This is good news, as fiber-optic cable is extremely expensive to purchase, install, and maintain. However, fiber-optic cable can do one thing that copper cables cannot: span extremely long distances. Fiber-optic cable can easily reach two miles at 100Mbps. For this reason, fiber-optic cable is often used to connect together buildings in a campus-like setting. But other than using it in situations when you need to span very long distances, you should avoid using fiber-optic cable.

> Twisted-pairs

Figure 4-5 UTP cable

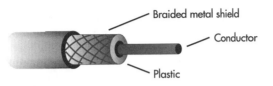

Figure 4-6 Coaxial cable

Twisted-Pair Cabling: The King of Network Cables

For the past several years, virtually all new networks have been built using some form of twisted-pair cabling. Usually, Category 5-grade twisted-pair is used, although quite a few networks exist in which Category 3-grade cable is installed. UTP is used instead of STP in almost all cases because it's less expensive, easier to install and maintain, and isn't much

Ask the Expert

Q: What is all this stuff about 10Base this and that?

A: The various Ethernet standards referred to as, for instance, 10Base-2, 10Base-T, 100Base-T, and so on contain in their name all you need to know about what they do. The first portion— the number—can be 10, 100, or 1000, and this number indicates the data rate (in Mbps) that the standard carries. The word *Base* means the network is *baseband* rather than *broadband*. (A baseband connection only carries one signal at a time, while a broadband connection carries multiple signals at a time). The terminating letter or number indicates what sort of cable is used, with *T* denoting twisted-pair, 2 denoting thin coaxial, and 5 denoting thick coaxial. Here's a quick reference guide to the different standards commonly seen:

- 10Base-2. 10Mbps, coaxial (RG-58) cable
- 10Base-5. 10Mbps, coaxial (RG-8) cable
- 10Base-T. 10Mbps, twisted-pair (two pairs, Cat-3 or higher) cable
- 100Base-T. 100Mbps, twisted-pair (two pairs, Cat-5) cable. Also, there is a variant called 100Base-T4 to designate four pairs.
- 100Base-TX. 100Mbps, twisted-pair (two pairs, Cat-5) cable
- 100Base-FX. 100Mbps, fiber-optic cable
- 1000Base-T. 1Gbps, twisted-pair (four pairs, Cat-5) cable
- 10GBase-X. 10Gbps, fiber-optic cable

affected by electrical interference. Both Ethernet and Token Ring networks use twisted-pair cabling. Note that different Ethernet types require different cables and that some higher-speed standards require STP.

When a new twisted-pair network is installed, a number of wiring components form the complete run from the workstation to the hub. As shown in Figure 4-7, the cabling starts at the hub, where a patch cable (usually 6–10 feet long) connects a port on the hub to a patch panel, using RJ-45 connectors on each end. On the other side of the patch panel, the twisted-pair cable is hard-wired to the patch panel connection, and then runs continuously to a wall jack (in an office, for instance), to which it is also hard-wired. The wall jack contains a RJ-45 connector on its other side, to which another patch cable connects, and then connects to the computer's Network Interface Card (NIC). The distance from the connector on the hub to the connector on the computer's NIC cannot exceed 100 meters of cable length.

Anywhere twisted-pair cabling isn't hard-wired, it uses RJ-45 modular connectors. These are just like the modular connectors you see on telephones, but they are larger and can accommodate up to eight wires. 10Base-T and 100Base-T uses four of those wires (two pairs: one for transmit and one for receive), while 1000Base-T uses eight of those wires.

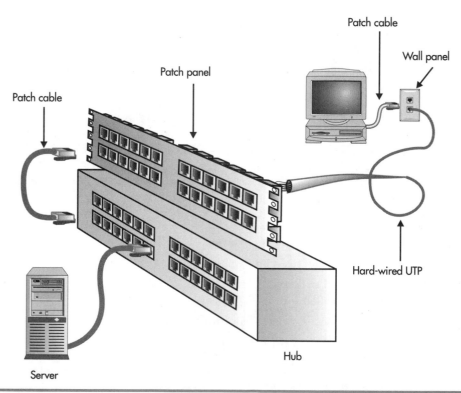

Figure 4-7 A typical twisted-pair network arrangement

The eight wires in the RJ-45 connector are numbered from one to eight. If you were to hold the connector in your left hand, with the pins in the connector facing up and pointed forward, pin 1 of the connector is the one furthest away from you (see Figure 4-8). Table 4-1 shows both the colors of standard Cat-5 cable that should be wired to each pin and 10Base-T assignments.

Most communications and network devices, including those designed to use RJ-45 connectors, are either *data communications equipment* (DCE) or *data terminal equipment* (DTE). If you have DTE equipment on one end, you need DCE equipment on the other. In a way, it's just like screws and nuts. Two screws don't go directly together and neither do two nuts. The same principle applies here: DCE equipment can't talk directly to other DCE equipment, nor can DTE equipment talk directly to DTE equipment.

The RJ-45 jack on a hub is DCE, while the RJ-45 jack on a computer's NIC is DTE. Note, you cannot communicate between DCE and DCE devices, or DTE and DTE devices using a standard twisted-pair/RJ-45 cable that has been wired, as described in Table 4-1. For instance, you cannot use a standard twisted-pair patch cable to connect directly from a network server to a workstation, or between two workstations, because those are all DTE devices. Instead, you must purchase or prepare a *crossover cable* that compensates for having, say, two DTE devices connect directly to each other. For 10Base-T networks, Table 4-2 shows you the wiring needed for a crossover cable.

TIP

You can easily purchase all the tools and parts needed to make twisted-pair/RJ-45 cables, and you should do so if you manage a network of any appreciable size (more than 50 workstations). Learning to use these tools and parts to make patch cables or to replace a failed cable can quickly become invaluable. This way, you can quickly make cables of any length you need. However, even though you should be able to do this, you're better off purchasing premade twisted-pair/RJ-45 cables to use with your network. Professionally made cables are more reliable and should give you fewer problems than the ones that you make yourself. Make your own cables when you're in a pinch.

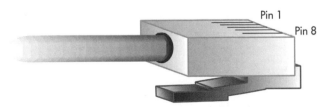

Figure 4-8 An RJ-45 connector

Pin Number	Wire Base Color	Wire Stripe Color	10Base-T Use
1	White	Orange	Transmit negative
2	Orange	White	Transmit positive
3	White	Green	Receive negative
4	Blue	White	N/A
5	White	Blue	N/A
6	Green	White	Receive positive
7	White	Brown	N/A
8	Brown	White	N/A

Table 4-1 10Base-T Wire Assignments for RJ-45 Connectors

What's All This About Cable Categories?

Twisted-pair network cables are rated in terms of their capability to carry network traffic. These ratings are defined by the Electronics Industry Association (EIA) and are referred to as Levels 1 and 2, and Categories 3, 4, 5, and 6. The different category levels are simply called Cat-3 through Cat-6. Table 4-3 shows the rated performance for each of these levels.

To achieve a particular performance rating in practice, you not only need cable certified to that performance level, but you must observe other requirements, including using connectors and patch cables that also meet the level of performance you want to achieve. For example, for a Cat-5 installation, you must have Cat-5 cable, connectors, patch panels, and patch cables. The entire circuit, from where the client computer connects to the hub connection at the other end, needs to be tested and certified to the performance level you need to achieve.

Pin	Wire Base Color	Wire Stripe Color	Pin	Wire Base Color	Wire Stripe Color
1	White	Orange	1	White	Green
2	Orange	White	2	Green	White
3	White	Green	3	White	Orange
6	Green	White	6	Orange	White

Table 4-2 Twisted-Pair/RJ-45 Crossover Cable Wiring

Level or Category	Rated Performance
Level 1	Not performance rated
Level 2	1Mbps
Category 3	10Mbps
Category 4	16Mbps
Category 5	100 Mbps to 1Gbps
Category 6	>1Gbps

Table 4-3 Twisted-Pair Performance Designations

TIP

You can use higher-rated cable systems for networks with lower requirements. For example, common practice these days is to use Cat-5 cable for all network wiring, even if the network only uses 10Base-T at 10Mpbs. Doing this makes good sense because cable plants are expensive to replace and using Cat-5 cable means you won't have to replace the network cabling when the network is upgraded eventually to 100Base-T or some higher standard. Also, Cat-5 cabling components are of higher quality than Cat-3 components, so your network cabling is likely to be more reliable.

Coaxial Cable

Many older networks (those built prior to circa 1992) still have coaxial cable installed. Most of this coaxial cable is the thin variety, which is RG-58 and is used with Thin Ethernet. A few may also use the thicker RG-8 cable for Thick Ethernet, but this is rare.

Thin Ethernet cabling is wired in a bus arrangement, where each network segment starts with a terminator that connects to the end of the cable, runs to each node in turn, and ends with another terminator on the other end. The terminators contain special 50-ohm resistors, and the network cable will not work unless both are installed.

All the connectors in a Thin Ethernet system are BNC connectors, a quick-release bayonet-style connector, both reliable and easy to use. BNC connectors come in a variety of different styles to enable you to make just about any network connection you need along the bus, including T-connectors, which have two female BNC connectors on each side of the crossbar of the *T* and a male BNC connector at the end of the shaft of the *T*. The two female connectors are used for the RG-58 cable coming into and out of a node, while the male

Ask the Expert

Q: **What is plenum-grade cable?**

A: In a building, the area between the ceiling of the rooms and the roof of the building is called the plenum space. Most buildings use ducts (big, flexible hoses) to provide conditioned air to the rooms in the building and they use the open plenum space for air returned from the rooms. Typically, the air returned from the rooms is partially reused by the air conditioning units to save energy, because it's already cooled or heated as appropriate—this saves a lot of energy over using 100 percent outside air. Occasionally, a building uses ducts for the return air, but the standard for office space is simply to use the plenum space.

Why is this discussion about office building air handling important in this module about cables? Because to run network cable through the ceiling of a building that uses the plenum for return air, you must either install the cable inside special piping called *conduit* (which is extremely expensive) or use plenum-grade cable. The difference between non-plenum cable and plenum cable is that the plastics used in plenum cable do not give off toxic fumes in case of a fire. Because most office buildings reuse the air in the plenum space, the last thing you would want to happen is to have them redistributing toxic fumes if a fire broke out somewhere in the building's roof or plenum space. A fire in a very small area could cause the fumes from the burning cable distributed to a very large area of the building because of how these ventilation systems work—most definitely a Bad Thing.

Make sure to check with your cabling contractor for details about the municipality in which you are installing network cable, but virtually all local codes in the United States require either conduit or plenum-level cable for buildings with plenum air returns. In addition to choosing the right kind of cable, it's also important for the cable installer to be familiar with, and comfortable with, doing any required wall penetrations that cross one-hour, fire-rated corridors or building fire zones. Those wall penetrations must be properly sealed to maintain the building's fire ratings.

connector attaches to a female BNC connector on the node's Ethernet card. There are also barrel connectors, with two female connectors on them; these are used to connect two Thin Ethernet wires together. Barrel connectors are also available in different shapes, including an elbow bend and a U-shaped bend, but most of the time the simple straight barrel connector is used. Figure 4-2, earlier in the chapter, shows the various parts of a Thin Ethernet BNC cable system.

Coaxial cable has a central *conductor*, which can be either a solid, single copper wire or a stranded set of wires. A white plastic material surrounds the central conductor, which is, in turn, surrounded by a metal foil, and then a braided wire *shield*. The shield is finally wrapped in the final plastic cable sheath.

TIP

Cable types must not be mixed in any coaxial network. If the network uses, say, RG-58A/U, then that is what you must always use—not any other coaxial cable. Not mixing RG-58A/U and RG-58/U is also a good idea because they have ever-so-slightly different signaling characteristics. (A/U cable uses a stranded center conductor, while /U—sometimes called C/U—uses a solid center conductor).

Learning to make coaxial cables with BNC connectors is fairly easy, but you need two special tools to make the job easy. First, you need a wire stripper that will cut the various parts of the cable to the right length. Many good strippers can do this for you automatically; check with your cable supplier to order one. You also need a crimper that both can crimp the central BNC pin onto the central conductor of the cable and can crimp the metal sleeve that holds the entire connector onto the wire. Again, you can buy special crimpers that can easily do both jobs. The best crimpers use a ratcheting mechanism to make exerting the proper amount of force easier for a solid, reliable connection.

Progress Check

1. When do you have to use plenum cable for a wiring installation?

2. Do you know what the following network types are and what type of cable they require? 10Base-2, 10Base-T, 100Base-T, and 1000Base-T.

---

1. When cable is run through a building's plenum space and the building uses the plenum space for HVAC return air. (Always check on your local jurisdiction's requirements, which may differ).

2. 10Base-2 uses RG-58 coax cable, 10Base-T requires Cat3 twisted pair cable, and 100Base-T and 1000Base-T use Cat5 or better twisted-pair.

Install and Maintain Network Cabling

Not only is the selection of a type of network cabling important, it's also important to install the cabling correctly. A proper cable plant installation should include all of the following:

- Proper cable and connectors for the type of network, including documentation of what components were selected and used.

- Complete labeling of all parts of the network, which should include the wall plates, cables, patch panel ports, patch cables, and hub port assignments.

- An *as-built* drawing of the building showing all the cabling routes and locations.

- A certification report showing that all the installed cables operate properly, using a special network test device.

- For bus-type networks, teaching users that they should not touch the coaxial cable for any reason whatsoever. The coaxial cable will cause all other nodes in the segment to fail if the cable is separated. Make sure that Facilities personnel also know this.

Making sure that a new cable plant installation is properly installed and well documented will save you time over the long run, by making the network more reliable and much easier to maintain and repair.

Choosing a Cabling Contractor

When building a new network, choosing a cabling contractor is extremely important. A contractor who does high-quality, well-documented work is desirable and, unfortunately, hard to find.

When choosing a contractor, make sure that he or she has a lot of experience installing networks like the one you're installing. In addition, assess the following issues as part of your selection:

- How will the contractor document the cable plant? What are his or her standards and do you think those documentation standards meet your needs? (Remember, no such thing exists as too much documentation for cable plants.)

- Will the contractor provide a set of as-built drawings showing how he or she installed the cables in the building? (If so, you should consult with the contractor before the work begins and reach an agreement that the final payment won't be made until these drawings are delivered. Contractors of all types are notorious for dragging their feet on providing these drawings once the work is finished.)

- How does the contractor install the cable to avoid electrical interference sources in the ceiling and walls?

- Does the contractor recommend a wiring solution that combines telecom wiring with data wiring? (Generally, keeping these two cable plants separate is best. They have different requirements and respond differently to different building conditions. What works fine for telephones may not work at all for network cable, and vice versa.)

- Has the contractor done any local installations that you can visit and view?

- Does the contractor also provide speedy post-installation support for new wiring drops? This is important, as many wiring contractors who specialize in new construction wiring are not good about returning to do the occasional single drop for new node locations. Ask for references regarding this important information.

- What equipment does the contractor use to certify the cable plant? What certification documentation will the contractor provide upon completion?

- Does the contractor also provide post-installation troubleshooting services?

Make sure to spend time finding the best local cable contractors available to you and compare them carefully. You may want to contact other companies like yours or computer user group members in your area to seek recommendations and experiences with different contractors. Try not to just rely on the references provided by the contractor; even firms that do sloppy work can usually put together a few good references.

TIP

For a large cabling job, make sure to negotiate an appropriate payment schedule. You should shoot for something along the lines of 30 percent on inception, 50 percent on completion, and 20 percent on delivery of as-built drawings, certification reports, and any other final deliverables. Make sure to keep no less than 15 percent for these final deliverables, to ensure that the cable contractor delivers them expediently. Contractors are notorious for dragging their feet on things like this after the wiring itself is done, so you need to make sure you have a way to motivate them to get *everything* done.

Solving Cable Problems

Cable problems can be extremely hard to diagnose and repair. Many cable problems are intermittent or result in reduced network bandwidth for the affected nodes. Tracking down the source of the problem can be difficult. At times, it's hard to know there even *is* a problem! Problems with network cabling typically exhibit themselves in the following ways:

- Abnormally slow network performance, particularly if one node is much slower than other, similar nodes (for star networks) or if all nodes on one segment have slower network performance than nodes on other segments (for bus networks).

- Sporadic disconnections from the network.

- Complete loss of network connectivity. This problem can also be intermittent.

Star networks are the easiest to troubleshoot. Because each node is on its own network cable leading to the hub, it's easier to isolate the problem down to several lengths of cable. If you're having trouble with a node on a star topology network, first determine if something is wrong with the computer or the cabling. Move the computer to a different location in the building and see if the same problems occur. If they do, then it's a sure bet the problem is in the computer, such as a failing NIC. Next, if the computer has normal network performance in a different location, try replacing the patch cable leading from the node to the wall. These cables can often become slightly damaged as furniture or computers are moved around. Next, in the wiring closet you can try connecting the patch panel from the node's location to a different port on the hub using a different patch cable. While wiring closet patch panels are less likely to fail, because they aren't moved around much, they can still have poor connections or wiring that can become problematic over time. Finally, if you have eliminated all other factors, you must consider replacing the cable leading from the wiring closet to the node's location. At this point, having a qualified network cabling contractor to assist you can be extremely helpful. The qualified network cabling contractor has equipment to test the cable in the wall and to determine if it's bad before pulling a replacement cable through the building. For troubleshooting help, you should expect to pay around $150 for a contractor to come out and test a length of cable. If for some reason they have to pull a new cable all the way to the location, you'll also have to pay for labor and materials for that work.

Coaxial networks can be much harder to troubleshoot, because many nodes share a single segment of the network. Usually, a problem in one part of the segment affects all nodes on the segment similarly. By far the most common problem on coaxial networks is loss of network connectivity for all the nodes in a segment. Someone disconnecting the network cable so it is not a continuous run invariably causes this loss. To track this problem down, you'll find 90 percent of the time that it's necessary to discover who's moving or rearranging offices, or which offices are being painted, or where other work of this type is being done in the building. The chances are excellent the problem is there. If this fails, then the troubleshooting job becomes much more difficult. There are two ways to track down cable breaks that aren't obvious:

● Use a coaxial cable scanner. These hand-held instruments can be attached to a coaxial network cable and can tell you how far along the cable any shorts or breaks are occurring. Keep attaching the cable scanner to the network cable in different locations until you can track down the problem.

● Get an extra terminator for the network and then disconnect the cable in a particular location and attach the terminator. See if the computers on the new, smaller segment can log into a server (a server must be available in the same segment; otherwise, you can use the PING command—if you're using the TCP/IP protocol on your computers—and try to ping another workstation in the complete segment). If they can, then you know the problem is further on along the cable. Move to a new location, attach the extra terminator, and try again. Eventually, you will find two nearby locations where the terminator will allow the network to work in one spot, but not in the next spot. You should find the cable problem somewhere between those two node locations. This approach requires patience, but it works fine in a pinch.

More troublesome still on coaxial networks is a problem that is causing poor network performance, but which is not causing any nodes actually to disconnect from the network. Such problems can be tough to find because they are often intermittent and they aren't usually easy to find with a cable scanner. When you have this type of problem, your best approach is to come up with a test that can quickly tell you how fast the nodes are communicating with the network. For example, you can time how long it takes to copy a particular file from the server. Then, use a terminator to close off a large part of the segment and perform the test again. Keep moving the terminator and retrying the test until you discover what part of the cable slows down network performance on the segment. Then, either replace all those portions or narrow your search further. This type of problem is usually caused by a poor connection in one of the male cable-end BNC connectors, although a flaky T-connector or barrel connector can also cause it. It's usually fastest—providing you narrow the problem to a small enough area—simply to replace all the cable and connectors in that location.

Having a second person to help you troubleshoot coaxial cable problems helps a lot, and you can find the problem much more quickly if you and the other troubleshooter have portable radios with which to communicate. One way to take advantage of this is to post one person in a fixed location at one end of the segment with a test computer, then have the other person move from location to location with a terminator. While the mobile troubleshooter maps out parts of the segment with the terminator, the stationary person can quickly test to see if any individual parts of the segment prove to be a source of the problem.

TIP

Before going to the trouble of pulling a new section of cable through the wall or replacing various cables and connectors, try simply running an extra cable from one location to another, such as out the door of one room, down the hallway, and into the room of another. Then, test to see if this "mapping out" of the suspect portion of the segment fixes the problem. If the problem goes away, then go ahead and have new cable run in the walls. If the problem is still there, you need to look further before replacing cable and connectors.

As a general rule, troubleshooting cable problems requires a careful step-by-step approach and a lot of patience. For coaxial cable systems, troubleshooting is made more difficult because a lot of network users are breathing down your neck while you're trying to concentrate and find the problem. You're lucky if you can find a coaxial network problem and solve it within an hour. Some problems, though, may take several hours (or more) to resolve.

CRITICAL SKILL
4.4 # Select and Install a SOHO Network

While this is a book focused on business networking, small office and home office (SOHO) networking is growing in importance, and no discussion about networking would really be complete without at least some coverage of home networking. Because people are purchasing and installing more and more computers for their homes, the question of home networking is becoming increasingly important to them.

Consider the benefits that a home network can bring a household with two or more computers:

- Printers can be shared, allowing all of the computer users in the home to make use of all of the printers. For example, some homes may have both color inkjet and black-and-white laser printers available. By sharing these printers through a home network, each person can make use of the most appropriate printer for any particular print job.

- A high-speed Internet connection can be shared. Many localities now have various high-speed Internet connections available in them, including DSL and cable networks. Both types can be configured to support multiple computers in a home. However, in order to take advantage of such connections, the computers must already be networked within the home.

- Files (or free storage space) can be shared. Sometimes a particular computer may start getting short on storage space. With a home network, however, all the computers in the home can use the available space on all of the other computers, possibly saving money that might otherwise need to be spent on replacement computers or additional hard disk drives.

● Backup devices can be shared. With a home network, critical files from all of the computers can be backed up over the network to a common tape drive or CD burner. Alternatively, critical files from each system can be copied onto one of the other systems as a form of backup, provided the computers have enough free space to permit this approach.

I'm sure you can see how these benefits would be helpful for homes with more than one computer. The question that follows, then, is this: What is the best way to select and install a home network?

Choose a SOHO Network

Due to the growth in interest in home networking, many companies are offering special home networking hardware and software. Additionally, in many cases, a home network can take advantage of traditional networking hardware and software. This section provides an overview of different home networking options.

Standard Network Hardware

It used to be that it wasn't really viable for home networks to use networking equipment designed for businesses, because business network equipment was too expensive and was designed to support only larger networks. A 24-port Ethernet hub would definitely be overkill for a home with two or three computers!

However, these days business network equipment is available in all shapes and sizes, and low-end solutions will work quite nicely in most homes. Small Ethernet hubs (both 10Base-T and 100Base-T) that can economically support two to four computers are readily available for around $50–$75.

If you consider all of the components that you would need for a small network, you'll find that you really don't need all that much:

● You need a central hub. You can install this hub in a convenient location, such as wherever the home's telephone wiring is located, or in a garage, closet, attic, or basement. You will need an available 110v outlet to power the hub in whatever location you select.

● Each computer needs a network interface card (NIC) that supports the type of network that you are installing. Most modern computers come with 10/100Base-T Ethernet cards built into them. If your computer doesn't have one of these cards, it's easy and inexpensive to purchase and install a standard NIC into most computers. The cost for a good Ethernet NIC these days is less than $50. Also, there are good Ethernet interfaces that can connect to a computer's USB port, and these are similarly inexpensive and work well.

● You will need to be able to cable the network. This is actually the hardest part, depending on the actual location of the computers and the ease with which you can run network cable to each location. If you aren't comfortable running such cable yourself, a good electrician or telephone wiring technician should be able to do a good job of this for you. The cost of professional wiring is about $100–$150 per network cable run, and this price should include all connectors, the cable, and extras such as wall plates and jacks.

● The operating system on most home computers—usually Windows 95, Windows 98, or Windows ME—is perfectly capable of handling all of the networking duties that you'll need for a home network. If you configure the operating systems for a peer-to-peer network, you'll be able to share printers and files through the system's built-in networking software. No additional software is needed.

All of these components are available separately, just as you would purchase them for a business. However, home networking kits are also available that include all of the components that you need, along with good instructions for setting up the home network. 3Com and Asante both make good home networking kits along these lines, and there are other good ones available, too.

TIP

A book like this can't really make detailed product recommendations, partly because products and technology change faster than books do. It's a good idea, therefore, to find recent reviews of products for home networking and use those reviews to help you decide on an actual product. Many good computer magazines have current product reviews, including some reviews of home-oriented products. Check your local library or the magazine rack at your local bookstore.

Other Home Network Options

A point made in the preceding section bears repeating: The hardest part of installing a home network is the wiring. Most people aren't qualified to install network cabling, nor do they want to start making holes in their walls and trying to figure out how to route cabling through their house (or under their house). Because this is the single greatest difficulty to installing a home network, many companies have come out with alternative network options that eliminate this problem, as follows:

● **Phoneline networks**   Home network kits are now offered that use a home's existing telephone wiring to provide a network connection between computers in a home. This option becomes attractive if there are telephone connections near each computer. Intel, 3Com, D-Link, and other companies offer phoneline network kits for the home.

● **Powerline networks**   Some companies are offering hardware that lets you network computers through a home's existing power wiring. The network equipment transmits its information through the power wiring, and all that's needed is to plug a special adapter into an available outlet near each computer. Powerline networks are typically slower than other network types (most claim speeds of about around 1Mbps) and they are subject to electrical noise from various types of equipment in the home. (One reviewer, in fact, had his powerline network crash every time his refrigerator's compressor came on.) You should choose a powerline network only as a last resort.

● **Wireless networks**   Another option is to use wireless technology. Several companies, including Netgear, D-Link, and Linksys, offer wireless home networking equipment. These networks, when using the latest technology, run at a pretty fast clip: 11Mbps, which is faster than 10Base-T and should be more than adequate for home use. If you decide to try a wireless home network, be aware that different factors in your home (for example, electrical interference from some appliance, or something in the walls that limits the connection between rooms or floors) may limit the network's speed or functionality. So, make sure that you can return or exchange the equipment if it doesn't work properly in your home.

Wireless solutions have been gaining a lot of steam in 2002, and they look to now be the favorite for home and small office networks that are eschewing hard-wired network solutions. There are two basic wireless standards that are in wide use: 802.11b and 802.11a. It's counter-intuitive, but in this particular case, 802.11a is a more advanced and faster standard than 802.11b (in this area only, think "b" for "basic" and "a" for "advanced"). 802.11b is presently in the widest use, and there are many good and relatively inexpensive solutions available that use this standard, including some rather nice combination units that combine an 802.11b wireless access point (also called a WAP, sort of like a wireless hub) along with a router intended to share a home's high-bandwidth Internet connection among multiple computers. The nice thing about the combination units is that one doesn't need to pay more for Internet service for multiple computers; the router makes it appear as if only one computer is on the connection.

There are some things about wireless about which you should be aware. First is that the two predominant standards operate at different data speeds. 802.11b operates at 11Mbps while 802.11a operates at 55Mbps. Second is that the particulars of the home and other installed equipment may interfere with a wireless network. This is most pronounced with 802.11b, which operates at 2.4GHz, the same frequency as many portable telephones and also where microwave ovens operate. (In fact, I tried to set up an 802.11b network at my home, and while it was easy to set up and connect, I kept getting dropped connections and I couldn't use my portable phone anywhere near the wireless network connections because it caused audible interference. 802.11a operates at 5GHz, which should be much less subject to interference.) Third, a wireless network potentially exposes you to security concerns. There are stories of people who drive around in cars with notebook computers and wireless network cards installed just looking for a free connection. Since most of these devices work in ranges greater than 300 feet, this is actually a possibility about which you should be concerned, albeit an unlikely one. Forth, this area is evolving very rapidly as of 2002, and a solution purchased today may not be compatible with equivalent hardware available in a couple of years.

4

Understanding Network Cabling

There are a lot of different ways to network computers in a home, and you need to consider several factors before choosing a type of network. Chief among these factors is the layout of the house and the locations of the computers. Also, consider whether you want to install extra wiring in the house, and whether you have a location for a central hub.

Generally, most people should first investigate standard networking hardware first, then wireless and phoneline networks, and finally try a powerline network as the last option. As always, assess your own needs carefully and make sure that you can exchange or return any home network equipment if it doesn't work properly in your home.

NOTE

For more on setting up a home network, see *Home Networking Survival Guide* by David Strom (McGraw-Hill/Osborne Media, 2001).

Module 4 Mastery Check

1. What are the three main network topologies?

2. What is an inherent advantage that Token Ring has over Ethernet?

3. When cabling a new network, what type of cable should you choose to run in most cases?

4. You would choose fiber-optic cable when you need to _____.

5. BNC connectors are used with what type of Ethernet network cable?

6. What is the modular connector used with 100Base-T networks called?

7. From the name 100Base-T, you can know which of the following statements are true?

    A. It is for a broadband network.

    B. It uses twisted-pair cable.

    C. It operates at 0.1 Gbps.

    D. It uses BNC connectors.

8. You need to understand the 5-4-3 rule for what type of network? What does the 5-4-3 rule mean?

9. True or false: A Token Ring network is logically and physically arranged in a ring configuration.

10. True or false: 1000Base-T networks require fiber-optic cable.

Module 5

Understanding Network Hardware

I f network wiring constitutes the nervous system of a network, then the devices discussed in this module represent the various organs. The network devices discussed in this module— including repeaters, routers, hubs, and such—are responsible for moving data from one network cable to another. Each device has different properties and uses. A good network design uses the right device for each of the various jobs the network must fulfill.

It is essential that you understand these basic components that go into building a network, as well as the job that each one performs.

CRITICAL SKILL
5.1 # Direct Network Traffic

The critical test of any network design is its capability to direct network traffic from one node to another node. You must connect the network's various devices in a configuration that enables the network to pass signals among the devices as efficiently as possible, taking into account the type of network and the different connectivity requirements for the network. Basic devices you use to connect include

- **Repeaters**, which extend the distance that network traffic can travel over a particular type of network media.

- **Hubs (concentrators)**, which are used to connect nodes to one another when you use a star topology, such as 100Base-T.

- **Bridges**, which are basically intelligent repeaters that direct traffic from one segment to another only when the traffic is destined for the other segment.

- **Routers**, which can intelligently route network traffic in a variety of important ways.

- **Switches**, which form fast point-to-point connections for all the devices connected to them. Connections from one port on a switch to another port are made on an as-needed basis, and are not echoed to ports that aren't involved in the traffic. By limiting the connections made, switches help eliminate traffic collisions caused by noncommunicating segments.

Putting together all the necessary pieces in the right way is the art of network design. Module 14 discusses important aspects of putting these pieces together so they work optimally, but you first have to know what these devices are and what they can do. The following sections discuss these essential network devices.

Repeaters

A *repeater* is a device that extends the distance of a particular network run. It takes a weak network signal in on one side, boosts the signal, and then sends it out its other side. You most often see repeaters on thin Ethernet networks, but they are available for virtually any network connection. For instance, if you have to run a 100Base-T Cat-5 cable longer than 100 meters, a repeater enables you to double that distance.

Repeaters operate at the physical layer of the OSI networking model. They do not have the intelligence to understand the signals that they are transmitting. Repeaters merely amplify the signal coming in either side and repeat it out their other side. (Remember, however, they also amplify any noise on the cable!) Repeaters are used to connect only the same type of media, such as 10Base-2 Thin Ethernet to 10Base-2 Thin Ethernet, or Token Ring twisted pair to Token Ring twisted pair.

Repeaters do have a small amount of intelligence that can be useful. They can segment one of their connections from the other when there is a problem. For example, consider two segments of Thin Ethernet that are connected using a repeater. If one of those segments is broken, the repeater still allows the good segment to continue working within itself. Users on the good segment will be unable to connect to resources on the broken segment, but they can continue to use the good segment without trouble. (Remember, though, this capability does you little good if your servers are on the broken segment and your workstations are on the good segment!) Figure 5-1 shows a network extension using repeaters.

TIP

Repeaters are usually used with 10Base-2 networks (Thin Ethernet), which are discussed in some detail in Module 4.

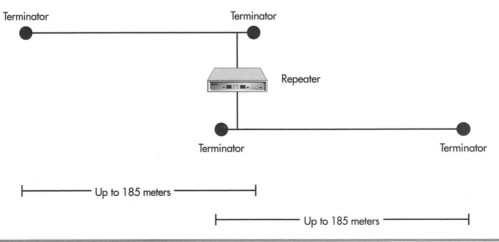

Figure 5-1 Using repeaters to extend network length

Hubs and Concentrators

Intelligent LAN concentrators—more simply called *concentrators* or, even more simply, *hubs*—are used to connect network nodes to network backbones. Nodes are connected to hubs in a physical star fashion (cables fan out from the hub to each node), whether they are used for a star topology or a ring topology network. (A simple network might consist of just a hub or two; smaller networks usually don't require a network backbone.)

NOTE

Module 4 contains a detailed discussion of bus, ring, and star topologies.

Hubs are available for virtually any network media type, with the higher-end hubs using replaceable modules to support multiple media types. For example, you can purchase a high-end hub chassis that can house both Ethernet and Token Ring modules.

You can purchase hubs in a variety of sizes, ranging from those that support only two workstations to those that support more than 100 workstations. Many network designers use stackable hubs, which usually support 24 node connections each. These hubs are often used in concert with switches, which are discussed in their own section of this module.

Hubs have two important properties. The first important property is that hubs echo all data from each port to all the other ports on the hub. Although hubs are wired in a star fashion, they actually perform electrically (logically) more like a bus topology segment in this respect.

Ask the Expert

Q: Should I use fewer large hubs, or more small hubs?

A: Larger hubs (or more often these days, switches) that can host hundreds of connections within a single chassis are generally more powerful than their smaller 24-port siblings, and they tend to have more built-in redundancy, such as backup power supplies in the unit and so forth. However, sometimes it's easier and less expensive to build a network using smaller 24-port hubs or switches, because you can simply purchase an extra 24-port unit as a hot-swap backup (a backup unit that can be quickly swapped in to take the place of a failed unit) that you can manually implement at a moment's notice. The only real disadvantage to this approach is that the redundancy is not automatic: If one 24-port hub/switch fails, you'll have to move its connections to the backup hub/switch, whereas a larger, more redundant unit can switch to redundant features automatically. As always, consider such trade-offs carefully for your particular company and its needs.

Because of this echoing, no filtering or logic occurs to prevent collisions between packets being transmitted by any of the connected nodes. The second important property that hubs possess is *automatic partitioning*, where the hub can automatically *partition* (in this context, *cut off*) any node having trouble from the other nodes, in effect shutting down that node. Such partitioning occurs, for example, if a cable short is detected, if the hub port is receiving excessive packets that are flooding the network, or if some other serious problem is detected for a given port on the hub. Automatic partitioning keeps one malfunctioning connection from causing problems for all of the other connections.

Hubs are becoming much more sophisticated. They often have a number of advanced built-in features, including the following:

- Built-in management, where the hub can be centrally managed over the network, using SNMP or other network management protocols and software.

- Autosensing of different connection speeds. For example, Ethernet hubs that can automatically detect and run each node at either 10 Mbps (10Base-T) or 100 Mbps (100Base-T) are common.

- High-speed uplinks that connect the hub to a backbone. These usually operate at 10 times the basic speed of the hub. (For example, for a 100-Mbps hub, the uplink ports might run at 1 Gbps.)

- Built-in bridging and routing functions, which make it unnecessary to use separate devices to perform bridging and routing.

- Built-in switching, where nodes on the hub can be switched instead of shared.

When ordering a hub, it's important to know how many nodes you want to connect, how much bandwidth each requires, and what type of network backbone is being used. Backbones can be anything from a shared 10 Mbps Thin Ethernet backbone, to 100 Mbps 100Base-TX backbones, up to higher-speed backbones. Your choice of a backbone technology depends on the total amount of bandwidth that you need and the various other network design criteria that you must meet.

Each hub is a separate *collision domain,* or an area of the network in which collisions can occur. Connecting all hubs together in some fashion generally results in a larger collision domain, encompassing all the hubs. The exception to this rule is a configuration where all the separate hubs are connected to a switch, which keeps each hub in its own collision domain. Figure 5-2 shows an example of a network using hubs.

Bridges

Bridges are, in a nutshell, more intelligent versions of repeaters. Bridges can connect two network segments together but they have the intelligence to pass traffic from one segment to

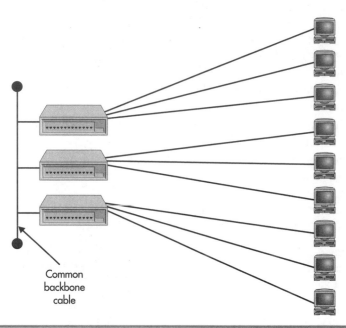

Common
backbone
cable

Figure 5-2 A typical hub arrangement

another *only when that traffic is destined for the other segment.* Bridges are, therefore, used to segment networks into smaller pieces. Some bridges are also available that can span different networking systems and media, such as from coaxial Thin Ethernet to twisted-pair Token Ring.

As you might recall, repeaters operate at the physical layer (Layer 1) of the OSI networking model. Bridges operate one layer higher, at the data-link layer (Layer 2). Bridges examine the media access control (MAC) address of each packet they encounter to determine whether they should forward the packet to the other network. Bridges contain address information about all the parts of your network, through either a static routing table that you program or a dynamic, learning-tree system that discovers all the devices and addresses on the network automatically.

TIP

Because they operate below the network layer at which protocols such as TCP/IP and IPX/SPX are defined, bridges don't really care about the network protocols they're carrying. They care only about the information required to operate at the data-link layer, which means that everything gets bridged or not bridged depending on its MAC address.

You should use bridges only on smaller networks, or in cases where you would otherwise use a repeater, but would benefit from keeping traffic on one segment from being transmitted on the other segment unnecessarily. Often routers or switches offer solutions that perform better and create fewer problems, so examine these other options before choosing a bridge.

Routers

Just as bridges are basically more intelligent repeaters, routers are more intelligent bridges. *Routers* operate at the network layer (Layer 3) of the OSI Model and are far more intelligent than bridges in sending incoming packets off to their destination. Because routers operate at the network layer, a connection across a router requires only that the higher layers use the same protocols. The router can translate from any of the protocols at Layers 1 through 3 to any other protocols at Layers 1 through 3 (provided the router has been configured and designed to do so). Routers can connect both similar and dissimilar networks. They are often used for wide area network (WAN) links.

Routers actually become a node on a network and they have their own network address. Other nodes send packets to the router, which then examines the contents of the packets and forwards them appropriately. (For this reason, routers often have fast microprocessors—usually reduced instruction set computer [RISC]-based—and lots of memory built into them to perform this job.) Routers can also determine the shortest route to a destination and use it. They can perform other tricks to maximize network bandwidth and dynamically adjust to changing problems or traffic patterns on a network.

TIP

To learn about the networks to which they're connected, and what they should do to route various types of packets properly, routers use a process called *discovery*. During the discover process, the router carefully "listens" to traffic on its ports, and also sends out advertisement packets letting other devices know of the router's presence.

Routers form the backbone of the Internet. When you use the TRACERT command to trace the route from a node to a destination, most of the addresses that appear for the hops are actually different routers, each one forwarding the packet to the next until it reaches its destination.

TIP

Routers can route only protocols that are *routable*. AppleTalk, NetBIOS, and NetBEUI are examples of protocols that are *not* routable, while TCP/IP and IPX/SPX are routable.

Routers must be programmed to function correctly. They need to have the addresses assigned to each of their ports, and various network protocol settings must be configured. Routers are usually programmed in one of two ways. First, most routers include an RS-232C port. You can connect a terminal or PC with terminal emulation software to this port and program the router in text mode. Second, most routers have network-based software that enables you to program the router, often using graphical tools. The method you use depends on the router and your security needs (you might want to disable network-based router programming so that unauthorized users cannot change the router's configuration). Figure 5-3 shows an example of a network that uses routers.

Switches

Switches, as their name implies, can switch connections from one port to another and they can do so rapidly. They are connection-oriented and dynamically switch among their various ports to create these connections. Think of a train yard with many trains coming in on some tracks and leaving on other tracks, and the switch being the yard manager who orders the track "switches" to take place so the trains get to their destination. A network switch is much like the yard manager, except that the switch directs packets rather than trains and uses Ethernet cabling rather than train tracks to transport its cargo.

TIP

Switches are a lot like bridges, except that they have many ports and otherwise look like a hub. You might think of a switch as a bridge with multiple ports.

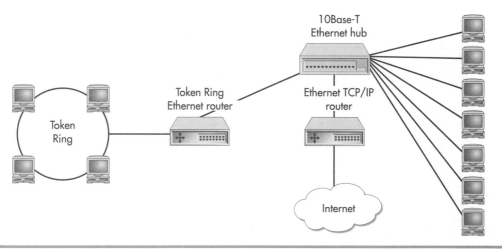

Figure 5-3 Example network using routers

Because switches form one-to-one connections between any two ports, all the ports coming into a switch are not all part of a single collision domain. In this sense, the switch acts as a sort of super bridge. Switches are often used to connect a number of hubs to a much faster backbone. For example, suppose that you have 10 hubs, each with 24 workstation nodes connected. If you simply connect all the hubs together on a common backbone, all 240 workstations would share a single collision domain, which could hurt performance quite a bit. Instead, a much better approach is to install a 12-port switch and to connect each hub to one of the ports on the switch. For instance, it is common to use 10Base-T Ethernet for workstation connections, but 100Base-T (or some other fast network connection) for the backbone. This further allows all the traffic being generated by each of the 10 hubs to continue to run at about 10 Mbps net connection speed to the servers, even though all the hubs are sharing the backbone. Figure 5-4 illustrates this approach.

TIP

Switches often are used simply to connect two given ports, but they are also intelligent enough to echo certain types of broadcast packets to all ports simultaneously.

Switches have become inexpensive and are blazingly fast. For local area network (LAN) connections, switches make more sense than routers, partly because of their cost and their relative simplicity. In fact, purchasing bridges has become difficult, as switches now dominate the market because they achieve the same benefits at a much lower cost and with much less complexity. Additionally, most new networks these days eschew hubs in favor of a 100 percent–switched approach. Since the differential cost for a 24-port switch versus a 24-port hub is now

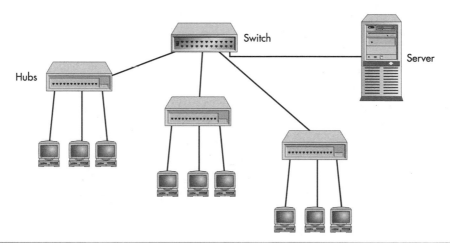

Figure 5-4 A network built using hubs and switches

relatively small, one can virtually eliminate network collisions by using a 100 percent–switch approach.

Gateways

Gateways are application-specific interfaces that link all seven layers of the OSI Model when they are dissimilar at any or all levels. For instance, if you need to connect a network that uses one of the OSI networking models to one using IBM's Systems Network Architecture (SNA) model, a gateway would perform this task admirably. Gateways can also translate from Ethernet to Token Ring, for example, although simpler solutions than gateways exist if you need such a translation. Because gateways have to translate so much, they tend to be slower than other solutions, particularly under heavy loads.

The primary use for gateways today is for handling e-mail. POP3 and SMTP are two examples of mail-handling protocols that are handled by gateways. Most e-mail systems that can connect to disparate systems either use a computer set up as a gateway for that chore, or let the e-mail server handle the gateway chores itself.

Progress Check

1. At which layer of the OSI model do repeaters, bridges, and routers operate?
   (Hint: They are all at different levels.)

2. For new networks, what type of device is often used in place of hubs?

CRITICAL SKILL
5.2 Protect a Network with Firewalls

Firewalls, also discussed in Module 10, are hardware devices that enforce your network security policies. This module also discusses firewalls because they often are installed hand in hand with routers. For instance, firewalls are sometimes installed with routers to create internetwork connections.

A firewall is a hardware device (which can be a computer set up for the task that runs firewall software, or a dedicated firewall box that contains a dedicated computer within it) that sits between two networks and enforces network security policies. Generally, firewalls sit between a company LAN and the Internet, but they can also be used between LANs or WANs when appropriate.

---

1. Repeaters operate at Layer 1, bridges at Layer 2, and routers at Layer 3.

2. Switches are now favored over hubs because they operate more elegantly and the incremental cost is extremely small.

There are basically two different types of firewalls: network-based and application-based. A network-based firewall operates at the packet level, and usually implements a technique called *packet filtering,* where packets between networks are compared against a set of rules programmed into the firewall before the packets are allowed to cross the boundary between the two networks. Packet filtering rules can allow or deny packets based on source or destination address, or based on TCP/IP port. Application-based firewalls, on the other hand, usually act in a proxy role between the two networks, such that no network traffic actually passes *directly* between the two networks. Instead, the firewall (usually called a *proxy firewall*) acts as a proxy for the users of one network to interact with services on the other network. This proxy interaction is usually done using a technique called *network address translation* (NAT), where the network addresses on the internal network are not directly exposed to the external network. In the application-based model, the proxy firewall takes care of translating the addresses so that the connections can take place.

TIP

Firewalls do not provide a network security panacea. The best firewall in the world won't protect your network from other security threats, such as some discussed in Module 10. However, they are an important part of network security, particularly for LANs connected to the Internet.

Firewalls come in all shapes and sizes, and range in cost from as little as a few thousand dollars to tens of thousands of dollars. In fact, these days one can even purchase small personal firewalls for home that cost less than $300 for hardware-based devices, or around $40 for firewall software that can be installed on a home computer. Different firewall devices have different features, and might encompass both network-based and application-based techniques to protect the network. Firewalls also usually serve as an audit point for the traffic between the two networks, using logging and reporting tools to help the administrator detect and deal with inappropriate network traffic.

CRITICAL SKILL
5.3

Connect RS-232 Devices with Short-haul Modems

While some might not consider a short-haul modem to be a true network device, it is a device that your network might require to provide point-to-point connectivity between a workstation and another device. Short-haul modems (sometimes called *line drivers*) enable you to connect two distant RS-232C devices to one another. Standard RS-232C cables are limited in distance to 50 to 100 feet. Short-haul modems allow the same connection to run as far as 5 miles using simple telephone-grade twisted-pair cabling.

Short-haul modems can often be perfect solutions when a computer needs terminal access to a remote device. For example, a user might need to access a terminal on a PBX telephone system, which uses an RS-232C port. You have two options to provide this remote access: You can install regular modems on each end and use a telephone connection to connect from the workstation to the PBX, or you can use two short-haul modems and run a twisted-pair cable between the two points. Depending on how frequently access is needed and how distant the device actually is, either approach can be good. Generally, short-haul modems are preferred when the two devices often or always need to be connected and running a twisted-pair wire between the locations is not prohibitively expensive or difficult. Short-haul modems are fairly inexpensive, costing about $100 each.

In most short-haul modem systems, two pairs of wire connect each short-haul modem, although one-pair variants exist. With the two-pair variety, one pair is used to transmit data and the other to receive data. Most short-haul modems are full duplex, allowing transmission to take place in both directions simultaneously.

To hook up two devices using short-haul modems, you use a standard RS-232C cable to connect each device to its short-haul modem. Then, you wire the twisted-pair wire to the short-haul modem, using the instructions that come with the modem. Finally, most short-haul modems require external power, so you need an available power outlet to plug them into. Figure 5-5 shows a sample of a short-haul modem connection.

TIP

If you frequently do RS-232C interfacing, you should invest in a device called a *breakout box*. This is a small device that has two RS-232C connectors on each end. In the box, each of the RS-232C pin signals is represented with a light-emitting diode (LED). Special patch posts and switches are available that enable you to reconfigure the RS-232C connection on the fly. Breakout boxes can be invaluable for achieving RS-232C communications between two devices that aren't communicating. They can show what is actually happening with the signals and enable you to try different cable configurations dynamically. Once you use the breakout box to figure out how to make the devices communicate, a permanent cable can then be made to those specifications.

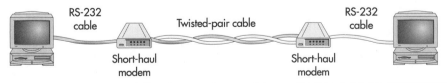

Figure 5-5 Short-haul modem connection

Module 5 Mastery Check

1. Two main types of firewalls exist, those that use _____ and those that use _____.

2. A gateway is used to make a connection where which layers of the OSI Model are dissimilar?

3. True or false: Repeaters examine packets passing between the two networks that they connect and decide whether or not to pass them along based on their destination address.

4. Which of the following statements about hubs are true?

   A. Each node connected to a hub is on its own private collision domain.

   B. Hubs can typically automatically sense a node's connection speed and adjust accordingly.

   C. Hubs are available only within stackable 24-port configurations.

   D. A hub is also called an intelligent LAN concentrator.

5. True or false: Hubs are always physically wired in a ring configuration.

6. If a network is designed with a backbone that runs at a faster speed than the hubs, the backbone typically runs at ____ times the speed of the hubs.

7. The Internet predominantly uses what type of device to form its various connections?

8. True or false: A firewall's sole job is to enforce network security policies that you create.

9. True or false: A router becomes a node on the network to which it connects.

10. Indicate which of the following protocols are able to be routed through a router: Appletalk, NetBIOS, NetBEUI, TCP/IP, and IPX/SPX.

Module 6

Making WAN Connections

Many companies have multiple locations that need to share network resources. For example, maybe the company's accounting system runs at the headquarters building where the accounting and MIS staff are located, but the warehouse across town still needs access to the accounting system for inventory picking tickets, data entry, and other order fulfillment and inventory tasks.

Or, perhaps the company uses a groupware system such as Lotus Notes that requires regular updates of information and messages from one site to another. In the real world, the situation can become even more complex. Some companies have offices all around the world, and each office has different requirements both to access and update data in other locations.

All of these are situations in which a *wide area network* (WAN) can be useful. Certainly, in a pinch multiple offices can send data to and receive data from each other by using Federal Express and identical tape machines, zip drives, JAZ drives, or other media, and simply send the data back and forth (assuming the application supports exchanging data in this fashion). But this sort of arrangement has some drawbacks, the biggest one being that it is comparatively slow.

There are many ways to connect LANs in one location to LANs in another location, and making such connections is the subject of this Module. First, you learn about basic concepts involved in linking LANs over a WAN. Then, the Module discusses different WAN technologies, along with the relative trade-offs that each requires.

Determine WAN Needs

Except in rare cases, WAN links are almost always expensive to maintain, particularly because bandwidth needs increase over time. Moreover, WAN links are generally much more prone to trouble than LANs because many additional possible points of failure exist. For these reasons, before you make your choice, it's important to assess the need for a WAN carefully and then study the different options available, their costs, and the trade-offs involved. Costs can vary wildly between different technologies, speeds, and other factors (including your location) so you have to rely heavily on cost and availability data from local providers for your own WAN analysis. Plus, prices and availability change almost every week, so make sure to get current data from your local providers before committing to a particular WAN technology.

TIP

Often, the need for a WAN can be satisfied using a technology called virtual private networks (VPNs). A VPN is a private network created through a public network, typically, the Internet. A VPN is called "private" because all of the packets between two points are encrypted, so even though the packets are transmitted over a public network, their information remains secure. And because VPNs use the Internet, they're usually much cheaper than dedicated WAN links, and often can make use of existing Internet connections for two (or more) locations. VPNs are discussed in detail in Module 9.

Analyze Requirements

Before beginning to look into different WAN technologies, you must have a firm grasp of the need for a WAN. Because of the cost and the time required to implement and maintain a WAN, you usually do not want to pursue one until the need is strong.

A company's first WAN is usually driven by a particular application, such as an accounting system. Then, once the WAN is operational, the company often begins to use the WAN for other applications. For example, a company might be transferring e-mail from one location to another using dial-up lines, but once the WAN that supports the accounting system is installed, they find it's easier to route the e-mail over the WAN link rather than maintain two separate connection schemes. Other WAN uses emerge this way, too, so it's important to analyze the primary application fully and then consider what other uses could be made of the WAN. If you fail to take into account all the uses that the company might have for the WAN, you might find that you've invested a lot of money in a solution that doesn't really meet all of your needs.

You need to answer a number of questions before you consider different WAN approaches:

- What are the locations that will participate in the WAN and what kind of WAN services are available to them? A sales office in Tahiti, for instance, is unlikely to be able to purchase the latest *x*DSL line.

- How much data needs to be transferred from each site to each other site, and in what time frame?

- How quickly does the data need to be transferred?

- Does the data transfer need to be synchronous or can it be asynchronous? For example, a warehouse clerk who is entering records directly into an accounting system located at another site requires a synchronous (real-time) connection, while a restaurant that needs to upload sales data to its headquarters at some time each night needs only an asynchronous connection.

- When do the data transfers need to be accomplished? Do they need to occur all the time? Do they need to occur once every 30 minutes, or follow some other schedule?

- What are the budget constraints?

Once you have the answers to these questions, you can then answer the questions that can guide you to a particular WAN technology. These issues are discussed in the following sections.

Switched or Dedicated?

A s*witched* WAN link is one that is not active all the time. For instance, a dial-up modem connection from one location to another would be a switched connection. Another example is an ISDN connection from one location to another. These are examples of connections that are formed only when you need them, and you usually pay for the time the connection is open, rather than the amount of data you're able to transmit over the connection. Figure 6-1 is an example of a switched WAN link.

Switched links can be either connection-based or packet-based. A *connection-based switched link* forms a connection as needed and makes a fixed amount of bandwidth available over that link. A *packet-based switched link* sends data packets into a network cloud in which they can follow a number of paths to their destination and then emerge from the cloud. Packet-switched networks can be more reliable because the data can take many different paths, but you are not guaranteed that each packet will arrive in a certain amount of time. A connection-based switched link just gives you one "pipe" from your source to your destination, but you can control what goes into the pipe and how long it will take to get to its destination.

A *dedicated* WAN link is one that is always up and running. Examples of dedicated WAN connections are DS1 (T-1) lines, *x*DSL lines, or leased telephone lines. You use a dedicated connection when you need the connection to be up all the time or when the overall economics show that such a connection is cheaper than a switched link. Figure 6-2 illustrates a dedicated WAN link.

Private or Public?

A *private network* is one that is exclusive to a particular company. No other company's data is sent over the private network. The advantages are that the data is secure, you can control how the network is used, and you can predict how much bandwidth you have available. A *public network* (or *external network*), such as the Internet, is a network through which many companies'

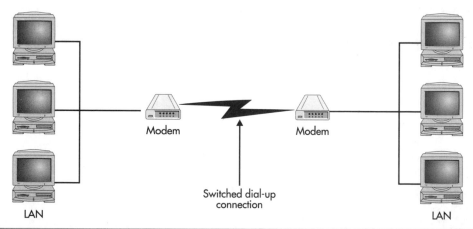

Figure 6-1 A switched WAN link

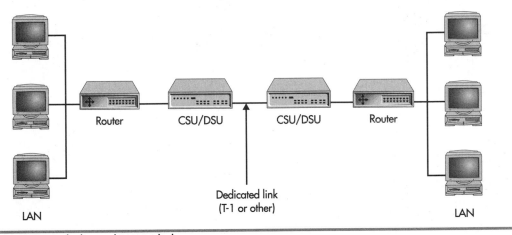

Figure 6-2 A dedicated WAN link

data passes. Public networks are less secure than private networks, but the advantages are that public networks are less expensive to use and you don't have to maintain the external network yourself.

Use a public network under the following conditions:

- You don't care if data occasionally takes longer to reach its destination or if the delay between sites is relatively unpredictable.

- You want the lowest cost network connection possible.

- The data does not need to be secure or you have the ability to make it secure over the public network. (Technologies exist that can provide such security, such as virtual private networks or some types of data encryption.)

Use a private network under these conditions:

- Data security is of utmost concern.

- You have a large, experienced staff to set up and maintain the public network.

- Cost is unimportant relative to the benefits that the network brings.

- You need full, reliable control over the network's bandwidth use.

Progress Check

1. Describe the main difference between a switched and a dedicated WAN link.

2. Is the Internet a private or public network?

CRITICAL SKILL
6.2 # Compare WAN Connection Types

Now that you understand some basics of WAN links, the remainder of this module provides an overview of different available WAN technologies and offers tips and advice on each type of link.

Plain Old Telephone Service (POTS)

Plain old telephone service (POTS) is the telephone service everyone knows. While not technically qualifying as a WAN connection (at least as most people think of WANs), POTS can still serve to link two or more sites together for certain low-bandwidth needs. Although it is among the slowest methods of establishing a network connection, POTS is ubiquitous and easily used throughout the entire world. POTS is also generally (but not always!) the least expensive way to connect.

POTS is carried over one set of twisted-pair wires (in other words, just two wires). In some cases, two sets of twisted-pair wires are used, but only the two main wires are used to carry the telephone signal and ring signals. The other two wires are used for other features, such as backlighting a keypad on a phone or providing a message-waiting light with some PBX systems. POTS connections currently use simple RJ-11 telephone jacks, which simply snap into place.

The maximum theoretical speed of basic analog POTS is 33.6 Kbps. Many factors can decrease this speed; chief among them is line quality. Telephone lines with static typically do not connect at the top speed of 33.6 Kbps, might lose their connections unexpectedly, lose data being transmitted, or pause for excessive periods of time as bursts of static inhibit the ability to transfer data.

When you are using POTS to establish a network connection, having matched modems at both ends is optimal. Matched modems from the same manufacturer more easily negotiate the highest possible data transmission rates and often can support "step-down" modes, which automatically use a slower speed when line noise unexpectedly becomes a problem.

---

1. A switched link is only formed when it is needed, while a dedicated link is open and available all the time, even when not being used.

2. The Internet is a public network.

POTS transmits analog signals, not digital ones. The data sent between systems is converted from digital data to analog data using a modem. The word *modem* is actually an acronym based on the device's function—modulator/demodulator. At each end of the connection, the sending system's modem modulates the digital data into an analog signal and sends the signal over the telephone line as a series of audible sounds. Then, at the receiving end, the modem demodulates the audible analog signal back into digital data for use with the computer.

Integrated Services Digital Network (ISDN)

The technology for Integrated Services Digital Network (ISDN), a high-speed digital communications network based on existing telephone services, has been around for more than 10 years. Because of extensive upgrades required at telephone company central offices (COs), however, ISDN has not become widely available until now, and even now it is usually available only in major metropolitan areas.

ISDN is available in two basic forms: the Basic Rate Interface (BRI) and the Primary Rate Interface (PRI). The ISDN-BRI connection is made up of three channels. Two channels are called *bearer channels* and carry data at speeds of 64 Kbps per channel. Bearer channels can also carry voice calls—that is, spoken telephone calls. (Each bearer channel can carry one voice call at a time.) The third channel, called a *data channel*, carries call setup information and other overhead communications necessary to manage the two bearer channels. The data channel carries 16 Kbps of data. Bearer channels are abbreviated as *B-channels*, while the data channel is abbreviated as a *D-channel*. Thus, an ISDN-BRI connection is often called a 2B+D connection, which reflects the number and the type of channels it contains.

An ISDN-PRI is made up of 24 B-channels and one D-channel. A PRI connection can carry a total of 1.544 Mbps, just like a T-1 line.

TIP

Different flavors of PRI configurations are available in different parts of the world. The configuration named *24B+D* is common, and you might also see variations such as 22 B-channels with a 64 Kbps D-channel, 24 56 Kbps B-channels, or even 30 standard B-channels (totaling 1.92 Mbps).

ISDN connections are usually formed as needed; they are switched. To use ISDN for a WAN link, you use on-demand ISDN routers at each end, which can "dial up" the other router when data is pending. Because ISDN has extremely fast call setup times, ISDN connections are formed much more quickly than POTS connections; forming an ISDN connection usually takes less than a second.

ISDN has not been as widely adopted as was once hoped; it is being eclipsed by xDSL and other connection types that offer better price/performance characteristics. Pricing changes occur regularly. ISDN prices also vary considerably in different parts of the country. Getting full pricing information from your own regional Bell operating company (RBOC) before choosing ISDN is important. Then, using your projected usage data, you should be able to calculate the cost to use ISDN.

Generally, the installation of an ISDN-BRI line, assuming no wiring changes are necessary, costs about $250. Some RBOCs might waive the installation charge if you sign an agreement to keep the ISDN line for one to two years.

TIP

In some parts of the country, from time to time, having an ISDN line installed takes a considerable amount of time—up to two months in some cases. Before choosing ISDN, get an accurate, written estimate from your RBOC on when it can complete the installation. Make sure you're prepared if the RBOC fails to meet its initial target date.

Monthly ISDN usage charges are similar to POTS charges. Long-distance ISDN call charges are similar to POTS charges. Remember, though, that connecting with two B-channels is equivalent to making two separate calls, and whatever charge exists for a single call will double when you use both B-channels.

Digital Subscriber Line (DSL)

A relatively new connection type becoming available is called a digital subscriber line (DSL). A number of different "flavors" of DSL exist; each name begins with a different initial or combination of initials, which is why DSL is often called xDSL. The available flavors include the following.

- **ADSL**   Asymmetric DSL allows for up to 8 Mbps of data to be received and up to 1 Mbps of data to be sent. Many RBOCs offer only up to 1.5 Mbps to be received (which is called the *downstream* direction) and 256 Kbps to be sent (called *upstream* direction), however, and distance from the CO might affect the speeds available at any particular location. At further distances, connections might be available only at much slower speeds (although in all cases ADSL is still faster than POTS connections using a modem).

- **HDSL**   High-speed DSL (HDSL) allows between 768 Kbps and 2.048 Mbps connections between two sites.

- **RADSL**   Rate-adaptive DSL (RADSL) allows for 600 Kbps to 12 Mbps of data to be received and 128 Kbps to 1 Mbps of data to be sent.

- **SDSL**   Symmetric DSL (SDSL) allows bidirectional rates varying from 160 Kbps to 2.048 Mbps.

- **VDSL**   Very-high-speed DSL (VDSL) allows up to 51 Mbps of data downstream and up to 2 Mbps upstream.

In this section, you learn about how *x*DSL works and about when you might be able to implement its extremely high-bandwidth capabilities. For these discussions, I focus on ADSL because it is the most prevalent and the least expensive. For WAN links, however, you should focus on SDSL if your WAN data needs are similar in both the downstream and upstream directions.

How xDSL Works

The twisted-pair copper wire that carries POTS is capable of carrying signals with up to a 1 MHz spread of frequencies. However, POTS uses only 8 KHz of that frequency bandwidth. The reason for this limitation is that, in the RBOC's CO switch, a card exists that interfaces with the analog signal that the twisted-pair wire sends to the phone company's digital network. This interface card allows only 4 KHz of signaling frequencies in each direction, even though the wire itself is capable of carrying a far broader frequency range.

*x*DSL works by opening up that 1 MHz maximum capability through the use of new *x*DSL interface cards that the RBOC can install in its CO switch. For lines that connect to those cards, the new frequency range is capable of carrying much more data than if the card were not installed. The distance from the computer equipment to the CO switch limits the data rate, however. Most *x*DSL implementations function optimally at up to 12,000 feet (about 2 miles). In particular, the 8 Mbps receive and 1 Mbps send data rates of ADSL are possible only within the 12,000-foot distance to the CO. Longer distances are possible, but not at the full possible data rate. For instance, running an ADSL connection at 18,000 feet—the distance at which 95 percent of telephone locations exist in relation to their CO switch— degrades the performance to about 1.5 Mbps, at best, in the receive direction. Only an estimated 50 percent of U.S. locations are within 12,000 feet of an RBOC CO switch. The good news is that some newer implementations of *x*DSL might be able to overcome the distance limitation. The situation is still developing, and longer-distance solutions probably won't be available along these lines until well into the year 2001, if not 2002.

ADSL

As mentioned, ADSL can support up to 8 Mbps of received data (also called *downstream* data) and up to 1 Mbps of sent data (also called *upstream* data). In addition to these two data channels, ADSL also carves out an 8 KHz channel for POTS, which can coexist with the ADSL data channels.

Specific implementations of ADSL vary in their data rate. Some of the slower implementations function only at 1.5 Mbps downstream and 256 Kbps upstream. In some cases, this speed might even decrease to 384 Kbps downstream and 64 Mbps upstream.

A lot of interest surrounds xDSL, particularly ADSL. The cost per megabyte of data transmitted is far less than POTS and is even considerably less expensive than ISDN. Even with all that interest, it will be, at best, several years before xDSL is more widely available. Right now, a number of RBOCs are rolling out xDSL, but still in limited markets.

No one knows yet how rapidly xDSL will catch on. The main limitation is in the implementation curve of the RBOCs, and the investment they need to make is considerable. Each xDSL line card (one required for each connection) is estimated to cost around $1,000. An RBOC might also have to upgrade each CO switch, at an estimated cost of between $250,000 and $500,000. While an RBOC can reasonably expect to recoup these costs in a relatively short period of time, the changes will require a great deal of capital.

Cynics note that ISDN has been possible for more than 12 years, but it is only now being more widely used. Will xDSL suffer the same fate? The jury is still out, but as of early 2002, it appears that xDSL is being adopted very quickly and is likely to be very successful.

Ask the Expert

Q: Why asymmetric DSL?

A: Many data access needs are asymmetrical. In other words, at any given time, a system often needs to receive more data than it needs to send, or vice versa. Most remote access connections, particularly Internet connections, are asymmetrical. The emphasis is on being able to receive data rapidly, rather than on sending data rapidly.

Because of this, ADSL is receiving the most interest among the xDSL implementations, simply because it offers more benefit within the same amount of frequency bandwidth. Most applications will work far better with the data rate being faster downstream than upstream.

Some xDSL implementations are symmetric, such as symmetric DSL and high-speed DSL. These xDSL connection types are more suited to uses where the exchange of data is roughly equal in both directions, such as two remote LANs that are connected to one another.

T-1/T-3 (DS1/DS3) Connections

More than 40 years ago, Bell Laboratories developed a hierarchy of systems that can carry digital voice signals. At the lowest level in Bell Labs' hierarchy is a connection called a *DS0* connection, which carries 64 Kbps of bandwidth. A connection that aggregates 24 DS0 channels is called a *DS1*, which can carry up to 1.544 Mbps when all channels are in use. The next common level is called a *DS3*, which carries 672 DS0 channels, for an aggregate total of 44.736 Mbps. The DS1 connection is commonly called a *T-1 connection*, which actually refers to the system of repeaters that can carry the DS1 traffic over a four-wire twisted-pair connection. (Surprisingly, a DS1 requires only two twisted-pairs, and not fiber-optic cable or anything exotic. To understand how much data can be carried over simple telephone wire, see the preceding section, "Digital Subscriber Line [DSL].")

DS1 connections are commonly used as digital connections between a company's PBX and a point of presence (POP) for a long-distance telephone carrier, and they are also commonly used to connect LANs to the Internet. A DS1 connection can handle up to 24 voice calls or as many as 24 data connections simultaneously. Or, using a multiplexer and a DS1, you can form one big 1.544-Mbps connection.

A popular technology called *fractional T-1* also exists, where a full DS1 is installed, but only the number of channels you pay for are turned on and available for use. Fractional T-1 is great because you can buy just the bandwidth you need and increasing the bandwidth (up to the maximum for a DS1) is just a phone call (and some more money!) away.

TIP

DS0, DS1, and DS3 WAN connections make use of frame relay signaling technology on the RBOC's side of the connection. Understanding the ins and outs of frame relay isn't especially important, although you should understand that when you install a DSx connection to the Internet for your LAN, you are really using frame relay services.

At your end of a DS1 connection are two key pieces of equipment: a CSU/DSU that converts the DS1 signals into network signals, and a router that directs packets between the DS1 and the LAN.

Asynchronous Transfer Mode (ATM)

Asynchronous Transfer Mode, commonly called just ATM, is a very high-speed technology for transmitting data between locations. ATM is a multiplexed, cell-based networking technology that collects data into entities called *cells* and then transmits the cells over the ATM network connection. ATM networks can carry both voice and data. ATM is very fast, with speeds ranging from 155 Mbps to 622 Mbps. Usually, ATM is used only by relatively large companies that need ATM's speed for their WAN links, or by companies that need to send enormous amounts of data through a network connection, such as a company that needs to transmit lots of video data.

X.25

X.25 connections have been available for a long time, but they are not typically used for WAN connections both because of the overhead involved and because the trade-off between price and bandwidth is not competitive with other solutions. Some older networks might still have X.25 connections in place, however, and they are commonly used in Europe. X.25 is a packet-switched WAN connection, in which data travels through an X.25 cloud, which works similarly to the Internet, but uses a private/public X.25 network. X.25 connections are typically relatively slow (56 Kbps), but in some cases might be faster.

The U.S. military originally developed and designed X.25 to make military voice traffic available even after a nuclear strike. As you might guess from this, X.25 is an extremely reliable, secure protocol for transmitting data. All frames (similar to packets) sent over X.25 networks are completely verified from one end of the connection to the other.

✓

Module 6 Mastery Check

1. DS1 and DS3 connections are more commonly called _____ and _____.

2. True or false: The theoretical maximum speed of POTS when analog lines are at each end of the connection is 64 Kbps.

3. True or false: An ISDN BRI connection typically uses three data channels and one bearer channel.

4. True or false: An ISDN PRI connection operates at speeds similar to DS1/T-1.

5. True or false: WAN links are usually much less expensive than LAN links.

6. To keep transmitted data secure over a public network, you can use _____ technology.

7. Two main types of connection types are switched and _____.

8. POTS is an acronym that stands for _____.

9. The most common form of xDSL is _____.

10. Data transfer needs tend to be either synchronous or _____.

Module 7

Understanding Networking Protocols

A network *protocol* is a set of rules that data communications over a network follow to complete various network transactions. For example, Transmission Control Protocol/ Internet Protocol (TCP/IP) defines a set of rules used to send data from one node on a network to another node. Simple Mail Transfer Protocol (SMTP) is a set of rules and standards used to transfer e-mail and attachments from one node to another. Dynamic Host Configuration Protocol (DHCP) is a protocol—a set of rules and standards—used to allocate IP addresses dynamically for a network, so they needn't be set manually for each workstation.

Many protocols are used in networking. In fact, in a sense, almost *every* activity on a network follows a protocol of one sort or another. Some protocols function at a low level in the OSI network model, others operate at a high level, and still others operate in between.

In this module, you learn about the essential networking protocols used to transmit and receive data across a network.

Explore TCP and UDP

As its name suggests, TCP/IP is actually two protocols used in concert with one another. *Internet Protocol* (IP) defines how network data is addressed from a source to a destination and in what sequence the data should be reassembled at the other end. IP operates at the network layer in the OSI Model. *Transmission Control Protocol* (TCP) is a higher-level protocol that operates one layer higher than IP, at the transport layer. TCP manages connections between computers. TCP messages are carried (encapsulated) in IP datagrams.

User Datagram Protocol (UDP) serves the same role as TCP, but offers fewer features. Both TCP and UDP packets are carried within IP packets, but the only reliability feature that UDP supports is the resending of any packets not received at the destination (UDP is connectionless). The chief advantage to UDP is that it is much faster for trivial network communications, such as sending a web page to a client computer. Because UDP doesn't offer many error-checking or error-handling features, it should be used only when it isn't that important if data occasionally gets mangled between points, or when an application program provides its own extensive error-checking and error-handling functions.

TCP and UDP Ports

Both TCP and UDP support the concept of *ports,* or application-specific addresses, to which packets are directed on any given receiving machine. For example, most web servers run on a server machine and receive requests through port number 80. When a machine receives any packets that are intended for the web server (such as a request to serve up a web page), the requesting machine directs those packets to that port number. When you request a web page from a web server, your computer sends the request to the web server computer and specifies that its request should go to port 80, which is where HTTP requests are directed. Hundreds of different ports have standardized uses, and defining your own ports on a server for specific

Ask the Expert

Q: What are datagrams, frames, and packets?

A: A *packet* is any collection of data sent over a network, and the term is usually used generically to refer to units of data sent at any layer of the OSI Model. (So, for instance, people talk about *IP packets*, even though technically the correct term is *IP datagrams*. In this book, *packet* is used generically. The persnickety definition of packet applies only to messages sent at the top layer of the OSI Model, the application layer.) Network layer units of data, such as those carried by IP, are called *datagrams*, while units of data carried at the data-link layer (Layer 1) are called *frames*.

applications is easy. A text file called SERVICES defines the ports on a computer. An example of a portion of Windows NT's SERVICES file follows (only selected entries are shown due to space constraints; the following is not a complete SERVICES file, but it illustrates what the file contains):

```
# Copyright (c) 1993-1999 Microsoft Corp.
#
# This file contains port numbers for well-known
# services as defined by
# RFC 1700 (Assigned Numbers).
#
# Format:
#
# <service name><port number>/<protocol>[aliases...][#<comment>]
#
echo              7/tcp
echo              7/udp
discard           9/tcp    sink null
discard           9/udp    sink null
systat           11/tcp    users            #Active users
daytime          13/tcp
daytime          13/udp
chargen          19/tcp    ttytst source    #Character generator
chargen          19/udp    ttytst source    #Character generator
ftp-data         20/tcp                     #FTP, data
ftp              21/tcp                     #FTP. control
telnet           23/tcp
smtp             25/tcp    mail             #SMTP
time             37/tcp    timserver
time             37/udp    timserver
```

```
tftp              69/udp                             #Trivial File Transfer
gopher            70/tcp
finger            79/tcp
http              80/tcp      www www-http           #World Wide Web
kerberos-sec      88/tcp      krb5                   #Kerberos
kerberos-sec      88/udp      krb5                   #Kerberos
rtelnet           107/tcp                            #Remote Telnet Service
pop2              109/tcp     postoffice             #POP-V2
pop3              110/tcp                            #POP v3-
nntp              119/tcp     usenet                 #NNTP
ntp               123/udp                            #Network Time Protocol
snmp              161/udp                            #SNMP
snmptrap          162/udp     snmp-trap              #SNMP trap
print-srv         170/tcp                            #Network PostScript
irc               194/tcp                            #Relay Chat Prot
ipx               213/udp                            #IPX over IP
ldap              389/tcp                            #Lightweight DAP
https             443/tcp     MCom
https             443/udp     MCom
who               513/udp     whod
cmd               514/tcp     shell
syslog            514/udp
printer           515/tcp     spooler
router            520/udp     route routed
netnews           532/tcp     readnews
uucp              540/tcp     uucpd
wins              1512/tcp                            #Windows Name Service
```

As you can see, most of the Internet services that you might be familiar with actually work through the use of TCP/UDP ports, such as HTTP for the Web, SMTP for e-mail, NNTP for Usenet, and so forth. The use of ports ensures that network communications intended for a particular purpose are not confused with others that might also be arriving at the same machine. Ports allow the receiving machine to direct arriving data appropriately. An example is a server that hosts web pages and also receives and processes e-mail. Packets arriving at port 80 will be sent to the web serving software, while those that arrive at port 25 will go to the e-mail software. Other services on the machine, such as Telnet and FTP, can also function concurrently through this mechanism.

IP Packets and IP Addressing

IP packets include addresses that uniquely define every computer connected to the Internet (see Figure 7-1). These addresses are used to route packets from a sending node to a receiving node. Because all the routers on the Internet know the network addresses to which they are connected, they can accurately forward packets destined for a remote network.

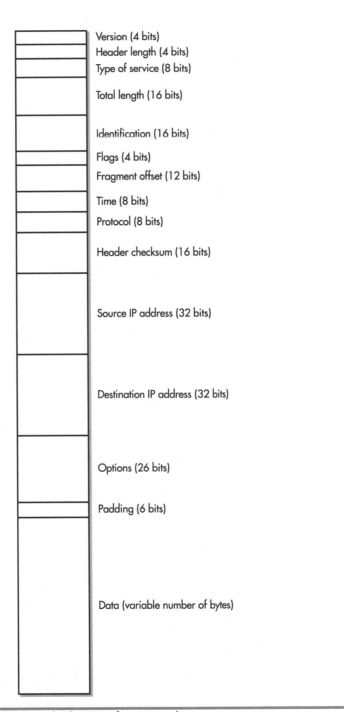

Figure 7-1 A schematic showing the layout of an IP packet

In addition to carrying its data, each IP packet contains a number of fields. These fields, in the order they occur, are

● **Version** This is the version of the IP protocol being used. This indicates, for instance, whether IP version 4 or version 6 is being used.

● **Header length** This field indicates the length of the header information before the data begins in the packet.

● **Type of service** This field is used for different things by different vendors. It can be used for such features as requesting high-priority routing, requesting highest possible reliability, and so forth.

● **Total length** This field indicates the total length of the packet.

● **Identification, flags, and fragment offset** These three fields are used to reassemble an IP packet that was disassembled at some point during transmission. These fields include all the information necessary for the correct reassembly of the packet at the receiving end.

● **Time to live** This field defines how many network hops the packet can traverse before it is declared dead and the routers stop forwarding it to other routers. This number is set when the packet is sent, and each router that handles the packet decrements the value by one. When the number reaches zero, the packet is dead and is no longer transmitted.

● **Protocol** This field indicates whether the IP packet is contained within a TCP or a UDP packet.

● **Header checksum** The header checksum is used to help ensure that none of the packet's header data (the fields discussed in this list) is damaged.

● **Source IP address** This field contains the address of the sending computer. It is needed in case a packet must be retransmitted, in which case the receiving node (or, in some cases, a router) knows from which node to request a retransmission.

● **Destination IP address** This field contains the address of the receiving node.

● **Options and padding** These final two fields of the header of the IP packet are used to request any required specific routing instructions or to specify the time that the packet was sent.

● **Data** The final field of an IP packet is the actual data being sent.

IP addresses are 32 bits long, allowing for a theoretical maximum number of addresses of 2^{32}, or about 4.3 billion addresses. To make them easier to work with and to help route them more efficiently, they are broken up into four *octets*, which are each one byte long. Thus, in decimal notation, IP addresses are expressed as *xxx.xxx.xxx.xxx*, where each *xxx* represents a number from 0 to 255. The numbers 0, 127, and 255 are usually reserved for special purposes, so typically these numbers are unavailable for assignment to nodes and the remaining 253 unique addresses are available for assignment in each octet.

Ask the Expert

Q: Is the Internet really running out of available addresses?

A: The current implementation of IP, called IP version 4 (IPv4), is approaching the point where running out of addresses is becoming a real possibility. In 1994, a proposal was issued to address this limitation. Called IP Next Generation (IPng and now IPv6), the new version of IP takes care of the addressing limitation by bumping up the address length from 32 bits to 128 bits. This allows 3.4×10^{38} (34 followed by 37 zeroes) unique addresses, which should leave plenty of room for all anticipated Internet addresses, even allowing for refrigerators, toasters, and cars to have their own IP addresses!

Addresses on the Internet are guaranteed to be unique through the use of an address registration service, presently administered by the Internet Corporation for Assigned Names and Numbers (ICANN). Actual registrations of domain names and addresses are handled through one of many *registrars*, which include companies such as INTERNIC, Network Solutions, and many others. ICANN is the overall authority.

ICANN assigns three major classes of addresses, called Class A, B, and C. For a Class A address, ICANN assigns the owner a number in the first octet; the owner is then free to use all possible valid combinations in the remaining three octets. For example, a Class A address might be 57.*xxx.xxx.xxx*. Class A addresses enable the owner to address up to 16.5M unique nodes. Class B addresses define the first two octets, leaving the remaining two open for the address's owner to use. For instance, 123.55.*xxx.xxx* would be a valid Class B address assignment. Class B addresses enable the holder to have 65K unique nodes. Class C follows this progression, defining the first three octets and leaving only the last octet available for the Class C owner to assign, enabling the owner to assign up to 255 unique nodes.

An Internet service provider (ISP) might own either a Class A or a Class B address, and then can handle a number of Class C addresses within their own address structure. Changing ISPs, even for a company that has a valid Class C address, means changing the company's address from a Class C address available through the first ISP, to a Class C address available from the second ISP.

As mentioned earlier, the addresses 0, 127, and 255 are reserved. Usually, address 0, as in 123.65.101.0, refers to the network itself, and the router that connects the network to other networks handles this address. The address 127 is a special *loopback address* that can be used for certain kinds of testing. The address 255 refers to all computers on the network, so a broadcast message to address 123.65.101.255 would go to all addresses within 123.65.101.*xxx*.

IP Subnetting

IP addresses are made up of two main components. The first—the leftmost—is the *network ID*, also called the *netid*. The other is the *host ID,* usually written without the space as *hostid*. The netid identifies the network, while the hostid identifies each node on that network. (Recall that in IP parlance, every node is called a *host* regardless of whether it's a server, client computer, printer, or whatever.)

For a Class C address, for instance, the netid is set in the first three octets, while the hostids use the fourth octet. For a Class B address, the first two octets are the netid, while the final two octets are hostids.

To understand how subnetting works, consider a company that has three networks in three different buildings, all connected by a 64-Kbps ISDN link. Each network has about 25 nodes on it. Each building has its own set of servers and printers for the workers in that building. The ISDN link between the networks is for the occasional need to transmit information between buildings, such as e-mail messages or accounting transactions. How should the company assign IP addresses in this situation?

One possibility is that the company could request a single Class C set of addresses, then assign those addresses across the three networks in some fashion. This seems like a simple solution, but it's actually a poor idea for a couple of reasons. Lots of network traffic typically gets sent to each hostid within a single netid. The slow ISDN link between the buildings would become a tremendous bottleneck in this situation, and the entire network would function very poorly.

Another idea is to use separate Class C addresses (netids) for each building. This is a relatively simple solution, and it would work just fine, except that possibly the company couldn't assign three separate Class C addresses, and it would be terribly wasteful of the available pool of IP addresses. In this situation, each building would be wasting more than 200 addresses for no good reason.

What if there were a way to divide up a Class C address so that each building could have its own *virtual* netid? Such a solution is what subnetting is all about. Subnetting allows you to subdivide a netid (usually that of a Class C address, but such subnetting can also be done with Class A or B addresses) across two or more networks.

TIP

To understand subnetting, you first need to understand the binary representation of IP addresses. For a quick overview of how binary numbers work, see Module 2.

Subnet Masks

If you look at a computer's IP configuration, you'll see that the computer always has both an IP address (such as 205.143.60.109) and a *subnet mask* (such as 255.255.255.0). It is the subnet mask that defines which part of the computer's IP address is the netid and which part is the hostid. To see this clearly, you need to represent the addresses in binary form:

```
Computer IP Address (Dec):    205        143        60         109
Computer IP Address (Bin):    11001101   10001111   00111100   01101101
Subnet mask (Dec):            255        255        255        0
Subnet mask (Bin):            11111111   11111111   11111111   00000000
```

The netid of an address, defined by the subnet mask, is whatever portion of the address that has a binary 1 set in the corresponding subnet mask. In the preceding example, the netid is the full first three octets (the first 24 bits), and the hostid is the last octet (the last 8 bits). Now you can see why 255 (decimal) is used so frequently in subnet masks: It is because 255 corresponds to having all bits set to 1 in an eight-bit number.

TIP

Subnet masks should always use contiguous 1s starting from the left and working to the right. The hostid portion should contain all contiguous 0's, working backward from the right to the left. While it is theoretically possible to build subnet masks that have interspersed 1's and 0's, it is never done in practice because it would quickly become too complicated to manage properly, and because there's no real reason to do so. Also, the portion of the hostid that is subnet-masked cannot consist of all 0s or all 1's. While certain implementations of IP do allow all 0's, such a configuration is not part of the accepted standard IP rules, and thus using such a hostid is risky because some devices on the network might not understand it.

Let's now return to the earlier example of the company with three buildings. What if the company could divide a single Class C address so that each building could use its own portion, and the routers connecting the buildings would understand which transmissions should be forwarded to the other buildings and which ones should not be? Such a configuration is where subnet masks are useful. A subnet mask allows you to "borrow" some bits from your hostids and then use those bits to create new netids. For the example given earlier, you would need to borrow three bits from the Class C address and use that address to create four separate netids. Examine how this configuration would work in binary format:

```
Subnet mask (Bin):    11111111   11111111   11111111   11100000
Bldg. 1 IP addresses: 11001101   10001111   00111100   100xxxxx
Bldg. 2 IP addresses: 11001101   10001111   00111100   011xxxxx
Bldg. 3 IP addresses: 11001101   10001111   00111100   101xxxxx
Subnet mask (Dec):    255        255        255        224
Bldg. 1 IP addresses: 205        143        60         129 - 158
Bldg. 2 IP addresses: 205        143        60         97 - 126
Bldg. 3 IP addresses: 205        143        60         161 - 190
```

The preceding example borrows three bits from the company's Class C address range, then uses this range of addresses to create up to six netids that the company can use, thus providing each building with 30 available hostid addresses. By using subnetting to designate each separate netid, the company can program the routers to send packets between networks only when the packets are supposed to be routed, and not otherwise.

Because subnet masks are usually created using contiguous bits for the mask itself, only nine subnet masks are commonly used, as shown in Table 7-1.

Note in Table 7-1 that some configurations are marked as "N/A" (not applicable). These subnet masks would result in no available addresses, because of the rule that the subnet portion of the netid cannot be all 0's or all 1's. For example, consider the subnet mask of 224, which uses three hostid bits for the subnetid. In theory, this configuration should result in eight subnets. However, the subnets represented by 000 and 111 aren't valid, and so they are lost. Likewise, 128 is not a valid subnet mask because that one bit would *always* be either a 1 or a 0.

TIP

As you learn about networking with TCP/IP, it is important that you understand how subnets work and the purposes for which they are used. However, if you need to implement subnets, you should initially work through the project with an experienced network engineer, who can help you avoid many possible pitfalls not explicitly described or shown in the preceding section. You might also want to pursue more detailed TCP/IP knowledge. Many books are available that are dedicated to the subject of TCP/IP and cover these subjects in much more detail.

Binary Mask	Decimal Equivalent	Number of Subnets	Number of Hostids per Subnet
00000000	0	1	254
10000000	128	N/A	N/A
11000000	192	2	62
11100000	224	6	30
11110000	240	14	14
11111000	248	30	6
11111100	252	62	2
11111110	254	N/A	N/A
11111111	255	N/A	N/A

Table 7-1 Most Common Subnet Masks

Progress Check

1. IP addresses are divided into two portions, the _____ and the _____.

2. How does a subnet mask affect an IP address?

CRITICAL SKILL
7.2 Demonstrate Understanding of Other Internet Protocols

Quite a few other protocols are used on the Internet that either rely on, or make use of, TCP/IP. In this section, you learn about these different protocols, what they do, and, when appropriate, how they work.

Domain Name System

If all you had to use to address computers over the Internet was their IP address number, trying to keep track of them and trying to use their correct addresses might make you a little crazy. To go to the web site for Yahoo!, for example, you would have to remember to type the address **http://204.71.202.160**. To solve this problem, a system called the Domain Name System (DNS) was developed. This system enables people to register domain names with ICANN and then use them to access a particular node over the Internet. Therefore, DNS is the service that allows you to open a web browser and type **http://www.yahoo.com** and then connect to a particular computer over the Internet. In this case, **yahoo.com** is the full domain name.

TIP

Domain names are given out on a first-come, first-served basis. However, ICANN gives preference to a holder of a valid registered trademark if a conflict develops. ICANN, upon being presented with valid trademark information and notice of the domain name that infringes on that trademark, goes through a process to assess the truth of the claim and, if necessary, takes a domain name away from its present holder and transfers the name to its rightful owner.

---

1. Network ID (netid) and Host ID (hostid)

2. Subnet masks control which bits of an IP address are used for the netid and hostid portions of the address.

Domains are organized in a tree arrangement, like a directory tree on a disk drive. The top level defines different *domain types*. The most common is the **.com** domain type, usually used with for-profit commercial entities. Other common domain types include

- **.edu** for educational institutions

- **.gov** for governmental entities

- **.mil** for military entities

- **.net** for Internet-related entities

- **.org** for nonprofit entities

- *.xx* for different countries—for instance, **.it** is for Italy, **.de** for Germany (Deutschland), and so forth

Within a domain name, entities are free to add other names before the beginning of the domain name. For example, if you had the domain **bedrock.gov**, you would be free to create additional names, such as **quarry.bedrock.gov** or **flintstone.bedrock.gov**.

As a matter of standards, the first portion of a domain name, preceding the actual domain name, indicates what type of service is being connected. For instance, **www.bedrock.gov** would be used for a World Wide Web server for **bedrock.gov**, while **ftp.bedrock.gov** would be used for an FTP server, and so forth. The standards for service types within the domain name are usually followed, but not always. The owner of the domain name is free to invent its own service types that meet some need of the owner. For example, some domain name holders refer to their e-mail servers as **smtp.domain.org**, while others might prefer to use **mail.domain.org**. The holders could also use anything else they wanted.

Domain names are resolved to IP addresses through the use of *name servers*, which are servers that accept the typed domain name, perform a database query, and then return the actual address that should be used for that domain name. Generally, each ISP maintains its own DNS servers (and many large companies and organizations maintain their own DNS servers as well). Any changes are propagated throughout all the Internet's DNS servers within a few days.

Dynamic Host Configuration Protocol (DHCP)

In the early days of TCP/IP-based networks, administrators defined each node's address in a file or dialog box. From then on, the address was fixed unless someone changed it. The problem was that administrators occasionally would mistakenly put conflicting addresses into other nodes on the network, causing a network's version of pandemonium. To resolve this problem and to make it easier to assign TCP/IP addresses, a service called Dynamic Host Configuration Protocol (DHCP) was invented.

Ask the Expert

Q: What's a host?

A: You might think a *host* is a server, and in some networking contexts, you would be right. However, in the jargon of Internet names and addresses, every computer that has an IP address is called a *host*. Thus the name, Dynamic Host Configuration Protocol. (Remembering that every computer is a host is particularly important in the UNIX and Linux worlds, where the term is much more common than in the Windows or Macintosh worlds.)

DHCP services run on a DHCP server, where they control a range of IP addresses called a *scope*. When nodes connect to the network, they contact the DHCP server to get an assigned address that they can use. Addresses from a DHCP server are said to be *leased* to the client that uses them, meaning they remain assigned to a particular node for a set period of time before they expire and become available for another node to use. Often, lease periods are for just a few days, but network administrators can set any time period they want.

You should not use DHCP for nodes that provide network services, particularly for servers that provide services over the Internet. This is because changing a TCP/IP address would make reliably connecting to those computers impossible. Instead, use DHCP to support client workstations that do not need to host services for other nodes.

Hypertext Transfer Protocol (HTTP)

The World Wide Web is made up of documents that use a formatting language called *HTML*, which stands for Hypertext Markup Language. These documents are composed of text to be displayed, graphic images, formatting commands, and hyperlinks to other documents located somewhere on the Web. HTML documents are displayed most often using web browsers, such as Netscape Navigator or Microsoft Internet Explorer.

A protocol called *Hypertext Transfer Protocol* (HTTP) controls the transactions between a web client and a web server. HTTP is an application-layer protocol. The HTTP protocol transparently makes use of DNS and other Internet protocols to form connections between the web client and the web server, so the user is aware of only the web site's domain name and the name of the document itself.

HTTP is fundamentally an insecure protocol. Text-based information is sent "in the clear" between the client and the server. To address the need for secure web networking, alternatives are available, such as Secure HTTP (S-HTTP) or Secure Sockets Layer (SSL).

Requests from a web client to a web server are connection-oriented, but they are not persistent. Once the client receives the contents of an HTML page, the connection is no longer active. Clicking a hyperlink in the HTML document reactivates the link, either to the original server (if that is where the hyperlink points) or to another server somewhere else.

File Transfer Protocol (FTP)

The acronym *FTP* stands for two things: File Transfer Protocol and File Transfer Program (which makes use of the File Transfer Protocol). It's sort of like, "it's a dessert topping *and* a floor polish," from the *Saturday Night Live* TV show. Because FTP (the program) makes use of FTP (the protocol), it can become confusing to know which is being discussed. In this section, I discuss the protocol. (When I'm referring to the program, I'll say so.)

FTP is an application-layer protocol used to send and receive files between an FTP client and an FTP server. Usually, this is done with the FTP program or another program that can also use the protocol (many are available). FTP transfers can be either text-based or binary-based, and they can handle files of any size. When you connect to an FTP server to transfer a file, you log in to the FTP server using a valid username and password. Many sites are set up, however, to allow something called *anonymous FTP*, where you enter the username *anonymous* and then enter your e-mail address as the password. For example, Microsoft maintains an FTP site you can use to download updates to its products. Located at **ftp.microsoft.com**, it is an example of a site that allows anonymous FTP.

To use the FTP program, on most platforms you type the command **ftp** followed by the address to which you want to connect. So, to use the Microsoft example, you would type **ftp ftp.microsoft.com**, then press ENTER. You then log in and you can use all of the FTP commands—PUT, GET, MGET, and so forth. Most FTP program implementations have online help to assist you with the various commands. Type **?** or HELP to access this feature.

NetNews Transfer Protocol (NNTP)

Usenet (NetNews) is a set of discussion groups devoted to an extremely wide variety of topics. More than 35,000 such groups are currently in existence. Usenet conversations are posted to Usenet servers, which then echo their messages to all other Usenet servers around the world. A posted message can travel to all the Usenet servers in a matter of hours and then be available to users accessing any particular Usenet server.

Usenet discussion groups are loosely organized into the branches of a tree. The following are some of the main branches:

- Alt, used for discussions about alternative lifestyles and other miscellaneous topics

- Comp, used for computer-oriented discussions

- Gov, for government-oriented discussions
- Rec, devoted to recreational topics
- Sci, for science-based discussions

Usenet groups can either be public, which are echoed to other Usenet servers, or private, which are usually hosted by a particular organization and require the user to enter appropriate login credentials before reading and posting messages.

The NNTP protocol is what makes Usenet possible. It allows for a connection between a Usenet reader (also called a *news reader*) and a Usenet server. It also provides for message formatting, so messages can be text-based or can also contain binary attachments. Binary attachments in Usenet postings are usually encoded using Multipurpose Internet Message Encoding (MIME), which is also used for most e-mail attachments. Some older systems use different methods to encode attachments, however, including one method called UUEncode/UUDecode and, on the Macintosh, a method called BinHex.

Telnet

Telnet defines a protocol that allows a remote terminal session to be established with an Internet host, so remote users have access similar to that which they would have if they were sitting at a terminal connected directly to the host computer. Using Telnet, users can control the remote host, performing such tasks as managing files, running applications, or even (with appropriate permissions) administering the remote system.

TIP

Telnet is a session-layer protocol in the OSI Model.

For Telnet to work, Telnet software must be running on both the host and client computer. You run the program Telnet on a client computer and run the program Telnetd on the host computer to allow the connection. Telnet is specific to the TCP protocol and typically runs on port 23 (although it can run on any port that has been enabled on the host system). Once users connect using Telnet, they must log in to the remote system using the same credentials they would use if they were using a directly connected terminal.

Simple Mail Transfer Protocol (SMTP)

E-mail had a somewhat rocky start on the Internet, with early e-mail programs sharing few standards with other e-mail programs, particularly in the handling of attached binary data.

The good news is that the situation is now much improved and most current e-mail software supports all the widely accepted standards.

The Simple Mail Transfer Protocol (SMTP) is used to send and receive e-mail messages from one e-mail server to another. Details on SMTP can be found in RFC 821. The SMTP protocol defines a dialog between a sending system and a receiving system.

An SMTP dialog starts when a sending system connects to port 25 of a receiving system. After the connection is established, the sending system sends a HELO command, followed by its address. The receiving system acknowledges the HELO command along with its own address. The dialog then continues, with the sending system issuing a command indicating that the system wants to send a message and the recipient for whom the message is intended. If the receiving system knows of the recipient, it acknowledges the request, and then the sending system transmits the body of the message along with any attachments. Finally, the connection between the two systems is terminated once the receiving system acknowledges that it has received the entire message. Figure 7-2 illustrates this process.

VoIP

An important emerging set of IP protocols concerns the transmission of voice and facsimile information over IP-based networks, called *Voice over IP*, or *VoIP* for short. VoIP is a protocol that allows analog voice data—for phone calls—to be digitized, and then encapsulated into IP packets and transmitted over a network. VoIP can be used to carry voice telephone calls over

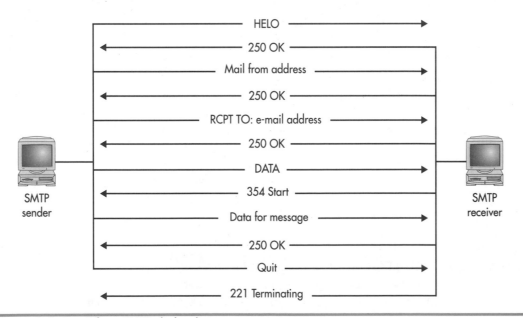

Figure 7-2 Part of an SMTP dialog between systems

any IP network, such as a company's LAN or WAN, or the Internet. There are important pros and cons to carrying voice traffic over a network using a packet-based protocol such as IP, as opposed to the switched connections that the telephone system normally uses. These pros and cons are discussed in detail in the following sections.

Benefits of VoIP

Sending voice data over IP networks has some very attractive possible payoffs.

More Efficient Use of Available Connections   Consider a large company with two main offices. At any given time, hundreds of voice conversations might be occurring between those two offices. Each traditional voice connection consumes one DS0 line, capable of carrying up to 56 Kbps of data were the line to be used digitally. Each conversation doesn't really use all of the available bandwidth on the line. Part of this is because most conversations have a lot of silent spaces—time between words or sentences, time where one party stops speaking and the other starts, and so forth. Plus, most conversations, were they encoded digitally, could be significantly compressed. Add all of this up, and each voice conversation is likely to use only one-third to one-half of the available bandwidth on a single DS0 circuit. If you were able to carry all of these voice conversations digitally, much less bandwidth would be required. Instead of 100 DS0 lines for 100 conversations, for example, the same conversations might use up only 25 to 33 DS0 lines if they were digitally packaged. Add up the cost savings, and you can see that many companies can save a significant amount of money by using VoIP.

VoIP Connections Are Packet-Oriented   When the user places a call, a single connection is formed between the caller and the receiver. This connection is static for the duration of the call. If the conversation were digitized and sent over a packet-oriented network, however, many possible paths would be available for each packet, and much more redundancy would be automatically available. For instance, if some portion of the network between the two points went down, the packets could still arrive at their destination through an alternate route, just as data packets do over the Internet. Also, available circuits would be used more efficiently, allowing more calls to be routed within a particular geographic area.

Disadvantages of VoIP

There are also some problems with VoIP that you need to consider.

No Guaranteed Delivery   VoIP does not guarantee delivery of IP packets over the Internet. For a digital transmission of data, this is no big deal; if a packet isn't confirmed as being received, it is simply retransmitted. For a real-time voice conversation, on the other hand, the loss of packets directly inhibits the conversation, and you can't go back in time to retransmit missing packets.

Packets Arrive out of Sequence Not only can IP packets simply fail to arrive at their destination on occasion, sometimes they arrive out of sequence due to other Internet traffic and other reasons. This is fine for transmitting things such as files, because they can be reassembled on the other end in the proper sequence. For a real-time application such as voice, however, having packets arrive out of sequence results in a hopelessly jumbled, and thus useless, transmission.

QoS Not Widely Implemented Real-time uses of the Internet, such as VoIP or multimedia streaming, and time-sensitive transmissions should be given priority over transmissions that are not particularly time-sensitive, such as the transmission of an e-mail message. Fortunately, IP has a quality of service (QoS) field that enables the user to prioritize traffic for such reasons. However, QoS is not widely implemented in all parts of the Internet.

VoIP's Development and Future

VoIP is a hot, emerging technology that is virtually certain to become an important part of the Internet and most companies' networks. However, there is still much work to be done toward actually implementing this technology widely and solving more certainly the problems outlined in this section. In other words, if you're learning about networking, you should be aware of VoIP—what it is and what it does—although most likely the technology will not become much of a factor in most networks for several years yet.

CRITICAL SKILL
7.3 Compare Important Proprietary Protocols

While Microsoft-based, Novell-based, and Apple-based networks can fully work with TCP/IP and all the previously discussed protocols, each type of network got its start supporting proprietary protocols unique to each company, and each of these protocols is still in wide use. All these companies have embraced TCP/IP and support it fully, both for servers and network clients. In the case of Microsoft and Novell networks, they can be easily deployed using only TCP/IP (as of Windows NT 4 and Novell NetWare 5). In theory, you could do the same thing with an Apple-based network, but you would lose a good deal of the Macintosh's network functionality if you did so. Because of this, an Apple-based network should support both AppleTalk (Apple's proprietary protocol) and TCP/IP.

Until just recently, Novell networks predominantly used the Internetwork Packet Exchange/ Sequenced Packet Exchange (IPX/SPX) protocols. These are derivatives of the Xerox XNS protocol. While different from TCP/IP, IPX/SPX is comparable to that protocol; IPX is analogous to IP, and SPX is analogous to TCP.

Microsoft networks were originally based on an IBM-developed protocol called *NetBIOS* (Network Basic Input/Output System). NetBIOS is a relatively high-level protocol that, in essence, extends the functionality of DOS to a network. Microsoft also used IBM's *NetBEUI* (NetBIOS Extended User Interface), an enhancement to NetBIOS.

Apple Macintosh computer networks originally supported only AppleTalk. The protocol was originally designed expressly for the purpose of sharing then-expensive Apple LaserWriter printers within small workgroups, using a low-bandwidth (230 Kbps originally) network media called LocalTalk. Over time, Apple extended AppleTalk somewhat to enable file sharing and other network functions, but AppleTalk is still an extremely inefficient network protocol that, even over Ethernet (called EtherTalk in Apple's implementation), works slowly. Still, if you have an Apple-based network, you have to live with the AppleTalk protocol.

Novell's IPX/SPX

Novell's IPX protocol was originally a derivative of the Xerox Network Systems (XNS) architecture and closely resembles it. While IPX can be used on any of the popular network media (Ethernet, Token Ring, and so forth), it was originally designed for Ethernet networks and works best with that media. In fact, the IPX protocol depends on Ethernet MAC addresses for part of its own addresses. IPX addresses are dynamic and are automatically negotiated with the server at login, rather than being statically set, as is the case with TCP/IP without DHCP services. An IPX network address comprises both a 32-bit network address and a 48-bit node address. In addition, another 16 bits are used for a connection ID, which allows up to 65,000 unique client/server connections between a client and a server. The address design of IPX theoretically allows for about 281 trillion nodes on each of 16 million networks.

IPX was originally designed only for LANs, but it has been enhanced to support WAN connections. While typically considered a "chatty" protocol that requires a lot of send/acknowledgment transactions, IPX has been enhanced with burst-mode capabilities, which increase the size of packets destined for a WAN and decrease the number of back-and-forth communications required. IPX can be routed, but only if the network includes an IPX-capable router.

NetBIOS and NetBEUI Protocols

IBM originally developed NetBIOS and NetBEUI to support small networks. Microsoft adopted the protocols as part of LAN Manager, a network operating system built on top of early versions of the OS/2 operating system.

Neither protocol is routable; each is suitable only for small LANs that do not rely on routers between different LAN segments. However, NetBIOS can be encapsulated within TCP/IP packets on Windows NT networks using a service called NetBIOS over TCP/IP (abbreviated as NBT, for NetBIOS over TCP/IP).

Microsoft LANs (prior to Windows 2000) rely on a NetBIOS service called *NetBIOS names* to identify each workstation uniquely.

In a simple NetBIOS implementation, names are registered with all workstations through a broadcast message. If no computer has already registered a particular name, the name registration succeeds. In a more complex Windows NT–based network that also uses TCP/IP, however, the NetBIOS names resolve to TCP/IP addresses through the use of Windows Internet Name Service (WINS). The names can also be resolved using static name definition entries contained in a file called LMHOSTS (LAN Manager HOSTS). Because many networking applications still use NetBIOS names, either WINS or LMHOSTS allows such applications to continue to function in a TCP/IP-only network. As far as the application is concerned, it is still working with NetBIOS, while TCP/IP performs the actual work in the background.

AppleTalk

AppleTalk has been extended in recent years into AppleTalk Phase II, which now allows routing of AppleTalk packets (assuming an AppleTalk Phase II–capable router). The Phase II variant can run over Ethernet, Token Ring, or Apple's LocalTalk media. Under Ethernet, AppleTalk uses a variant of the 802.2 frame type called Ethernet *SNAP* (SubNetwork Access Point).

While Apple Macintosh computers can use both TCP/IP and IPX/SPX through the addition of special software, the Macintosh operating system is dependent on AppleTalk, so both TCP/IP and IPX/SPX are translated at each node into AppleTalk messages before being passed to the operating system. This translation process is one of the reasons that Apple Macintosh computers tend to be slower than other types of computers over network connections. Still, the approach works and is relatively easy to set up and maintain.

✓ *Module 7 Mastery Check*

1. What are the following protocols used for?

   A. SMTP

   B. DHCP

   C. DNS

   D. TCP/IP

2. TCP/IP addresses are composed of _____ parts, called _____.

3. To take a range of TCP/IP addresses, such as a Class C, and subdivide it, you use _____.

4. Which of the following protocols are routable, assuming an appropriate router is in place?

   A. TCP/IP

   B. IPX/SPX

   C. NetBIOS

   D. NetBEUI

5. FTP stands for both _____ and _____.

6. A single computer that uses TCP/IP internally routes incoming data to the appropriate service or program through the use of _____.

7. DNS stands for _____.

8. Web pages are transmitted using a protocol called _____, which stands for _____.

9. Every TCP/IP address always has a corresponding _____ that indicates which part of the address is the netid, and which is the hostid.

10. A TCP/IP address range that fixes the first two octets and leaves the remaining two octets open for the user to allocate is called a Class ___ address.

Module 8

Exploring Directory Services

In the early days of LANs, finding server resources was pretty simple. Most organizations started with just a file server and a print server or two, so knowing what files, printers, and other services were in which locations on the LAN was easy.

These days, the situation is considerably more complex. Even relatively small organizations might have multiple servers, each one performing different jobs, storing different sets of files, providing different Internet or intranet services, hosting different printers, and so forth.

Directory services work to bring organization to this far-flung network clutter. In this module, you learn about what directory services do and how they work. You also learn about directory services in use today and slated for use in the near future. With directory services becoming more and more central to the administration of networks, learning this information becomes an increasingly important part of designing, deploying, and managing networks.

CRITICAL SKILL
8.1 # Define Directory Service

In most networks, you optimize the function of different services by hosting them on different computers. Doing so makes sense. Placing all your services on one computer is a bit like placing all your eggs in one basket: If you then drop the basket, you'll break all your eggs. Moreover, you can achieve optimal performance, more reliability, and higher security by segregating network services in various ways. Most networks have quite a few services that need to be provided and often these different services run on different servers. Even a relatively simple network now offers the following services:

- File storage and sharing

- Printer sharing

- E-mail services

- Web hosting, both for the Internet and an intranet

- Database server services

- Specific application servers

- Internet connectivity

- Dial-in and dial-out services

- Fax services

- Domain Name System (DNS) service, Windows Internet Naming Service (WINS), and Dynamic Host Configuration Protocol (DHCP) services

- Centralized virus-detection services

- Backup and restore services

This is only a short list. Larger organizations have multiple servers sharing in each of these functions—with different services available through different means in each building or location—and might have additional services beyond those discussed here.

All this complexity can quickly make a network chaotic to manage. If each one of the individual servers requires separate administration (with, for instance, separate lists of users, groups, printers, network configurations, and so on), then you can easily see how the job can become virtually impossible in no time.

Directory services were invented to bring organization to networks. Basically, directory services work just like a phone book. Instead of using a name to look up an address and phone number in a phone book, you query the directory service for a service name (such as the name of a network folder, or a printer), and the directory service tells you where the service is located. You can also query directory services by property. For instance, if you query the directory service for all items that are "printers," it can return a complete list, no matter where the printers are located in the organization. Even better, directory services enable you to browse all the resources on a network easily, in one unified list organized in a tree structure.

One important advantage of directory services is that they eliminate the need to manage duplicates of anything on the network because the directory is automatically shared among all of the servers. For example, you don't have to maintain separate user lists on each server. Instead, you manage a single set of user accounts that exists in the directory service and then assign them various rights to particular resources on any of the servers. Other resources work the same way and become centrally managed in the directory service. Not only does this mean that you have only one collection of objects to manage, but also it means that users have a much simpler network experience. From the user's perspective, they have only one network account with one password, and they don't have to worry about where resources are located or keep track of different passwords for different network services or servers.

TIP

In this module, the term *network resource* refers to any discrete resource on a network, such as user accounts, security group definitions, e-mail distribution lists, storage volumes, folders, and files. The term *directory* in this module refers to the directory that a directory service uses, rather than a directory on a hard disk.

To provide redundancy, directory services usually run on multiple servers in an organization, each of the servers having a complete copy of the entire directory service database. The separate databases are kept synchronized through a process called *replication*, in which changes to any of the individual directory databases are transparently updated to all the other directory service databases. Because a directory service becomes central to the functioning of a network, this approach lets the network as a whole continue to operate if any single server with directory services on it crashes. Servers that do not actually host a copy of the directory still make use of it by communicating with the directory servers. For instance, if a user tries to open a file hosted on a server that doesn't actually host the directory service, the server will automatically query the directory service on another server to authenticate the user's access request. To the user, this happens behind the scenes.

You should know about five important directory services:

- *Novell eDirectory* (previously called Novell Directory Services or NDS) is the network directory service that has been popular for the longest time. eDirectory runs on NetWare 4.*x* and greater servers, and is also available for other server operating systems (such as Solaris, Linux, and Windows NT), enabling you to use eDirectory as a single directory service for managing a multivendor network.

- *Windows NT domains* are not actually complete directory services, but they provide some of the features and advantages of directory services.

- *Microsoft's Active Directory* debuted with the Windows 2000 Server line of products. This is a true directory service and it brings the full features of a directory service to a network predominantly built using Windows 2000 Server.

- *X.500 Directory Access Protocol* (DAP) is an international standard directory service that is full of features. However, X.500 provides so many features that its overhead makes deploying and managing it prohibitive. Consequently, X.500 is in an interesting position: It is an important standard, yet, paradoxically, it is not actually used.

- The *Lightweight Directory Access Protocol* (LDAP) was developed by a consortium of vendors as a subset of X.500 to offer an alternative with less complexity than X.500. LDAP is in wide use for e-mail directories and is suitable for other directory service tasks. The most recent versions of eDirectory—and also Active Directory—are compatible with LDAP.

Forests, Trees, Roots, and Leaves

One thing common to all directory services is a tree-based organization (with the tree usually depicted upside-down with the root at the top), somewhat similar to the organization of directories on a hard disk. At the top of the directory tree is the *root* entry, which contains other entries. These other entries can be containers or leaves. A *container object* is one that contains other objects, which can also include more containers and leaves. A *leaf object* represents an actual resource on the network, such as a workstation, printer, shared directory, file, or user account. Leaf objects cannot contain other objects. Figure 8-1 shows a typical directory tree.

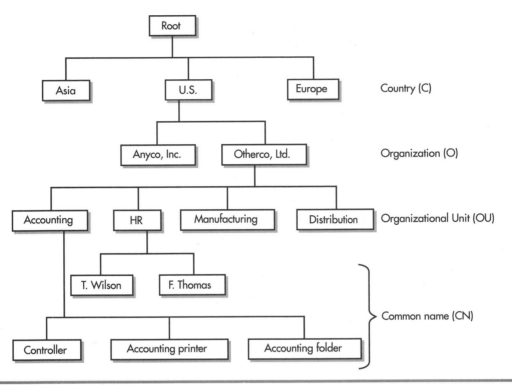

Figure 8-1 A typical directory tree

All the objects in a directory tree have *attributes* (sometimes called *properties*), which vary depending on the type of object to which the attribute is attached.

For example, a *printer leaf object* might contain attributes that describe the printer, who can administer the printer, what the printer's name is on the network, and so forth. A *user account leaf object* might contain attributes that include the full name of the user account, its password, and resources that the user can access. The details of what attributes attach to what leaf or container objects vary among all the directory services, although they generally use similar attributes.

Department of Redundancy Department

Keeping directory services running is essential for any network that relies on them. Because they contain all details about accounts, resources, and security, the absence of directory services means the network won't work—at all! Because the directory services become so important to a network, you must protect them with some degree of redundancy. Keeping duplicate copies of the directory on multiple servers provides the necessary redundancy. This is done using one of two approaches: primary/backup (master/slave) and multimaster. In the *primary/backup model,* a single primary database contains the primary (or "real") directory on one server, while other servers hold one or more backup copies. If the primary copy stops working for some reason, the backups can continue to provide directory services to the network without the user even knowing that the primary copy isn't available. Windows NT uses a primary/backup approach. In the *multimaster model,* multiple directory servers exist, but they are all peers to one another. If one goes down, the other peers continue to operate normally. The advantage of the multimaster model is that each directory server can fully participate in doing the work of the directory service. Windows 2000 Server uses the multimaster approach.

Directory servers, whether they use the primary/backup or multimaster approach, must keep in sync with changes on the network. This synchronization is provided through a process called *replication,* which automatically duplicates any changes to the directory on one server to all the other directory servers.

A potential problem exists with any replication process, though: If two changes are made to the same leaf object on two different directory servers and the changes are different, what does the system do when the changes "collide" during replication? Different directory services handle this problem in slightly different ways. In the case of eDirectory, the time stamps of the changes drive which of two conflicting changes will win. (Because of this, servers running eDirectory must carefully keep their time synchronized; this synchronization is also handled during replication.) Microsoft's Active Directory doesn't use time stamps, but instead uses sequence numbers in a clever scheme that avoids the potential problems of a time-stamp approach. (Even though eDirectory servers synchronize their time, their time can still become out of sync between synchronizations.)

Some directory services also allow a concept called *partitioning*, in which different directory servers keep different parts of the entire directory tree. In this case, a controlling directory server usually manages the entire tree (called the *global catalog* in Active Directory), and then other directory servers can manage smaller pieces of the total tree. Partitioning is important for networks with multiple LANs connected by a WAN. In such cases, you want to host a partition that relates to a particular LAN locally, yet still allow access to the entire tree for resources accessed over the WAN. Each LAN hosts its own partition, but can still access the total tree when needed. You arrange the partitions (and set the scheduled replication times) to make the best use of the WAN's performance, which usually is slower than that of a LAN.

Progress Check

1. In what basic ways does a directory service simplify a network?

2. What are the names of the essential object types of a directory structure?

CRITICAL SKILL
8.2 Describe Specific Directory Services

Quite a few different directory services are available. Choosing one usually goes hand in hand with choosing a main network operating system, although this isn't always the case. Both eDirectory and Active Directory can handle non-Novell and non-Microsoft servers, respectively. Consequently, even a network that currently uses mostly Windows NT servers might still rely on eDirectory for directory services through the use of Novell's eDirectory for Windows NT product. Using a single directory service with different network operating systems often happens because an organization starts out favoring a particular network operating system and then later finds itself forced to support additional NOSs, but the organization still wants to maintain a coherent, single directory service to manage both network operating systems.

Earlier in the module, the main directory services were listed. Here they are again:

● Novell eDirectory

● Microsoft's Windows NT domains

● Microsoft's Active Directory

● X.500 Directory Access Protocol (DAP)

● Lightweight Directory Access Protocol (LDAP)

These are the predominant directory services that you will encounter, although you should be aware that others exist. For example, you should also be aware of StreetTalk, a directory service product from a company called Banyan. StreetTalk has been in existence for a long time as part of the Banyan Vines network operating system (which is essentially a UNIX-based NOS). StreetTalk is available for Novell servers as well as Vines servers. Banyan-based networks are rarely used anymore, though, so you're unlikely to encounter StreetTalk.

---

1. Directory services vastly simplify network administration and also the use of the network.
2. Forests, trees, roots, and leaves

eDirectory

Novell eDirectory (formerly called Novell Directory Services, or NDS) has been available since 1993, being introduced as part of NetWare 4.x. With many organizations having tens or hundreds of NetWare servers, this product was a real boon and was rapidly implemented, particularly in larger organizations that desperately needed its capabilities. eDirectory is a reliable, robust directory service that has continued to evolve since its introduction. Version 8.7 is now available and it incorporates the latest directory service features.

eDirectory uses a master/slave approach to directory servers and also allows partitioning of the tree. In addition to running on Novell network operating systems, eDirectory is also available for Windows NT, Windows 2000, Solaris, and Linux systems. The product's compatibility with such a variety of systems makes eDirectory a good choice for managing all these platforms under a single directory structure.

You manage the eDirectory tree from a client computer logged in to the network with administrative privileges. You can either use a graphical tool designed to manage the tree called *ConsoleOne,* another graphical tool called *NWAdmin,* or a text-based tool called *NETADMIN.* Each allows full management of the tree, although the graphical products are much easier to use, and with Netware 5.x, can be run on the server console.

The eDirectory tree contains a number of different object types. The standard directory service types—countries, organizations, and organizational units—are included. The system also has objects to represent NetWare security groups, NetWare servers, and NetWare server volumes. eDirectory can manage more than a billion objects in a tree.

Windows NT Domains

Windows NT 4 introduced a directory service feature organized around the use of domains. The Windows NT domain model breaks an organization into chunks called *domains,* all of which are part of an organization. The domains are usually organized geographically, which helps minimize domain-to-domain communication requirements across WAN links, although you're free to organize domains as you wish. Each domain is controlled by a *Primary Domain Controller* (PDC), which might have one or more *Backup Domain Controllers* (BDCs) to kick in if the PDC fails.

All changes within the domain are made to the PDC, which then replicates those changes to any BDCs. BDCs are read-only, except for valid updates received from the PDC. In case of a PDC failure, BDCs automatically continue authenticating users. To make administrative changes to a domain that suffers PDC failure, any of the BDCs can be *promoted* to PDC. Once the PDC is ready to come back online, the promoted BDC can be *demoted* back to BDC status.

Windows NT domains can be organized into one of four domain models. You choose an appropriate domain model depending on the physical layout of the network, the number of users to be served, and other factors. (If you're planning a domain model, you should review the white papers on Microsoft's web site for details on planning large domains, because the process can be complex and difficult.)

The four domain models are

- **Single-domain model**   In this model, only one domain contains all network resources.

- **Master domain model**   The master model usually puts users at the top-level domain and then places network resources, such as share folders or printers, in lower-level domains (called *resource domains*). In this model, the resource domains trust the master domain.

- **Multiple master domain model**   This is a slight variation on the master domain model, in which users might exist in multiple master domains, all of which trust one another, and in which resources are located in resource domains, all of which trust all the master domains.

- **Complete trust model**   This variation of the single-domain model spreads users and resources across all domains, which all trust each other.

TIP

A good white paper on designing Windows NT 4 domains, while keeping Active Directory in mind, can be found at: http://www.microsoft.com/technet/winnt/ winntas/technote/planning/nt4tont5.asp.

Explicit trust relationships must be maintained between domains using the master or multiple master domain models, and must be managed on each domain separately. Maintaining these relationships is one of the biggest difficulties in the Windows NT domain structure approach, at least for larger organizations; if you have 100 domains, you must manage the 99 possible trust relationships for each domain within each domain, or a total of 9,900 trust relationships. For smaller numbers of domains (for example, less than 10 domains), management of the trust relationships don't become much of a problem, although they can still cause difficulties.

Active Directory

Windows NT domains work relatively well for smaller networks, but they can become difficult to manage for larger networks. Moreover, the system is not nearly as comprehensive as, for example, eDirectory. Microsoft recognized this problem and has developed a new directory service called Active Directory, which is a comprehensive directory service that runs on Windows 2000. Active Directory is fully compatible with LDAP (versions 2 and 3) and also with the DNS used on the Internet.

Active Directory uses a peer approach to domain controllers; all domain controllers are full participants at all times. As mentioned earlier in this module, this arrangement is called *multimaster* because there are many "master" domain controllers but no "slave" controllers.

Active Directory is built on a structure that allows "trees of trees," which is called a *forest*. Each tree is its own domain and has its own domain controllers. Within a domain, separate organization units are allowed to make administration easier and more logical. Trees are then aggregated into a larger tree structure. According to Microsoft, Active Directory can handle millions of objects through this approach.

Active Directory does not require the management of trust relationships, except when connected to Windows NT 4.x servers that are not using Active Directory. Otherwise, all domains within a tree have automatic trust relationships.

X.500

The X.500 standard was developed jointly by the International Telecommunications Union (ITU) and the International Standards Organization (ISO). The standard defines a directory service that can be used for the entire Internet. Because of its broad applicability, the X.500 specification is too complex for most organizations to implement. Also, because of its design, it is intended to publish specific organizational directory entries across the Internet, which is something most companies would not want to do. Just the same, the X.500 standard is an extremely important standard and most directory services mimic or incorporate parts of it in some fashion.

The X.500 directory tree starts with a root, just like the other directory trees, and then breaks down into country (C), organization (O), organizational unit (OU), and common name (CN) fields. To specify an X.500 address fully, you provide five fields, as in the following:

```
CN=user name, OU=department, OU=division, O=organization, C=country
```

For example, you might configure the fields as follows:

```
CN=Bruce Hallberg, OU=Networking Books, OU=Computer Books,
O=McGraw-Hill,C=USA
```

LDAP

To address the complexity problems involved with full X.500 DAP, a consortium of companies came up with a subset of X.500, called the Lightweight Directory Access Protocol (LDAP). LDAP's advocates claim that it provides 90 percent of the power of X.500, but at only 10 percent of the cost. LDAP runs over TCP/IP and uses a client/server model. Its organization is much the same as that of X.500, but with fewer fields and fewer functions.

LDAP is covered predominantly by RFC 1777 (for version 2) and RFC 2251 (for version 3). Some other RFCs also describe aspects of LDAP; however, 1777 and 2251 are the two main documents. The LDAP standard describes not only the layout and fields within an LDAP directory, but also the methods to be used when a person logs into a server that uses LDAP, or to query it or update it. (Because directory services might fulfill many simultaneous authentications, queries, and—more importantly—might accept simultaneous updates, it is important that these methods be clearly defined to avoid collisions and other potentially corrupting uses of the directory by client applications and administrative tools.)

LDAP Models

The following four basic models describe the LDAP protocol:

- The *Information Model* defines the structure of the data stored in the directory.

- The *Naming Model* defines how to reference and organize the data.

- The *Functional Model* defines how to work with the data.

- The *Security Model* defines how to keep the data in the directory secure.

The Information Model describes a number of aspects of the directory. First is the directory's *schema*, which is the template for the directory and its entries. Next are the *classes* allowed for entries in the directory. Classes are categories to which all entries are attached. Next, the Information Model defines *attributes,* which are items of data that describe the classes. An example of an attribute is CN or OU, which are attributes used for all entries in the directory. The next aspect described by the Information Model is the *syntax* for the attributes. The syntax specifies exactly how attributes are named and stored, and what sort of data they are allowed to contain (such as numbers, string text, dates and times, and so forth). Finally, *entries* are defined. An entry is a distinct piece of data, like an object, that can be either a container or a leaf.

TIP

Microsoft uses nomenclature to describe LDAP that differs from the terms defined in the RFCs. Most notably, Microsoft calls an *entry* an *object,* and calls an *attribute* a *property.* These names refer to the same things, and you should be aware of this when reading the RFCs or other documents about LDAP and comparing the information to that found in documents from Microsoft.

The Naming Model defines the names that serve as primary keys for entries in the directory. The Naming Model defines *distinguished names* (DNs), which are full names of entries, as well as *relative distinguished names* (RDNs), which are components of Distinguished Names. The following is an example of an LDAP DN:

```
CN=Bruce Hallberg, OU=Networking Books, OU=Computer Books,
O=McGraw-Hill, C=USA
```

Each component of the DN, such as the CD, OU, or O entries, is an RDN.

The Functional Model for LDAP defines how LDAP accomplishes three types of operations: Authentication, Interrogation, and Updates. Authentication is the process by which users prove their identity to the directory, Interrogation is the process by which the information in the directory is queried, and Updates are operations that post changes to the directory.

Finally, the Security Model controls how the directory is used in a secure fashion. For most implementations of LDAP, a security protocol called Simple Authentication and Security Layer (SASL) is used. RFC 2222 describes SASL.

LDAP Organization

An LDAP tree starts with a root, which then contains entries. Each entry can have one or more *attributes*. Each of these attributes has both a *type* and *values* associated with it. One example is the CN, which contains at least two attributes: FirstName and Surname. All attributes in LDAP use the text string data type. Entries are organized into a tree and managed geographically and then within each organization.

One nice feature of LDAP is that an organization can build a global directory structure using a feature called *referral*, where LDAP directory queries that are managed by a different LDAP server are transparently routed to that server. Because each LDAP server knows its parent LDAP server and its child servers, any user anywhere in the network can access the entire LDAP tree. In fact, the user won't even know he or she is accessing different servers in different locales.

✓ *Module 8 Mastery Check*

1. As a user of a network, a directory service on a network is primarily useful for

_____.

2. As a network administrator, a directory service on a network is primarily useful for

_____.

3. True or false: Windows NT domains are full directory services.

4. True or false: Novell's eDirectory directory service can be used to manage Windows NT and Windows 2000 servers, as well as Linux and Solaris servers.

5. LDAP stands for _____.

6. The LDAP protocol is based on the _____ directory service.

7. Which of the following are benefits of the LDAP directory service relative to the X.500 directory service:

    A. LDAP has many more features than X.500.

    B. LDAP enjoys broad support by other directory services that are often compatible with LDAP.

    C. LDAP is simpler and easier to implement than X.500.

8. True or false: It is often a good idea to run directory services on multiple servers so that redundancy exists.

9. Microsoft's Active Directory handles redundancy using a _____ approach.

10. Microsoft's Windows NT domains handle redundancy using a _____ approach.

8

Exploring Directory Services

Module 9

Connections from Afar: Remote Network Access

In preceding modules, you learned about networking systems together through a LAN and through a WAN, and about the technologies that go into both types of networks. You also need to know about another important type of network connection: remote access to a network. With today's travel-happy corporate cultures and with companies needing to support such things as working from home and small remote offices, remote access has become more important than ever. Unfortunately, it's also one of the most difficult parts of a network to get right, as you will see in this module.

One of the big problems with remote access is that it can seem as though all the remote users have different needs and all the different solutions available speak to different needs, and none of those solutions takes care of *all* the needs. Spending some time analyzing your company's needs and finding solid solutions that meet those needs is usually nontrivial and requires a fair amount of time and effort. The following section describes one way in which you might categorize different remote access needs, which is the first step to finding a remote access solution (or solutions) for your network.

CRITICAL SKILL
9.1 Classify Remote Users

Users who require remote access fall into one of a number of different categories. Each category of remote user often has different needs, and different technologies and remote access solutions are often needed to satisfy these different needs completely. Most important to remember is that you need to know what categories of remote users *you* have to support. Every company has a different mix of remote users, who have different needs from company to company. Moreover, even when needs are identical, the solutions you employ might change based on other criteria. For instance, you might handle access to an accounting system from a remote location differently, depending on whether it's a client/server or a monolithic application.

I suggest that you classify your remote access users into one of four categories:

- Broad traveler
- Narrow traveler
- Remote office user
- Remote office group

You need different strategies to support these different types of users. If you're working in a small company, you likely won't have to support all these categories right off the bat.

Ask the Expert

Q: What is a client/server application?

A: Client/server applications consist of processes (programs) that run on both the server side and the client side and that work in concert. For example, a database server performs queries for the client, and then transmits to the client only the results of that query. The client's job is just to display the results and maybe format them for printing. A monolithic application, on the other hand, performs all of its work on one computer, typically the client computer. The server for a monolithic application serves up only the files needed for the application to run and the data files that the application manipulates. Generally, client/server applications require much less bandwidth to work at acceptable speeds than monolithic applications. A 56-Kbps modem connection might be adequate for a client/server application, such as an accounting system, whereas that same modem would be totally inadequate for that same application designed to be monolithic.

The most common type of remote access user is called the *broad traveler*. This is someone who normally is based in a main office that usually has LAN access, but who occasionally or frequently travels on business. Travel takes this person to virtually any place in the world, so the traveler must contend with different telephone systems, long-distance carriers, and other geographic challenges (see Figure 9-1). Often, this type of user mostly needs e-mail access, but also needs occasional access to stored or e-mailed files. This type of user might or might not have a dedicated portable (laptop) computer. The user might normally use a desktop computer on the LAN but have a laptop computer for traveling, might use a single laptop both on the LAN and when traveling, might check out laptop computers from a shared pool when travel needs arise, or might even rent a laptop computer for an occasional travel need. These different approaches further complicate providing services to the traveler.

Another common type of remote access user is called a *narrow traveler*. This is someone who travels to relatively few locations, such as from corporate headquarters to the company's manufacturing plants or distribution centers. The nice thing about this type of user is that you can predict the sites from which the user might need to access data, and thus can make local support available to help. For instance, you might have a way for the user to log in to the distribution center's LAN and access e-mail and files at the headquarters location through an existing WAN link, as shown in Figure 9-2. This type of user needs e-mail, file access, and often access to a centralized application, such as an accounting system.

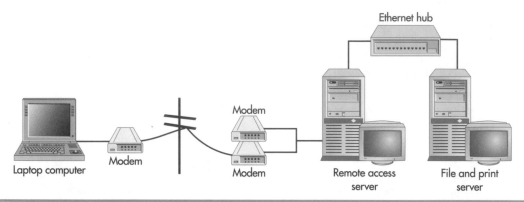

Figure 9-1 A typical remote access session

The third common type of remote access user is the *remote office user*. This user is in a single location and needs access to the corporate LAN for e-mail and possibly for application access (see Figure 9-3). This person usually does not need file access, except to send files through the e-mail system, because this person maintains local file storage. This user is in a single location, so you can pursue certain high-speed links that aren't feasible for the travelers. A person telecommuting from home would fall into the category of remote office user.

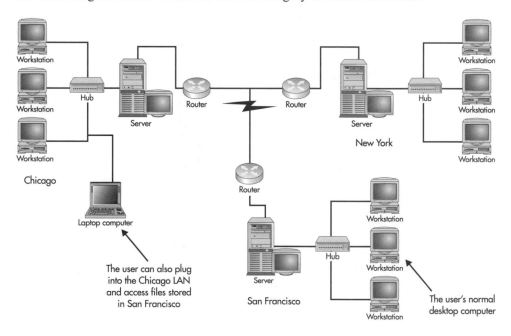

Figure 9-2 A WAN used by a "narrow traveler"

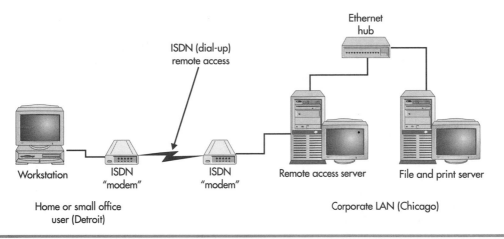

Figure 9-3 A remote office user's network setup

The fourth type of remote access user is something of a hybrid. Sometimes a small group (two to five people) stationed in a remote location need certain services from the corporate LAN. These services aren't cost-effective for this group to have locally, yet these users have a small local LAN for printer and file sharing, as seen in Figure 9-4. This type of remote access user needs a combination of services: partly they are like any user of a remote LAN, and partly they are like a remote office user. They usually require a mixture of both types of solutions for proper support.

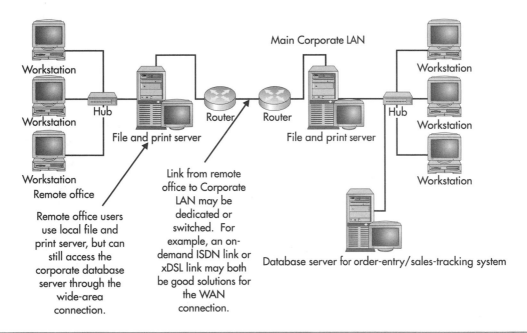

Figure 9-4 Supporting a small remote office that requires LAN access

Determine Remote Access Needs

Before implementing any remote access system, you need to define clearly what the different types of remote users in the company need. Examples of needs you should meet include

- Easy remote access to e-mail and to files stored in e-mail

- Remote access to stored private or shared files on the LAN

- Remote access to a centralized application, such as an accounting system or a sales order system

- Remote access to groupware programs or custom applications

- Internet access

- Intranet/extranet access, including any hosted web-based applications on those systems

- Remote access to any of the previous features from a fixed location, such as a remote sales office

- Remote access to any of the previous features from anywhere in the world

To understand your specific remote access support needs, it's important to interview all the potential users (or at least a representative subset) and find out how to categorize them as described earlier. Chances are that you must support remote access through more than one mechanism. How you categorize the users and their needs will suggest which mechanisms make sense.

To interview the users, make sure you carefully probe all possible needs. For example, if you ask them if they need remote access to the files stored in their LAN directories and they reply, "not really," that's not an adequate answer. You need to pin them down by asking such questions as, "Will you *ever* need remote access to files? What if you had only e-mail access? Could your assistant e-mail you any needed files?" You also might want to consider taking this tack: Once you have come up with different remote access needs in your company, try to survey the users in writing to inquire about their specific needs. Not only should you get less ambiguous answers, but you also get important documentation to justify the required expenses and effort in acquiring and setting up the remote access systems needed.

When examining remote access needs, you need to estimate bandwidth requirements and tolerances for the different users. This is important for planning and also for appropriately setting user expectations. For example, if salespeople want minute-to-minute access to a sales tracking system and also frequently want to download 4MB file packages to use for quotations, you have to explain the limitations of modem speeds and telephone connections to reduce these users' expectations. Or, you can find different solutions to meet their needs that are consistent with the amount of bandwidth you can offer.

You can estimate a particular application program's bandwidth requirements in a few good ways. The first involves actually measuring the application's bandwidth needs. On the LAN, you can monitor the amount of data being sent to a particular node that uses the application in the way it would be used remotely. You can measure the data in a number of ways. For a Windows PC, you can run System Monitor or Performance Monitor on the client and look at the network traffic that the PC is consuming (see Figure 9-5). You can also measure the volume of data from the server. For a Windows NT or 2000 server, you can use Performance Monitor to measure bytes transmitted to and from the client. For a Novell server, you can use the console Monitor application and watch the amount of data being sent and received by the client's server connection.

If the bandwidth requirements of an application are simply too great to handle over the type of remote connection that you have to use (such as a 33.6-Kbps modem connection), you need to explore other alternatives. These include using a remote control solution (discussed in greater detail later in this module) or using the application in a different way. For example, you might load the application onto the remote computer rather than use it across the LAN. Also, perhaps the data needs of the user don't need to be up to date and minute to minute, and you can set up a procedure whereby the user receives weekly data updates on a CD-ROM or through some other mechanism.

The ways that you can satisfy remote access needs are virtually limitless. However, the key is to assess the needs carefully and to work creatively, given your available or proposed remote access technology, to find ways to satisfy the remote user's needs.

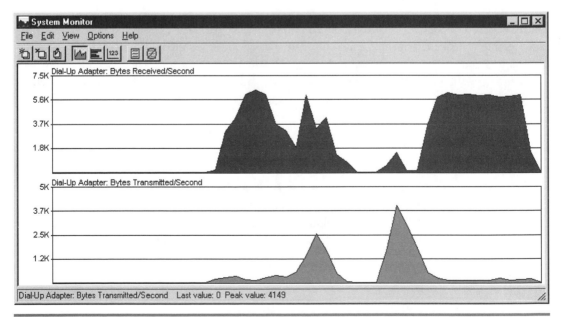

Figure 9-5 Using Windows System Monitor to look at the bandwidth that an application is using

Progress Check

1. What is the most common type of remote access user, and what characteristics define them?

2. Name three specific remote access needs for which you may need to provide a remote access solution.

Describe Remote Access Technologies

A variety of different ways exist to accomplish remote access connections for users. Sometimes these different technologies are appropriate for some users but not for others. Sometimes the choices you have are restricted by how the remote user needs to access the data. For example, a remote user at a single location can fairly easily set up a high-speed link to the corporate LAN, while a traveling remote user might be limited to using modems and dialup telephone connections.

The following sections discuss different techniques and technologies, along with the pros and cons of each. The ones that you implement depend on the needs you've identified, your budget, and the existing infrastructure of your network.

Remote Node Versus Remote Control

Remote users can connect to a network in two basic ways: remote node and remote control. A *remote node connection* is one in which the remote computer becomes a node on the network. Data flows between the remote node and the network much as it would for a LAN-connected user, albeit usually at much slower rates. When you connect to an ISP to access the Internet, you are using a remote node connection.

A *remote control connection* is one in which a remote user takes control of another computer directly connected to the LAN, with only the screen, keyboard, and mouse information being transmitted through the connection. Because the remote control computer is directly connected to the LAN, its network performance is just as fast as that of any other LAN workstation. The information actually transmitted—the screen information, keyboard data, and mouse data— usually doesn't require much bandwidth. (One exception to this rule is a highly graphical application, such as a CAD drawing program.) Remote control connections also have ways

---

1. The "broad traveler" is the most common type of remote access user in most companies. The broad traveler is usually based at a central location, but travels to any number of places around the country or world and needs remote access when traveling.

2. Any three of the following: e-mail, file browsing and upload/download, access to a centralized application, Internet (Web) access, extranet/intranet access, or access to a groupware or custom application.

to transfer files back and forth from the remote computer to the controlled computer, so files can still be downloaded from the LAN to the remote computer and vice versa.

Remote control is accomplished using special applications designed for this purpose. Examples of remote control software include PCAnywhere, Carbon Copy, and ReachOut, as well as Windows NT Terminal Server (or Terminal Services for Windows 2000) and Citrix MetaFrame. You run the remote control software on both the LAN-connected computer and the remote computer. The connection is established over a dialup line or through the Internet.

Two types of remote control applications are available. The first runs on a single computer and supports a single remote computer at a time. PCAnywhere and Carbon Copy are examples of this type. Another type allows multiple sessions to run on a single computer, so you can allow more than one user making use of a single computer connected to the LAN. Windows NT Terminal Server, Windows 2000 Terminal Services, and Citrix MetaFrame are examples of this type. The multiuser solutions use the LAN computer's multitasking capabilities to construct multiple virtual PCs, windows, and desktops, sort of like a mainframe with multiple terminal sessions.

Remote control is the best bet when the remote users need to access applications that don't work well over lower bandwidth connections. And, because most applications don't run well over slower connections, remote users will usually find that a LAN-connected application works better with remote control than with remote node.

Any of the remote connection technologies can work with both remote node and remote control. You can connect to a remote control system through modems connected directly to the remote control computer, through ISDN lines, over the Internet, or even over a LAN or WAN link.

How do you know whether to choose remote node or remote control connections? Consider these points:

- When a remote user needs only LAN file access and e-mail access, a remote node connection can meet these needs and is often simpler to set up and maintain on both sides of the connection.

- If a remote user needs to run an application that is LAN-connected, choose remote control. A few applications might be able to run reasonably well over a remote node connection, provided the application itself is already installed on the remote computer and the application must access only relatively small amounts of data through the remote link. For example, accessing e-mail through Microsoft Outlook works fine over a remote node connection, provided the remote users already have Outlook installed on their local computer.

- Many applications now are being web-enabled, so a remote user can use a web browser to access and use such applications. These types of applications run equally well—more or less—over a remote node or remote control connection. For example, Microsoft Exchange Server supports a number of connection types, including web access to mailboxes and calendars, through a feature called Web Outlook. Many client/server accounting systems now are also starting to implement web access.

● If you need to maintain an application directly for the users, remote control might be the way to go because it leaves the application on the LAN-connected machine, where you can easily access it to make configuration changes or perform other maintenance. The remote user runs only the remote control software and instantly benefits from any work you do on the LAN-connected machine. This capability can provide a real advantage if your network's users aren't comfortable doing their own maintenance or troubleshooting on the software. With such a connection, you can more easily handle any problems that arise without having to travel to some remote location or requiring users to ship their computers to you for repair or maintenance.

Whether you choose remote node or remote control, you then have to determine how the users will connect to the LAN. A variety of different ways exist to make this connection, as discussed in the following sections.

To Modem or Not to Modem, That Is the Question . . .

Remote users can connect to your network in two ways: by connecting to devices connected to the network in some fashion, or by connecting to an ISP and then accessing the network over the LAN's Internet connection. For example, users can use a modem to dial in to a modem connected to the LAN that you maintain. Alternatively, users can use a modem to connect to a modem managed by an ISP, and then make use of the LAN's connection to the Internet to get into the LAN.

Manage Your Own Modems

For small networks, it can often be easiest simply to add a modem or two to a computer set up to accept remote connections, then let the users use those modems to connect. You can set up the modems on individual PCs that run remote control software, on PCs that run remote node software (such as Windows NT's RAS), or on special LAN-connected interfaces built for the purpose of providing remote node connections. You can also build your own "modem farms" with tens or hundreds of modems, using special hardware that supports such uses.

Take Advantage of Someone Else's Modems

Usually, it's a real hassle to manage your own modems because not only do you have to manage the modems themselves, but also the remote node software and hardware, the telephone lines used, and all the problems that can occur at any time. If a LAN already has a high-speed link to the Internet, such as through a fractional T-1 or full T-1, it can be easier to let the remote users dial in to a local ISP and then connect to the LAN through the Internet. Such a setup has many advantages:

- **No need to support modems directly**   You don't have to worry about managing the modems. If users can't connect, they can call the ISP for connection help. Larger ISPs have round-the-clock support staff in place to provide such help, which beats getting beeped at 2:00 A.M. because a user in Europe can't connect.

- **No long-distance tolls**   The user usually has only to make a local call to connect to the ISP, saving money on long-distance charges compared to dialing the LAN directly.

- **Minimal impact on LAN performance**   Using the LAN's Internet connection usually doesn't affect the LAN users who also use that connection, for two reasons. First, many remote users connect to the LAN outside normal working hours when the Internet connection probably isn't being used much. Second, because the remote user is connected to the ISP usually through a slow 33.6 or 56-Kbps modem connection, the total impact to your high-speed Internet link is minimal, even during working hours.

- **High-speed connections**   Your users can take advantage of whatever high-speed Internet links are available to them and you don't have to worry about having to implement matching technology on the LAN side. A user can use an xDSL line, a cable modem, or an ISDN line, and then connect to an ISP that supports that high-speed connection. On the LAN side, the high-speed connection (for example, a T-1) remains the same.

- **Better global access**   Users traveling internationally will have better luck making connections to a local ISP than over an international telephone connection. Using a modem internationally is problematic at best—connection speeds are slow, the quality of the line is usually not good, and delays added by satellite connections (most international telephone traffic goes through a satellite) cause additional problems. And, of course, the cost can be prohibitive. I once spent hundreds of dollars just checking e-mail from Singapore to the United States several times in one week. Singapore telephone rates are much higher than U.S. rates; originating calls from Singapore cost $2 to $3 per minute (although even the standard U.S. rate of $0.75 per minute to Singapore would have been expensive). A far better solution would have been to dial in to a Singapore-located ISP modem (most large ISPs such as CompuServe or AT&T have a presence in most countries) and use the Internet to get to the U.S.-based LAN. Such a solution would have been cheaper, more reliable, and faster. (At the time, however, those types of connections weren't really possible, as they now are.)

When you allow remote users to access the LAN through the Internet, you usually use a technology called virtual private network (VNP). This is a network link formed through the Internet between the remote user dialed in to an ISP and the company LAN. VPNs use sophisticated packet encryption and other technologies, so the link from the user to the LAN is secure, even though it is being carried over a public network. VPN solutions range from simple ones that can be implemented on Windows 2000 Server essentially for free (using the

RRAS service, included with the latest versions of Windows NT Server, or the equivalent service in Windows 2000) to stand-alone specialized VPN routers that can support hundreds of users. Figure 9-6 shows how a VPN connection works.

TIP

Windows 98 and Windows ME include built-in support for client-side VPN connections. You can also get support for Windows 95 by downloading version 1.3 (or later) of Windows 95's Dial-Up Networking software. Also, many makers of stand-alone VPN routers enable you to license VPN software for the remote users. Some charge a per-license fee for the software, while others include a license for unlimited remote users as part of their VPN router.

Higher-Speed Remote Links

Modem connections are fairly slow, usually running at only up to 33.6 Kbps. While many applications can be made to work reasonably well over this speed connection, the trend is that this speed is becoming more and more inadequate, even for just transferring files (application files seem to keep growing with each new version of an application). Modems are still the lowest common denominator for remote access, however, because standard POTS (plain old

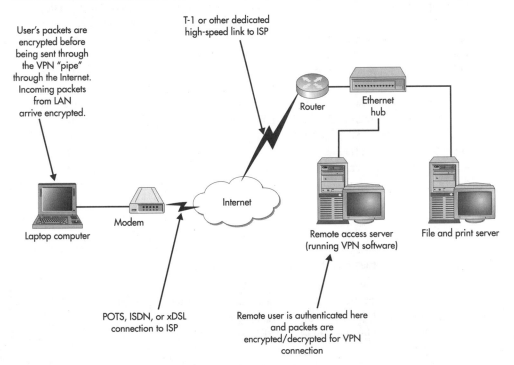

Figure 9-6 A typical VPN connection

telephone service) connections are available virtually everywhere and modems work reasonably well, all things considered.

TIP

Modems available these days are typically rated at up to 56 Kbps. There is an important caveat in this rating, however: It requires that the other end of the connection have a digital connection. Moreover, the 56-Kbps rating is a maximum available in the downstream direction; upstream never exceeds 33.6 Kbps even when connected to an ISP that uses 56 Kbps–capable digital connections on its end. You can't achieve 56 Kbps over standard telephone lines, even if you have matched 56-Kbps modems at both ends; the maximum you will get is 33.6 Kbps in both directions over standard telephone lines with standard modems on each end.

In a nutshell, users who travel to different locations need to rely on modem connections. No standard high-bandwidth connection exists yet that is ubiquitous enough to find in most hotels. For remote users who are at a single location, however, higher-speed connections become feasible. Home users in many metropolitan areas can now get high-speed DSL and cable modem connections to the Internet. And using a VPN, they can benefit from these higher speeds when connecting to the corporate LAN. Even for users who don't have DSL or cable modems available in their area, ISDN is usually an option from the local telephone company.

Remote users using DSL or cable modems are "hard-wired" to a particular ISP for their connection, so they have to use a VPN approach to connecting to the LAN. ISDN users, on the other hand, have the choice of either connecting to an ISDN-capable ISP or to ISDN "modems" hosted on the LAN. Through a process called *bonding*, ISDN users can achieve speeds up to 128 Kbps, although this consumes two B-channels (and doubles the call charges!). Still, such speeds are better than the 33.6 Kbps that you can otherwise achieve through a modem.

NOTE

ISDN and DSL technology are discussed in more detail in Module 6.

Virtual Private Networks

This module has already mentioned VPNs, but their importance to remote access calls for a dedicated section to explore them more fully. VPN is an extremely important technology that is in widespread use. A VPN network connection is carried over a shared or public network— which is almost always the Internet—and encrypts the data so that only the VPN client and server can read it. VPN connections cost much less than dedicated connections, such as the WAN technologies discussed in Module 6, because they take advantage of the cost efficiencies of the Internet without compromising security.

VPN connections are used in two important ways:

- To form WAN connections using VPN technology between two networks that might be thousands of miles apart, but which each have some way of accessing the Internet

- To form remote access connections that enable remote users to access the LAN through the Internet

The emphasis in this module is on remote access, but it's important to know that VPNs support WAN connections in much the same way as they support a remote access connection. The main difference for a WAN VPN connection is that it connects two networks together, rather than a user and a network, and relies on different hardware (typically) than a remote access connection uses. A WAN VPN connection takes advantage of the existing Internet connection for both LANs, and might run virtually 24 hours a day. A remote access connection, on the other hand, is usually formed when needed, and uses less expensive hardware on the remote side, such as a dialup modem or perhaps a higher-speed Internet connection, such as xDSL, ISDN, or cable modem.

TIP

In some circumstances, a VPN might even be an appropriate way to segregate users in a single location from other users, by using the company's intranet to host the VPN tunnel. Such a scheme might be appropriate, for example, if one group of users accesses data that is so sensitive that it must be separated from the rest of the company in some fashion. In such cases, the sensitive network can be separated from the corporate LAN, except for a firewall that allows VPN connections from the sensitive LAN to the corporate LAN, but not vice versa. This configuration would still allow users on the sensitive LAN to access general corporate network services.

VPN Protocols

A VPN connection has several requirements. First, both sides of the VPN connection must be connected to the Internet, usually using the Point-to-Point Protocol (PPP). (Other public or private networks can also carry VPNs, but this discussion will stick with the Internet because it's the most frequently used network for this purpose.) Second, both sides must have a networking protocol in common. This protocol is usually IP, but can also be IPX, NetBEUI, or AppleTalk. Third, both sides must establish a *tunnel* through their existing PPP connections, through which their data packets will pass. The tunnel is formed using a *tunneling protocol*. Finally, both sides must agree on an encryption technique to use with the data traversing the tunnel. A variety of different encryption techniques are available.

The three most popular tunneling protocols used for VPNs are Point-to-Point Tunneling Protocol (PPTP), Layer 2 Tunneling Protocol (L2TP), and Internet Protocol Security (IPSec).

PPTP is a Microsoft-designed protocol that can handle IP, IPX, NetBEUI, and AppleTalk packets. PPTP is included with current versions of Windows, starting with Windows 95, and is also supported by Windows NT's Routing and Remote Access Service (RRAS, a free upgrade to Remote Access Service) and by Windows 2000. For a Windows-oriented network, PPTP is the way to go. L2TP is a newer protocol that is an Internet Engineering Task Force standard, and will probably become the most widely supported tunneling protocol because it operates at Layer 2 of the OSI model, and thus can handle all Layer 3 protocols, such as IP, IPX, or AppleTalk. IPSec, while probably the most secure tunneling protocol, seems to be most popular for LAN-to-LAN VPNs and for UNIX-oriented VPNs, due to its reliance on IP. IPSec is a Layer 3 protocol and is limited to handling only IP traffic.

TIP

While IPSec works only with IP packets, an L2TP VPN can also carry the resulting IPSec packets, because they can be handled like the other major Layer 3 packets, such as IP, IPX, and AppleTalk packets.

Types of VPNs

Three major types of VPNs are in use today. The first type uses a router with added VPN capabilities. VPN routers not only can handle normal routing duties, but they can also be configured to form VPNs over the Internet to other similar routers, located on remote networks. This method is used to create VPN WAN links over the Internet, usually between multiple company locations.

The second major type of VPN is one built into a firewall device. Most popular firewalls, such as CheckPoint's Firewall-1 or Watchguard's Firebox, serve not only as firewall devices but also can serve as VPN hosts. Firewall VPNs can be used both to support remote users and also to provide WAN VPN links. The benefit of using a firewall-based VPN is that you can administer your network's security, including both standard firewall security and VPN security, entirely within the firewall. (For example, you could configure the firewall to allow connections to the network only when they are made as part of a valid VPN connection.)

The third major type of VPNs includes those offered as part of a network operating system. The best example of this type is Windows NT's RRAS, Windows 2000, and NetWare 5 running Novell's BorderManager software. These VPNs are most often used to support remote access, and they are generally the least expensive to purchase and install. (In the case of Windows NT and Windows 2000, the NOS includes VPN services.)

VPN Clients

Both sides of a VPN connection must be running compatible VPN software using compatible protocols. For a remote access VPN solution, the software you install depends on the VPN itself. Dedicated VPN solutions also sell client software that you can distribute to your users. Usually, this software carries a per-copy charge, typically around $25–50 per remote computer supported. (Some VPNs include unlimited client licenses, but the VPN is licensed to accept only a certain number of connections at a time.)

If you are using a Windows NT or Windows 2000 VPN and some version of Windows 95 or later on the remote computer, then you can take advantage of the VPN software included for free with those operating systems.

✓ Module 9 Mastery Check

1. True or false: It is often easy to find one good remote access solution that will meet the needs of all the users needing remote access.

2. True or false: Client/server applications are typically more amenable than monolithic applications to being used over a remote access connection.

3. The three things that most remote users need are _____, _____, and _____.

4. When you are connecting to the Internet using a dialup line, you are typically using a remote_____ type of connection.

5. When you are remotely controlling a computer program running at a distant site, you are typically using a remote_____ type of connection.

6. Name two situations in which remote control connections are best (compared to remote node connections).

7. Name four reasons you should consider using an ISP for dialup access, having users access the LAN through the company's high-speed Internet connection.

8. VPNs work by taking advantage of an existing network connection (usually over the Internet) and then creating an encrypted _____ through which the data packets pass.

9. True or false: IPSec is limited to only TCP/IP traffic, while PPP and L2TP can both handle a variety of different network protocols in addition to TCP/IP.

10. You can set up a simple (but functional) VPN service using _____ software included with _____ operating system.

Module 10

Securing Your Network

Most things you learn about networking are relatively straightforward and can be accomplished. Do you want a new file and print server? You install it and set it up, and it either works or it doesn't. If it doesn't work, you proceed to troubleshoot it, fix any issues, and ultimately you complete the task. Network security, on the other hand, is a horse of a different color. You can *never* really finish the project of securing a network and you can't *ever* be completely certain that a network is secure. How much money you invest in securing a network, how much time you devote to the job, or how much fancy security hardware and software you install doesn't matter: No network is ever completely secure. (Amusingly, there's a corollary to this: The only completely secure network is the one nobody can use.)

Having said that, network security is one of the most important jobs facing any network administrator. Good network security helps prevent all the following:

● Company secrets, such as proprietary designs or processes, from falling into the wrong hands (both internally and externally)

● Personal information about employees from falling into the wrong hands

● Loss of important information and software

● Loss of use of the network itself

● Corruption or inappropriate modification of important data

The preceding is a list of only some of the more important things that network security can prevent. If you spend any time thinking about all the information that is stored on and that flows through networks with which you work (and you *should* spend time thinking about this), you'll probably come up with additional dangers to avoid.

This module overviews the subject of network security. Its aim is to familiarize you with important network security ideas and concepts, and also various technologies involved in network security. If you are responsible for a network's security, you should pursue more detailed information, and you should also seriously consider hiring a specialist on this subject to help you secure your network. Even if you don't have primary responsibility to keep your network secure, the security of the network is everyone's job, and, if you're an IS professional, security is an even more important part of your job.

Secure Your Network from Internal Threats

Internal security is the process of securing your network from internal threats, which are generally much more common than external threats. Examples of internal threats include the following:

- Internal users inappropriately accessing information to which they should not have access, such as payroll records, accounting records, or business development information

- Internal users accessing other users' files to which they should not have access

- Internal users impersonating other users and causing mischief, such as sending e-mails under another person's name

- Internal users accessing systems to carry out criminal activities, such as embezzling funds

- Internal users compromising the security of the network, such as by accidentally (or deliberately) introducing viruses to the network (viruses are discussed in their own section later in this module)

- Internal users "sniffing" packets on the network to discover user accounts and passwords

To deal with threats such as these, you need to manage the network's security diligently. You should assume that, in the population of internal users, at least some exist who have the requisite sophistication to explore security holes in the network and that at least a few of those might, at some point, have reason to do so.

TIP

One of the more unpleasant parts of managing security is that you need to think in a way where you expect the worst of people, and then you must take steps to prevent those actions you expect. It's not a happy mindset, but it is required to do a good job in the security arena. Remember, too, that you're likely to get better results if you hire an outside firm to help manage the network's security. Not only should the outside firm have a higher skill level in this area, but its people will be used to thinking as security people and they will have invaluable experience gained from solving security problems at other companies. Perhaps even more important, using an external firm doesn't put employees in the position of being in an adversarial relationship with the rest of the employees.

Account Security

Account security refers to the process of managing the user accounts enabled on the network. A number of tasks are required to manage user accounts properly, and the accounts should be periodically audited (preferably by a different person than the one who manages them daily) to ensure that no holes exist. Following are a number of general steps you should take to manage general account security:

- Most NOSs start up with a user account called "Guest." You should remove this account immediately because it is the frequent target of crackers. You should also avoid creating accounts that are obviously for testing purposes, such as "Test," "Generic," and so forth.

● Most NOSs start up with a default name for the administrative account. Under Windows NT, the account is called Administrator; under NetWare, it is called either Supervisor or Admin (depending on which version you are using). You should immediately rename this account to avoid directed attacks against the account. (Under NetWare 3.*x,* you cannot rename the Supervisor account.)

TIP

As a safety measure, also create a new account to be a backup of your administrative account. Call it whatever you like (although less obvious names are better), give the account security equivalence to the administrative account, and safely store the password. Should something happen that locks you out of the real administrative account, you can use the backup account to regain access and correct the problem.

● You should know the steps required to remove access to network resources quickly from any user account and be sure to explore *all* network resources that might contain their own security systems. For example, accounts will be managed on the NOS (and possibly on each server) and also in specific applications, such as database servers or accounting systems. Make sure that you find out how the system handles removed or deactivated accounts. If you delete a user account in order to remove access, some systems don't actually deny access to that user until they log out from the system.

● Work closely with the Human Resources department so that it is comfortable working with you on handling security issues related to employee departures, and develop a standard checklist to use for standard HR-related employment changes that affect IT. The HR department might not be able to give you much—if any—advance notice, but it needs to understand that you need to know about any terminations *immediately,* so you can take proper steps. Along the same lines, you want to work out a set of procedures on how you handle accumulated e-mails, files, and other user access both for friendly departures and terminations. Your relationship with the appropriate people in the HR department is crucial in being able to handle security well, so make sure that you establish and maintain mutual trust.

● Consider setting up a program whereby new users on the network have their assigned permissions reviewed and signed off by their supervisor. This way, you won't mistakenly give someone access to things he or she shouldn't have.

Another important aspect of account security is account password security. Most NOSs enable you to set policies related to password security. These policies control how often the system forces users to change their passwords, how long their passwords must be, whether users can reuse previously used passwords, and so forth. At a minimum, consider these suggestions for password policies:

- You should consider requiring users (through network password policy settings) to change their main network password every 90 to 180 days (30 days is a common recommendation, but this might be too frequent in most environments).

- You should set the reuse policy so that passwords cannot be reused for at least a year.

- You should require passwords that are *at least* six characters long. This yields, on a random basis, 36^6 possible permutations, or a bit more than 2 billion possibilities. Using eight characters yields 36^8, or almost 3 trillion, possibilities. And if the NOS uses case-sensitive passwords, then the possibilities are much larger: 62^6 (57 billion) and 62^8 (218 trillion), respectively. Even 2 billion possibilities is a lot. If someone were able to try one password a second, he or she would have to spend 63 years to try that many permutations. Or, with an optimized program that can try 5 million possibilities a second, it would take about a year to crack an 8-character mixed-case password using brute force.

TIP

Many password-cracking programs rely on dictionaries of common words and names to reduce dramatically the number of possibilities they have to try. Because of this, encourage users to create passwords that are not words in any language or, if they are words, that they have numbers and other nonalphanumeric characters inserted somewhere in the word so a "dictionary attack" won't easily work. Also, for networks that support mixed-case passwords, encourage users to use mixed-case characters.

- Make sure that you turn on any policies that monitor for and deal with people entering in wrong passwords. Often called *intruder detection,* this type of policy watches for incorrect password attempts. If too many attempts occur within a set period of time, the system can lock out the user account, preventing further attempts. I like to set this type of feature to lock an account any time five incorrect passwords are entered within an hour and then to lock the account until it's reset by the administrator. This way, if someone is entering in a large number of incorrect passwords, he or she will have to talk with the administrator to reopen the account, and you can find out why this situation developed and then correct it. Usually, the user forgot their password and tried a number of incorrect passwords, but someone else may be trying to guess the password, so it deserves to be examined (by asking the user if the incorrect password attempts were theirs) to rule out the latter possibility.

- Novell NetWare and Windows NT enable you to establish limits on when and where a user can log on to the network. You can establish times of day that a user is allowed to log on and you can also restrict a user account to a particular network node. Doing so for all users on the network is usually overkill, but you might want to consider restricting the administrative account to several different workstations, so someone at a different workstation (or coming in through a WAN connection) cannot log in to the account, even if that person somehow knows the password.

TIP

Consider performing periodic password audits, wherein you actually test the security of your network passwords using commercially available tools designed to crack user passwords (these tools won't work without the administrator password and frequently require physical access to the server). Password audit programs can crack the passwords on your network using a variety of approaches and will report how long each one took to crack. Truly secure passwords are not crackable in any reasonable amount of time. Amazingly, when you first conduct such an audit, you may be surprised to discover that many of the passwords in use on your network are not secure and are cracked in a matter of seconds. I recommend a great program for Windows-based networks called LC4 from a company named @Stake (**http://www.atstake.com**). You can use what you learn from a program like LC4 to tweak your own password policies to be more secure.

There's an interesting catch-22 concerning network security policies: If you make them *too* strict, you can actually *reduce* the security of your network. For example, suppose that you set the network to force a password change once a week and to disallow the reuse of passwords. Most users will be unable to remember from week to week what password they're using and they will naturally resort to writing down their password somewhere in their office. Of course, a written password is much less secure than a remembered password. The trick with network security is to strike a balance between security and usability.

File and Directory Permissions

The second type of internal security that you need to maintain for information on your network involves the users' access to files and directories. These settings are actually a bit tougher to manage than user accounts because you usually have at least 20 directories and several hundred files for every user you have on the network. The sheer volume of directories and files makes managing these settings a more difficult job. The solution is to establish regular procedures, then follow them and then periodically spot-audit parts of the directory tree, particularly areas that contain sensitive files. Also, structure the overall network directories so that you can, for the most part, simply assign permissions at the top levels. These permissions will "flow down" to subdirectories automatically, which makes it much easier to review who has access to which directories.

NOSs allow considerable flexibility in the permissions that they let you set on files and directories. Using the built-in permissions, you can enable users for different roles in any given directory. These *roles* control what the user can and cannot do within that directory. Examples of generic directory roles include the following:

● **Create only** This type of role enables users to add a new file to a directory, but restricts them from seeing, editing, or deleting existing files, including any they've created. This type of role is perfect to enable a person to add new information to a directory to which they shouldn't otherwise have access. The directory becomes almost like a mailbox on a street corner: You can put only new things in it. Of course, another user will have full access to the directory to retrieve and work with the files.

- **Read only**   This role enables users to see the files in a directory and even to pull up the files for viewing on their computer. However, the users cannot edit or change the stored files in any way. This type of role is good for material published to users who need to view the information, but which they should not change. (Users with read privileges can copy a file from a read-only directory to another directory and then do whatever they like with the copy they made. They simply cannot change the copy stored in the read-only directory itself.)

- **Change**   This role lets users do whatever they like with the files in a directory, *except* they cannot give other users access to the directory.

- **Full control**   Usually reserved for the "owner" of a directory, this role enables the owner(s) to do whatever they like with the files in a directory and, further, enables them to grant other users access to the directory.

These roles are created in different ways on different NOSs. Modules 16 and 19 provide more details on how Windows 2000/NT and NetWare handle directory permissions.

Just as you can set permissions for directories, you can also set security for specific files. File permissions work similarly to directory permissions. For specific files, you can control a user's ability to read, change, or delete a file. File permissions usually override directory permissions. For example, if users had change access to a directory, but you set their permission to access a particular file in that directory to read-only, they would have only read-only access to that file.

Practices and User Education

The third important type of internal security concerns the most insecure part of any network: the people. You should be concerned about two things here. First, you need to establish good security practices and habits. It's not enough to design and implement a great security scheme if you do not manage it well on a daily basis. To establish good practices, you need to document security-related procedures and then set up some sort of process to make sure that the employees follow the procedures regularly. In fact, you're far better off having a rudimentary security design that is followed to the letter than having an excellent security design that is poorly followed. For this reason, keep the overall network security design as simple as possible consistent with the needs of the company.

You also need to make sure—to the maximum extent possible—that the users are following prudent procedures. Some of these you can easily enforce through settings on the NOS, but you must handle others through education. Some tips to make this easier are as follows:

- Spell out for users what is expected of them in terms of security. Provide a document for them that describes the security of the network and what they need to do to preserve it. Examples of guidelines for the users include choosing secure passwords, not giving their passwords to anyone else, not leaving their computers unattended for long periods of time while they are logged in to the network, not installing software from outside the company, and so forth.

- When new employees join the company and are oriented on using the network, make sure that you discuss security issues with them.

- Depending on the culture of the company, consider having users sign a form acknowledging their understanding of important security procedures that the company expects them to follow.

- Periodically audit users' security actions. If the users have full control access to directories, examine how they've assigned permissions to other users.

- Make sure that you review the security logs of the NOS you use. Investigate and follow up on any problems reported.

TIP

It's a good idea to document any security-related issues you investigate. While most are benign, occasionally you might find one in which the user had inappropriate intent. In such cases, your documentation of what you find and what actions you take might become important.

While it's important to plan for the worst when designing and administering network security, you also need to realize that most of the time security issues arise from ignorance or other innocent causes and not from malicious intent.

Progress Check

1. True or false: Setting strong security settings for your network and making sure users follow good security practices will result in a completely secure network.

2. True or false: The strictest security settings available to you will result in the highest level of security on your network.

---

1. False. No network is ever completely secure.

2. False. The trick is to strike a balance between security and usability. Making your network security settings *too strict* can result in reduced security, as users might then try to circumvent the intent of the settings. For instance, if you set the most draconian password policy available for your network, the typical result would be to reduce your overall security as users will simply write down their passwords to keep in their office.

CRITICAL SKILL
10.2 Secure Your Network from External Threats

External security is the process of securing the network from external threats. Before the Internet, this process wasn't difficult. Most networks had only external modems for users to dial in to the network and it was easy to keep those access points secure. With the advent of the Internet and the fact that nearly all networks are connected to it, however, external security becomes much more important.

Earlier in this module, you read that no network is ever totally secure. This is especially true when dealing with external security for a network connected to the Internet. Almost daily, hackers discover new techniques that they can use to breach the security of a network through an Internet connection. Even if you were to find a book that discussed all the threats to a specific type of network, the book would be out of date soon after it was printed.

Three basic types of external security threats exist:

- **Front-door threats**   These threats arise when a user from outside the company somehow finds, guesses, or cracks a user password and then logs on to the network. The perpetrator could be someone who had an association with the company at some point or could be someone totally unrelated to the company.

- **Back-door threats**   These are threats where software or hardware bugs in the network's OS and hardware enable an outsider to crack the network's security. After accomplishing this, the outsider often finds a way to log in to the administrative account and then can do anything he or she likes.

- **Denial of service**   These are attacks that deny service to the network. Examples include committing specific actions that are known to crash different types of servers or flooding the company's Internet connection with useless traffic (such as a flood of ping requests).

NOTE

A fourth type of external threat exists: computer viruses, Trojan horses, worms, and other malicious software from outside the company. These threats are covered in their own section later in the module.

Fortunately, you can do a number of things to implement strong external security measures. They probably won't keep out a determined and extremely skilled hacker, but they can make it difficult enough that a hacker will probably give up and go elsewhere.

Ask the Expert

Q: What are the most common network security devices?

A: Here are some important security devices with which you should be familiar:

- **Firewall** A system that enforces a security policy between two networks, such as between a LAN and the Internet. Firewalls can use many different techniques to enforce security policies.

- **Proxy server** A server that acts as a proxy (an anonymous intermediary), usually for users of a network. For example, it might stand in as a proxy for browsing web pages, so that the user's computer isn't connected to the remote system except through the proxy server. In the process of providing proxy access to web pages, a proxy server might also speed web access by caching web pages that are accessed so that other users can benefit from having them more quickly available from the local proxy server, and might also provide some firewall protection for the LAN.

- **Packet filter** Usually built into a router or a firewall, a packet filter enables you to set criteria for allowed and disallowed packets, source and destination IP addresses, and IP ports.

Front-Door Threats

Front-door threats, in which someone from outside the company is able to gain access to a user account, are probably the most likely threats that you need to protect against. These threats can take many forms. Chief among them is the disgruntled or terminated employee who once had access to the network. Another example is someone guessing or finding out a password to a valid account on the network or somehow getting a valid password from the owner of the password.

Insiders, whether current or ex-employees, are potentially the most dangerous overall. Such people have many advantages that some random hacker won't have. They know the important user names on the network already, so they know what accounts to go after. They might know other users' passwords from when they were associated with the company. They also know the structure of the network, what the server names are, and other information that makes cracking the network's security much easier.

Protecting against a front-door threat revolves around strong internal security protection because, in this case, internal and external security are closely linked. This is the type of threat where all the policies and practices discussed in the section on internal security can help to prevent problems. You can also take additional steps to stymie front-door threats:

- Keep network resources that should be accessed from the LAN separate from resources that should be accessed from outside the LAN, whenever possible. Here's an example: Maybe you're lucky enough that you never need to provide access to the company's accounting server to external users. You can then make it nearly impossible to access that system from outside the LAN, through a number of measures. You can set up the firewall router to decline any access through the router to that server's IP or IPX address. If the server doesn't require IP, you can remove that protocol. You can set up the server to disallow access outside normal working hours. Depending on the NOS running on the server, you can restrict access to Ethernet MAC addresses for machines on the LAN that should be able to access the server. You can also set the server to allow each user only one login to the server at a time. The specific steps that you can take depend on the server in question and the NOS it is running, but the principle holds true: Segregate internal resources from external resources whenever possible.

- Control which users can access the LAN from outside the LAN. For example, you might be running VPN software for your traveling or home-based users to access the LAN remotely through the Internet. You should enable this access only for users who need it and not for everyone who is likely to need it.

- Consider setting up a separate remote access account for remote users, and make this account more restrictive than their normal LAN account. This might not be practicable in all cases, but it's a strategy that can help, particularly for users who normally have broad LAN security clearances.

- For modems that users dial in to from a fixed location, such as from their homes, set up their accounts to use dial-back. *Dial-back* is a feature whereby you securely enter the phone number of the system from which users are calling (such as their home phone numbers). When the users want to connect, they dial the system, request access, and then the remote access system terminates the connection and dials the preprogrammed phone number to make the real connection. Their computer answers the call and then proceeds to connect them normally. Someone trying to access the system from another phone number won't be able to get in if you have dial-back enabled.

- If an employee with broad access leaves the company, review user accounts where he or she might have known the password. Consider forcing an immediate password change to such accounts once the employee is gone.

TIP

An important aspect of both internal and external security is physical security. Make sure that the room in which your servers are located is physically locked and secure.

People trying to access the network who have not been associated with the company at some point often try a technique euphemistically called *social engineering,* which is where they use nontechnological methods to learn user accounts and passwords inside the company. These techniques are most dangerous in larger companies, where not all the employees know each other. An example of a social engineering technique is calling an employee and posing as a network administrator who is trying to track down a problem and who needs the employee's password temporarily. Another example is to sort through a company's trash looking for records that might help the culprit crack a password. Make sure to instruct your company's employees carefully to never give out their password to anyone over the telephone and also that bona-fide IT people usually never need to ask anyone's password.

Back-Door Threats

Back-door threats are often directed at problems in the NOS itself or at some other point in the network infrastructure, such as its routers. Make no mistake about it, all NOSs and most network components have security holes. The best thing you can do to prevent these problems is to stay current with your NOS software and any security-related patches that are released. You should also periodically review new information about security holes discovered in the NOS software you use (and don't rely on the vendor's web site for the best information on this!). A good web site to use to stay current on security holes is the one maintained by the Computer Emergency Response Team (CERT), located at **http://www.cert.org**. Aside from finding advisories on security holes, you can also discover much valuable security information on the site.

Web servers are a frequent target for hackers. Consider the following tips to help protect against threats to web servers:

- You're better off if you can host the company's web site on an external server (such as an ISP's system) than on your own network. Not only is an ISP better able to provide the server service 24 hours a day, seven days a week, but it also has better security. Also, you needn't worry about allowing web server access to your LAN from outside the company, which can sometimes leave open other holes.

- Make sure that you implement a strong firewall router for your network. Firewall routers are discussed in more detail in Module 3. You should also have someone knowledgeable of the specific firewall and web server you implement test your configuration or help with the configuration. Remember, firewalls also need to have their software kept current.

- Make absolutely certain that you've carefully reviewed the security settings appropriate for your web server and have implemented all of them, and that you audit these settings occasionally.

Ask the Expert

Q: What is a demilitarized zone?

A: When you place computers between your firewall (on the other side of the firewall from your network) and your connection to an external network, such as the Internet, the area between those two devices is called the *demilitarized zone*, or *DMZ* for short. Usually, an organization will place their public web server in the DMZ, and that computer will not have any sort of confidential information on it. This way, if the security of that computer is broken, the attacker hasn't gained entry to the network itself.

- Consider placing a web server designed for people outside the company outside of your firewall (in other words, between the firewall and the router that connects you to the Internet—this area is called a "demilitarized zone"). This way, even if someone is able to break into the web server, he or she won't have an easier time getting to the rest of your network.

- Safely guard your e-mail traffic. E-mail is one of the most commonly used means to get viruses or Trojan horse programs into a company. Make sure you run virus-scanning software suitable for your e-mail server, and that the virus signatures are updated at least *daily*.

Denial of Service Threats

Denial of Service (DoS) attacks are those that deny service to a network resource to legitimate users. These are often targeted at e-mail servers and web servers, but they can affect an entire network. DoS attacks usually take one of two forms: They either deny service by flooding the network with useless traffic, or they take advantage of bugs in network software that can be used to crash servers. DoS attacks against an e-mail server usually flood the server with mail until the e-mail server either denies service to legitimate users or crashes under the load placed on it.

To help prevent DoS attacks, again make sure to keep your various network software current. Also, use settings on your firewall to disallow Internet Control Message Protocol (ICMP) traffic service (which handles ping requests) into the network and deny access to servers from outside the LAN that needn't be accessed from outside the LAN. For example, the company's accounting system server probably doesn't need to be accessed from outside the LAN. In such a case, you would configure the firewall or packet-filtering router to deny all outside traffic to or from that server's IP address.

An Innocent DoS

I once witnessed an innocent problem that resulted in a denial of service to a multinational company's entire e-mail system. The situation that caused this attack was as follows: A user at Company A had set their e-mail system always to send mail with a return receipt requested. When this user went out of town, they created a rule in their e-mail Inbox that replied to all messages with a message saying that the user was out of the office. While the user was gone, a user at Company B sent the Company A user a message, to which the automatic reply was sent. However, the Company A user had their default settings always to request delivery receipts (which are often generated by the receiving server for Internet e-mail, and not by the user reading the message). Thus, the mail server at Company B dutifully sent back a receipt that it had received the sender's message. Of course, the user at Company A's Inbox rule then replied automatically to the receipt message, which generated another return receipt, and so forth. Before anybody noticed what was going on, some 50,000 messages had flooded Company B's e-mail system, which crashed under the load. Because Company B had a somewhat fragile configuration, the crash affected some 30,000 employees around the world, who went without e-mail for a couple of hours because of this attack.

This attack resulted from an innocent misconfiguration by the user at Company A. If they had instead used the e-mail system's "Out of Office" feature, the system would have generated only one automatic message for any given sender, and the problem would not have occurred. Innocent or not, however, this sort of situation can easily be exploited by someone who actually wants to cause trouble.

CRITICAL SKILL
10.3 Protect Your Network from Viruses and Other Malicious Software

Unfortunately, an increasing array of malicious software is circulating around the world. Many different types of this software exist, including the following:

- **Viruses**   A computer *virus* is a program that spreads by infecting other files with a copy of itself. Files that can be infected by viruses include program files (COM, EXE, and DLL) and document files for applications that support macro languages sophisticated enough to allow virus behavior (Microsoft Word and Excel are common targets of macro-based viruses).

- **Worms**   A *worm* is a program that propagates by sending copies of itself to other computers, which run the worm and then send copies to other computers. Recently, worms have spread through e-mail systems like wildfire. One way they spread is by attaching to e-mails along with a message that entices the recipients to open the attachment. The attachment contains the worm, which then sends out copies of itself to other people defined in the user's e-mail address book, without the user knowing that this is happening. Those recipients then have the same thing happen to them. A worm like this can spread rapidly through the Internet in a matter of hours.

- **Trojan horses**   A *Trojan horse* is a program that purports to do something interesting or useful and then performs malicious actions in the background while the user is interacting with the main program.

- **Logic bombs**   *Logic bombs* are malicious pieces of programming code inserted into an otherwise normal program. They are often included by the program's original author or by someone else who participated in developing the source code. Logic bombs can be timed to execute at a certain time, erasing key files or performing other actions.

More than 20,000 known viruses exist today, with more being written and discovered daily. These viruses are a major threat to any network, and an important aspect of your network administration is protecting against them.

To protect a network from virus attacks, you need to implement some sort of antivirus software. Antivirus software runs on computers on the network and "watches" for known viruses or virus-like activity. The antivirus software then either removes the virus, leaving the original file intact, quarantines the file so it can be checked by an administrator, or locks access to the file in some other fashion.

Antivirus software can be run on most network computers, such as fileservers, print servers, e-mail servers, desktop computers, and even computerized firewalls. Antivirus software is available from a number of different vendors, with three of the most notable being Symantec (Norton AntiVirus), TrendMicro (PC-cillin), and Network Associates (McAfee VirusScan). Your best bet is to make sure you run antivirus software on all your servers and set up the software so that it is frequently updated (every few days, or better yet, daily). (You can set up most server-based antivirus software to update its list of known viruses securely over an Internet connection automatically.) Also, because e-mail is the chief mechanism of transmission for computer viruses these days, make especially sure that you run antivirus software on your e-mail server.

You might also want to run antivirus software on your workstations, but you shouldn't rely on this software as your primary means of prevention. Users can and will disable such software on occasion, and workstation-based antivirus software can cause other support problems, such as interacting with other desktop software (or the desktop OS) in ways that cause problems. Instead of relying on such software as your primary protection, consider desktop antivirus software as a supplement to your server-based software.

Find Other Security Resources

Even in an entire book devoted to the subject of network security, you can't learn all you need to know to make a network as secure as possible. New threats are discovered constantly and the changing software landscape makes such information quickly obsolete. Instead, in this module you learned about common security threats and read advice that can help you formulate and implement good security practices. You should especially consider retaining an outside security consultant to help you set up your security plans and to review and audit them on a regular basis.

Finally, if you're responsible for network security, you should know it's a job that never sleeps and you can never know enough about it. You need to spend time learning more of the ins and outs of network security, particularly for the NOSs that you use on your network. The following books can help further your network security education:

- *Network Security: A Beginner's Guide*, by Eric Maiwald (ISBN 0-07-213321-4, McGraw-Hill/Osborne, 2001).

- *Hacking Exposed: Network Security Secrets and Solutions*, Third Edition, by Stuart McClure, Joel Scambray, and George Kurtz (ISBN: 0-07-219381-6, McGraw-Hill/Osborne, 2001).

- *Windows NT Security Handbook,* by Tom Sheldon (ISBN: 0-07-882240-8, McGraw-Hill/Osborne, 1998).

- *Windows 2000 Security Handbook,* by Tom Sheldon and Phil Cox (ISBN: 0-07-212433-4, McGraw-Hill/Osborne, 2001).

- *Internet Firewalls and Network Security,* Second Edition, by Chris Hare and Karanjit Sayan (ISBN: 1-56205-437-6, New Riders Publishing, 1996), is an older book, but has an excellent explanation of true "security" (that is, DoD levels). The book also describes how to develop network security policies in a company and explains packet filtering and firewall technology.

- *The Happy Hacker,* by Carolyn P. Meinel (ISBN: 0-929408-21-7, American Eagle Publishing, 1998), is an excellent introduction to hacking. The book applies a "how-to" approach, and teaches both novices and moderately experienced network security persons what to look for on a daily basis.

Module 10 Mastery Check

1. Which is the more common threat for which you need to plan network security: internal or external?

2. What steps should you take with a network operating system's default Guest and Administrator accounts?

3. True or false: The strictest security settings you can set in your network are always the best for overall security.

4. An attack that makes part or all of a network unusable is called
   a _____.

5. True or false: To protect against computer viruses, you only need to run antivirus software on your network's desktop computers.

6. True or false: It is better to keep any web servers you maintain for use by the outside world outside your demilitarized zone.

7. In typical file access permissions, what is the difference between change rights and full-control rights?

8. True or false: A good security program can make virtually any network completely secure.

9. When an outside person tries to learn a user's account name and password by, for example, posing as a network support person on the telephone, the practice is called
   _____.

10. A _____ is a device or computer that sits between two networks and enforces a security policy between those two networks.

Module 11

Network Disaster Recovery

Network servers contain vital resources for a company, in the form of information, knowledge, and invested work product of the company's employees. Most companies, if they were suddenly and permanently deprived of these resources, would not be able to continue their business uninterrupted and would face losing millions of dollars, both in the form of lost data and the effect that such a loss would have. Therefore, establishing a network disaster recovery plan and formulating and implementing the network's backup strategy are the two most important jobs in network management.

This module discusses these two topics. You will learn about the issues that you should address in a disaster recovery plan, and also about network backup strategies and systems. Before getting into these topics, however, you should read about the City of Seattle's disaster recovery experiences.

Notes from the Field: the City of Seattle

This book's Technical Editor, Tony Ryan, had a personal experience with network disaster recovery. Tony works in the IT department for the City of Seattle. On February 28, 2001, the city experienced an earthquake that caused the city's disaster recovery plans to be tested. What follows is Tony's discussion about the City of Seattle's disaster recovery operations, and how they handled the problems that occurred in the wake of the earthquake. This is an excellent example of why you need disaster recovery planning, and how that planning needs to encompass all possible disaster events.

Notes on the Seattle 2001 Earthquake and Its Disaster Recovery
By Tony Ryan

Seattle has seen some very unusual and attention-grabbing events over the past few years. Notable among them were the World Trade Organization conference of 1999 and the violent demonstrations that accompanied it, which were broadcast worldwide on television and the Internet. Also, riots broke out during Mardi Gras celebrations in 2000. However, nothing compared to the potential and realized damage wrought by the 6.8 earthquake that struck Wednesday, February 28, 2001.

The EOC Situation
The City of Seattle has an Emergency Operations Center, or EOC, which is activated during any event or crisis that has a potential impact on public safety, or that might otherwise affect any number of services provided by the City to its citizens. Sometimes that EOC can be activated ahead of time, for example, for the Y2K event and the anniversary of the WTO demonstrations.

Looking at the preparation made for those events and comparing it to what happens during unplanned events such as the earthquake, helps to illustrate some important principles about IT disaster recovery and disaster preparedness.

Never Assume

During the preparations for Y2K, members of my staff were asked to augment the staff normally assigned to support the EOC's desktop and laptop PCs and printers. The staff who normally support the EOC are from a different IT organization than ours, and as can be expected, their way of doing things differed from ours for a number of valid reasons. However, once my staff had a chance to look at the EOC's environment, they were able to share some new perspectives and methods that were welcomed and adopted by EOC support staff, and all involved had a new idea of what would be expected to be the "standard" way of configuring EOC PCs. Examples ranged from hard-coding certain models of PC NICs to run better on the switches in their wiring closet to developing and implementing a base image for all the laptops to be deployed in the building. The Y2K event, as a result, was lauded as an example of ideal cooperation between IT groups and excellent preparation overall. It was a very calm Saturday morning!

Change Management?

Between events, however, there was a great deal of time and opportunity for things to change. The facility might have been used for other business purposes; equipment such as laptops might have been loaned out, or customers could have come in and used the equipment; and other IT groups beside ours might have assisted the staff and performed alterations to the configurations that went undocumented or were not communicated to all involved.

The Results

Whatever it was that might have happened remains unknown. What we did discover following the earthquake was that when customers who normally use the EOC in emergency situations went to use the equipment, in some cases, the machines did not work as expected. Software could not be loaded on this PC; that laptop doesn't connect to the network anymore; some PCs were not the same, or had been swapped for less-powerful processors. Things had changed, and the result was that some of the emergency work IT professionals such as web support technicians had to perform took more time than we had anticipated. Ironically, the Web played a crucial role in our overall communications "strategy." The impact of that equipment not immediately working was not yet evident, however, the following events illustrate how they might have been.

A few minutes after the earthquake struck, several of the downtown buildings in which City of Seattle employees work were evacuated due to fear of structural damage. While no one was injured, and amazingly only two keyboards were broken throughout all the buildings in which we provide support, imagine a couple thousand very frightened and concerned people streaming onto the sidewalks and streets, flooding cellular telephone networks in frantic attempts to contact loved ones, and looking for any possible focus for communication—especially managers such as myself and other supervisory staff, all possessing varying levels of training in disaster preparedness.

Luckily, the Mayor's Office had sent representatives to the gathering sites indicated for staff to walk to in such events, and informed everyone in the core buildings that were directly affected that they were to go home. With that announcement, the CTO announced to all to "check the Web" for information, meaning the City's internal web site. But what if the EOC PC had been swapped out (let's say) for a Pentium 133 with 64MB RAM and that PC could not run Microsoft's FrontPage2000? If that web site had to be updated with news and official information on a routine basis, the results could have been at best inconvenient and confusing.

Contingency and Costs

Because we are a publicly funded entity, we are very careful about how we spend our customers' money, as it is subject to great scrutiny (and rightfully so). Customers often do not have the funds to afford both modern PC equipment to run the latest version of Windows and a spare PC to sit in the closet, "just in case." After the earthquake, a couple of buildings were temporarily unavailable for occupancy until inspectors had a chance to examine the damage to see if the buildings were safe for employees. One of those buildings actually houses a lot of our IT staff, and as a result, not only were we trying to find "spare PCs" for our customers to use (while they looked for office space), but we as IT support staff found ourselves doing the same thing. The direct impact: We found it difficult in a few cases to support our customers as quickly as our service-level agreements required, especially since we could not immediately re-enter our building to gather our PCs or other necessary equipment.

Lesson Learned: Keep Spares…At Least a Few

So it seems that you either pay up front…or pay later. It makes sense to keep a percentage of PCs available for these rainy-day events; 10 to 15percent of replaceable inventory should work. Consider that businesses of any kind are obligated in such situations to perform a kind of "triage" as to which of their business functions are most critical and which can be postponed—until their entire stock of equipment can be reconnected or replaced—and 10 to 15 percent is justified.

Have a Plan for Communications and How You Will Communicate

Following the CTO's announcement, some asked, "What about those who don't have web access at home?" As IT staff, we asked, "What if the web servers themselves had all been destroyed?" (In fact, ceiling debris in the room in which they are housed fell very close to them, but the servers were not damaged and the service was never down.) Still others asked, "What about those who missed the message and don't know to check the Web? These items and "what to do in the event of" could be addressed with a clear, ever-ready communications plan. Ironically, such plans had been developed down to the last detail for other events, but in the case of a real "emergent" event, we as a department had not identified a plan to follow. A priority for our department now is to re-examine that situation and develop a plan, using communications plans developed for the Y2K event and the like as models.

Another point: As previously mentioned, our staff are not responsible for supporting the EOC on a routine basis. We are more than happy to be directed to assist in that support, and as evidenced, have done so on a few occasions. Almost immediately following the earthquake, I received a page indicating that I was to dispatch technicians to the EOC to support the City officials who report there during emergencies. While our team was under no agreement with the EOC to provide support even "on demand," I immediately asked two of my senior technicians, who had worked at the EOC in the past, to respond. They reported for duty there and supported the facility until the assigned staff arrived. There was never a doubt that we would pitch in whenever asked, but I made it a point to ask our divisional director if developing some clearer expectations, or even an SLA, between our staff and the EOC would be appropriate, and he agreed. I did find out that those in the EOC are granted power by legislation to use "all" City resources in the event of an emergency, but a clear agreement could also permit me to identify a rotating on-call staff person who could be proactive and call the EOC in such instances.

I must point out that none of these preparations can substitute for dedicated, intelligent people. The shining example is one of my technicians who supports programmers responsible for the City's payroll application. He had the presence of mind to come early to work the day after the quake, and he somehow persuaded the construction crew and inspectors to permit him access to the building. He walked up 13 flights of stairs, picked up a PC and peripherals, carried it back down the stairs and to another building and configured it to work on the segment in the new building so the programmer could run the operations necessary for the City's payroll run that weekend, and employees could receive their checks on time, as expected. You cannot ask for more than that.

CRITICAL SKILL
11.1 Plan for Disaster Recovery

A disaster recovery plan is a document that explores how a network recovers from a disaster that either imperils its data or stops its functioning. A company's external financial auditors often require annual disaster recovery plans, because of the data's importance to the business and the effect that such a network failure would have on a company. Moreover, disaster recovery plans are also important because they force the manager of the network to think through all possible disaster scenarios. By taking these scenarios into account, the manager can make more effective plans to protect the network's data from loss and to restore full operations of the business as quickly as possible. As mentioned in the introduction to this module, planning for disaster recovery and managing the company's backup systems are a network manager's two most important jobs.

Most companies do not have extremely long disaster recovery plans. For a single network of up to several hundred nodes and 15 or so servers, such a plan usually consists of about 10–20 pages or fewer, although its length varies depending on the complexity of the company's network operations. (Fortune 500 companies, for instance, may have disaster recovery plans that are several hundred pages long, when all sites are considered in aggregate.) One strategy to keep disaster recovery plans concise and to maximize their usefulness is to focus on problems that, while remote, are at least somewhat likely to occur. Alternatively, you can focus on disaster results rather than trying to cover every possible disaster. (Focusing your plan on disaster results means contemplating such things as loss of a single server, loss of the entire server room, loss of all of the customer service workstation computers, and so forth, without worrying about what possible disasters might cause those results.)

The following sections discuss the minimum key issues that a disaster recovery plan should address. Depending on your own company, your plan may need to address additional issues.

Assess Needs

Before drafting the actual plan, you should first assess what needs the plan must meet. These needs will vary depending on who requires input into the disaster recovery planning process, and what issues these people want the plan to address. Consider these types of needs:

- Formally planning for contingencies and ensuring that all possible disasters have been considered, and defining countermeasures in the plan.

- Assuring the company's external accounting auditors that the company has considered and developed plans to handle disasters.

- Informing the company's top management about the risks that exist for the network and its data in different situations, and how much time you expect to need to resolve any problems that occur.

- Soliciting input from top management of the company as to recovery priorities and acceptable minimum requirements to reestablish services.

- Formally planning with the key areas of your company's business (for example, manufacturing, customer service, sales) considerations surrounding different types of computer-related disasters or serious problems.

- Satisfying customers of the firm that the firm's data operations are safe from disaster.

Once you have identified the needs that the plan must meet, you can then begin the planning process with a clear vision of what the plan needs to address. You will also know which other people from the different parts of the company to involve in the planning process.

Disaster Scenarios

You should start your planning process by considering different possible disaster scenarios. For example, consider the following disasters:

- A fire in your server room—or somewhere else in the building—destroys computers and tapes.

- A flood affecting your server room destroys any computers or backup batteries low enough to the floor to be affected. (Remember that floods may well be caused by something within the building itself, such as a bad water leak in a nearby room or a fire that activates the fire sprinklers.)

- An electrical problem of some kind causes power supplies to fail.

- A structural building failure of some kind affects the network or its servers.

- Any of the preceding problems affects computers elsewhere in the building that are critical to the company's operations. For example, such an event may happen in the manufacturing areas, in the customer service center, or perhaps in the telephone system closet or room.

While none of these events is very likely, it is still important to consider them all. The whole point of disaster recovery planning is to prevent or minimize serious losses, and the process is much less useful if you consider only those disasters that you think are the most likely.

After considering disasters such as those mentioned, you should next consider serious failures that could also affect the operations of the network. Here are some examples of these:

- The motherboard in your main server fails, and the vendor cannot get a replacement to you for three or more days.

- Disks in one of your servers fail in such a way that data is lost. If you are running some kind of redundant disk (RAID) scheme, plan for failures that are worse than the RAID system can protect. For example, if you use RAID 1 mirrored drives, plan for both sides of the mirror to fail in the same timeframe. If you are using RAID 5, you would plan on any two drives failing at the same time.

 NOTE

RAID disk arrays are discussed in detail in Module 12.

- Your tape backup drive fails and cannot be repaired for one to two weeks. While this doesn't cause a loss of data in and of itself, it certainly increases your exposure to such an event.

You should plan how you would respond to these and any other possible failures. If the motherboard in your main server fails, you may want to make plans to move its drives to a compatible computer temporarily. If your disks fail, you should design a plan under which you can rebuild the disk array and restore data from your backups as rapidly as possible. If your tape backup drive fails, you will likely want to find out how quickly you can acquire an equivalent drive, or whether the maker of the tape drive can provide reconditioned replacement drives quickly in exchange for your failed drive. For all of these failures, you will also want to consider the cost of keeping spare parts available, or even entire backup servers, so that you can restore operations as rapidly as possible. You should consider and investigate all of the following types of possible responses:

- Should you carry a maintenance contract? (If so, make sure you thoroughly understand its guarantees and procedures.)

- Should you stock certain types of parts on hand so that they are readily available in case of failure?

- Are other computers available that might work as a short-term replacement for a key server? What about noncomputer components that are important, such as routers, hubs, and switches?

- If you need to take temporary measures, are the affected employees trained to do their jobs with the replacement, or with no system at all if necessary? For example, if a restaurant's electronic systems are down, can the restaurant (and the servers, kitchen staff, cashiers, and so on) still operate the business manually until the system is repaired?

The process of considering possible problems, such as disasters or failures of key pieces of equipment, and then making plans for handling them is certainly the meat of disaster recovery planning. However, your written plan should also discuss or address other issues, which are covered in the following sections.

Communication

An important part of any disaster recovery plan concerns how you will handle communications. Without effective communications, your attempts at handling the disaster will be hampered, and other people will not be able to do their jobs as well as they might otherwise.

Start by first listing all of the different parties who may need to be notified of a problem, its progress toward resolution, and its final resolution. Your list might look something like this:

- The board of directors

- The chief executive officer or president

- The vice presidents of all areas

- The vice president or head of an affected area

- Your supervisor

- Employees affected by the problem

For each of these parties—and any others you may identify—you next need to consider what level of problem requires their notification. The board of directors, for example, will likely not need to know about a disaster unless it is likely that it will have a material effect on the company's performance. Your supervisor, on the other hand, probably wants to be notified about every problem, and certainly any affected employees need to be notified.

Once you have listed the notification parties and what they need to be informed about, you should then consider *how* you will inform them. If you're the primary person resolving the disaster, it's best to delegate notification to someone else who is less directly involved so that you can focus on resolving the problem as quickly as possible. For example, the job of communicating with the appropriate people should be delegated to your supervisor or to an employee who works in your department and is free to handle this job. Whoever has this job should be clear on the communication procedures, and he or she should have access to the necessary contact information—such as home phone numbers, pager numbers, cell phone numbers, and so forth—for situations that require notification after working hours. You may also want to consider setting up a telephone tree for rapid notification.

The written disaster recovery plan should include all of the preceding information.

Offsite Storage

Offsite storage is an important way of protecting some of your backup tapes in the event that a physical disaster, such as a fire, destroys all of your onsite copies. Because offsite storage is such an important aspect of disaster protection, it should be discussed in your disaster recovery plan.

TIP

If you do not yet have an offsite storage procedure, you should seriously consider adopting one. While fireproof file cabinets can protect tape media from small fires, they are not necessarily invulnerable to very large or hot fires. Plus, tapes are more sensitive to smoke and heat than the papers that a fireproof file cabinet is designed to protect.

Companies that provide offsite storage of files often also offer standardized tape storage practices. These usually work on a rotation basis, where a driver for the storage company comes to your office periodically—usually weekly—and drops off one set of tapes and picks up the next set of tapes. The companies typically use stainless steel boxes to hold the tapes, and the network administrator is responsible for keeping the boxes locked and safeguarding the keys. You need to decide which tapes you should keep onsite and which ones to send offsite. One rule of thumb is always to keep the two most recent complete backups onsite (so that they're available to restore deleted files for users) and send the older tapes offsite. This way, you keep on hand the tapes that you need on a regular basis, and you minimize your exposure to a disaster. After all, if a disaster destroys your server room and all of the tapes in it, you probably won't be too worried about losing just a week's worth of data.

TIP

The amount of data that you can accept exposing to a disaster will vary widely depending on the nature of your company's business and the nature of the data. Some operations are so sensitive that the loss of even a few minutes worth of data would be catastrophic. For example, a banking firm simply cannot lose any transactions no matter what. Businesses that need to protect supersensitive data sometimes enlist a third-party vendor to provide offsite *online* data storage. Such a vendor replicates a business's data onto the vendor's servers over a high-speed connection, such as a T-1 or T-3. These vendors usually also offer fail-over services, where their computers can pick up the jobs of your computers should your computers fail. Alternatively, if a business runs multiple sites, it might set up software and procedures that enable it to accomplish the same services using its own sites.

Critical Components for Rebuilding

Your plan should describe what computer equipment and software will be required to resume operations if the entire building is a loss. This list should roughly estimate the cost of the equipment and how it can be procured rapidly. By preparing such a list, you can reduce the time required to resume operations in a temporary facility. Also, if your company purchases insurance against business interruptions, you will need these estimates for that insurance policy.

CRITICAL SKILL
11.2 Back Up and Restore Your Network

A network disaster recovery plan is worthless without some way of recovering the data stored on the server. This is where network backup and restore comes in. If you're a network administrator, or aspire to become one, then you should already know about the importance of good backups of the system and of important data. If you don't know this, then it's probably the most important lesson that you can take away from this book: Making regular backups is a requirement when using computers—period.

You don't have to work with computers for very long before you observe firsthand the importance of good backups. Computers can and do fail, and they sometimes fail in ways that render the data stored on them unrecoverable. Or, perhaps some strange turn of events causes certain important files to be deleted or corrupted. In cases such as these, jobs are saved or lost based on the quality of the backups in place and the ability to restore that important data.

Assess Needs

Before designing network backup procedures, you first have to assess the needs of the company. In particular, you need to understand the company's backup needs very well. Questions such as the following may help in understanding the needs that you must meet:

- How dynamic is the data stored on the servers? How often does it change, and in what ways does it change?

- How much data needs to be backed up, and at what rate is the amount of data growing?

- How much time is available to make the backup? Make sure that you avoid situations where you need to back up terabytes of data using a system that can handle only megabytes per hour.

- If a partial or complete restoration from a backup is required, how quickly must it take place? As a rule of thumb, restoring data takes about twice as long as backing it up, although in some cases the times may be approximately equal. In other words, if it takes your backup system 10 hours overnight to back up the entire network, it will take 10–20 hours to restore that data—and this estimate doesn't include the time required to resolve whatever problem made it necessary to restore data in the first place.

- How coherent does the backed up data need to be? In other words, does a collection of data files need to be handled as a single unit? For example, a directory containing a bunch of word processing files isn't terribly coherent; you can restore one, many, or all of them without much concern about how those restorations will affect other files. On the other hand, a collection of database files for a high-end database is often useless unless you can restore *all* of the files in the set, and from *exactly* the same point in time. (High-end databases—such as Oracle's—that require this kind of backup will have their own detailed instructions for how backups must be made.)

- What is the required trade-off between cost and recoverability? You can design backup systems that operate minute to minute so that if something fails, the systems will lose no data and management can place a high degree of confidence in this fact. (A bank, for instance, requires this kind of high-end backup system.) However, such backup systems cost a lot of money and require a lot of administration. Most companies would gladly trade that sort of extreme cost for some lower degree of recoverability, such as nightly backups of the system. What does your company need and what is it willing to pay for?

- How many levels of redundancy does the company need in its backups? Most backups are made onto tapes and support servers that use RAID arrays, so the tapes are actually the *second* level of protection. In some cases, multiple tapes may be required, each with a separate copy of the backup. Or, another way to proceed for maximum redundancy is to copy backups to an offsite storage company over some sort of network connection.

When making your assessment, it is important to involve the senior management of your company in the process. At a minimum, you should present your findings and seek management's agreement or input.

Acquire Backup Media and Technologies

Once you have some idea of your backup needs, you can then proceed to acquire the necessary hardware and software to create and manage your backups.

Assuming that you need to purchase new backup hardware for a system, there are a number of proven, good choices, depending on your actual needs. When choosing a backup technology, consider the following factors:

- Reliability of the hardware and the media

- Cost of the hardware and the media

- Storage capacity

- Likely frequency of restorations

- The importance of fitting the entire backup onto a single piece of media

Table 11-1 reviews different types of backup technologies, their approximate costs, and the relative pros and cons of each. Note that prices of drives, media, and costs per megabyte in Table 11-1 are approximations.

Name	Approximate Cost of Drive	Approximate Cost of Media	Media Capacity	Pros and Cons
ZIP drives	$150 ($0.75–1.50/MB)	$15 each ($0.075–$0.15/MB)	1–200MB	+ Random access – Very small capacity – Slow speed
JAZ drives	$500 ($0.50/MB)	$100 ($0.10/MB)	1GB	+ Random access – Small capacity – Slow speed
CD-ROM/RW drives	$200 ($0.32/MB)	$1–5 ($0.002–$0.008/MB)	640MB	+ Random access – Small capacity – Slow speed – CD-ROM media is not reusable
DVD-ROM/RW drives	$500 ($0.083/MB)	$10 ($0.001/MB)	6GB	+ Random access + Large capacity - Slow speed

Table 11-1 Backup Technologies

Name	Approximate Cost of Drive	Approximate Cost of Media	Media Capacity	Pros and Cons
QIC-80/Travan drives	$250–500 ($0.05–0.03/MB)	$30 ($0.003/MB)	5–20GB	+ Very low drive cost/MB – Slower than other tapes
DAT DDS-1 drives	$500 ($0.167/MB)	$20 ($0.007/MB)	2–4GB	– Higher drive cost/MB than QIC/Travan – Low tape capacity
DAT DDS-2 drives	$800 ($0.10/MB)	$25 ($0.003/MB)	8 GB	+ Lower tape cost/ MB than DDS-1 or QIC/Travan
8mm tape	$1,500 ($0.188/MB)	$50 ($0.006/MB)	8GB	+ Proven technology – No longer cost-competitive with newer DAT/QIC capacities – Relatively slow tape seek times for restoration of individual files
Mammoth (8mm)	$4,000 ($026/MB)	$90 ($0.0006MB)	150GB	+ Proven technology + High tape density + Fast – Not in wide use (compared to DLT)
Digital linear tape (DLT)	$3,000 ($0.038/MB)	<$50 ($0.0005/MB)	80GB	+ Very reliable + Very fast + High per-tape capacities + Extremely low media cost/MB
Super digital linear tape (SDLT)	$5,000 ($0.023/MB)	$80 ($2.75/GB)	220GB	+ Very reliable + Very fast + High per-tape capacities + Extremely low media cost/MB
Ultrium	$5,000 ($0.023/MB)	$80 ($2.75/GB)	220GB	+ Very reliable + Very fast + High per-tape capacities + Extremely low media cost/MB – New tape format

Table 11-1 Backup Technologies *(continued)*

If your company can afford DLT and can make use of its capacities (smaller DLT drives are also available), you should definitely look into purchasing this technology. DLT tapes are rock-solid, can be used a rated million times, and are said to have a shelf life of 30 years. Moreover, the drives are fast both for backups and restorations. Finally, robotic autochangers are available for DLT drives, which means that there is plenty of head room if you outgrow the limit of the size drive you own. Also, the robotic systems are relatively inexpensive, and range from small systems that can hold five tapes up to large libraries that can hold tens or hundreds of tapes.

Some newer backup technologies, such as SuperDLT (220GB per tape) and Ultrium (200GB per tape), promise to up DLT's ante. For very large networks, these emerging technologies may make sense, and their use will become more widespread in the next few years.

Choose Backup Strategies

After acquiring all the necessary information, you can plan a backup rotation strategy, which addresses how backup media is rotated. Backup rotations are designed to accomplish the following goals:

- Rebuild the system, with the most recent possible data, in case of a catastrophic failure

- Restore files from older tapes that may have been accidentally erased or damaged without anyone noticing the potential loss of data immediately

- Protect against backup media failure

- Protect the data from an environmental failure, such as a fire, that destroys the original system and data

Most network operating systems maintain special bits for each file on the system. One of these is called the *archive bit,* which indicates the backup status of the file. When a user modifies a file, its archive bit is set to "on," indicating that the file should be backed up. When the backup is accomplished, the archive bit is cleared. Using this archive bit and your backup software, you can make the following types of backups:

- A *full backup*, where all selected directories and files are backed up, regardless of their archive bit state. Full backups clear the archive bit on all of the backed-up files when they are finished.

- An *incremental backup*, where only files with their archive bit set are backed up. This backs up all files changed since the last full or incremental backup. Incremental backups clear the archive bit of the backed-up files; those files will not be backed up during the next incremental backup unless they are modified again and their archive bits are reset to the "on" state.

- A *differential backup*, which is similar to the incremental backup in that it backs up only files with their archive bits set. The key difference in a differential backup is that the archive bits are left turned on. Subsequent differential backups will back up those same files again, plus any new ones that have been modified.

In a perfect world, it would be nice always to perform full backups. If the system were to fail, then you would need only the most recent backup tape to restore the system fully. However, for a number of reasons, performing a full backup may not always be feasible. For one thing, perhaps there is inadequate time to perform a full backup each day. Another reason is to extend the life of your media and tape drive by reducing the amount of work that they do. You need to weigh these concerns against the increased time it takes to restore from a combination of full and incremental or differential backups, however, and the increased possibility of being unable to restore backups properly using a combination approach (for example, if a full restoration required a full backup from the previous week, plus four incremental backups since then, you're counting on having all five tapes be perfectly good and you're somewhat more exposed to a bad tape).

One common way to mix these types of backups is to perform a full backup of the system once a week, and perform only incremental or differential backups each day of the week. Examine the following examples:

- You perform a full backup every Friday night and incremental backups on Monday through Thursday. If the system fails Monday morning before any data is entered, you need to restore only the full backup from the previous Friday night. If, however, the system fails on Thursday morning, for example, you have to restore four tapes sequentially in order to retrieve all of the data: the full backup from the previous Friday, then the incremental tapes from Monday, Tuesday, and Wednesday nights. Moreover, to guarantee the integrity of the data, you must be able to restore *all* of those tapes, and in their proper sequence. Otherwise, you run the risk of ending up with mismatched data files. In this scenario, you have four media-based points of failure, which might entail more risk than you care to take.

- You perform a full backup every Friday night, and differential backups Monday through Thursday. In this scenario, if the system fails Monday morning, you just restore the tape from the previous Friday night. However, if the system fails on Thursday morning, you have to restore only two tapes: the last full backup from Friday night, plus the differential backup from Wednesday night. Because differential backups back up all changed files since the last full backup, you never need to restore more than two tapes, thereby reducing the number of possible points of media failure.

The general rule of thumb is this: Incremental backups generally minimize the amount of time needed to perform each daily backup, but they take longer to restore and pose a greater risk of media failure. Differential backups take longer to make, but reduce the time required to restore and reduce the risk of media failure.

So, to determine the best backup scheme for your system, you need to balance the nature of the data and the amount of risk you're willing to take against the cost of each backup, the capacity of the tapes, and the amount of time it takes to make each regular backup.

The most common backup rotation scheme is called Grandfather-Father-Son (GFS). A common way to implement this scheme is to use at least eight tapes. You label four of the tapes as "Monday" through "Thursday," and four others "Friday 1," "Friday 2," up to "Friday 4." Every Monday through Thursday, you use one of those labeled tapes, replacing the data stored the previous week. Each Friday tape corresponds to which Friday in the month you are on: On the first Friday, you use Friday 1, and so forth. Finally, on the last day of each month you prepare a month-end tape, which you do not reuse, but instead keep offsite in case an environmental failure destroys the system and all locally stored tapes.

There are three main variations of the GFS scheme. In the first, you simply make a full backup of the system each time that you perform a backup. This variation offers the greatest amount of media redundancy and the minimum amount of restoration time. In the second, you perform a full backup on each of the Friday tapes and the monthly tape, but perform only incremental backups during the week. In the third, you do much the same thing, but use differential backups instead of incremental backups.

TIP

If your data is extremely critical and not easily reconstructed, you can often perform full backups every night and also squeeze in a quick incremental backup at lunch time. This way you can't lose more than a half day's worth of data instead of a full day's.

You can also choose rotation schemes that are simpler than GFS. For instance, you may use just two or three tapes, then rotate them in sequence, overwriting the old data each time you do so. This lets you restore any of the previous three days data. The shortcoming of this scheme is that sometimes you may need to go back further in time to restore data that had been erased or damaged without anyone immediately noticing. You can combat this problem by using several tapes that you rotate weekly or monthly.

One factor to keep in mind when considering different tape rotation schemes is the *granularity* of your backups. Generally, granularity refers to the flexibility that you retain to recover data from earlier tapes. In the standard GFS scheme, where full backups are made all the time, you can restore a file from any given day for a week's time, for any given end of the week (Friday) for a month's time, or for any given month for a year's time. You could not, however, restore a file that was created three months ago in the middle of the month and erased (or damaged) before the month was over, because a clean copy wouldn't exist on *any* of the backup tapes.

Ask the Expert

Q: Why is it important to consider the granularity of a backup scheme?

A: One reason to consider granularity carefully is the possibility of data becoming corrupted and the situation not being noticed. For instance, I once worked with a database file that had been corrupted several weeks earlier, but which had been continuing to function and seemed normal. After problems started to develop, however, the database vendor's technical support staff discovered that a portion of the database that wasn't regularly used had become lost and wasn't repairable. The problem was caused by a bad sector on the database's hard disk. The only way that the support people could recover the database and ensure that it was clean was to restore backups, going further and further back in time, until they found a copy of the database that didn't have the damage. They then reentered the data that had been added since the nondamaged copy was made. Because of the increasing time span between backups as the support people dug further and further back in time, the amount of data that we needed to reenter grew almost exponentially.

The best advice for choosing a rotation scheme for important data is this: Unless there are reasons to do otherwise (as already discussed), use the GFS scheme with full backups every time. This maximizes the safety of your data, maximizes your restoration flexibility, and minimizes the risk of media failure. If other factors force you to choose a different scheme, use the discussions in this module to arrive at the best compromise for your situation.

✓ Module 11 Mastery Check

1. What is meant by the term "backup rotation granularity"?

2. True or false: If a network's servers are running fine, backups are unnecessary.

3. Name five concerns that a disaster recovery plan should address.

4. How many times are DLT tapes rated to be able to be used?

5. What is the most common backup rotation scheme called?

6. For a network server that employs _____, backup tapes are actually the second level of defense against hardware failure.

7. A backup that backs up all files with the archive bit set, but leaves the archive bit unchanged is called a _____ backup.

8. True or false: High-end databases can have their files backed up just like the files of any other application.

9. There are two newer tape technologies that are successors to DLT and that have higher capacities. They are called _____ and _____.

10. True or false: One of the most important topics to address in a disaster recovery plan is communications.

Module 12

Purchasing and Managing Server Hardware

CRITICAL SKILLS

L ots of different *types* of servers exist—file and print servers, application servers, web servers, communications servers, and more. What all servers have in common, though, is that multiple people rely on them and that they are usually integral to some sort of network service. Because servers are used by tens or hundreds (or thousands!) of people, the computers you use for servers need to be a cut—or two—above just any old workstation. Servers need to be much more reliable and serviceable than workstations. Plus, they need to perform in different ways from workstations.

In this module, you learn about network server hardware. You learn about what distinguishes a server from a workstation, about different server hardware configurations, and about preparing a server for use in your network.

Explore What Distinguishes a Server from a Workstation

With high-performance desktop computers selling for $2,000–3,000, it can be hard to see how a computer with the same processor can cost in excess of $10,000 just because it's designed as a "server." Server computers truly are different from workstations, however, and they incorporate a number of important features not found in workstations. These features are important to a server's job, which is to serve up data or services to a large number of users as reliably as possible.

Server Processors

Much of the performance of a server derives from its *central processing unit*, or CPU. While servers are also sensitive to the performance of other components (more so than a workstation), the processor is still important in determining how fast the server will be.

Servers can run using one processor or using many. How many processors you choose for a server depends on many factors. The first is the network operating system (NOS) you use. You need to carefully research how many processors are supported on your proposed NOS if you wish to use multiprocessing.

If you plan to use Windows NT Server, Windows 2000 Server, or Windows .NET Server, you can use multiple processors, depending on which edition of those NOSs you plan to run. Windows NT Server can handle up to eight processors, although you might need a custom version of Windows NT available from the maker of the server system, because most multiprocessor systems have certain custom features that the operating system must support. Windows 2000 Server can handle up to four processors, while Windows 2000 Advanced

Server can handle up to eight processors, and Windows 2000 Datacenter Server can handle up to 32 processors. For Windows .NET Server, both the Standard and Web editions support up to 2 processors, Enterprise edition supports up to 8, and Datacenter edition supports up to 32. If you plan to use UNIX, then it depends—some versions of UNIX support multiple processors, while others do not.

Another factor to consider is the job that the server does and whether the server's tasks are presently bottlenecked by the processor. File and print servers tend not to need multiple processors. While they benefit from fast processors, the advantage is not as great as you might think. It's far more important for a file and a print server to have lots of RAM and a fast disk subsystem. Database servers, on the other hand, are processor-hungry and definitely benefit from as many processors as possible running at the fastest possible speed. (It's also important for the database server software to be built in such a way that it can make use of multiple processors.) Web servers tend to be modest in their processor requirements—they rely on fast busses, fast network connections, lots of RAM, fast disks, and that's about it. A fast processor (or multiple processors) is nice on a web server, but it might be overkill.

Managing multiple processors requires a lot of overhead work on the part of the operating system. Because of this, having twice as many processors in a computer doesn't double its processing capability; instead, double the processors might improve the computer's speed by only about 50 percent. Depending on your operating system, there is also a point of diminishing returns, past which additional processors won't give you much additional performance. Part of this has to do with how the operating system handles multiple processors. Another part has to do with the number of threads doing work in the operating system (threads cannot be shared between processors, so if only two main threads are doing all the work on the system, more than two processors won't improve your performance by any meaningful amount).

To determine the number of processors you should use for any given task, you should consult with the maker of both the network operating system you plan to use and makers of the primary applications you plan to run on the server. You might also want to discuss these issues with other companies that are performing similar work with the proposed server application. For instance, for a database server for an accounting system that supports hundreds of users, you should talk to other sites that use the same software and have roughly the same number of users, to learn about their experiences and suggestions. It's vital to double-check your proposed server configurations in this way, because different uses of a server might require far more—or far less—hardware resources than you might estimate. If you can find another company doing about the same thing and with approximately the same load, you can drastically improve your confidence in a proposed server hardware configuration's ability to meet your needs.

Ask the Expert

Q: What's a thread?

A: Operating systems that multitask often do so using a mechanism called a *thread*. In fact, all modern operating systems use threads, including Windows 9*x*, Windows NT/2000, OS/2, NetWare, and many versions of UNIX. In operating systems that make use of threads, each running program runs as a *process*, which has its own memory resources and is kept separate from other processes in the computer. However, the process is divided into different units of work, called threads. These threads have access to all the resources of the process in which they run and are the actual "agent of work" within the process. For example, a word processor such as Microsoft Word might have a main thread that accepts typed input from the user and displays it on the screen, another that handles any printing chores, and others that constantly check spelling and grammar in the background as the user works. In this example, the application Word is a single process with multiple threads. In a multithreaded operating system, every process always has at least one thread.

The Intel Pentium Family

Intel's Pentium family has a variety of different processors, ranging from the basic Pentium all the way up to the Pentium 4 Xeon processor. Current server-class computers are shipping with Pentium 4 or Pentium 4 Xeon processors. The Xeon series of processors are optimized for server-type duties and are more amenable to running in a multiprocessor system.

Pentium 4 Xeon processors are currently available in speeds ranging from 1 GHz up to 2 GHz. The design of the Xeon processor allows for 8 to 32 processors in a Pentium 4 Xeon system. For certain applications, having such a large number of processors can be an advantage. The Xeon processor family is packaged in a Single Edge Contact Cartridge, which is much larger than the packaging used for the Pentium non-Xeon processors. The Xeon processors also generate quite a bit more heat than their non-Xeon brethren, mostly due to the much larger cache memory and other features that boost Xeon processor performance in a server. (It's a good thing that most servers can monitor their in-case heat levels; sometimes these chips can heat up to more than 170° Fahrenheit.)

The next big jump in server processors will likely come from Intel's new Itanium processor family, previously known as the IA64 architecture. The Itanium family is based on a 64-bit architecture that uses something Intel calls EPIC (Explicitly Parallel Instruction Computing). This architecture relies heavily on compiler techniques to arrange the byte-level code so that it can execute as efficiently as possible in parallel (meaning multiple processor instructions execute at the same time).

Intel Clones

Two companies make processors that are essentially clones of Intel's processors. Advanced Micro Devices (AMD) makes the K6 series of processors, which perform on par with Intel Pentium II and III processors, and also the Athlon line, which competes primarily with Pentium III and 4 processors. A company called Cyrix also makes a line of Intel-compatible processors, called the Via MII series.

The problem with Intel clone chips is that, despite their manufacturers' protestations to the contrary, they won't ever be 100 percent compatible with Intel's processors. Because software vendors *usually* certify their software against only Intel processors, such vendors are certain to be slow to respond to any problems that crop up with the clones. Because of this issue, clone chips are not typically used in server-class machines, where reliability and serviceability are of paramount importance.

TIP

Before choosing any server hardware, ensure that the maker of the network operating system you plan to use certifies the entire system, including the processor. It is also wise to make sure that the maker of any applications you plan to run on the server also certifies the hardware you are choosing (most server application makers insist only that the hardware be certified for the operating system, but it's wise to double-check).

PowerPC

Originally, Motorola, IBM, and Apple teamed up to design and use the PowerPC processor, a RISC-based processor that is actually manufactured by Motorola. Today, the PowerPC is used in Apple Macintosh computers and some UNIX-based servers from IBM and Motorola. If you're running a Macintosh-based network, you are almost certainly using the PowerPC processor in both your desktop computers and any Apple-built servers.

Bus Capabilities

For most servers, the name of the game is moving data—usually, *lots* of data. File and print servers might need to serve up hundreds of files simultaneously to hundreds of users, and to coordinate and handle the data needs of all those users. Database servers might manage databases that are many gigabytes or terabytes large, and they must be able to retrieve large chunks of data from their databases and provide it to users within milliseconds. Application servers might perform both processor-intensive and disk-intensive operations while providing application services to users.

Just as networks often have fast backbone segments connecting many slower segments together, a computer relies on its bus to do the same sort of work. A bus is the data transfer "backbone" of a computer system, to which the processor, memory, and all installed devices connect. At any given time, a server might be moving megabytes of data from its disks to the network cards, to the processor, to the system's memory, and back to the disks as it performs its tasks. All these components are connected together by the system's bus, so optimizing that portion of the computer as much as possible makes sense. The bus, in fact, might handle about five times more data than any single component in the system, and it needs to do so quickly. While it's true that a modern PCI bus can handle 33 MHz at 32 bits, this just isn't enough in a high-end server. Many servers must handle multiple NICs (each running at speeds up to 100 Mbps, or even 1 Gbps) and multiple disk controllers running at speeds up to 40 Mbps. If those devices are busy at the same time, even a PCI bus will quickly get saturated.

Thus, server manufacturers need to get around bus speed limitations. The manufacturers use several schemes to do so. One way is by using multiple buses in a single system. For example, some of HP's NetServer servers use three PCI busses that can all run at full speed simultaneously. Just by using a little planning in placing certain peripherals on the different busses, you can greatly increase the system's overall speed.

A consortium of hardware vendors, including Compaq, HP, IBM, Dell, and many others, is also working on an improvement to PCI called PCI-X. PCI-X offers a 133-MHz bus at 64 bits, or up to 1,066 MBps throughput (yes, that's mega*bytes* per second). PCI-X systems should start appearing soon.

NOTE

PCI-X is being designed to be backward-compatible with standard PCI, but using a slower PCI card on the PCI-X bus will "throttle down" the bus to run at the slower speed. Instead, such systems are expected to support both a standard PCI bus for PCI cards and the PCI-X bus for PCI-X cards.

Other bus enhancements are also in the works. Some vendors are working on an initiative called System I/O, which promises speeds of up to 6 GBps (gigabytes per second) and the capability to use more than one channel (called a *link)* to go even higher. Intel is also working on a competing specification called Next Generation I/O (NGIO) with speeds of around 2.5 GBps per channel. NGIO can be arranged in a "fabric" configuration (where short paths exist between all components in the system) allowing much higher speeds depending on how the channels are configured.

RAM

Another important part of any server is its installed memory. Servers rely heavily on caching data from the network and from the server's disks to achieve the best possible performance, and they rely heavily on their random access memory (RAM) to do this. For example, most network operating systems cache the entire directory of files they store for quick access. They also keep requested files in cache for an extended period of time, in case the data from the file is needed again. They also buffer writes to the system's disk through write caches in RAM, and perform the actual disk writes asynchronously, so the disks are not as much of a bottleneck as they otherwise would be. For most servers, 256MB of RAM should be considered a bare minimum. For heavy-duty database servers supporting hundreds of users, you might want to install more than 1GB of RAM to achieve the best possible performance.

TIP

How much RAM do you really need for your server? This is hard to say because a lot depends on how the server is used. The good news is that both Windows NT Server/Windows 2000 Server and Novell NetWare provide statistics showing how the memory in the system is used. You can use this information to help determine when more memory would be beneficial. For Windows NT/Windows 2000, use Performance Monitor to see how memory and the system swap file are being used. For Novell NetWare, use the cache statistics in the console's MONITOR program.

RAM comes in three varieties: nonparity, parity, and error checking and correcting (ECC). Parity RAM uses an extra bit for every byte to store a checksum of the byte's contents. If the checksum doesn't match when the memory is read, the system stops and reports a memory error. Nonparity memory eliminates the parity bit and therefore can't detect any memory errors. Inexpensive workstations sometimes use nonparity RAM as a cost-cutting technique, although you should avoid its use whenever possible, even on workstations.

Parity-based memory has two problems. First, the system can only detect memory errors; it can't correct them. Second, because only one bit is used to store the parity, it is possible to "fool" the parity mechanism with a more severe error. For instance, if two bits simultaneously changed polarities, the parity system wouldn't detect the problem. ECC memory is designed to address these problems. Systems using ECC memory can detect up to two bits of errors and can automatically correct one bit of error. Most current servers use ECC memory because of the added protection that it offers.

Another type of RAM is Rambus dynamic random access memory (RDRAM). RDRAM is faster than other types of RAM. After some initial problems with RDRAM-based motherboards, Intel and Rambus seem to have the kinks worked out of RDRAM, and you can expect it to be used more broadly on servers. However, currently most servers ship with synchronous dynamic RAM (SDRAM), which is thought to be more reliable and consistent than RDRAM, and also happens to be much less expensive.

Disk Subsystems

The third crucial performance subsystem for a server is its disk drives. Hard disk drives are usually the slowest components of any system, and because most of the server's work involves the hard disks, they are the components most likely to bottleneck the system. Also, the data stored on a server is usually critically important to the company, so it's also important to have the most reliable disk configuration you can afford.

Disk Interfaces: SCSI Versus EIDE

Two types of disk interfaces are in widespread use today: Enhanced Integrated Drive Electronics (EIDE) and Small Computer Systems Interface (SCSI). For a workstation using Windows 9x, EIDE performs on par with a SCSI-based disk system. For a server running Windows NT/2000 or Novell NetWare, however, SCSI offers clear performance advantages. It would be beyond this section's scope to go into all of the details separating IDE from SCSI. However, SCSI systems perform much better when they have simultaneous access to more than one hard disk, and when they are used on an operating system—such as NetWare, Windows NT/2000, or even UNIX—that can take proper advantage of SCSI's features.

TIP

SCSI is pronounced "scuzzy." For a while, Macintosh users tried to adopt the pronunciation "sexy," but it never took hold. (SCSI first saw widespread use on the Macintosh, at least in the personal computing world.)

Many varieties of SCSI-based disk systems are available, as follows:

- **SCSI-1** The basic SCSI specification can transfer data to and from the disks at approximately 5 MBps using an 8-bit transfer width. Advances in SCSI technology have made SCSI-1 obsolete and it is not used on current systems. (This is good because most SCSI-1 implementations weren't compatible with one another.)

- **SCSI-2** This is the basic SCSI interface in use today. It extends the SCSI specification and adds many features to SCSI, and it also allows for much faster SCSI connections. In addition, SCSI-2 greatly improved the SCSI compatibility between different SCSI device manufacturers.

- **Fast-SCSI** With Fast-SCSI, the basic SCSI-2 specification is enhanced to increase the SCSI bus speed from 5 MHz to 10 MHz and the throughput from 5 MBps to 10 MBps. Fast-SCSI is also called *Fast Narrow-SCSI*.

- **Wide-SCSI** Also based on SCSI-2, Wide-SCSI increases the SCSI-2 data path from 8 bits to either 16 or 32 bits. Using 16 bits, Wide-SCSI can handle up to 20 MBps.

- **Ultra-SCSI**   Also called SCSI-3, this specification increases the SCSI bus speed even higher—to 20 MHz. Using a narrow, 8-bit bus, Ultra-SCSI can handle 20 MBps. It can also run with a 16-bit bus, increasing the speed further to 40 MBps.

- **Ultra2 SCSI**   Yet another enhancement of the SCSI standard, Ultra2 SCSI doubles (yet again) the performance of Ultra-SCSI. Ultra2 SCSI subsystems can scale up to 80 MBps using a 16-bit bus.

- **Ultra160 SCSI**   By now you should know the story: Ultra160 SCSI again doubles the performance available from Ultra2 SCSI. Ultra160 SCSI (previously called Ultra3 SCSI) is named for its throughput of 160 MBps.

- **Ultra320 SCSI**   An emerging standard, Ultra320 SCSI will move data at a rate of 320 MBps.

TIP

A new storage connection technology, called Fibre Channel, can use either fiber-optic or copper cable, is a much more flexible connection scheme than SCSI, and promises throughput many times faster than even that of Ultra320 SCSI. Based loosely on a network paradigm, Fibre Channel will initially be expensive to implement, but large data centers will benefit greatly from its advances over SCSI.

As you can see from the preceding list, a dizzying array of SCSI choices is available on the market today. Because of all the different standards, it's a good idea to make sure you purchase matched components when building a SCSI disk subsystem or when purchasing one as part of a server. Make sure the controller card you plan to use is compatible with the drives you will use, that the card uses the appropriate cables, and that it is compatible with both the server computer and the network operating system you will use. The good news is that once you get a SCSI disk subsystem up and running, it will run reliably and with excellent performance.

Disk Topologies: It's a RAID!

The acronym *RAID* stands for redundant array of inexpensive disks. RAID is a technique of using many disks to do the work of one disk and it offers many advantages compared to using fewer, larger disks.

The basic idea behind RAID is to spread a server's data across many disks, seamlessly. For example, a single file might have portions of itself spread across four or five disks. The RAID system manages all those parts so you never know they're actually spread across all the disks. You open the file, the RAID system accesses all the appropriate disks and "reassembles" the file, and provides the entire file to you.

The immediate benefit you get is that the multiple disks perform much more quickly than a single disk. This is because all the disks can independently work on finding their own data and sending it to the controller to be assembled. A single disk drive would be limited by a single disk head and would take much longer to gather the same amount of data. Amazingly, the performance of a RAID system *increases* as you add more disks, because of the benefit of having all those disk heads independently working toward retrieving the needed data.

If you think about a simple RAID array with data spread across many disks, you'll probably notice that, while it improves performance, it also increases the chance of a disk failure. Using five disks to do the work of one means that five times more chances exist for a disk failure. Because the data is spread among all the disks, if one fails, you might as well throw away all the data on all the remaining disks because it's useless if a big chunk is missing. Fortunately, different RAID schemes address this problem, as you see in the following discussion.

There are many different ways to use multiple disks together in some sort of RAID scheme and, accordingly, a number of *RAID levels* are defined, each of which describes a different technique, as follows:

- **RAID 0** This scheme is a configuration whereby data is spread (*striped*) across multiple disks, although *with no redundancy.* Losing one drive in a RAID 0 array results in the loss of data on all the disks. RAID 0 is appropriate only for improving performance, and should be used only with nonessential data. RAID 0 arrays can stripe data across two or more disks, as shown in Figure 12-1.

- **RAID 1** This type of array doesn't stripe data across multiple disks. Instead, it defines a standard whereby data is mirrored between disks. Two disks are used instead of one, and the data is kept synchronized between the two disks. If one of the disks fails, the remaining disk continues working just fine, until the failed drive can be replaced. RAID 1 is often simply referred to as *mirroring*. An enhancement to RAID 1 is called *duplexing*; the data is still duplicated between two disks, but each disk has its own disk controller, adding another level of redundancy (because you can lose either a disk or a controller and still keep operating). Duplexing can also improve performance somewhat, compared to straight mirroring. Some RAID 1 implementations are also intelligent enough to read data from either disk in such a way that whichever disk has its drive head closest to the data performs the read request, while the other one sits idle. However, all writes must occur simultaneously for both disks. Figure 12-2 shows a typical RAID 1 array layout.

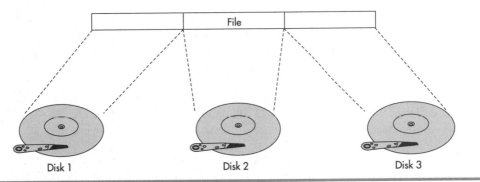

Figure 12-1 A RAID 0 array stripes data across multiple disks.

TIP

You can combine RAID levels 0 and 1 to achieve the performance benefit of RAID 0 with the high level of redundancy of RAID 1. Imagine a series of RAID 1 arrays with two disks each. Combine each of these RAID 1 arrays so that data is striped across them, and you have what is called a RAID 10 array (with *10* referring to a combination of RAID 1 and RAID 0).

- **RAID 2**   You won't see RAID 2 implemented in the real world. RAID 2 is a technical specification that stripes data across multiple disks and then uses a Hamming Code ECC that is written to a set of ECC disks. The ratio of data disks to ECC disks is quite high with RAID 2: There are four data disks for every three ECC disks. RAID 2 isn't used because of its inefficiencies.

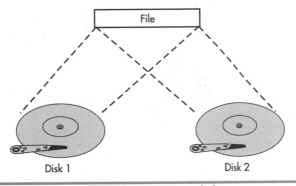

Figure 12-2 A RAID 1 array mirrors data between two disks.

● **RAID 3** This is where RAID starts to get interesting; RAID 3 implementations used to be fairly common, although these days you see RAID 5 used much more often than RAID 3. RAID 3 stripes data across multiple data disks and then uses an exclusive OR (XOR) bit-wise operation against all the stored data on each data disk to come up with ECC data, which is written to a single ECC drive. So, for example, you can have four data drives and one ECC drive to back them up. Figure 12-3 shows a RAID 3 array. The XOR data has an interesting mathematical property. If you remove one of the data drives, you can take the remaining data, plus the data on the ECC drive, and reconstruct what is missing from the failed drive. RAID disk controllers do this automatically if a drive fails, although the drives operate at a much slower rate than normal because of the overhead of having to reconstruct the data on the fly. A more useful technique is to replace the failed drive and then use the ECC data to rebuild the lost data.

TIP

If more than one drive is lost from a RAID 3 or a RAID 5 array, all the array's data will be lost. Still, these arrays provide good protection at relatively low incremental cost.

● **RAID 4** This is another of the RAID standards that isn't used in the real world. RAID 4 is similar to RAID 3, except data is not striped between the different data drives. Instead, each block of data is written whole to a single data drive, with the next block being written to the next data drive, and so forth. RAID 4 still uses a single ECC disk for all the data drives, but otherwise it is too inefficient to be of much benefit, particularly when compared to RAID 3.

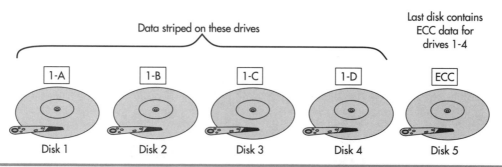

Figure 12-3 A RAID 3 array stripes data across multiple disks, with an ECC disk to protect the data.

● **RAID 5** RAID 5, depicted in Figure 12-4, is the current standard for RAID systems (RAID 1 also remains a current standard, but it has different applications). Recall how RAID 3 worked, with data striped to a set of data disks, and the ECC code written to a single ECC disk. RAID 5 improves on this scheme by interleaving the data and ECC information across all the disks. The big advantage of this approach over RAID 3 is that it doesn't rely on a single ECC drive for all write operations, which becomes a bottleneck on RAID 3 systems. Because all the drives share the ECC work, performance with RAID 5 is slightly better than with RAID 3. There is a small drawback to this, though, that most commentators miss. In RAID 3, if you lost a data drive, the system slowed down (usually dramatically) as the data was reconstructed on the fly. If you lost the ECC drive, however, the system would still run just as fast as if no drive were lost. With RAID 5, if you lose a drive, you're always losing part of your ECC drive (because its job is spread among all the disks) and you get a slowdown no matter what.

TIP

Server manufacturers make a big to-do about how the design of a RAID 5 system will allow a system to continue running if a drive fails. While this is technically true, the performance of a server in that condition is poorer than otherwise—possibly so poor that no one would want to use the server. RAID 5 does excel, however, at rebuilding the missing data once the failed drive is replaced. While this process might take several hours to complete, it gives you added peace of mind. This process might keep you from losing data and having to restore from a recent tape backup, which you might otherwise have to do if you didn't have some level of RAID protection on your server.

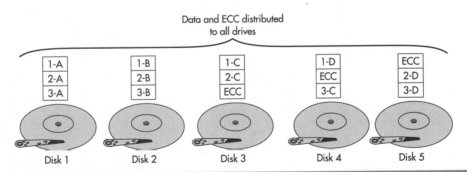

Figure 12-4 A RAID 5 array stripes data across multiple disks, and alternately uses all disks for ECC data.

Which level of RAID should you use on your network server? Most network administrators favor RAID 5 because it requires only 20 to 25 percent of the total disk capacity for the redundancy function. Yet it performs well and offers a measure of safety. However, RAID 3 and RAID 5 arrays do occasionally fail to recover data properly (although they very rarely lose data). For this reason, you usually should opt for either RAID 1 or RAID 10 for network servers that store important data.

In general, the different RAID configurations offer different levels of reliability. Ranked from best to worst purely in terms of the system's likelihood of losing data would be RAID 1, RAID 10, and then RAID 5 and RAID 3. There are always trade-offs, though. A system with 20 disks using just RAID 1 would be unwieldy to manage, because you would have 10 logical drives to manage and use efficiently. However, if you configured those same 20 disks as two RAID 5 arrays, you would be able to manage more efficiently the two logical disks that would result.

You must make your own decision based on the importance of the data, the required levels of performance, the capabilities of the server, and the budget available to you. One thing you should *never* do, though, is trust that any RAID level replaces regular, tested, reliable tape backups of network data!

I2O

Short for Intelligent I/O, I2O (often written I_2O) is an emerging standard that moves the I/O processing from the computer's processor to the disk controller. I2O promises to improve the performance of disk subsystems somewhat, although not as much as many of its proponents suggest. At the end of the day, the I/O processing still must be done; it's just done on the disk controller with I2O. Where I2O does benefit systems is by relieving some of the load on the computer's central processor, freeing it to do other tasks.

Server State Monitoring

An important feature of most servers is the capability to monitor its own internal components and to notify you if any problems develop or appear to be developing. Higher-end servers can typically monitor the following:

- Proper fan operation
- System voltage
- Memory errors, even if corrected by ECC memory
- Disk errors, even if corrected automatically

- In-case temperature

- Operating system hangs

- Computer case opening

Any of these errors might indicate a current or impending problem with the server. For example, a one-bit memory error that is corrected by the system's ECC memory might not cause a problem for the server because it was corrected, but it might indicate that a RAM chip or bank of RAM is starting to experience trouble. Similarly, climbing temperatures in a case might not cause an immediate problem, but might indicate that a fan isn't operating properly, has a blocked intake, or is facing another problem, and ultimately temperatures higher than those allowed for in the server design will cause a failure.

Server state monitoring solutions can alert you to problems either via an e-mail or through a pager, so you can resolve them. Some even operate if power is lost to the server or even the server room (this is called "lights-out" capability). Many high-end servers also offer "prefailure" warranties that state that the manufacturer will replace any components reporting even minor errors, so you can replace them before trouble actually strikes. For those servers you depend on to be the most reliable possible, such monitoring features can be a real lifesaver.

Hot-Swap Components

Most servers these days include hot-swap components that you can replace while the system continues to operate. Usually, hot-swap components are limited to disks, power supplies, and fans, all of which are running in a redundant configuration. For example, a system might have two power supplies; if one fails, the system still operates normally and you can replace the failed power supply without having to turn off the server. Similarly, most RAID disk configurations enable you to replace a failed drive without shutting down the server, provided the disks are installed in a hot-swap configuration.

TIP

Many RAID disk systems enable you to install a stand-by disk, and the system itself uses that stand-by disk to replace any failed drive automatically. Of course, you would then replace the actual failed disk as soon as possible, where it then becomes the stand-by disk for the disk array.

Progress Check

1. True or False: Basically, computers designed to be used as servers are the same as those designed to be used as workstations.

2. Which RAID level offers more redundancy: RAID 0 or RAID 1?

There's more to choosing a server than simply finding the fastest possible computer on which to base your server. Because servers are usually important to a company, their selection requires some thought and research. You need to define your needs properly, know how you want to use the server, and know what software you plan to run on the server.

NOTE

Throughout this module and most of this book, *Windows Server* means both Windows NT Server 4 and Windows 2000 Server. When important differences exist between these two products, those differences will be clearly noted.

CRITICAL SKILL
12.2 Choose Servers for Windows 2000 Server and NetWare

In this section, you learn about the basics of defining server needs, selecting a server, and purchasing a server.

Define Needs

Before looking at different server models, you need to understand clearly the needs that the server has to meet. Otherwise, you risk either under- or over-purchasing hardware, both of which can cause problems and might lead you to spend more than you needed to spend. Under-purchasing leads to additional, unplanned purchases, which might include adding more disks or more memory, or even having to replace the server much too soon. Over-purchasing means you spent more for a server than necessary, which might lead your company to deny your request for a particular server. Instead, you need to find the "sweet spot" for specifying

---

1. False. While the essential architecture of a server computer is the same as that used by a workstation, server computers are very different in their reliability and manageability.

2. RAID 1 (mirroring) offers redundancy, while RAID 0 (striping) does not.

just the right server for your needs; then you can defend your required configuration and its cost. You can't do any of this unless you have clearly defined your needs.

To specify the needs for a server clearly, you must be able to answer all the following questions:

- *What is the useful life of the server?* How long do you expect to use the server? Will you replace it in two, three, or four years? (Most servers are used for two or three years before being replaced.) Everyone should agree on this timeframe because if you plan to replace the server in two years, you can get by with a smaller server than if you need one to last three or four years. If you specified a server capable of meeting two years' needs, however, you don't want to get to the end of two years and then find out that your company won't approve a replacement.

- *What job will the server perform?* Will it be a file and print server, a web server, a database server, or some other kind of server?

- *How many users does the server have to support and what are the needs of those users?* For example, with a file and print server, you must estimate the storage and bandwidth requirements needed to satisfy all the planned users' requests. For a database server, you must know how quickly the server needs to respond to various database operations.

- *How reliable must the server be?* What are the consequences (costs and impacts) if the server crashes for one or more hours, or for a day or two?

- *Will you use clustering for the server?* Clustering is a technique whereby multiple servers share the same essential job. If one fails, everything keeps working, albeit at a slower rate. Once the failed server is repaired, it can then be added back to the cluster.

- *How safe must the data on the server be from loss?* This is different from the preceding question because you might have cases in which a server must never lose data, even if it isn't a big deal if the server goes down for a few hours. In such a situation, you would use a RAID-1 or RAID-10 configuration, but you might not care too much about, say, redundant power supplies. You might also explore some kind of hierarchical storage scheme, where data is automatically copied to tape or optical disk in real time, or where you make several live incremental backups of files each day.

- *If the server fails, what are your backup plans?* Do you plan to keep a hot-spare server (one that's ready to be swapped in at a moment's notice for a failed server) available or do you plan simply to rely on the server manufacturer's service capabilities? Also, sometimes if a server fails, other existing servers might temporarily meet some of its needs. For example, in a Windows NT network, if your Primary Domain Controller (PDC) fails, you can have Backup Domain Controllers (BDCs) that can pick up the slack while the PDC is down. Or, you might have redundant printer queues defined on another server, ready to be made available if the primary print server fails.

- *How do you plan to back up the server?* Do you plan to have a tape drive on the server itself or do you plan to back it up over the network to some other server's backup device?

Do you plan to make backups while the server is being used or overnight when it's not being used? These are important questions to answer because if you host the backup device on the server, you also need to have backup software on the server. If you plan to back up a server while it's being used, you need a fast backup system connected to a fast server bus to minimize the impact to the users during the day. If you plan to back up a server over a network connection, you need a network connection fast enough to handle the amount of data on the server. Think carefully about your backup plans when specifying a server.

- *How could the demands placed on the server change over time?* Is the company aggressively hiring more employees so that the server might have to support twice as many users a year from now and four times as many users two years from now? Make sure you understand the company's overall plans and factor them into your assessment of server needs. Also, even in companies where the number of users is relatively static, the amount of storage required by each user will still grow rapidly. Estimate that current storage requirements could double every 18 months, everything else being equal. If you have historical data for how much storage users consume, this data can help you estimate your system's requirements even more accurately. (And don't forget to anticipate any new network services that could more rapidly increase your storage needs!)

- *Does the new server need to work with any existing hardware?* If you have to reuse a network backup device, for instance, you should make sure that the new server can properly support it (and vice versa).

- *How much physical room do you have available to house the server?* Are you compelled by space requirements to go with the smallest server possible?

Once you answer these questions and any others that might crop up, you're ready to start looking at different servers that can meet the needs you defined.

Select the Server

Aside from choosing the types of equipment you need for a server, you must remember three basic prerequisites that all your server purchases should meet: compatibility, compatibility, and compatibility. If your network operating system starts displaying error messages on a particular server, you'll need fast responses to these types of problems. If you built a server yourself by buying a motherboard, a disk controller, a video card, and so forth, you're not going to get effective support, either for the hardware or for any compatibility problems that crop up with the software. For both Novell and Microsoft network operating systems, make sure that each part of the server—as well as the entire system collectively—is certified by Novell or Microsoft for its respective network operating system. For Novell, go to the following URL and check that any planned hardware is certified through Novell's YES! program:

```
http://developer.novell.com/npp/advanced.htm
```

For Microsoft operating systems, go to the following URL to look at Microsoft's Hardware Compatibility List (HCL) and make certain that the hardware you like is certified:

```
http://www.microsoft.com/hcl
```

When selecting servers, you often select a manufacturer first and then select the actual model you need. This is because, everything being equal, you're slightly better off if all your servers are from the same maker. Managing servers from one manufacturer is much easier than managing servers from many manufacturers. You can do a better job of stocking spare parts that might fit into all of your servers, and you can build a better relationship with the manufacturer or a particular dealer, which might hold additional benefits. For example, Dell lets companies certify their in-house technicians on Dell hardware (including servers), and then lets them order parts more directly, bypassing the first level of support (the first support people are the "first level" and their main job is to intercept the easy questions that beginners ask), and also provides other benefits.

Be conservative in selecting servers and server brands. You should stick with the top names in the industry. For servers, the best makers are Compaq, Dell, Hewlett-Packard, and IBM. When you select a server, you should stick with the "majors" for many reasons, including these:

- They have much more established service organizations and practices.

- They are likely to offer higher-quality support.

- Because so many other networks are based on their equipment, their technical support databases probably already contain any problems you encounter and they probably have fixes available.

- The NOS vendor is also more likely to have data on any problems concerning one of the top servers.

- They have much better in-house engineering, and their servers are likely to perform better and to be more reliable.

These are just the biggest reasons. You might remember a time when the mantra in management information systems (MIS) departments was, "Nobody ever got fired for buying IBM." A similar mindset actually makes sense when buying servers, not only because the purchase is more defensible, but because buying from major manufacturers actually makes better business sense, for the reasons cited in the preceding list.

Remember these general differences when you select a server for either NetWare or Windows NT Server: First, while any server is RAM-hungry, Windows NT Server works better with more RAM than an equivalent NetWare server. If everything else is equal, plan on giving Windows NT 50 to 100 percent more RAM than a NetWare server. Also, database servers are RAM-hungry and for databases of any appreciable size (10GB or larger), so plan on using at least 512MB of RAM (1GB isn't out of the question for the best possible performance).

You need to remember that NetWare 3.x and 4.x are uniprocessor NOSs, while Windows NT and Windows 2000 can operate with up to 8 or 32 processors. NetWare 5.x can also support up to 32 processors. Still, for a NetWare server, you probably want the fastest Pentium Xeon processor you can find, while a Windows NT/2000 Server will work very well with two or four slower processors. Also, remember that with single-processor servers, NetWare tends to perform better than Windows NT/2000 Server. Depending on the actual application, NetWare outperforms Windows NT/2000 Server by 15 to 30 percent, even if you've already added more RAM to the Windows NT/2000 Server configuration (see the "Server Processors" section at the beginning of this module for more information about multiprocessing on NetWare 4.11).

Both Windows NT/2000 Server and NetWare can implement certain RAID levels themselves. For the best performance, however, you should select a disk controller that can take this burden off the NOS. High-throughput disk controllers also often have a significant amount of RAM on them for caching disk data, and they usually have their own processor to help handle their chores. Moreover, you always want to use SCSI-based disk subsystems on a server. A workstation running Windows 98 performs equally well with either EIDE or SCSI, but a server can take advantage of SCSI's features to improve performance significantly over EIDE disk interfaces.

Choosing your actual disk configuration is relatively straightforward. You start by determining your current and planned space requirements, and then you consider your performance and reliability needs to choose a particular RAID level that makes sense (see the "Disk Topologies: It's a RAID!" section earlier in this module for more information). Once you know these things, you can choose the amount of disk space you need and ensure that the server you want can handle your current and planned disk space needs. Remember this tip: You're better off knowing what your disk needs will be over time and planning to purchase additional disk space as the need arises. This is because the capacity of disk drives is increasing at a rapid rate, while prices are falling at a rapid rate. Buying a 20GB drive a year from now, for example, will be much less expensive than purchasing the same drive today. Just make sure that the server you select can handle all the drives that you plan to purchase, and then install those drives as needed to save your company money. For NetWare servers, also remember that the optimal amount of RAM depends on the amount of disk space in the server, so you want to plan on purchasing more RAM when you add any significant amount of disk space. But, happily, the same rule of thumb for disks holds true for RAM: Prices are spiraling downward, and tomorrow's RAM will almost certainly be much less expensive than today's RAM.

If you plan to purchase a server for Windows NT/2000 Server or NetWare 5.*x,* you might also want to consider selecting a system that accepts additional processors. This way, if you find the system is becoming bottlenecked at the processor level, you can install additional processors to reduce or remove that bottleneck.

Purchase the System

Once you decide on the server you want, purchasing it is relatively straightforward: Shop around and get the best price on the system you want. Make sure that the suppliers you approach offer the level of support you need, both for presales selection assistance and for post-sales support.

TIP

Remember, it's not really "cricket" to rely on the expertise of a particular supplier to help you select a server and answer any presales questions you have, and then to purchase the server from some mail-order supplier with the best price. Try to be fair in your dealings. You should not abuse vendors with higher support capabilities in this fashion; if you do so, they might not be around to help you with after-sales issues that arise, or to help you with future purchases. This is not to say that you should pay a lot more for a piece of hardware from such vendors—just take into account the vendor's level of service when you evaluate different price quotes, and remember that price isn't everything.

Depending on your company's financial practices, you might want to consider leasing a server. Doing so brings you several benefits. First, leasing conserves your company's cash: Instead of shelling out $20,000 all at once, you can pay it off over time. Also, the annual impact of a lease is much lower than with a purchase, and leasing might make it easier to fit a particular server within your budget. Leases also have a hidden benefit: They force you to consider whether to replace a server at the end of the lease term (usually three years). They also usually make it easy to return the server to the leasing company and then lease a new server with which you can move forward. In the end, you pay about as much for leasing as buying (all things considered), and leases can help discipline a company to keep its computer equipment relatively current. The only drawback to leasing is that you must have enough time to replace the server at the end of the lease, when you might prefer to do it several months before or after the lease is up. Still, in some companies, the benefits of leasing far outweigh the disadvantages. Discuss leasing with your financial department before ordering a server.

And don't spend a lot of money on the monitor! You don't spend enough time looking at the monitor (unless you misconfigure the server) to warrant even a 17-inch monitor for the console. A 15-inch monitor will do.

CRITICAL SKILL
12.3 Install Servers

The actual practice of setting up a server is mostly specific to the server itself and the NOS that you plan to use. In subsequent modules, this book describes basic installations of NetWare, Windows 2000 Server, and Linux.

When you set up a new server, remember to plan on extensively testing its hardware prior to implementing it. While most servers are reliable right out of the box, the fact is that if some part of the server is going to fail, it almost always fails shortly after being set up and used. I prefer to test servers for at least a week, even before installing the NOS onto the server. Most servers come with diagnostic software that you can configure to operate continuously, testing the system's processor, video subsystem, disk surfaces, and RAM, and log any errors that crop up. Right after pulling a server from its box and installing any components that you need to install, plan on putting the server into a diagnostic loop using its diagnostic software and letting it run those tests for as long as possible. In no case should you test the server for less than several days (try to shoot for a week of testing).

After finishing the testing, you can install the NOS. During this phase, pay careful attention to any peculiarities of the server and to any error messages reported by the NOS or the server during the installation process. You must resolve these errors fully prior to going live with the server. In particular, watch out for any intermittent messages, such as a message that there was a parity error in the system's RAM or an unexpected lockup of the server during installation. Even if those problems don't recur, consult with the maker of the server and get advice on the problem. (Be sure you carefully write down any messages or other things that you notice if this happens.) Servers have a tendency to fail at the most inopportune times, so make sure that you have complete confidence in it before making it available to users. It might make sense also to let the server run its production software configuration for several days as an added test before putting it into use.

Especially make sure to have all potential NLMs (NetWare Loadable Modules), NT services and processes, or UNIX/Linux daemons running together as part of the testing. When you combine third-party software for these platforms, there are numerous opportunities for bugs or incompatibilities to appear that the vendors do not anticipate (despite the NOS vendors' stamp of approval).

Most server manufacturers have made it easy to install their server and to install the NOS onto the server. Companies such as Compaq even ship their servers with special CD-ROMs that mostly automate the process of installing various NOSs onto the server and also install any needed support files that the NOS needs to work optimally with the server hardware. Prior to installing a NOS onto a server, make sure to read the server's documentation carefully and to take advantage of any automated tools provided by the server manufacturer.

TIP

The top-tier server makers (Compaq, Hewlett-Packard, and Dell, for example) maintain e-mail notification systems that let you know about any new patches they release or any serious problems they have with a particular model. These e-mail services are extremely useful, so you should plan on signing up for them immediately on receipt of any new server.

Here's something else to think about: Sometimes servers are built and then sit around in inventory for several months before being sold. Consequently, the server might not come with the most current software. Before installing the server, check the maker's web site for any updates that aren't in your package and consider whether to install those updates during your implementation process.

CRITICAL SKILL
12.4 Maintain and Troubleshoot Servers

To do the best job of maintaining and troubleshooting servers, you need to take steps to do two things: decrease the chance of failure and improve your chance of rapidly resolving any failures that do occur. Problems are inevitable, but you can greatly decrease your odds of having them and you can also greatly improve your chances of resolving them quickly by taking steps *before* you actually have any problems.

To decrease the chance of failure, make sure to follow all the advice previously given: Use reliable, tested servers and components. You should also take these additional steps:

● Whenever possible, try to reduce the number of jobs that a server must do. Although building a single server that will be a file and print server, a database server, an e-mail server, and a web server is certainly possible, you're much better off (from a reliability standpoint) segregating these duties onto smaller, separate servers.

● Set up a practice of frequently viewing the server's error logs. If the server NOS supports notification of errors (such as to a pager), implement this feature. Many failures start with error messages that might precede the actual failure by a few hours, so getting an early heads-up might help you keep the server running or at least enable you to resolve the problem at the best possible time.

● If a server supports management software that monitors the server's condition, make sure to install the software.

● Most RAID arrays that support hot-swap of failed drives also require that the NOS have special software installed to support this feature fully. Make sure that you install this software before any failures occur.

- NOS software is among the most bug-free available, but it's still a truism that there is no such thing as completely bug-free software. Over time, any NOS will eventually fail. While many servers run for up to a year without trouble, you're better off establishing a practice of periodically shutting down the server and bringing it back up again. This practice eliminates small transient errors that might be accumulating and could eventually lead to a server crash, such as memory leaks in the NOS. The best frequency for such restarts is monthly.

CAUTION

Make sure that you do a backup before shutting down the server and restarting it. The greatest chance of hardware failure occurs when the system is powered back up again.

It's a good idea to make three good backups and test restores prior to putting a server into use. It might seem redundant, but you never know when you might need to restore your data.

You can also do some general things to improve your ability to resolve any server failures rapidly. The most important is to maintain for each server an extensive binder (or file box), which I call a "rebuild kit." This binder should contain the following:

- All purchase data for the server, including your purchase order and a copy of the supplier's invoice.

- A printout of the server's configuration. Most servers' setup programs can generate a detailed list with all components and their versions. Compaq's Insight Manager is great for this.

- All software needed to rebuild the server completely from scratch. This includes the setup software for the server, the NOS software, device driver disks, and any patch disks you need or have applied. Remember to add to the box any new drivers or patches that you get during the life of the server so that they will be available.

- Contact information for service on the server, including any extended warranty contract numbers or other information that you need to get service.

- Note paper, for documenting all changes to the server's configuration and any error messages that appear. Write all the information clearly, noting the date, the time, and any other details that you (or someone else) might need to fix the server if it fails.

- A printout or document noting anything special about the server or how you configured the disk drives, including NOS settings. You need these settings if you have to rebuild from scratch. Knowing these settings might enable you to recover the data on the server's disks so that you don't have to restore the data from backup tape.

CAUTION

You need a strong backup plan for any server, with appropriate tape rotations and regular tests of your ability to restore data from the tapes you make. The goal is never to have to use these tapes, but they give you an absolutely critical safety net if the server's disks crash and lose their stored data.

Even if you're the best computer troubleshooter in the world, you should plan on working with the service department of your server's manufacturer to troubleshoot any problems. Doing so can save you because the people in this department have extensive databases available to them of the problems others have experienced. They also are familiar with the steps needed to help prevent data loss as you work to troubleshoot the problem. Troubleshooting a server on your own, no matter how experienced and knowledgeable you are, is usually a mistake.

✓ Module 12 Mastery Check

1. True or false: All servers benefit from having multiple processors installed.

2. Describe what the following RAID levels do:

   A. RAID 0

   B. RAID 1

   C. RAID 5

3. Name three things that server state monitoring can track.

4. Which type of RAM offers a greater degree of safety from data loss: parity or ECC?

5. Which of the following disk technologies offers the highest performance?

   A. Ultra160 SCSI

   B. Ultra2 SCSI

   C. EIDE

   D. Wide-SCSI

6. Generally speaking, how much improvement in server processor performance does doubling the number of processors in a server gain?

   A. 25 percent

   B. 50 percent

   C. 100 percent

   D. 200 percent

7. Which of the following methods is the best way to determine how many processors you need in a server for a given task?

   A. Use one processor for every 250 users

   B. Keep adding processors until the processor utilization drops to 15 percent for each processor while the load is placed on the server

   C. Ask the vendor of the main server application or other users of the same application about their experience with the application and how their server is configured

   D. For a 10MHz network, use one processor, for a 100MHz network, use two processors, and for a 1GHz network, use four processors

8. In a server computer, what does a "bus" do?

9. True or false: For a server, the best type of RAM to use is parity RAM.

10. True or false: For most servers, you're fine using IDE-based disk subsystems.

Module 13

Purchasing and Managing Client Computers

Desktop computers are really where the "rubber meets the road" when it comes to networks. These machines are the users' primary interface to the network and the resource on which users most rely to get their jobs done. In fact, the network is designed to support the desktop computers' work, rather than the other way around. Maintaining desktop computers is also the task on which you often spend the most time in managing a network, so their purchase, implementation, and management are important. You can have the best network in the world, but if your desktop computers aren't up to the task, the network's users won't be productive.

This module focuses on the management of desktop computers. Chances are that if you're reading this book, you already know about the bits and bytes that make up desktop computers and desktop operating systems. You're probably already a wizard with Windows or the Macintosh, and you're comfortable installing new computer hardware and repairing problems on desktop computers. If you don't know about these things yet, many good books exist that cover the technologies in desktop computers in more detail than this book can provide. In this module, the major concern is how desktop computers integrate with the network and how you can get the most out of them when you're managing or setting up a network.

CRITICAL SKILL
13.1 Choose Desktop Computers

Choosing desktop computers involves many considerations. Making good choices here will pay big dividends over time. When purchasing new desktop computers, you have the opportunity to select machines to reduce your support burden, improve end-user productivity, and—overall—conserve your company's cash. The following sections explore the different factors that go into choosing desktop computers.

Desktop Platforms

You need to know what desktop computer platform you will use. Generally, companies tend to gravitate toward either PC-based desktop computers or Macintosh-based desktop computers. (These days, it is increasingly rare to find companies that depend much on Macintoshes as a staple of their desktop computer diet.) In a few rare cases, a few companies might alternatively gravitate toward Linux- or UNIX-based desktop computers, but you'll usually choose between PCs and Macintoshes.

Advantages and disadvantages exist for each platform. Regardless of the specific pros and cons, you're *much* better off if you can keep the company standardized on a single desktop computer platform. Companies that have purchased their desktop computers in accordance with individual user preferences end up with real support headaches, which arise from many different sources. Supporting two desktop platforms is more than twice as difficult as supporting one platform. Why? Consider the following:

- You need to maintain expertise in two platforms, and in their applications and platform-specific peculiarities. In a small company, you need more people to keep the requisite levels of expertise on both platforms than you would need if you had to support only one platform.

- You need to stock more spare parts and expansion hardware. Generally, components that work in a PC won't work in a Macintosh, and vice versa.

- You need to license and inventory more software titles (on average, twice as many).

- Problems that would never occur with one platform or another occur when you have to support both, even in the network itself. Supporting two platforms is more complex than supporting one, so the servers must run additional software, must allow for the different ways that each platform works, and so forth. All this increases the complexity of the network, and increased complexity means less reliability for everyone.

- Interplatform incompatibilities cause problems for users who have to work together. Even if they use the same application (such as Microsoft Word) on both PCs and Macintoshes, platform differences still exist. For example, even Adobe fonts with the same name look and paginate differently on Macs and PCs. Users might painstakingly format a document in Word, Excel, FrameMaker, or other applications available on both platforms, only to find that the other platform doesn't present their work in exactly the same way. When users frequently need to interact with one another with their files formatted for a variety of platforms, the incompatibilities become a real problem.

- In some cases, you might be unable to find software titles with matching versions available for both platforms. This usually means users who are using a particular application won't be able to interact with users who are using the other platform's functionally equivalent application. For example, Microsoft Access is available only for Windows, not for the Macintosh. Many other examples also exist.

- You will be limited in the programs you can develop for widespread use. For example, try developing a Microsoft Access–based application and then having Macintosh users use it. They can't, because Microsoft Access doesn't exist on the Macintosh and there's no real way to use the same database application on both platforms in such cases. You can probably exchange data, but not the program written in Access. The same situation exists for virtually all programming languages: They are almost universally platform-specific, despite the efforts of their makers to make them platform-neutral. Examples of this kind of problem are much more common than not. (One exception to this rule would be a SQL-based application that makes use of something such as an Oracle database server, but this type of software doesn't make sense to use for simple applications.)

These examples should convince you that you're better off running the *wrong* desktop platform than running *two* desktop platforms. If you're in a company where two desktop platforms are in use, you should work toward implementing a standard platform. This process is difficult and time-consuming, but is important both for increasing overall company productivity and keeping information systems (IS) costs at a reasonable level. If you're setting up a network from scratch, make sure you have an agreement to standardize on a single platform. Make sure that support for this standardization goes all the way to the CEO; otherwise, the company might hire some vice-president who insists on another platform. If you don't have this support worked out in advance, you might have trouble implementing the standard.

TIP

If you move into PC management, you will probably be called on to perform *cost analyses* to determine which platform to choose or to justify why you chose the one you did. These exercises include costs of new hardware and software, dealing with legacy applications or systems to which the platform must connect, and maintaining and supporting the platform, as well as predicting the viability of the platform in one, two, five, and ten years. Remember that the CFO is usually the CTO or CIO's boss, since IT/IS has historically been considered a cost center rather than a profit center.

After deciding whether or not to standardize on a single platform, your next decision is which one to choose. Most often, a company has a history with a particular platform, so sticking with that platform is usually the easiest solution, unless a good reason exists for a change. If you're lucky enough to be setting up a company network for the first time, then you get to help choose a platform. This choice should always be driven by what the users need to accomplish, what applications they need to run, and what platform best supports those applications. You need to consider the full range of applications that the company is likely to need, but the users' needs should be the primary driver. For most companies, this means you'll strongly lean toward PCs as the standard. However, for some companies, Macs are still a good idea. Generally, Macs make sense in companies that have a strong artistic or graphic bent to their makeup, such as a web design firm, a graphic design house, and so forth.

TIP

As you have probably already noticed, many people want to make a platform decision based on the platform that they like the best. Many people happily call themselves "PC fanatics" or "Mac fanatics." For some of these people, the issue rises almost to the same level of importance to them as a religion. Such fervent brand loyalty should never influence you in making a smart business decision. However, the presence of such strong opinions also means that you must tread carefully when discussing platform issues with the system's users!

If no need exists that strongly suggests a particular platform, then, for many reasons, you should lean toward choosing PCs. PCs are the most price-competitive, are in the widest use, attract the largest assortment of software and hardware developers, and have much more infrastructure to support them. Also, for certain important business application software categories, good solutions are available on the PC platform but not on the Mac platform (in some other instances, although the Mac platform offers similar solutions, they are inferior to those available for the PC).

TIP

While this book aims to be platform-neutral, the fact is that more than 90 percent of networked desktop computers are PCs. While this book is just as applicable to Macs as PCs, the remainder of this module assumes a PC environment.

Reliability and Serviceability

The most important features to look for in any desktop computer are its reliability and another closely related feature, its serviceability. Studies have shown that the actual cost of a desktop computer is a small percentage of its lifetime cost, which includes software costs, training costs, and support costs.

Ask the Expert

Q: What is TCO?

A: TCO is an abbreviation standing for total cost of ownership. It takes into account the lifetime cost for a purchase, including maintenance, depreciation, training, software development, and so forth.

Anything you can do to minimize support costs will pay a hefty (although not easily measured) premium over the lifetime of your desktop computers. You should not only consider the cost of support and repair, but also the cost to the company when users lose work because of computer crashes or when they lose the ability to work productively for a period of time because their computer is being repaired. All of these kinds of problems contribute to the TCO of a technology selection.

Author's Note

I once joined a company that had been purchasing "no-name" clones for its desktop computers. In my first week, I set up five brand new units still in boxes, only to find that three of them were dead on arrival (DOA). That same week, the company's chief financial officer (CFO), who was working on an important financing activity, had his computer crash repeatedly (losing unsaved work each time) until I finally swapped his entire computer for one of the new ones that actually worked. Was the money saved on those computers (about $400 per unit) worth it? What was the cost to the company for all these mishaps? The answer is simple: far more than the company saved. I immediately changed the company's brand to a more reliable one (the CFO was sympathetic!) and got rid of the existing machines as quickly as possible. Don't be penny-wise and pound-foolish when you purchase computers.

When assessing reliability, you need to look at the whole picture. Reliability comes from several things. First, reliability means the computer uses tested, high-quality components. Second, reliability means those components are engineered to work well together. You can make a cake with the best ingredients available, but if your recipe isn't good, you still get a bad cake. Computers are no different. Even the best components don't always work well together. Top-tier manufacturers test all the components that go into their systems and ensure that they're compatible with one another. Third, reliability means that you use a reliable combination of software on the unit and that whenever possible you use software that has been certified on the computers.

Serviceability is closely related to reliability. *Serviceability* simply means that working on or repairing a particular computer is relatively fast and easy. Features that enhance serviceability are easy-opening cases requiring no tools, quickly replaceable internal components—such as hard disks, memory, or video cards that require simple or no tools—and other features, such as easily updated Basic Input Output Software (BIOS) in the computer. Serviceability is also strongly influenced by the services available from the computer's maker. Does the computer manufacturer stay current in offering updates to its computers? Does their web site offer a lookup that lets you find out the configuration of a computer based on its serial or service ID numbers? Is technical information about its systems readily available or does the vendor tend to gloss over any discovered problems? How quickly can you get replacement parts? Does the manufacturer include onsite service for a period of time that reduces your support burden? What is the warranty on any given computer? Is the vendor sufficiently successful and stable that you can expect the company to be around for the entire useful life of the unit? What other value-added services are offered if problems occur?

TIP

PC Magazine performs an annual survey of reliability and serviceability for the major computer and printer manufacturers, based on survey responses from thousands of readers. This information is extremely valuable when selecting a computer manufacturer and you should pay close attention to the results.

Other factors that strongly influence serviceability are often overlooked. How many computers does the maker sell and is the specific model that you are buying widely used? These factors are important because a widely used computer is more likely to be supported when new software or hardware comes out, because companies that make software and hardware know they must ensure that their products work properly with these computers. Suppose that you use computers from a small, local company (or, even worse, build the computers yourself), and some software package or operating system that comes out in a year or two fails to work properly on your machines. The maker of the software or hardware might say something like, "Well, we haven't tested on that computer, so we don't know why our product isn't working right." While the maker might act in good faith to resolve the problem, the problem might take much longer to resolve than on a widely used system, and it might never be resolved. On the other hand, if you're using a top-tier computer, such as one from IBM, Compaq, Dell, HP, or Gateway, the vendor of the new product probably knows how to resolve any problems that arise and has already done so before the product was shipped.

TIP

If your company runs an application that is vital to its business but that is not widely used, it sometimes pays to find out what computers the application maker uses. If you know that the application maker has built the application using a particular make, you can reduce your risk of having trouble with that application by considering using the same brand yourself.

You can also improve serviceability if you standardize on a particular manufacturer, because then you can focus your resources on supporting that line of computers. Those people who support the desktop computers in the company will find it easier to stay up to date with the peculiarities of that manufacturer and will become more comfortable working with those computers. Also, your company's support staff will be able to solve a problem once and then apply the solution to many computers, rather than having to troubleshoot many different types of problems on many different types of computers. Finally, there might be service-quality benefits when you establish a strong ongoing relationship with a computer manufacturer.

If you support many computers, make sure that they are as consistent as possible. Not only do you want to ensure (as much as possible) that they are the same model and the same configuration, but you also want to make sure that the manufacturer uses the same components for all computers of a particular model. Some manufacturers are not careful about this; they will slip in different motherboards or NICs without any notice. For someone buying a single computer, this isn't a problem, but when you have to support 500 or 5000 computers that are all supposed to be exactly the same but aren't, it becomes a huge problem, because then you have to keep track additionally of different drivers and configuration information. Also, if you install and maintain computers through the use of disk images (such as those made by Norton Ghost), you will have to maintain different images for all of the different *submodels* of the computer.

Price and Performance

Once the preceding priorities are satisfied, you can then strike the appropriate balance between performance and price. You need to take into account the useful life that you plan for new purchases and make certain to purchase systems that will be productive over that useful life. In determining this balance, don't look at how well a particular configuration can handle today's needs, but how well it can handle tomorrow's needs.

Some people might disagree, but I firmly believe that price should be your *last* priority when you purchase computers. Although purchase price is important, you first need to determine your needs and then find the most reasonably-priced computers that best fulfill those needs. Different strategies exist for getting the best price. These strategies range from straightforward bargaining and competitive bids, to slightly under-purchasing on the performance side, but planning to upgrade the existing computers when needed (at least in terms of RAM and hard disk space, both of which decrease pretty rapidly in price over time).

Ask the Expert

Q: What does "useful life" mean?

A: The term "useful life" refers to the length of time that a particular asset, such as a computer, will be able to perform useful work. The useful life of a computer will change depending on the computer, the software it needs to run, the user who uses it, and the budget available to upgrade or replace it. A programmer needing the latest and greatest hardware and software all the time will get a relatively short useful life out of a computer, while a person who uses a computer only for word processing and doesn't care about running the latest software will get a much longer useful life out of a computer. For most desktop computers, the useful life is around 3–4 years, although exceptions to this rule of thumb are easy to find.

TIP

Don't forget to estimate the cost involved to replace a computer or to upgrade a computer when you choose a system. It might be less expensive overall to purchase a more capable computer now that you won't need to upgrade or replace as quickly, when you factor in the labor costs and user productivity impact from installing a replacement.

You can estimate that the demands placed on a desktop computer will double every 24 months or so, taking into account your planned useful life. Set your performance levels to meet that need. (People used to assume performance requirements doubled every 18 months, but this seems to be slowing a bit in recent years.) For example, suppose that you've determined that today's user requires 10GB of disk space, 512MB of RAM, and a Pentium 4 1.7-GHz processor. In 24 months, your users are likely to be clamoring for 20GB of disk space, 1GB of RAM, and a Pentium 4 4-GHz processor (or its equivalent). In another 24 months (about four years from purchase), these demands will double again, to 40GB of disk space, 2GB of RAM, and the equivalent of a Pentium 4 8-GHz processor. These projected demands might seem unlikely today, but when you look back at the needs of four years ago, such forward-looking projections look reasonable.

TIP

I once worked out the "18–24 month doubling formula" back to the dawn of PCs (not to date myself too much!), with machines containing 64KB of RAM, 8088 or 6502 processors, and—if they were lucky—a 5MB hard disk. The formula turns out to be extremely accurate!

Using this way of estimating performance needs, you should be able to find a "sweet spot" between price, performance, and useful life that minimizes your costs and maximizes the benefits that your users will receive.

Progress Check

1. True or false: You can always be assured that every computer of a single make and model will use the same internal components.

2. The most important factors to consider in purchasing a desktop computer are its
   _____ and its _____.

---

1. False. While most large manufacturers are sensitive to using the exact same components for every copy of a particular model of a computer (especially on their desktop computers that are targeted for business use), not all manufacturers respect this idea. You should always ask about this prior to choosing a computer system for widespread deployment.

2. Reliability and serviceability.

13.2 Determine Network Workstation Requirements

Computers connected to a LAN differ slightly from computers that are stand-alone. They have additional hardware installed in them and they run additional network software. This section explores these differences.

Network Workstation Hardware

All network computers need an installed network interface to connect to the network. Such an interface usually takes the form of a network interface card (NIC), but some computers have the NIC integrated onto the system's motherboard. Each NIC is specific to the type of network it supports. NICs are available for Ethernet networks, Token Ring networks, and even other networks. NICs are also usually specific to the cable media you have installed. For example, Ethernet NICs are available for 10Base-2 media, 10Base-T media, or 100Base-T media, with 1000Base-T NICs now beginning to appear. Some NICs also support multiple media types, which can be a blessing if you're in the middle of migrating from one media type to another. For example, some Ethernet NICs support 10Base-2, 10Base-T, and 100Base-T on a single NIC.

Network Workstation Software

Network workstations also need networking software to work with the network. This software consists of several components: a driver for the NIC, driver software for the protocols being used, and a network requestor (sometimes called a network *redirector*). Workstations acting in a peer-to-peer fashion also have peer software that provides network services to other workstations. Additionally, network service software might be needed, such as that required to use a particular network directory service such as Novell's eDirectory.

For Windows-based computers, you can choose to use software that is included with Windows to connect to both Novell networks or to Windows NT/2000-based networks. You can also use Novell's network software for Novell-based networks. Both sets of network software work well, although differences exist.

For Novell-based networks, Microsoft's networking software consumes less memory than Novell's, but it doesn't offer as many features and doesn't integrate with the Novell servers quite as well. Still, it's reliable and performs well. Novell's client software (called Client 32) works well and makes good use of the Novell server's features, and is also more secure than Microsoft's Novell network software.

When using the Microsoft software with NetWare 4.*x* or greater servers, you must also run service software to access Novell's directory service. This software is included both with Windows and Client 32.

Under Windows, you manage the network software through the Network Properties dialog box for Network Neighborhood or through the Network object in the Control Panel (which also accesses the Network Properties dialog box). Figure 13-1 shows an example of this dialog box.

The Network Properties dialog box contains a number of entries, including the following main categories:

● **Client**   You might have client software installed for Novell networks or Microsoft networks. This client software interacts with the servers to request network services. In Figure 13-1, you can see that the Client for Microsoft Networks is an installed component.

● **Network interface**   This entry represents the driver software that is installed for any installed NICs or for "virtual NICs" used to connect to a network through a modem. In Figure 13-1, you can see the 3Com Etherlink driver listed in the installed components.

● **Protocols**   This software adds support for any needed networking protocols, such as TCP/IP, IPX/SPX, or NetBEUI.

● **Services**   Any additional network service software, such as that used for NDS, also appears in the Network Properties dialog box.

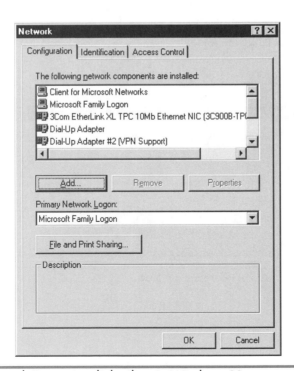

Figure 13-1 The Network Properties dialog box in Windows 98

Purchasing and Managing Client Computers

13

You add new entries, whether they are clients, protocols, or services, by clicking the Add button on the dialog box. This accesses the Select Network Component Type dialog box, shown in Figure 13-2. You choose which type of component you want to install and click the Add button.

After choosing which type of component you wish to install, click the Add button. You then see a Select dialog box that lists the available software of that type. Figure 13-3 shows how this dialog box looks if you are installing an additional network protocol. Choose the protocol to install, then click the OK button.

NOTE

When using Novell Client 32 software, you instead use the Client 32 setup program. The results will appear in—and can be managed in—the Network Properties dialog box, but they are installed separately.

After choosing the software to add, you return to the Network Properties dialog box, from which you can choose to install additional network software. After you have completed all your choices, you click OK in the Network Properties dialog box to save the settings and actually install the software into the operating system. The program prompts you for any needed installation diskettes or CD-ROMs. After the installation completes, you need to restart the computer to begin using the software.

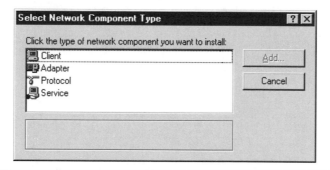

Figure 13-2 Selecting a network component type

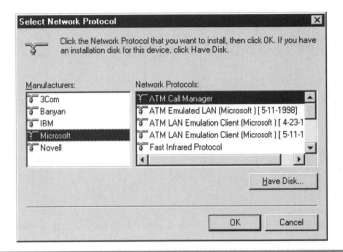

Figure 13-3 Choosing a protocol to add

TIP

First, install the client software you wish to use, either the one for Novell networks or the one for Microsoft networks. Doing so automatically loads the protocols on which the requestor relies, which saves time if your network uses the default protocols.

In the Network Properties dialog box, entries are *bound* to other entries, enabling them to work together. For example, protocols are bound to NICs, which enables the protocol to send and receive that type of packet through the NIC. Clients are bound to protocols, enabling that network requestor to use a particular protocol. By default, this binding is done for you automatically when you install the components. If combinations of protocols exist, NICs, and requestors that you do not use, you can delete those particular bindings.

TIP

Install only the network components you actually need in the Network Properties dialog box. Adding unnecessary components—such as networking protocols that you aren't using—only unnecessarily reduces the performance of the network workstation.

Module 13 Mastery Check

1. Generally speaking, computer capabilities double every _____ to _____ months.

2. True or false: You are better off running the wrong desktop computer platform than running two desktop computer platforms.

3. Generally, Macs make sense in companies that have a strong _____ or _____ bent.

4. True or false: The purchase price of a computer represents the main portion of its lifetime cost.

5. True or false: The most important consideration when purchasing a desktop computer is getting the lowest price.

6. True or false: If a computer uses the best components available, you are assured of a highly capable and reliable computer.

7. Serviceability is the assessment of the ease of _____ a computer system.

8. True or false: When you install a network workstation, you should choose to install all of the available networking software for the operating system in question.

9. The general average useful life of most desktop computers is around _____ to _____ years.

10. TCO is an abbreviation standing for _____.

Part II

Hands-On Knowledge

Module 14

Designing a Network

Networking professionals rarely have the opportunity to walk into a company and design a new network from the ground up, but those who do are certainly lucky. While such an effort involves long hours, stress, deadlines, and the nagging worry that maybe they're forgetting something, in return they get to shape the computing environment of a large number of users, and—in many companies—set the tone for how efficiently the company itself can function in coming years. In some companies that rely heavily on information technology, a smoothly running network might even determine whether or not the company will be successful. It's an enormous responsibility, but also one of the most rewarding jobs you can have.

Of course, designing a network from the ground up is more the exception than the rule. Mostly, networks start small and simply grow over time. Networks are almost like skin cells, where you're sure to replace each one of them every few years, but only a few at a time. Networks do the same thing: They grow over time and, if you measure them now and then again in a few years, it seems as though an entirely new network has been built. But the process is usually evolutionary rather than revolutionary. Exceptions exist to this rule, though. For example, one company might move to a new building, decide to scrap the old network during the process, and put in a new one at the new location. Likewise, a well-funded start-up company that goes from 5 to 500 employees in six months is likely to see the need for a new network.

Regardless of whether you're building a brand new network from scratch or renovating an existing network, the tools you use are much the same and the process of designing the network is also much the same. The concept is actually simple: You assess the needs that the network must meet and then you meet those needs. In practice, this process is much more involved, but the idea is straightforward. Even in an evolving network, using network planning to formulate a long-term plan to renovate the network makes sense. So, understanding what you must examine when you build or renovate a network is important.

Network design is not really an exact science. Getting it exactly right the first time is nearly impossible, even with the best design tools and resources available. This is because every network has different demands placed on it, and these demands often interact in surprising ways. Moreover, predicting what new demands will be placed on the network over time, how users will use the network resources, or what other changes you might have to make is almost impossible. The entire situation is both fluid and chaotic. The trick is to do a good job of estimating needs and then do the best job possible to create a design to meet those needs. Having fallback plans is also important, in case some part of the network doesn't perform the way you intended. For instance, once the network is up and running, you might find that the distribution of bandwidth across segments is poor. You want to know in advance how you can measure and address these types of problems. You might also find storage requirements are much higher or lower than you expected. You need to know what to do if this happens. The real point is this: Network design is a process, and often an iterative process. Your job as a network designer is to get as close as possible to the needed design and then fine-tune the design as needed.

A lot of the network design process is what you decide to make of it. There are simple network design processes, and there are horrendously complex processes that involve dozens of people, complex statistical modeling, and even network simulation software to test a planned design and see if it holds together. In this module, you learn a relatively comprehensive process that is straightforward and simple. Using the information in this module, along with a good dose of experience, will yield a flexible network that should easily meet the needs of hundreds of users.

TIP

You can't design a network of any size without plenty of experience running similar networks. You can manage the overall process by understanding the methodology, but you can't create a good design without experience. If you're new to networking and you have to design a network, make sure you get experienced people on the team—either as consultants or as part of a supplier-led team—and listen carefully to their experience and knowledge. Listening well pays off with a design that will work, rather than one that might look good on paper but won't hold up to actual use.

This module relies on all the information you learned in the preceding modules. Think of this module as the one that brings together into a coherent whole all the information that you have already learned. Preceding modules have focused on the bits and bytes of networks, while this module is the view from 30,000 feet where you start to see how everything works together.

CRITICAL SKILL

14.1 Assess Network Needs

The importance of doing a good job in assessing the needs that a network must meet cannot be overstated. Many adages exist concerning the importance of knowing your goals. "Measure twice and cut once," is one that carpenters use. "Ready, fire, aim," is one that pokes fun at people who don't properly set goals. And hundreds of others exist. The point is this: Before worrying about what network topology to use, what NOS platform to use, how to structure your hubs, bridges, and routers, and what grade of wiring to install, you must know what the network needs to accomplish. Doing a proper job can be tedious, but assessing needs is where you should place the most emphasis during a design process. Failing to do so almost certainly will result in a network that isn't productive for its users.

TIP

Many information systems (IS) professionals are, at heart, technologists who love to play with the latest technologies. Be careful to avoid giving in to the temptation to design the network around the "hot" technologies and then try to figure out how the needs fit into those technologies (many people mistakenly try to do this). Instead, start with the needs and then find out what technologies support those needs.

When assessing needs, you are trying to come up with detailed answers to the following questions:

- How much storage space is required?
- How much bandwidth is required?
- What network services are required?
- What is the budget for the project?

These basic questions are fairly easy to answer as a whole, but you need to break them down further to make sure no holes in the network design could lead to problems. For example, it might be easy to determine that the network must be able to support up to 100 Mbps of bandwidth, but you need to know how and when that bandwidth is used. If the accounting department is using 90 percent of the bandwidth when communicating to the accounting server, for example, then naturally you want to put the accounting system's server and its users on their own network segment. You won't recognize such issues and how to address them unless your assessment leads you to determine with some degree of detail how the network resources will be used.

The following sections discuss what you should examine as you learn what a given network must be able to do. No particular order exists in which you should examine these issues and you might find that you must cycle through the list several times to get a complete picture. You also might find a particular company's needs require more or less analysis in each category. Common sense is required when you design a network. The following suggestions are guidelines to start you on the right path.

Applications

A good place to start with a network design is to list and understand the applications that will run on the network. Ultimately, a network is only as good as the work it helps people accomplish, and people do their work most directly through the application software they use. If the applications don't work right, then the users won't work right, so the network has to support the planned applications properly.

Most networks have both common applications and department- and user-specific applications. Most companies usually meet the common application needs through a suite of desktop applications, such as Microsoft Office or Lotus SmartSuite. The following is a list of applications that most companies simply install for all users, whether or not each user needs each one:

- Word processor
- Spreadsheet
- End-user database

- Presentation graphics

- E-mail

- Personal information manager (calendar, contact list, and so forth)

- Virus-scanning software

Your first order of business is to determine a number of things about the common applications. You need to know whether all users need to have the entire suite installed, how often different users plan to use the different applications, how many files they will create and store, how large those files might be, and how those files will be shared among users. For example, in a 1,000 user population, you might determine that 90 percent will use word processing to generate an average of 10 documents a month, with each document averaging 100KB, and the users probably will want to keep two years' worth of documents on hand at any given time. Yes, these will be educated guesses, but it's important to come up with reasonable estimates. Experience with similar user populations and companies can pay off handsomely in determining these estimates. With this information alone, you know immediately that you need about 24MB of storage per user, or 21.6GB for the word processing population of 900 users, just for word processing documents. For applications where users frequently will share files, you might have to factor in that most users keep personal copies of some files that they also share with others.

TIP

You can help reduce overall network storage requirements by establishing shared directories in which different groups of people can store and access shared files.

Then you come up with the same estimates for the other applications, taking into account their expected size, frequency of creation, and long-term storage requirements.

TIP

Don't get bogged down in "analysis paralysis," worrying about whether you can scientifically prove that your estimates are accurate. Instead, make sure that the estimates are reasonable to other network professionals. At a certain point, you need to justify the network design and cost, and, to do this, having reasonable estimates is necessary. Just avoid overdoing it.

After determining the common applications, move on to department-specific applications. This step gets trickier for new networks in new companies because you might not know what applications will be used. For existing companies, you have the advantage of already knowing what departmental applications you need to support. Different departmental applications can have wildly different impacts on the network. For example, an accounting system designed around shared database files needs a different network design than one using a client/server database design. The former relies more on fileserver performance and is more likely to be bandwidth-sensitive than an efficient client/server application that runs on a dedicated server. If a departmental application is not yet selected, talk with the managers of that department to get their best estimates and then proceed.

Following are common departmental applications you should consider:

- Accounting

- Distribution and inventory control

- Manufacturing/MRP

- Information technology

- Electronic commerce

- Human resources

- Payroll and stock administration

- Publishing

- Marketing support

- Legal

- Other line-of-business applications specific to the company's industry

For each of the departmental applications you identify, you need to ask several questions: How much storage will they consume? Where will the applications be run from (from local computers with data on a server or completely centralized where both the data and the application run on a central computer)? Will they have their own dedicated servers? How much network bandwidth will the application need? How will all these factors change as the company grows?

Finally, while you might not formally include them in your plan, consider user-specific applications that might be run. For example, you might estimate that people in the company's research and development (R&D) group are all likely to run two or three unknown applications as part of their job. If you decide that user-specific applications will have a significant impact on the network, then you should estimate their needs just as you have the other types of applications. If you decide they will have minimal impact, then you might decide either to include a small allowance for them or none at all.

Project 14-1 Perform an Application Assessment

In this project, you will perform an application assessment for a fictional company.

ACME Industries is a company that manufactures a number of products, such as magnetic bird seed, giant slingshots, and fake train whistles used by coyotes in Arizona in their pursuit of roadrunners. They have two facilities: one in which all of their manufacturing and distribution is done, and a corporate headquarters that houses all of the office-based functions of the company (such as the executives, salespeople, accounting, and so forth). The company is moving both locations and you are tasked with helping to design the networks in each location. The applications in use are already selected and consist of the following:

Manufacturing Facility (25 employees)	Headquarters Facility (25 employees)
Microsoft Excel	Microsoft Word
	Microsoft Excel
	Microsoft PowerPoint

In reality, virtually any company in the world will have more complex requirements than those noted; however, the steps that you follow to assess the applications will be the same.

Step by Step

1. Create a table (either on paper or in Excel). In the rows, create a section for each facility, and list one application in each of the rows. For example:

Manufacturing	
Microsoft Excel	
Headquarters	
Microsoft Word	
Microsoft Excel	
Microsoft PowerPoint	

(continued)

2. Create the following columns for the table:

- Number of users
- Number of files per user per day
- Average size of files
- Number of days to keep online

When complete, your table should resemble the one shown in Figure 14-1.

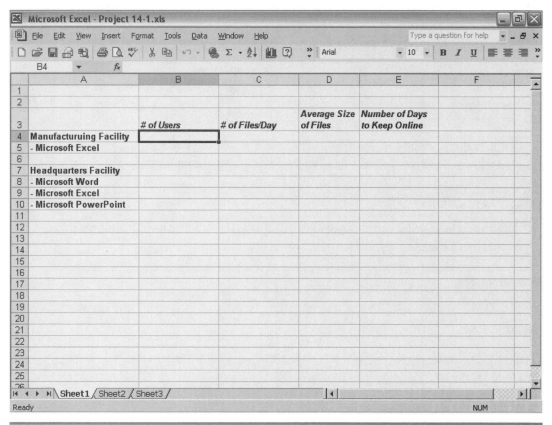

Figure 14-1 The table after Step 2

3. Complete the table using the example values shown in Figure 14-2. In a real assessment, you will need to come up with appropriate real-world estimates for these values.

4. Using Excel, or a calculator, calculate the total storage requirements for each application and for each facility. Figure 14-3 shows these values. Note that in the example, size values are all in kilobytes.

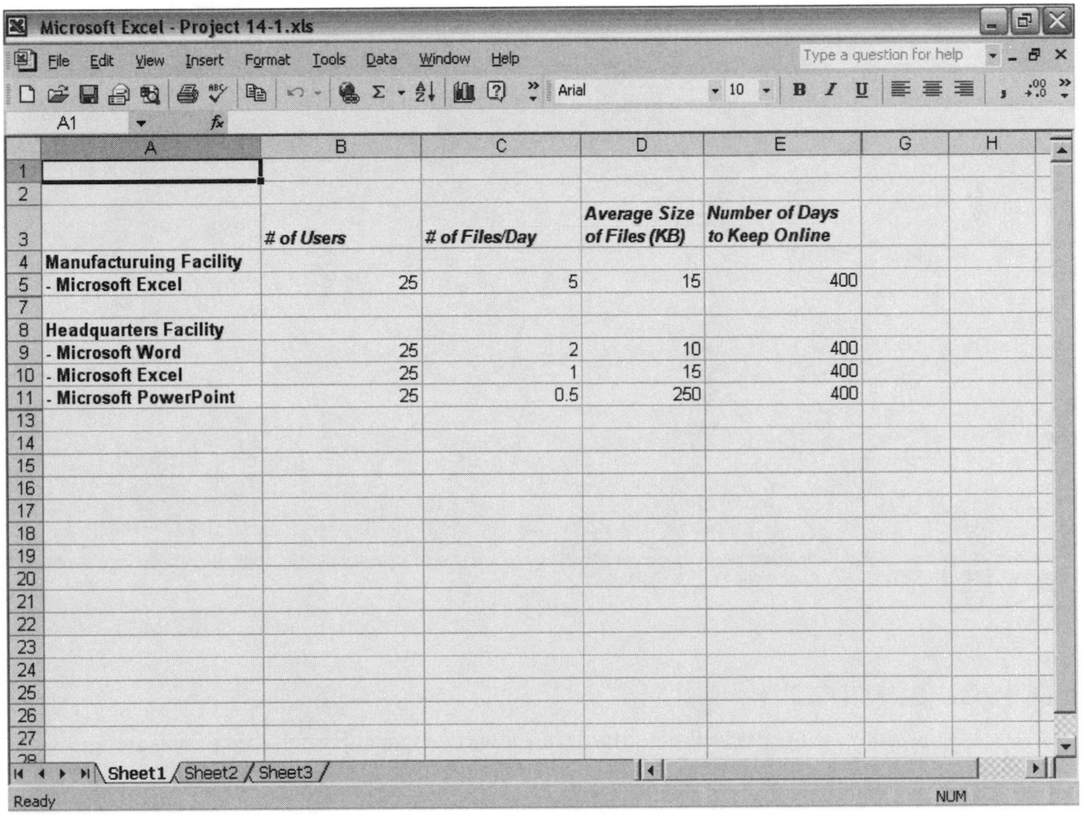

	# of Users	# of Files/Day	Average Size of Files (KB)	Number of Days to Keep Online
Manufacturuing Facility				
- **Microsoft Excel**	25	5	15	400
Headquarters Facility				
- **Microsoft Word**	25	2	10	400
- **Microsoft Excel**	25	1	15	400
- **Microsoft PowerPoint**	25	0.5	250	400

Figure 14-2 Example values for the assessment table

(continued)

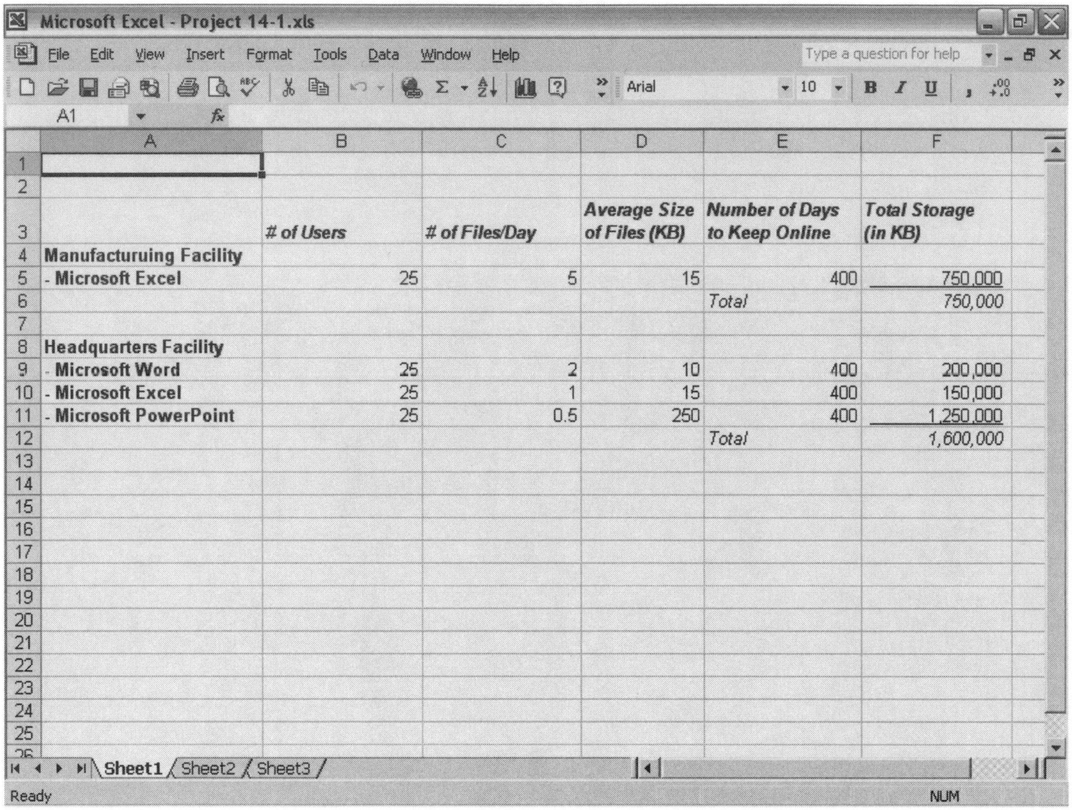

	A	B	C	D	E	F
1						
2						
3		# of Users	# of Files/Day	Average Size of Files (KB)	Number of Days to Keep Online	Total Storage (in KB)
4	**Manufacturuing Facility**					
5	- **Microsoft Excel**	25	5	15	400	750,000
6					Total	750,000
7						
8	**Headquarters Facility**					
9	- **Microsoft Word**	25	2	10	400	200,000
10	- **Microsoft Excel**	25	1	15	400	150,000
11	- **Microsoft PowerPoint**	25	0.5	250	400	1,250,000
12					Total	1,600,000

Figure 14-3 Total file storage requirements

Project Summary

While overly-simplified, this project illustrates how you can approach calculating storage requirements for a network. In the real world, you will also add in a "fudge factor" to allow for inaccuracies in your model. You will have to come up with a fudge factor that you're comfortable with for the actual environment, and this will be guided by the importance of the storage requirements, the budget available, and any other factors that you think important. I typically recommend increasing your totals by at least 50 percent. In some cases, particularly if the incremental storage cost is minimal, you might increase your totals by 100 percent.

Using the model shown in this step-by-step, you would need a minimum of 750 MB of disk storage for the manufacturing facility, and 1.6 GB for the headquarters facility. In the real world, you would likely purchase a fileserver with 2 GB+ for the manufacturing facility, and 5 GB+ for the headquarters facility, which should allow plenty of room for errors in the model and for unforeseen growth.

Users

Once you know what applications the network must support, you can estimate how many users need to be supported and what applications each user will use. Estimating total users will likely be easier because the company should already have a business plan or long-range budget from which you can derive these estimates. Your user estimates should be reasonably granular: Know the number of users in each department in the company as well as the company's total number of users.

You should estimate how many users will need to be supported immediately, in one year, in three years, and in five years. Even though five years is a distant horizon to use for an estimate, this information is important to know during the design process. Different growth rates suggest different network designs, even at the inception of the network. A company estimating it will have 100 users immediately, 115 users in one year, 130 users in three years, and 150 users in five years needs a different network design than a company estimating 100 users immediately, 115 users in one year, 300 users in three years, and 1,000 users in five years. In the latter case, you must invest more in a design that is more quickly scaleable and you are likely to spend much more at inception to build the network, even though the network will have the same number of users in the first two years.

Knowing the number of users isn't enough, though. You need to know more about the users. At a minimum, consider the following questions to determine if any of the following will be important factors for the users generally or for subgroups of the users:

- **Bandwidth requirements**   Aside from the bandwidth required to save and retrieve files, send and receive e-mail, and perform an average amount of browsing on the Internet, do any users need significant amounts of bandwidth? For example, will scientists download a fresh copy of the human genome from the Internet once a week? Will groups of users need to exchange large quantities of data among different sites? Will any users be running video conferencing software over your LAN and WAN/Internet connection? How much web browsing do you expect the network's users to do? Will people be sending large attachments frequently through Internet e-mail?

- **Storage requirements**   Will any group of users need significantly more storage capacity than the overall average you already determined? For instance, will an electronic imaging group catalog millions of documents into image files on a server? If so, how many people need access to that data? Will the accounting group need to keep the previous 10 years of financial information online? Will the company use or install an executive information system where all the managers have query capability into the company's accounting, distribution, and manufacturing systems, and, if so, how much additional bandwidth or server performance could that capability require?

- **Service requirements**   Will any groups of users need additional network services not needed by most users? For example, does part of the company do work of such sensitivity that it should be separated from the rest of the LAN by a network firewall? Will a subset of users need direct inward fax capability?

When examining user bandwidth requirements, remember to look at the timeliness of the bandwidth needs. If certain known activities require a lot of bandwidth and must be carried out during the normal workday, that high-bandwidth use might interfere with the performance of the rest of the network. Therefore, make sure to estimate both average and peak bandwidth needs.

Network Services

Next, you should look at the services that the network must provide. These can vary widely in different companies. A very basic network might need only file and print services, plus perhaps Internet connectivity. A more complex network will need many additional services. Consider which of the following types of services the network you are designing will need to provide, as well as any others that are specific to the company:

- File and print services
- Backup and restore services
- Internet Web browsing
- FTP and Telnet
- Internet or external e-mail
- Internet security services
- Dial-out from LAN through a modem pool
- Dial-out to LAN through a modem pool
- Fax into LAN (manually distributed or automatically distributed)
- Dynamic Host Configuration Protocol (DHCP) services
- Centralized virus-protection services
- WAN services to other locations
- Streaming Internet radio and other media
- Voice over IP (VoIP)

For each service, you must answer a number of questions. First, you need to know the storage and bandwidth requirements for each service, and any other impacts they will make. For instance, a fax-in service might itself require a small amount of storage space, but all the fax bitmaps that users will end up storing might have a large impact on total storage needs. Second, you need to know how the service is to be provided. Usually, this means that you need to know what server will host the service. Some services require such little overhead that you can easily host them on a server that does other jobs. A DHCP server, which requires minimal resources, is a good example of such a service. On the other hand, an e-mail system might require such high resources that you must plan to host it on its own dedicated server. Third, you need to know what users or groups of users need which services. This is because, to minimize backbone traffic, you might need to break the network down into smaller segments and locate frequently used services for a particular user population on the same segment as the users use.

Progress Check

1. Name the three key capability requirement areas you should always consider when designing a network.

2. True or false: A proper network design methodology will let you design a network in a linear fashion.

Security and Safety

The preceding considerations are all related to the bits and bytes required by different parts of the network. Security and safety concern the company's need to keep information secure—both inside and outside a company—and to keep the company's data safe from loss. You need to know how important these two issues are before attempting to set down a network design on paper.

For both these considerations, a trade-off exists between cost and effectiveness. As mentioned in earlier modules, no network is ever totally secure and no data is ever totally safe from loss. However, different companies and departments have different sensitivities to these issues, indicating that more or less money should be spent on these areas. Some applications might be perfectly well suited to keeping their data on a striped RAID 0 array of disks, where the risk of loss is high (relative to other RAID levels), because the data might be static and easy to restore from tape if the disk array is lost. Other applications might require the highest level of data-loss safety possible, with fail-over servers each having mirrored RAID 1 or RAID 10 arrays and online tape backup systems updating a backup tape every hour or for every transaction. Similarly, some companies might work with data that is so sensitive that they must install the best firewalls, perhaps even two levels of firewalls, and hire full-time professionals dedicated to keeping the data secure. Other companies might be happy if they are only reasonably secure.

The point is that you must determine how important these issues are to the company for which you are designing the network. Then, you can propose different solutions to address these needs and factor these needs into the rest of your design.

---

1. Bandwidth, storage, and services.
2. False. The process of designing a network is almost always iterative.

Growth and Capacity Planning

The final area to consider is the expected growth of the network, particularly if the company expects this growth to be substantial. As mentioned earlier in this module, a network designed for a rapidly growing company looks different from one for a slowly growing company, even if both companies start out at the same size. In the former case, you want a design that you can quickly and easily expand without having to replace much of the existing hardware and software. In the latter case, you can get by with a simpler network design.

You want to consider the impact of growth on the different parts of the network that you've already examined (applications, users, and services), because linear growth does not always mean a matching linear impact to the network. Assuming linear growth, the impact to the network might be much lower, or much higher, than the curve.

For example, you saw in Module 4 how Ethernet uses a collision detection mechanism to manage network traffic. In that module, you also learned that Ethernet scales linearly, but only up to a point. Once the network starts to become saturated, performance starts to drop rapidly because of the chaotic nature of Ethernet's collision detection scheme. Consider a 10-Mbps Ethernet network transmitting 3 Mbps of traffic. This traffic probably flows smoothly, with few collisions and few retransmissions required. Push the network demand up to 4–5 Mbps, however, and its performance grinds to a halt as the network becomes saturated and you end up with as many collisions and retransmissions as real data. In fact, the amount of good data flowing over a saturated Ethernet network will actually be less than the amount flowing over a less-saturated network.

You can also find examples where an increase in demand doesn't cause a corresponding increase in network or server load. For example, the server load for a complex e-mail system might increase only by a small amount if you doubled the number of users because the system's overhead generates most of the load. Or, the storage requirements for an accounting system might not double just because you keep twice as much data in it to accommodate the overhead that might consume most of the existing space. Alternatively, that same accounting system might consume four times as much storage space if you double the data storage, because its indexing scheme is relatively inefficient. The point is that you need to know how different applications scale with increased use. The vendors of the main applications you will use should be able to provide useful data in this regard.

TIP

Be careful not only to consider how applications behave as they scale, but how they behave as they are scaled *in your planned network environment*. Different network operating systems, network topologies, and client and server computers will all affect how well a particular application can support growth.

Project 14-2 Develop a Scenario Plan

Project 14-1 showed a basic approach to assessing network storage requirements. When performing any important planning activity, you should also do something called "scenario planning," in which you explore how changes to the model will affect the answers you come up with. This lets you assess the impacts of different possible future scenarios and develop plans to meet those possibilities should they occur.

Step by Step

1. Starting with the model you built in Project 14-1, assess the different storage requirements using the following changes:

   - Increase users at both locations to 100.

   - Increase the size of the average PowerPoint file to 1MB

   - Increase the number of Excel files generated at the headquarters facility to three per day

2. Based on the changed resulting storage totals for each location, consider how you would meet the increased needs.

The three changes shown, all very reasonable changes that may occur after setting up a network, increase the storage requirements at the manufacturing facility by a factor of four and at the headquarters by a factor of ten. How would you address these needs if they became apparent only several months after setting up the network that you planned earlier? Many possibilities exist:

- Add additional disk drives to the servers.

- Replace existing disk drives in the servers with larger-capacity units.

- Add an external storage cabinet to any servers that already have the maximum internal storage installed.

- Install network-attached storage (NAS).

- Add incremental servers, dividing up the data that each must hold.

Project Summary

For a real network planning job, you should conduct careful scenario planning to take into account possibilities such as those shown in this example, and you should have at least a basic idea of the ways in which you would propose meeting those increased needs and the costs and effort involved in each.

Meet Network Needs

Once you complete your assessment (by this point, you're probably sick of the assessment process!), you can then start working on finding ways to meet all the needs you've identified. This process is largely holistic and is not worked through by following a series of steps and ending up with a single answer, like an equation. Instead, you should start by mapping out the various parts of the network, considering the three main topics discussed in this section, and "build a picture" of the network design. The design that you create will incorporate all you learned during the assessment process, taking into account your experience and the advice you get to devise a concrete design that results in an equipment list, specifications, and a configuration.

Seeking criticism of your design from other network professionals, who might have valuable experience that you can then factor into your design, is important. No single networking professional exists who has seen and had to cope with all possible design needs, so you want to combine the advice of as many seasoned people as you can.

Choose Network Type

You probably want to start the design by choosing a network type. This should be a relatively straightforward decision, based on the overall bandwidth requirements for the network. For most new networks, you almost certainly will decide to use one of the flavors of Ethernet. Ethernet is by far the most common type of network installed today and it's an easy default choice.

You also need to decide what level of Ethernet you need. For wiring to the desktop, you should choose 100Base-T. It is reliable, and provides plenty of capacity for most needs. For your network backbone, you can usually use a higher-bandwidth connection, such as 1000Base-T, without incurring too much additional cost.

Choose Network Structure

Next, decide how you plan to structure the network. In other words, how will you arrange and wire the various hubs, switches, and routers that the network needs? This is probably the trickiest thing to determine because it's hard to predict how much data must flow from any given set of nodes to any other set of nodes. Still, you should have estimates based on your assessment work that will help. If you can identify expected heavy traffic patterns, you should also draw a network schematic with these patterns indicated to help you sort it out. Remember the following tips:

- Ethernet's CDMA/CD collision handling means that an Ethernet network will handle only about one-third of its rated speed. In other words, a 10Base-T segment, which is rated at 10 Mbps, will handle about 3.3 Mbps in practice. The same holds true for 100Base-T, which will handle about 33 Mbps of actual data before starting to degrade.

- Whenever possible, use "home run" wiring for all nodes to a single wiring closet or server room. ("Home run" wiring means that each network cable runs from each workstation to a single location.) Doing so enables you to change the network structure more easily (for example, to break segments into smaller segments) as needs change.

- Except in the smallest networks, plan on a network backbone to which the hubs connect. An Ethernet switch rather than a nonswitching hub should handle the backbone, so each hub constitutes a single segment or collision domain. You still must plan to keep each segment's traffic below the Ethernet saturation point, but this structure will give you plenty of flexibility to meet this goal.

- These days, Ethernet switches are becoming inexpensive enough that you can actually use them as hubs. It's not at all unreasonable to use current hardware to wire everything at 100Base-T using only switches, and it's not much more expensive than using a combination of hubs and switches.

- The physical building might dictate how you structure your network. For example, a building larger than 200 meters in any dimension probably means you won't be able to employ a home-run wiring scheme for all your nodes. This is because twisted-pair Ethernet usually reaches only 100 meters (that includes routing around building obstructions, patch cables, and other things that make the actual cable distance longer than you might measure on a map of the building).

- For multifloor buildings that are too big for a home-run wiring scheme, consider running the backbone vertically from floor to floor and then have a wiring closet on each floor that contains the hubs to service that floor's nodes. The wiring from the closet on each floor then fans out to each of the nodes on that floor.

- Consider running the backbone speed at 10 times the hub/desktop network speed. If you're using 10Base-T hubs to connect to the desktop computers, plan on a 100Base-T backbone. If you're using 100Base-T to the desktop, consider a gigabit network connection such as 1000Base-T for the backbone.

- Most of the time, most nodes do the majority of their communication to one or two servers on the network. If you are planning department-specific servers or if you can identify similar patterns, make sure that each server is on the same segment as the nodes that it primarily serves.

- If your servers tend not to be assigned to support departments and instead support the entire company, make sure that the servers are directly connected to the backbone's Ethernet switch.

- If you have any high-bandwidth users, consider keeping them on a segment separate from the rest of the network (if appropriate) and also consider upgrading the speed of that segment to 100 Mbps or 1,000 Mbps if needed.

- As you start to implement the network, carefully watch the ratio of collision packets to data packets. If the number of collisions on any segment climbs to 5 to 7 percent of the total number of packets, performance is starting to suffer; you need to investigate the cause and find a way to decrease this ratio. You can usually do so by breaking the segment into smaller pieces, or by configuring capable switches into what is called a virtual LAN, or VLAN, unless you know of another way to reduce the amount of traffic.

Choose Servers

When choosing servers for a network, start by determining what network operating system you will use. For PC-centric networks, the decision is usually between Novell NetWare 5 and Windows 2000 Server. Whenever possible, avoid using both, because supporting two NOS systems makes managing the servers much more difficult. You're better off compromising on a single NOS platform than trying to support both.

Next, list the various network services that your servers must provide. You need to look for efficient ways to host these various services on your servers, balancing a number of factors:

- All else being equal, using more small servers to host fewer services each is more reliable than using fewer large servers to each host many services.

- Conversely, having more small servers increases your chance of having a server fail at any given time.

- Using more small servers is more expensive and requires more maintenance than using fewer large servers.

- If you plan to use more than one server, consider which services should be redundant on another server or how you plan to deal with the failure of any server.

Using your assessment information, you can easily determine how much storage capacity your servers will need. However, it's much harder to know how capable each server should be in terms of processor power, installed RAM, and other features, such as bus configuration. For these specifications, you need to rely on the advice of the NOS vendor and the manufacturer of the servers that you are considering. Fortunately, both Microsoft and Novell have published tests and recommendations for sizing servers given different service and user loads. Many first-tier server manufacturers also have such data to help you choose an actual server model and its specifications.

Module 14 Mastery Check

1. The most important task when designing a network is _____.

2. Most networks are built

   A. All at once

   B. Slowly, piece by piece, over time

3. When designing a network from scratch, you should estimate how the needs will change over (choose all correct answers):

   A. One year

   B. Three years

   C. Five years

   D. Ten years

4. True or false: When designing a network, you should assess how critical the data stored on the network will be for the company, and how the use of the network will impact the company's ability to accomplish its goals.

5. An accounting system designed around _____ needs a different network design than one using a _____ design.

6. Know the number of _____ in the company as well as the company's total number of users.

7. True or false: Dynamic Host Configuration Protocol (DHCP) is a network service that requires such little overhead that you can easily host it on a server that does other jobs.

8. True or false: For most new networks, you almost certainly will decide to use one of the flavors of Ethernet.

9. True or false: When choosing servers for PC-centric networks, the decision is usually between Novell NetWare 5 and Windows 2000 Server.

10. To achieve maximum speed for a network at minimal incremental cost, you should always consider designing the backbone to run at _____ times the speed of the individual node connections.

Module 15

Installing and Setting Up Windows 2000 Server

In this module, you learn how to install Windows 2000 Server. Before you install Windows 2000 Server, however, you first must conduct a variety of preinstallation checks that prepare the system for the process. Next, you perform the actual installation, providing necessary information that the installation program needs. Finally, you test the installation by having a client computer log in to the server properly and perform some basic network duties. All these steps are described in detail in this module.

TIP

This module and the two following modules provide an overall introduction to Windows 2000 Server. Certain advanced installation scenarios and techniques are not described here. To learn about other features and choices available when installing, administering, or using Windows 2000 Server, consult a dedicated Windows 2000 Server book, such as *Windows 2000: The Complete Reference* by Kathy Ivens and Kenton Gardinier (ISBN: 0-07-882582-2, McGraw-Hill/Osborne).

CRITICAL SKILL
15.1 Distinguish Windows 2000 Versions

Windows 2000 is an entire family of products, all built on essentially the same programming code, but with significant feature and tuning differences. Windows 2000 is an upgrade from the Windows NT line of products, which ended with Windows NT 4.

The desktop version of the product family is called *Windows 2000 Professional.* Windows 2000 Professional is made to run on business desktop computers and is not an upgrade for Windows 9*x*/Windows ME. Windows 2000 Professional supports the following broad features:

- Runs on systems with a minimum of 64MB of RAM (Microsoft claims that Windows 2000 Professional runs faster overall than Windows 9*x*/ME on systems with 64MB of RAM—an impressive claim that you should verify for yourself)

- Supports up to 4GB of physical RAM

- Supports one or two processors

- Works with Windows 2000 Server to take advantage of Active Directory and Intellimirror

- Includes support for plug and play (PnP) devices (PnP was not really supported in Windows NT)

- Includes all Windows NT's features, including a preemptive, protected, multiprocessing operating system

- Fully supports mobile computer features, including power management

## 15

Windows 2000 Server Standard Edition is the mainstream server version of Windows 2000. It includes all the power of Active Directory, as well as the following features:

- New management tools (compared to those provided with Windows NT) based on the Microsoft Management Console (MMC)

- Windows Terminal Services, which allows Windows 2000 Server to host graphical applications, much like a mainframe hosts applications for dumb terminals

- Internet and web services (DHCP, DNS, Internet Information Server, and Index Server)

- RAS and VPN services

- Transaction and messaging services

- Support for up to four processors

- Support for the latest versions of the standard network protocols

Windows 2000 Advanced Server is the mid-range offering of Windows 2000 Server products. It enhances the features of Windows 2000 Server by adding the following:

- Support for up to 8GB of installed RAM

- Network load balancing (for example, Advanced Server can share a heavy TCP/IP load among a number of servers and balance their loads)

- Windows 2000 clustering

- Support for up to 8 processors

- Support for 2-node clusters

The most powerful version of Windows 2000 Server is the Datacenter Server version. This version is used when extremely large databases need to be hosted for thousands of users or when other extremely heavy demands need to be placed on Windows 2000 Server. Datacenter Server includes all the features of the other versions of Windows 2000 Server, plus the following:

- Support for up to 64GB of installed RAM

- Support for up to 32 processors

- Support for 4-node clusters

CRITICAL SKILL

15.2 Prepare for Installation

Before installing Windows 2000 Server, you first must prepare the server computer that you will use and make important decisions about the installation. This preparation stage consists of a number of tasks, including the following:

● Make sure the server hardware is certified for use with Windows 2000 Server.

● Make sure the server is properly configured to support Windows 2000 Server.

● Carry out any needed preinstallation testing on the server hardware.

● Survey the hardware prior to performing the installation.

● Decide how you will install Windows 2000 Server, after gathering all the configuration information you will need during the installation.

● Back up the system prior to an upgrade.

These tasks are discussed in the following sections.

Check Hardware Compatibility

Microsoft maintains an extensive Hardware Compatibility List (HCL) that lists different hardware components and their testing status on various Microsoft products, such as Windows 2000 Server. To avoid problems with your server, it is important you make sure that the server itself and any installed peripherals have been tested with Windows 2000 Server and work properly. The latest version of the HCL can be found at http://www.microsoft.com/hcl. You can also find a text-based copy on the Windows 2000 Server CD-ROM. Using the web HCL is preferred, however, because it might have more current data than the file included on the installation CD-ROM.

Check the Hardware Configuration

Purchasing a computer for use as a server can be a complex task. You have to contend with the myriad details of installed RAM, processor configuration, disk configuration, and so forth, as well as factor in your anticipated needs to come up with a reasonable server configuration.

NOTE

Module 12 contains information about different server technologies and about specifying a server for general use.

Ask the Expert

Q: What if my hardware isn't listed on the HCL?

A: If a particular hardware component in your planned server isn't listed on the HCL, all is not lost. For one thingp, the HCL might not have the most current data, and the hardware that you wish to use might be certified, but not yet listed. It's best to check with the hardware's maker, because that company will know the current status of the hardware's certification. Also, products not listed in the HCL might work fine with Windows 2000. If you are deploying a server for testing purposes or to support limited services, and you are comfortable doing so, you can still proceed to install Windows 2000 Server and begin working with it. You should not do this for production servers that many people will depend on, however. Not only might an undiscovered incompatibility cause serious problems with an uncertified server, but you will be unable to get the highest level of support from Microsoft for hardware that is not yet certified. For this reason, you should avoid deploying important servers that are not yet certified by Microsoft.

Windows 2000 Server requires the following *minimum* hardware configuration:

- One 133-MHz Pentium class processor or greater

- 256MB of RAM

- About 1GB of free disk space for the installation process

- A CD-ROM or network connection from which Windows 2000 Server is installed; if you are using a CD-ROM drive, Microsoft recommends one that is 12*x* speed or faster

The preceding are the minimum requirements specified by Microsoft. You should carefully consider using more capable hardware than that specified, particularly for any kind of server (even one that will support only a few users).

Instead, follow this advice when configuring a server for Windows 2000:

- Start with at least a single fast Pentium IV processor running at 1,000 MHz or greater. Pentium 4 Xeon processors are a benefit in a server and you should carefully consider the price of such systems relative to the expected performance improvement (all else being equal, a Pentium 4 Xeon family processor will perform about 15 to 20 percent faster than an equivalent Pentium 4 processor). Also, consider using a system that has either two or more processors or the capability to add additional processors later if your needs grow faster than expected.

- Windows 2000 Server runs best on systems that have plenty of RAM. For a server, make sure you have at least 384MB of RAM. If you plan on supporting all the different services available with Windows 2000 Server (such as Terminal Services, RAS, DHCP, DNS, and so forth), then 512MB of RAM might be a better choice than 384MB of RAM. One gigabye of RAM is not an unreasonable amount, particularly for servers that will experience heavy loads. (Don't forget, you can start with 384MB of RAM and install more if needed, and possibly at a less expensive price than when you first purchase the server.) Do *not* attempt to run Windows 2000 Server on a system with less than 256MB.

- A fast SCSI-based disk subsystem is important, particularly for servers that will store a lot of data. See Module 12 for more information on choosing SCSI systems, using different RAID levels, and other important disk information.

- Windows 2000 Server requires a lot of disk space for its initial setup. The formula to determine the amount of disk space is 850MB + (RAM in MB * 2). In other words, you need 850MB, plus another 2MB of disk space for each megabyte of installed RAM in the server. This is a minimum amount required for installation. Installing the server onto a system that will use FAT32 (File Allocation Table) formatted disks requires an additional 150MB or so because FAT32 stores files less efficiently than NTFS. Installing Windows 2000 Server from a network installation point also requires more disk space: Estimate about 150MB of additional disk space if you will be installing over a network connection rather than from CD-ROM.

Use the information in Module 12 to help you size your server, but remember this rule of thumb: Get the most capable server you can afford and make sure it is expandable to meet your future needs, through the addition of more RAM, more processors, and more disk space. Even with all of that, it is common for servers to be replaced three to four years from the date they were placed into service.

Test the Server Hardware

You found all your server hardware in the Windows 2000 Server HCL, you made sure your server is adequately sized, you purchased it, and you have your shiny new Windows 2000 Server CD-ROMs sitting there, all ready to be installed. Is it time to start the installation yet? Well, not quite. Before installing any NOS, particularly on a server that will be used for production, make sure you carry out hardware testing (also called *burn-in*) on the server before installing Windows 2000 Server. Computer hardware tends to be most reliable after it has been running for a while. In other words, failures tend to happen when equipment is new, and the chance of hardware failure decreases rapidly after the hardware has been up and running for 30 to 90 days. Because of this, it's a good idea to test new servers for at least a week (testing for two weeks is even better) before proceeding to install the NOS. Doing this can help provoke any early failures in the equipment, during a time when they're easy to fix and they won't affect any users or the network. Moreover, many servers have a 30-day return or exchange policy from their manufacturer, so if you discover problems, you'll have a chance to return the system and perhaps start over with a different model.

You test the hardware using diagnostic software that should have come with the server or is available from the maker of the server. Most such diagnostic software enables you to choose which components of the system are tested and enables you to test them in an endless loop, logging any discovered errors to a floppy disk or to the screen. You should focus the tests on the following components:

- Processor(s)

- System board components (interrupt controllers, direct memory access [DMA] controllers, and other motherboard support circuitry)

- RAM

- Disk surfaces

TIP

Server-testing software often enables you to choose between nondestructive and destructive testing of the disks. (Destructive means any data on the disks is erased during the testing.) Destructive testing is best to discover any errors on the disks. This is one reason that you want to carry out this testing before you install your NOS.

If the diagnostic software allows you to do so, you can usually safely skip testing components such as the keyboard or the display. Your primary concern is that the unit continues running properly when it is under load for an extended period of time. You also want to make sure that the RAM is working properly and that no bad sectors show up on the disks during testing. It's also a good idea during testing to power the unit on and shut it down a number of times, since the impact to the unit of initially powering on often can provoke a failure in any marginal components.

Survey the Server Prior to an In-Place Upgrade

The Windows 2000 family of products takes advantage of PnP (Plug and Play) hardware, and can detect and automatically configure any PnP devices to work with Windows 2000 Server during the installation. PnP is not perfect, though. For one thing, you might have installed components that are not PnP devices, and Windows 2000 will be unable to configure those devices. Also, sometimes PnP devices can conflict with other devices, or the drivers for a specific device might not allow proper configuration for some reason. Because of these imperfections, it's important to survey the components installed in the server before installing Windows 2000 Server as an upgrade. Performing a survey is not really important when setting up a new server.

For the survey, write down all the installed devices, along with the resources that each one uses in the server. The resources include the IRQ channel, DMA channel, and memory I/O addresses used by each device. Then, if a device isn't working properly after you install Windows 2000 Server, you might be able to configure the device manually to known settings that work.

TIP

Some server computers come with utilities such as Compaq's SmartStart. Such utilities handle the server at a hardware level and keep the information in a space separate from the NOS. Server utilities such as Compaq's make life much easier when you are trying to troubleshoot a hardware problem with the server.

Make Preinstallation Decisions

After configuring, checking, preparing, and testing your hardware, you can actually begin installing Windows 2000 Server. During this process, you first spend time making a number of important preinstallation decisions that you must be prepared to specify during the installation. The following sections discuss these choices.

Upgrade or Install?

You can upgrade a server running Windows NT Server 3.51 or 4.0 to Windows 2000 Server and maintain all your existing settings, user accounts, file permissions, and so forth. You can also perform a full installation where you wipe out any existing NOS on the server. You must perform a full installation to a new server or to one running any NOS other than Windows NT Server. If you are running an upgradeable version of Windows NT Server, however, pros and cons exist to both approaches.

NOTE

If you are running Windows NT Server 4 Enterprise Edition, you can upgrade only to Windows 2000 Advanced Server.

The main benefit to upgrading is that all your existing settings under Windows NT Server will be maintained and automatically carried forward into your Windows 2000 Server installation. These include networking details, such as TCP/IP configuration information, as well as security settings that you might have tediously set up over time. In fact, if the server can be upgraded, you should plan on doing so, unless you need to change something fundamental in the server, such as changing from FAT to NTFS.

FAT or NTFS?

Windows 2000 Server supports hard disks formatted using either File Allocation Table (FAT16 and FAT32) or NT File System (NTFS). Important advantages exist to using NTFS under Windows 2000 and, in some cases, it is required. You would want to install Windows 2000 Server onto a disk that uses the FAT file system only when the system must be used in a dual-boot setup, where it retains the capability to boot another operating system, such as Windows 98. Even in cases where you need to maintain dual-boot capability, though, you're better off maintaining a primary FAT partition for the other operating system and setting up an extended partition with NTFS to hold Windows 2000 Server. In such cases, Windows 2000 automatically installs dual-boot support that enables you to choose which operating system to use when the system is started.

TIP

If you are installing Windows 2000 Server onto a system that has only a single FAT partition and you want to dual-boot Windows 2000 Server with that other operating system, but you want to establish a new NTFS partition for Windows 2000 without having to destroy the existing FAT partition, you can use ServerMagic from PowerQuest to accomplish this. ServerMagic enables you to resize an existing FAT partition without losing any of its data and it also fully supports FAT and NTFS partitions. Without a product such as ServerMagic, you instead have to back up the FAT partition, destroy it as you repartition the hard disk, and then restore the other operating system (and all applications and files) to the new, smaller FAT partition.

NTFS is required for any Windows 2000 Servers that will function as Domain Controllers and also is the only file system that enables you to take full advantage of Windows 2000's security features. Moreover, NTFS is optimized for server performance and performs better than FAT under almost all circumstances.

Domain Controller, Member Server, or Stand-Alone Server?

Before deciding this question, you need to understand two important concepts in Windows 2000 networks: domains and workgroups. A *domain* is a sophisticated administrative grouping of computers on a Windows 2000 network that makes it possible to administer the network's resources from a single point and to implement strong security. Domains enable you to manage multiple Windows 2000 or Windows NT servers more easily. A *workgroup* is a simple collection of computers on a network and is suited only to pure peer-to-peer networks.

You can configure Windows 2000 Servers in one of three modes to support either domains or workgroups, as follows:

- Domain Controllers hold the domain's Active Directory information and authenticate users and access to resources. Most Windows 2000 networks have at least one domain and therefore need at least one Domain Controller.

- Member servers are part of a domain, but do not hold a copy of the Active Directory information.

- Stand-alone servers do not participate in a domain but instead participate in a workgroup.

Prior to Windows 2000, Windows NT servers that were Domain Controllers had to be designated as either Primary Domain Controllers (PDCs) or Backup Domain Controllers

(BDCs). Windows 2000 with Active Directory simplifies matters significantly so that all Windows 2000 Domain Controllers are simply that: Domain Controllers. Each Domain Controller holds a copy of the Active Directory data and can perform all the functions of the other Domain Controllers. Previously, the PDC performed all administrative tasks, whereas the BDCs simply kept read-only copies of the domain information to continue authenticating security on the network in case the PDC failed. Windows 2000 Server, on the other hand, uses the concept of *multimaster domain controllers*, which all seamlessly operate the same way as the other Domain Controllers.

TIP

Except in the smallest of networks, it's a very good idea to have two Domain Controllers. This way, all of your domain information is preserved and available to the network should one of the Domain Controllers crash. Domain information is automatically synchronized between the available Domain Controllers.

Per Seat or Per Server?

Another important choice to make when installing Windows 2000 Server is how the server will manage its Client Access Licenses (CALs). Windows 2000 Server supports two different ways of managing CALs: Per Server and Per Seat. *Per Server licensing* assigns the CALs to the server, which will allow only as many connections from computers as there are installed CALs on that server. *Per Seat licensing* requires purchasing a CAL for each of your client computers, which gives them the right to access as many Windows 2000 servers as they wish; the servers will not monitor the number of connections. Generally, Microsoft recommends that you use Per Server licensing when running a single server and Per Seat licensing when running multiple servers. If you are unsure of which mode to use, Microsoft recommends that you choose Per Server because Microsoft lets you change to Per Seat mode once at no cost (whereas changing from Per Seat to Per Server has a price). Carefully review licensing options with your Windows 2000 reseller to determine the most economical way to license your network servers properly.

Wait! Back Up Before Upgrading!

If you are installing Windows 2000 Server as an upgrade to another NOS, such as Windows NT Server, it's vital that you fully back up the server prior to installing Windows 2000 Server. (It's a good idea to make two identical backups, just in case.) You should use whatever backup software you normally use for your existing NOS, making sure the software can properly restore the previous NOS in case you need to "unwind" the upgrade process and revert to your starting point. Even when you are performing an upgrade to Windows NT and will not be reformatting any of the disks, making a preinstall backup is good insurance in case of trouble.

Progress Check

1. What are the three different Windows 2000 Server configurations with respect to support for workgroups or domains?

2. What are the four versions of Windows 2000 called?

CRITICAL SKILL

15.3 Install Windows 2000 Server

There are a number of ways to begin the installation of Windows 2000 Server. You can

- Configure the server computer to boot from the Windows 2000 Server CD-ROM
- Begin the installation while running Windows NT Server
- Begin the installation while running Windows 95 or 98
- Prepare boot diskettes and use them to begin the installation process
- Install from a network installation point that has been previously set up

When setting up a new server, you have only two real choices to begin the installation: boot from the Windows 2000 Server CD-ROM or prepare boot diskettes. Most servers can boot from their CD-ROM drives, which is the best way to perform the installation. If you find that you instead need to prepare boot diskettes, you can do so by running the MAKEBOOT.EXE program found on the Windows 2000 Server CD-ROM. The example installation in this module assumes that you are booting the installation process from the Windows 2000 Server CD-ROM.

Run the Windows 2000 Server Setup Program

The following sections describe the process of running the installation program for Windows 2000 Server and installing it onto a server. If you are learning about Windows 2000 Server and have a suitable computer to use, you should take the time to install Windows 2000 Server so that you understand how the process works. Or, if you like, you can read along through the following descriptions in order to familiarize yourself with the installation process. (I recommend actually

---

1. Domain controller, member server, and stand-alone server (stand-alone servers may participate in a workgroup, but not a domain).

2. Professional, Standard Server, Advanced Server, and Datacenter Server.

performing an installation such as the one described here, and then "playing with" the resulting server as a way of more quickly and completely learning about Windows 2000 Server.)

When you boot from the Windows 2000 Server CD-ROM, the program first presents a text-based screen that walks you through the early installation choices you will make. You first press ENTER to confirm that you wish to install Windows 2000 Server, or press F3 to exit the installation program.

The program then prompts you to choose whether you wish to install Windows 2000 Server or to repair an existing Windows 2000 Server installation. You press ENTER to choose to install Windows 2000 Server.

Next, the program requires that you agree to the Windows 2000 Server license agreement. Press F8 to agree to the license and proceed.

The next screen begins the meat of the installation process. You see a screen listing all available disk partitions to which you can install Windows 2000 Server. You can perform the following actions at this point:

- Use the arrow keys and press ENTER to select an existing disk partition.

- Press the letter C on the keyboard to create a new disk partition from unpartitioned disk space (a new server installation usually requires that you create a partition).

- Press the letter D on the keyboard to delete an existing partition (you usually must do this only when removing all vestiges of a previous operating system, after which you will create the installation partition you need).

When you press the letter C to create a partition, the program prompts you for the size of the partition you wish to create. By default, the program offers the maximum size partition. To accept this choice, simply press ENTER, at which point the program creates the new partition. You then return to the screen listing all partitions, and the program displays the new partition that you created as "New (Unformatted)." Choose this partition and press ENTER to proceed.

After you select the new partition, the program prompts you to choose a disk format: either FAT or NTFS. For most servers, you use only NTFS partitions, so choose NTFS and press ENTER to continue. The installation program then formats the partition for you.

NOTE

A brief discussion about choosing between FAT and NTFS appears earlier in this module, in the section "FAT or NTFS?"

After the format completes, files necessary to continue the installation of Windows 2000 Server are automatically copied to the new partition. After copying the files, the program automatically restarts the system, and the graphical portion of the installation starts automatically.

The graphical setup program walks you through various installation choices you must make during the setup process. Although you can modify most of these choices later, it's best if you can make the correct choices the first time during the initial installation of Windows 2000 Server. The remainder of this section continues the installation process and discusses the choices that the program presents.

The graphical setup program first attempts to detect and set up all the basic devices installed in the computer. This process takes five to ten minutes.

Once the basic devices are installed and set up, you are prompted to choose the locale and keyboard settings you wish. These choices default to English (United States) and U.S. Keyboard Layout (if you're using a copy of Windows 2000 Server purchased for the United States), so you can usually just click the Next button to continue.

Next, the program prompts you to enter your name and organization name. Most companies prefer that you *not* personalize the operating system to a particular individual. Instead, use a name such as "IT Department" and then enter your company's name in the field provided. Click Next to continue.

The program then prompts you to choose either Per Server or Per Seat licensing. Refer to the discussion earlier in this module, in the section "Per Seat or Per Server?" which discusses this choice. Then choose the appropriate option button. If you choose Per Server, select the number of licenses you own. Then click Next to continue.

The next dialog box is important. You enter the name of the computer to which you are installing Windows 2000 Server; you also enter the initial Administrator password. The computer name that you choose will be the name of the server and the name seen by users when they browse the servers on the network. If possible, you should choose a name that you won't need to change later. For the Administrator password, choose a good, strong password that could not easily be guessed. The Administrator password is the key to doing anything you need to do with the server, so you need to choose a password that will be secure. As a rule of thumb, choose an Administrator password with eight or more characters, including both letters and numbers. Make sure it's also a password you will remember! After completing the fields, click Next to continue.

Next, the program displays a dialog box that lists all the different components that you can optionally install with Windows 2000 Server. If you are following along and performing a sample installation of Windows 2000 Server to learn about the installation process, only basic choices related to setting up a file and print server should be selected. However, the following is a list of all the choices (you can choose to add these components after the main installation is complete):

- **Certificate Services (1.5MB)**   Certificate Services are used to enable public-key applications. You do not need to install this option unless you have an application that requires these services.

- **Cluster Services (2.2MB)**   Windows 2000 Cluster Services enable two or more servers to share a common workload and to provide fail-over support in case one of the servers experiences a hardware failure. You do not need to install this option unless you are building a high-availability server cluster.

- **Internet Information Server (ISS) (28.7MB)**   IIS allows a Windows 2000 Server to operate as a web and FTP server. Choosing this option installs IIS along with a number of support features related to IIS. You do not need to install IIS for a file and print server.

- **Management and Monitoring Tools (15.7MB)**   Choosing this option installs supplemental management tools, including the following:

  - Connection Manager components for managing RAS and dial-up connections

  - Directory Service Migration Tool for migrating from NetWare Directory Services (NDS) to Windows 2000 Active Directory

  - Network Monitor Tools, which you can use to perform rudimentary network packet analysis and decoding

  - Simple Network Management Protocol, which lets the Windows 2000 Server report management information to an SNMP management computer on the network

TIP

For a basic fileserver or print server, it's a good idea to choose to install the Network Monitor Tools, which you can select as part of the Management and Monitoring Tools installation option. First, select Management and Monitoring Tools in the dialog box, and then click on the Details button and choose Network Monitor Tools.

- **Message Queuing Services (2.4MB)**   These services queue network messages used with certain client/server applications. Unless such an application requires you to do so, you needn't install this tool.

- **Microsoft Script Debugger (1.6MB)**   This option adds tools that enable you to debug 'scripts written in VBScript and JScript. Because you might occasionally need to access the Internet through a web browser on the server (to download driver updates, for example) and because you might develop server-based scripts written in VBScript or JScript, you should choose to install this tool.

- **Networking Services (3.6MB)**   This installation choice is a catch-all for a wide variety of network services that you might choose to install on your server. In particular, you should consider selecting several of these options for a fileserver or print server. First, consider installing Dynamic Host Configuration Protocol (DHCP), which allows the server to manage a range of IP addresses and to assign addresses automatically to client computers. Second, consider installing Windows Internet Name Service (WINS), which provides name resolution and browsing support to client computers that are running pre-Windows 2000 operating systems (such as Windows NT and Windows 9*x*) and are using only the TCP/IP protocol. Neither of these options is required for a basic fileserver or print server, however.

- **Other Network File and Print Services**   This option enables you to install the additional support required to share the server's files and printers with Macintosh computers and UNIX-based computers. You needn't select this option if all your client computers are running some version of Windows.

- **Remote Installation Services (RIS) (1.4MB)**   With RIS, you can remotely install Windows 2000 Professional onto network computers that support a feature called *remote boot.* You need a dedicated partition on the server to host the Windows 2000 Professional disk images. You do not need this tool for a basic file and print server.

- **Remote Storage (3.5MB)**   This feature enables you to configure a Windows 2000 Server disk to move rarely accessed files automatically onto an available tape drive or writeable CD. The operating system can automatically recall these files if they are needed. Most servers do not need this tool.

- **Terminal Services (14.3MB) and Terminal Services Licensing (0.4MB)**   These two options enable a Windows 2000 Server host multiple Windows sessions for remote computers, in which the applications execute on the server and the client computer handles only the display and keyboard/mouse input for the application. Windows Terminal Services works somewhat the same as mainframes, where all the work is performed on the mainframe and the client acts only as a terminal to the mainframe. You do not need these options for fileservers or print servers.

TIP

Understanding and administering Terminal Services can be complicated and requires some techniques not readily apparent at first glance. Taking a course or purchasing a book on Terminal Services is probably a good suggestion, especially if using Terminal Services as an exclusive remote control or remote access solution.

After choosing from the preceding options, click Next to continue. The program then prompts you for information about a modem attached to the server, if one exists. You can provide your area code and any number you need to dial to get an outside line, and indicate whether the phone line supports tone dialing or pulse dialing. Complete the requested fields and click Next to continue.

Next, the program prompts you to enter the correct date and time, as well as the time zone in which the server resides. Update these fields if necessary and click Next to continue.

The program next prompts you to select your network settings. You can choose between Typical settings or Custom settings. For a small network, you can usually safely choose the Typical settings option. Choosing Custom settings enables you to define details, such as exactly what networking components will be installed and how each is configured. For this example of a basic installation of Windows 2000 Server, Typical settings is chosen.

Next, the program prompts you to choose between setting up Windows 2000 Server as a member of a workgroup or a domain. A discussion about the differences between these two choices appeared earlier in this module, in the section "Domain Controller, Member Server, or Stand-Alone Server?" You cannot join the new server to a domain, however, unless the domain already exists and a Domain Controller is available to authenticate (allow) the new server into the domain. For a new server, even one that will be a Domain Controller, therefore, choose Workgroup and click Next to proceed.

The setup program then completes its portion of the installation of Windows 2000 Server, using the information you provided.

Project 15-1 Install Windows 2000 Server for Learning

In this project, you will install Windows 2000 Standard Server onto a computer running Windows ME. This is a good way to start to learn about Windows 2000 Server without having to dedicate a computer to running it. When complete, you will be able to dual-boot to either Windows 98 (or other Win9x operating systems, like Windows ME) or Windows 2000 Standard Server.

Step by Step

1. On the computer that already has an earlier version of Windows installed, make sure that it has adequate capacity to install and run Windows 2000 Server. This topic is discussed earlier in this module, but basically the computer should have a Pentium 133MHz or faster processor, 256MB of RAM, and about 1GB of free disk space.

2. Insert the Windows 2000 Server CD-ROM and boot the computer to the CD-ROM drive. (On some computers, you may have to change your BIOS settings to enable booting from CD-ROM.)

3. Follow through the text-based portion of the installation process. When you are prompted for a disk partition on which to install Windows 2000 Server, you can choose any available disk partition that has adequate space, including the partition that already contains Windows. Do not choose to format the disk if you are installing to the partition that contains Windows; Windows 2000 Server will install and run on a FAT- or FAT32-formatted partition. If, however, you have an available partition that you don't mind erasing, you can choose to format that partition with NTFS and to install Windows 2000 Server to that partition. Provided the main partition is unchanged, dual-boot will still work in this configuration.

4. Restart the computer at the end of the text-based installation portion to begin the graphical portion of the installation.

5. Follow through and complete the basic questions asked during the beginning of the graphical installation, such as choosing a locale and keyboard and entering your name.

6. When prompted, choose Per Seat licensing for a stand-alone learning server.

7. When prompted, enter in a name for this server (this is the name by which the server will be seen on the network) and assign an Administrator password (make sure it's one you won't forget).

8. When prompted, make appropriate choices about what Windows 2000 Server services to install. For a good all-around server on which to begin learning about Windows 2000 Server, choose Internet Information Server, Management and Monitoring Tools, and Networking Services.

9. Complete the remainder of the installation, choosing Typical when prompted for the networking portion of the server setup, and either Domain Controller or Stand-Alone Server when prompted for the server type. Do NOT choose Domain Controller if you are performing this installation in a functioning company network without checking first with the network administrator (and probably not even then to avoid causing problems on the network). If you are using a small home network, however, you can experiment with working with a Domain Controller by choosing that option.

After the graphical portion of the installation completes, you are prompted to restart the computer. When the computer restarts, you will see a menu that lets you choose to boot to either Windows 2000 Server (this will be the default choice) or the existing version of Windows.

Project Summary

In this project, you installed Windows 2000 Server in a common configuration used to learn about the network operating system. Once complete, you can start to explore the various administrative tasks on the server, using the following module as a basic guide. Assuming that you do this on a computer on which you do other work, you installed Windows 2000 Server in such a way that you can still access your existing productive Windows operating system.

Complete Windows 2000 Server Setup

After the main setup program completes, the system restarts to the Windows 2000 Server login prompt. To log in to the server, press CTRL-ALT-DEL. You log in as Administrator, using the password you defined as part of the setup process in the preceding section. The Windows 2000 Server desktop then appears, along with the Windows 2000 Configure Your Server program (called the Server Configuration program for the remainder of this section), which walks you through the remaining steps required to get the server operational. Figure 15-1 shows the Server Configuration program running on the Windows 2000 desktop.

If you are setting up a single server for a small network—the assumption made for the example in this module—you can choose the option marked "This is the only server in my network," as shown in Figure 15-1. For more complicated Windows 2000 installations, choose "There are already one or more servers operating in my network," which requires more detailed setup knowledge.

(continued)

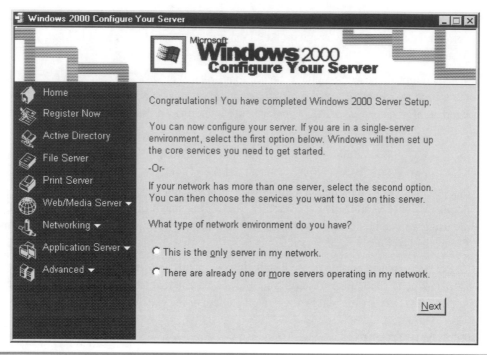

Figure 15-1 The Windows 2000 Server Configuration program

You then see a confirmation screen (shown in Figure 15-2) that confirms you want to set up the server with Active Directory, DHCP, and DNS services, which are standard for a single server in a network. If you like, you can read more about these services by clicking the links shown in the Server Configuration dialog box. Once you are done, click Next to proceed.

Next, the program prompts you for the name of the domain you will create and any Internet domain of which the server needs to be aware. The domain name cannot have spaces and you should choose a simple name, one you can work with easily. Many companies choose the name of their company, or some abbreviation thereof, for their domain name. You also enter any Internet domain name that exists for your network. The Internet domain name is one owned by your company. For example, if you work for a company called Acme Corporation, you can call your Windows 2000 domain ACME, and your Internet domain would probably be acme.com. (If your company doesn't have an Internet domain name registered, enter **local** in the field instead.) For this example, the Windows 2000 domain name will be OMH and the Internet domain name will be **local**. Enter your information and click Next to continue. After a pause, the program warns you that the choices you have made will now be installed and the server will be restarted. Click Next a second time to do this. Note that the program might prompt you for a Windows 2000 Server CD-ROM during this process.

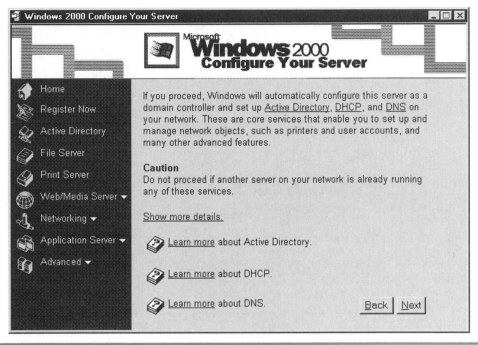

Figure 15-2 Confirming the installation of core network services

After the system installs the components needed and restarts, you need to complete some final steps in the Server Configuration program (shown in Project 15-2), after which you will be done installing the server.

Project 15-2 Completing a Network Server Configuration

This project shows you how to complete the configuration of a network server. This is distinct from the installation of Windows 2000 Server, and involves making choices about the network that the server will service, as well as enabling some important services. In this example, you are configuring a server that is acting as a Domain Controller. The configuration is something that you run whenever you want, although typically it immediately follows installation.

Step by Step

1. Right-click the desktop object My Network Places and choose Properties from the pop-up menu.

2. Right-click the Local Area Connection object and choose Properties from the pop-up menu. This opens the Local Area Connection Properties dialog box, shown in Figure 15-3.

(continued)

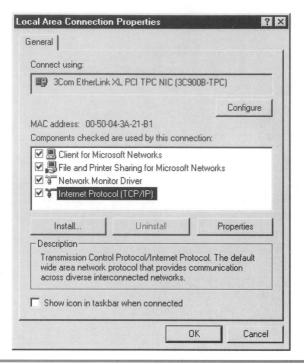

Figure 15-3 The Local Area Connection Properties dialog box

3. Choose the Internet Protocol entry and click the Properties button.

4. Click the Use the Following IP Address option button.

5. Enter the correct IP number for this server to use as its IP address. If you don't have an existing range of numbers and your network isn't directly connected to the Internet, use 10.10.1.1.

6. Enter the correct subnet mask. If your network hasn't used subnet masks before, choose 255.0.0.0.

7. In the Preferred DNS Server field, enter the IP address that you just assigned to the server. In this example, 10.10.1.1 is used. At this point, the Internet Protocol (TCP/IP) Properties dialog box should look like that shown in Figure 15-4. Click OK to close the various Properties dialog boxes already opened.

8. You now need to authorize DHCP services. Open the Start menu, then choose Programs, Administrative Tools, and DHCP. You then see the DHCP Manager program, as shown in Figure 15-5.

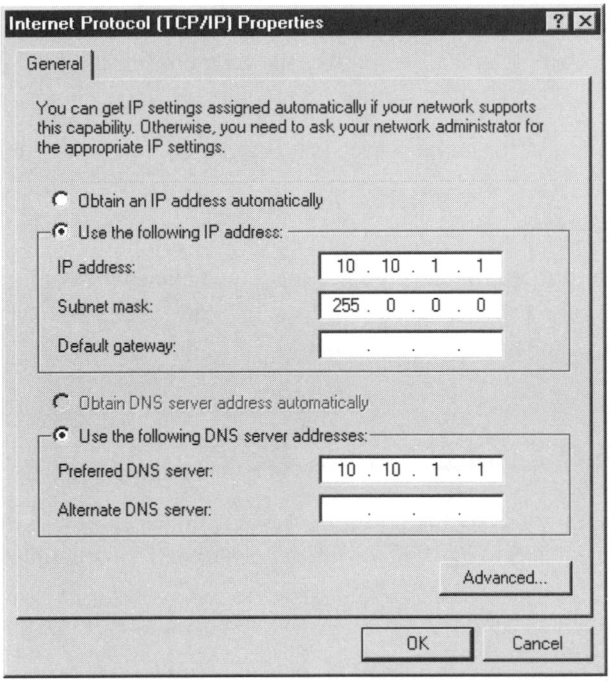

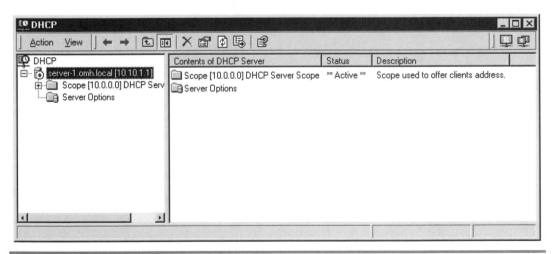

Figure 15-4 The Internet Protocol (TCP/IP) Properties dialog box with sample choices

Figure 15-5 The DHCP Manager program

(continued)

9. Expand the tree in the left pane. Then, right-click the server shown in the pane, choose All Tasks, and then Authorize. This authorizes the server to fulfill DHCP requests and enables the server to parcel out IP addresses to client computers on the network.

10. Shut down and restart the server for the preceding changes to take effect.

Project Summary

Congratulations! By completing this project you have finished the configuration of a Windows 2000 Server acting as a Domain Controller. You now have a server capable of serving the needs of many users and of performing a number of useful tasks.

CRITICAL SKILL
15.4 Configure a Server Client

Before you can *really* finish setting up a new server, you need to test its ability to allow a client computer to connect to it. To do this, you need to perform the following steps:

1. Create a test user account.

2. Create a shared resource on the server for the client computer to access.

3. Configure a Windows 9*x* client to connect to the server.

4. Actually log in to the server with the client computer and verify that everything is working properly.

The following sections explain how to carry out these tasks.

Create a User Account

The first order of business to confirm server functionality is to create a test user account, with which you can log in to the server from a network computer. You can use the Administrator account for this if you wish to skip this step, but using a sample user account is better.

Start by opening the Start menu, then Programs, then Administrative Tools. Then, finally select the entry called Active Directory Users and Computers. This opens the Windows Management Console application with the Active Directory Users and Computers settings, as shown in Figure 15-6.

As with most Windows programs, the left pane enables you to navigate a tree (in this case, the tree of user and computer objects) and the right pane shows the details for the selected branch of the tree. To add a user, right-click the server in the left pane, choose New, and then choose User from the pop-up menu. You then see the Create New Object (User) dialog box shown in Figure 15-7.

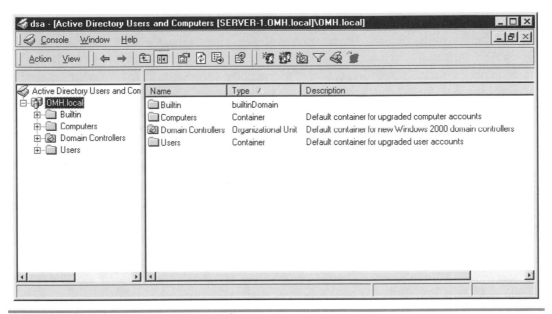

Figure 15-6 Active Directory Users and Computers

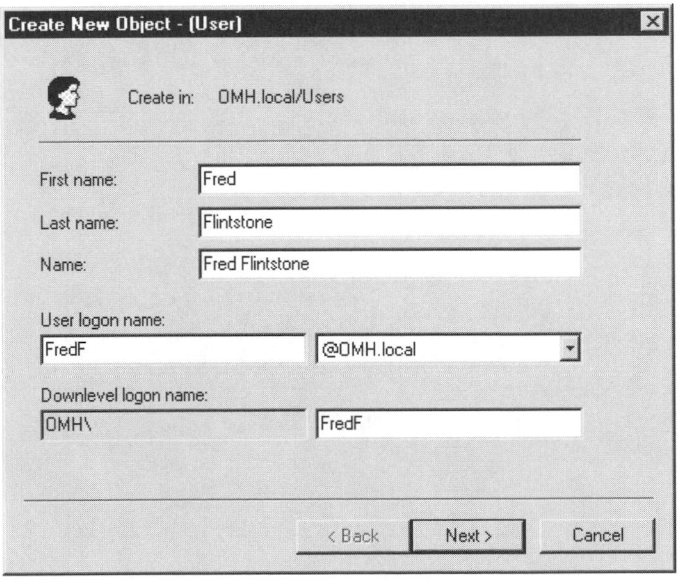

Figure 15-7 Create New Object (User) dialog box

Enter the first and last name for the user you wish to create and then enter a logon name in the User Logon Name field. The program generates the remaining fields automatically based on the information you just entered, although you can change their settings if you want. In the example shown in Figure 15-7, the user FredF will log in to Active Directory using the user account **fredf@omh.local**. After entering in the information, click Next to continue.

Now enter a starting password for the account you just created. For this example, simply use the password **password**. (Remember to remove this test user account after you finish with your testing. You don't ever want to leave a user account active on the system with a password that others can easily guess.) Click Next to continue and then click Finish to complete creating the user account.

Create a Shared Folder

The next step is to create a resource—in this case a folder—that the test user should be able to access from a computer on the network. Windows 2000 Server shares folders through a mechanism called a *share*. A *share* is a browseable resource that remote users can access, provided they have sufficient privileges to do so.

To set a folder so it can be accessed over the network, create a normal folder on one of the server's disk drives. Right-click the folder and choose Sharing from the pop-up menu. This displays the Sharing tab of the folder's Properties dialog box, as shown in Figure 15-8.

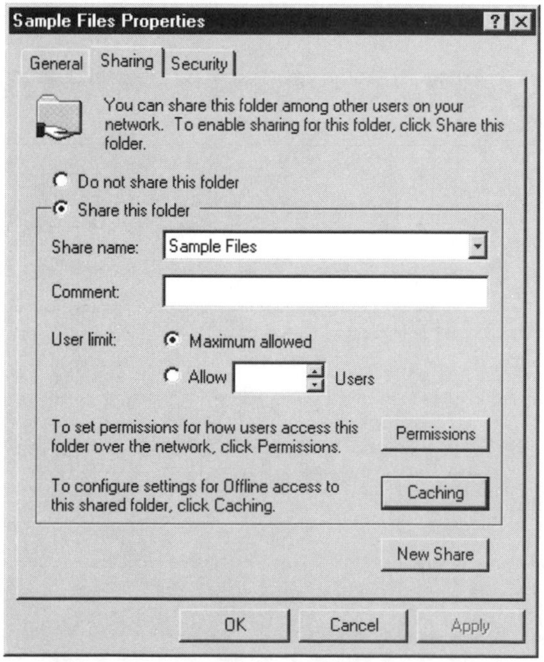

Figure 15-8 The Sharing tab of a folder's Properties dialog box

To make the folder shared, first click the Share This Folder option button. Next, review the share name (which is automatically assigned based on the folder name) and modify it if you like. Then click OK to finish sharing the folder.

TIP

By default, new shares created on the server allow everyone full control of their contents. To change this default setting, you need to click the Permissions button and then modify the permissions. This is discussed in more detail in Module 16.

Set Up a Windows 9x Client to Access the Server

To set up a Windows 95 or Windows 98 client to access the new server, follow these steps:

1. In the Control Panel, open the Network object. This activates the Network dialog box.

2. Click the Add button, choose Client in the Select Network Component Type dialog box, and then click Add to bring up the Select Network Client dialog box.

3. In the Select Network Client dialog box, choose Microsoft from the list of manufacturers, and then choose Client for Microsoft Networks in the right pane (see Figure 15-9). Click OK to continue.

4. After a short while, the Network dialog box reappears in the foreground, with both the Client for Microsoft Networks and the TCP/IP protocol installed, as shown in Figure 15-10.

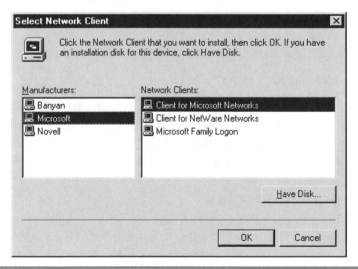

Figure 15-9 Choosing to install Client for Microsoft Networks

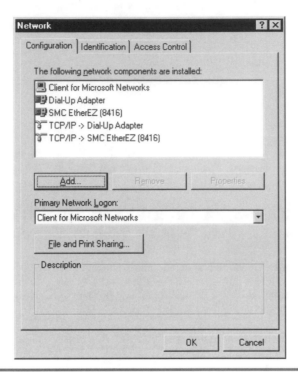

Figure 15-10 The Network Properties dialog box with installed components

5. Select Client for Microsoft Networks and click the Properties button.

6. In the Client for Microsoft Networks Properties dialog box, select the checkbox Log Onto Windows NT Domain, and then type the name of the domain in the field provided. For the example used in this module, the domain name is simply OMH.

7. Click OK to close the Network dialog box.

Once you close the Network dialog box, you might be prompted for your Windows 9*x* CD-ROM so that the necessary components can be installed. After the installation of the network components is complete, the program prompts you to restart the computer, which you must do before the network settings are made active.

Test the Client Connection

After completing the preceding steps, you can now log on to the domain being administered by Windows 2000 Server and browse the files that you placed into the shared folder.

When the computer restarts after you complete the steps in the preceding section, the program prompts you to log in to the domain before displaying the Windows 9*x* desktop.

Enter the test user account name (FredF), the domain name (OMH), and the password that you assigned (password) to log in to the domain. If you have entered the information correctly, you will log in to the domain. If any problems occur, such as an unrecognized username, password, or domain name, the program warns you and gives you a chance to correct them.

Once Windows 9*x* starts, you should be able to open Network Neighborhood and see the server that you installed included in the list of servers. When you open the server, you can see any shares on the server to which you have access. Among those folders, you will see netlogin and sysvol, as well as the folder that you created and shared. You should be able to open the sample share and see the files that you placed in the folder. You should also be able to manipulate those files, delete them, rename them, open them, and so forth just as if you were working with files on a local hard disk.

TIP

Sometimes a server might not appear automatically in Network Neighborhood, particularly if it has recently been installed. If you encounter this problem, open the Start menu, choose Find, and then choose Computer. Type the name of the server that you set up in the Find dialog box and click Find Now. After a moment, the server should appear in the Find dialog box and you can double-click to open it.

✓ *Module 15 Mastery Check*

1. Which of the following are valid Windows 2000 Server configurations?

    A. Member server

    B. Domain Controller

    C. Domain partner

    D. Stand-alone server

    E. Primary Domain Controller

2. In what general circumstances does Microsoft recommend choosing either Per Seat client licensing or Per Server client licensing?

3. True or false: All Windows 2000 Server's file and folder security features are available on the FAT32 file system.

4. Name the three different server versions of Windows 2000 Server.

5. Prior to setting up a new server, you should spend 1–2 weeks performing a

    _____.

6. True or false: You can install Windows 2000 Server as an in-place upgrade to Netware 5 or Netware 6.

7. True or false: The Administrator account is a temporary account used only for the initial setup of Windows 2000 Server.

8. Prior to installing Windows 2000 Server as an in-place upgrade from Windows NT, you should first perform both a _____ and _____.

9. How much available disk space do you need to install Windows 2000 Server?

10. What is the name of the resource that lets you know whether a computer is compatible with Windows 2000 Server?

Module 16

Administering Windows 2000 Server: The Basics

nstalling and setting up Windows 2000 Server is only the tip of the iceberg. Far more important and time-consuming is the process of administering the server. This process includes regular and common duties such as adding new users, deleting old users, assigning permissions to users, performing backups, and so forth. These topics are the subject of this module. Learning how to do all these things and to do them well will ensure that the network and the server remain productive and secure.

CRITICAL SKILL
16.1 # Review Network Security

Before delving into the administrative activities discussed in this module, you should spend some time thinking about network security and how it relates to your specific company. Network security is an important subject, and administering a server must be predicated on maintaining appropriate security for your network.

The key here is to remember that every network has an appropriate level of security. The security requirements for a Department of Defense (DoD) contractor who designs military equipment will be different from the security requirements for a company that operates restaurants. The important thing, therefore, is first to determine the appropriate security needs of your network. Many beginning network administrators forget this important fact and set up their networks to follow the strongest security measures available. The problem with this approach is that these measures almost always reduce the productivity of people using the network. You need to strike a balance between productivity and security, and the answer will be different for every company.

For example, Windows 2000 Server enables you to set various security policies that apply to users. These include forcing password changes at intervals you specify, requiring that passwords be of a certain minimum length, causing new passwords always to be unique and not reuses of old passwords, and so on. You could set up these policies to require passwords that are at least 20 characters long and that must be changed weekly. If users don't resort to writing down their passwords so they can remember them from week to week, these settings would be more secure than shorter, less-frequently changed passwords. A 20-character password is virtually impossible to crack using standard methods, and weekly password changes reduce the chance that someone else will discover a user's password and be free to use it for an extended period of time. The problem with policies this strict, however, is that users will frequently forget their passwords, be locked out of the system for periods of time, and require a lot of help from the network administrator (you!) to clear up these problems each time they occur. For a DoD contractor, these trade-offs might be worthwhile. For the restaurant operator, however, they would be inappropriate and would end up hurting the company more than they help. So, the point to remember is that network security should always be appropriate to the company and its specific network, and that it is important to define appropriate security levels early on and to get the necessary support from management for the trade-offs you think appropriate.

A related point is this: Sometimes security that is too strong results in reduced security over the long run, at least for certain things. For example, in the preceding example with the frequently changing, 20-character passwords, you can be assured that a large percentage of users will have to write down their passwords so they can remember them and gain access to the system. The problem here, of course, is that a written password is far less secure than one that is remembered, because someone else can find the written password and bypass security easily after doing so.

The final point—and the reason you should pay attention to this subject before learning about administration—is that you should determine the appropriate network security early so that you can allow for it as you administer the network on a daily basis. Network security doesn't have to take up much of your time, provided you set up your administrative procedures so they presuppose the level of security you require. For example, if you know what your password policies will be on the network, it takes only a few seconds to ensure that each new user has those policies set for their account. If you know that you maintain a paper-based log of changes to security groups in the network, then it takes only a second to follow this procedure as you change group membership occasionally. Failing to determine these security practices and policies early on will result in having to undertake much larger projects as part of a security review or audit. Security is an area where you're much better off doing things right the first time!

CRITICAL SKILL
16.2 Administer User Accounts

For anyone—including the administrator—to gain access to a Windows 2000 Server, he or she must have an account established on the server or in the domain (a *domain* is essentially a collection of security information shared among Windows 2000 servers). The account defines the *user name* (the name by which the user is known to the system) and the user's password, along with a host of other information specific to each user. Creating, maintaining, and deleting user accounts is easy with Windows 2000 Server.

TIP

Every account created for a Windows 2000 Server domain is assigned a special number, called a Security ID (SID). The server actually recognizes the user by this number. SIDs are said to be "unique across space and time." This means that no two users will ever have the same SID, even if they have the same user name or even the same password. This is because the SID is made up of a unique number assigned to the domain and then a sequential number assigned to each created account (with billions of unique user-specific numbers available). If you have a user called Frank, delete that account, then create another account called Frank, both accounts will have different SIDs. This ensures that no user account will accidentally receive permissions originally assigned to another user of the same name.

To maintain user accounts, you use the Active Directory (AD) Users and Computers management console. You can open this console by clicking the Start menu, choosing Programs, then selecting Administrative Tools. Once the console is open, open the tree for the domain you are administering and then click the Users folder. Your screen should look similar to Figure 16-1 at this point.

To accomplish activities in the console, you first select either a container in the left pane or an object in the right pane, then either right-click the container or object or open the Action pull-down menu and choose from the available options. Because the available options change based on the selected container or object, first selecting an object with which to work is important.

Add a User

To add a user with the AD Users and Computers console, start by selecting the Users container in the left pane (with the tree open to the domain you are administering). Then, right-click the Users container, choose New from the pop-up menu, and then choose User from the submenu. You see the Create New Object (User) dialog box shown in Figure 16-2.

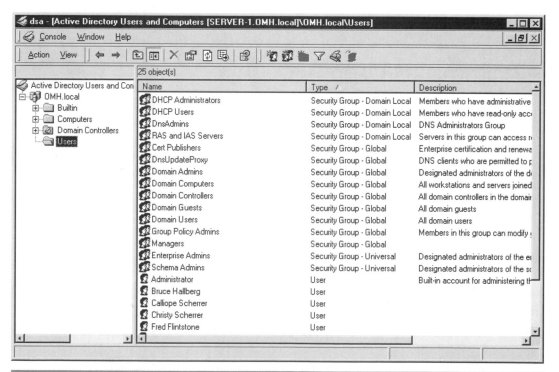

Figure 16-1 The Active Directory Users and Computers console

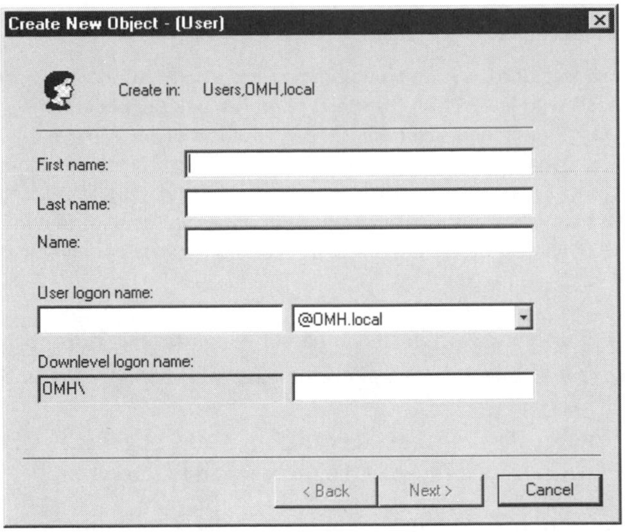

Figure 16-2 Use the Create New Object (User) dialog box to add a new user

Fill in the First Name, Last Name, and User Logon Name fields. Then, click the Next button to move to the next dialog box, which is shown in Figure 16-3.

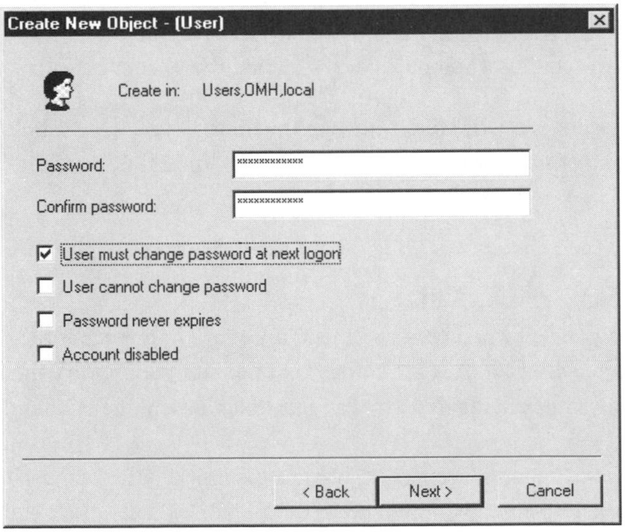

Figure 16-3 The second dialog box for adding a new user

TIP

You should establish standards by which you assign logon names on your network. Small networks (those with fewer than 50 users) often just use people's first names, followed by the first initial of their last names when conflicts arise. A more commonly used convention is to use the user's last name followed by the first initial of their first name. This latter standard allows far more combinations before conflicts arise, and you can then resolve any conflicts that arise by adding the person's middle initial, a number, or some other change so that all user names at any given time on the system are unique.

In the second dialog box, which has no name, you enter the initial password that the account will use. You also select several options that will apply to the account, as follows:

- **User Must Change Password at Next Logon**   Selecting this checkbox forces users to choose their own password when they first log in to the system.

- **User Cannot Change Password**   You might select this option for resource accounts if you do not want to enable the user to change their password. Generally, however, you should not select this option; most sites allow users to change their own password, and you want to enable them to do so if you've also set passwords to automatically expire.

- **Password Never Expires**   Choose this option to allow the password to remain viable for as long as the user chooses to use it. Activating this option for most users is generally considered a poor security practice, so consider carefully whether you should enable this option.

- **Account Disabled**   Selecting this option disables the new account. The administrator can enable the account when needed by clearing the checkbox.

After entering the password and selecting the options you want, click Next to continue. You will then see a confirmation screen. Click Next a final time to create the account or click Back to return to make any needed changes.

Modify a User Account

The dialog boxes you see when creating a user account are much simpler than the one you see when modifying a user account. The dialog box in which you modify the information about a user contains many other fields that you can use to document the account and to set some other security options.

To modify an existing user account, right-click the user object you wish to modify and choose Properties from the pop-up menu. You then see the tabbed dialog box shown in Figure 16-4.

In the first two tabs, General and Address, you can enter some additional information about the user, such as his or her title, mailing address, telephone number, e-mail account,

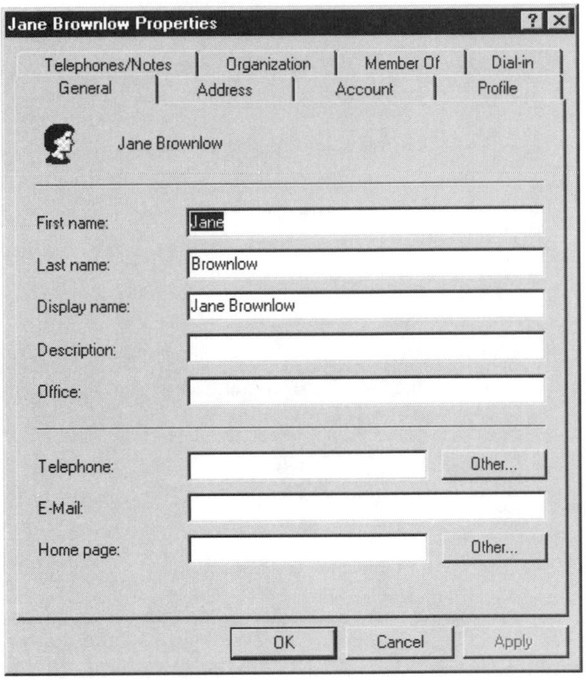

Figure 16-4 A user's Properties dialog box

and so forth. Because Active Directory also integrates with new versions of Exchange Server, this information might be important to enter for your network.

The third tab, Account, is where you can set some important user account options. Figure 16-5 shows the Account tab.

The first line of the dialog box defines the user's Windows 2000 logon name, as well as the Windows 2000 domain in which the user has primary membership. The second line defines the user's Windows NT logon name, which the user can optionally use if he or she needs to log in to the domain from a Windows NT computer or use an application that doesn't yet support Active Directory logins. (Although you can set these two logon names to be different, doing so rarely is a good idea.)

Clicking the Logon Hours button displays the dialog box shown in Figure 16-6. In this dialog box, you select different blocks of time within a standard week and then click the appropriate option button to permit or deny access to the network for that time period. In Figure 16-6, the settings permit logon times only for normal work hours, with some cushion before and after those times to allow for slightly different work hours. By default, users are permitted to log on to the network at any time, any day of the week. For most networks, particularly smaller networks, permitting users to log on at any time is generally acceptable.

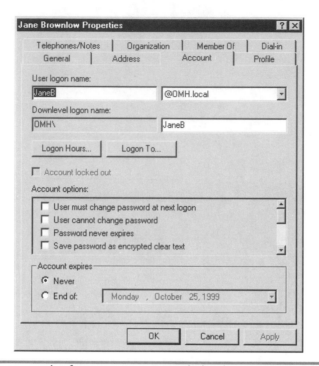

Figure 16-5 The Account tab of a user's Properties dialog box

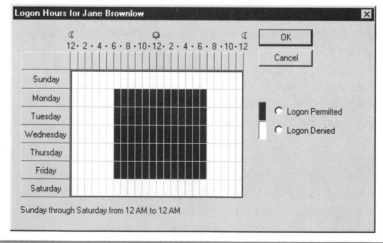

Figure 16-6 Setting logon time restrictions for a user

Another button on the Account tab of the user's Properties dialog box (refer to Figure 16-5) is the Logon To button, which opens the Logon Workstations dialog box shown in Figure 16-7. By default, users can log on to any workstation in the domain, and the domain authenticates them. In some cases, a system might require stricter security, where you specify the computers to which a user account can log on. For example, you might set up a network backup account that you use to back up the network, then leave this account logged on all the time in your locked computer room. Because the backup account has access to all files on the network (or it couldn't do its job), a good idea is to limit that account to log on only to the computer designated for this purpose in the computer room. You use the Logon To button to set up this type of restriction.

TIP

The Logon To feature works only if the network uses the NetBIOS or NetBEUI protocols. This feature will not work with TCP/IP-only networks.

You should be aware that allowing a user named George (for example) to log on to another user's computer does not mean that George can log on with the other user's permissions or access anything that only the other user can access. This simply means George can use the listed physical computer to log on to his own account from that computer.

The Account Options section of the Account tab enables you to select various binary (On/Off) account options. Some of the options, such as requiring a user to change his or her

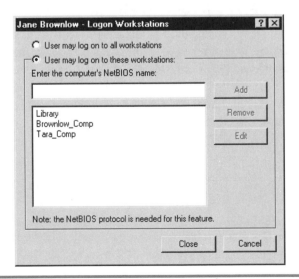

Figure 16-7 Restricting the computers to which a user can log on

password at the next logon, you set as you add the account. Some options listed are unique to the user's Properties dialog box. The two most important of these additional options are Account Is Disabled and Account Is Trusted for Delegation. Account Is Disabled, if selected, disables the user account while leaving it set up within Active Directory. This option is useful if you need to deny access to the network, but might need to reenable the account in the future. (Also, Account Is Disabled is handled as a high-priority change within the domain, and it takes effect immediately, even across large numbers of domain controllers.) Because deleting an account also deletes any permissions the user might have, you should always disable an account if you might need to grant access to the network again to that user. (For example, if someone is on vacation, you could disable the user's account while he or she is gone and then clear the Account Is Disabled checkbox when the user returns.) You must select the second option, Account Is Trusted for Delegation, if you want to designate the user account to administer some part of the domain. Windows 2000 Server enables you to grant administrative rights to portions of the Active Directory tree without having to give administrative rights to the entire domain.

The last option on the Account tab of the user Properties dialog box is the expiration date setting, Account Expires. By default, it is set to Never. If you wish to define an expiration date, you may do so in the End Of field. When the date indicated is reached, the account is automatically disabled (but not deleted, so you can reenable it if you wish).

Another tab that you will use often in the user's Properties dialog box is the Member Of tab, in which you define the security groups for a user. Figure 16-8 shows this tab. Security groups are discussed later in this module.

Delete or Disable a User Account

Deleting a user account is easy using the Active Directory Users and Groups Management console. Use the left pane to select the Users folder and then select the user in the right pane. Either right-click the user and choose Delete, or open the Action pull-down menu and choose Delete.

Disabling an account is just as easy. As before, first select the user account. Then, right-click it and choose Disable Account, or open the Action pull-down menu and choose Disable Account.

TIP

If you need to delete a large number of accounts, you can save time by selecting them all before choosing the Delete or Disable Account commands. Just be sure you haven't selected accounts that you don't want to delete or disable!

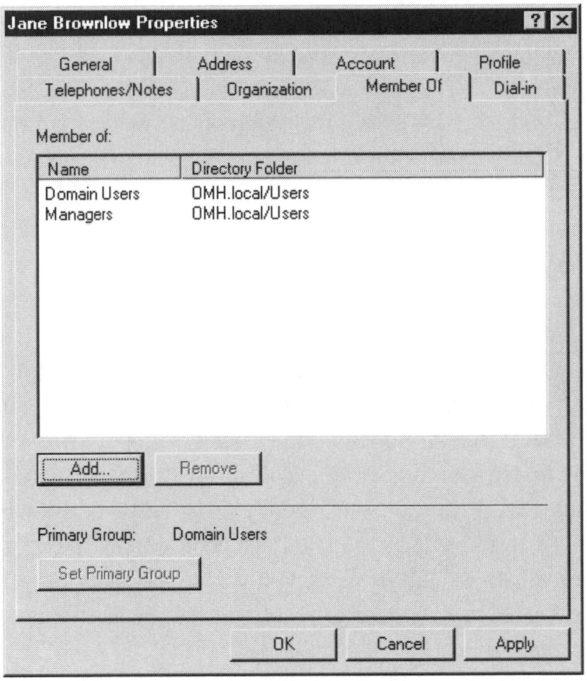

Figure 16-8 Controlling a user's membership in groups

CRITICAL SKILL
16.3 Work with Windows 2000 Security Groups

On any network, you usually have to administer permissions to many different folders and files. If you were able to grant access only by user account, you'd quickly go crazy trying to keep track of all the necessary information. For example, suppose that a group of people, such as an accounting department, has different permissions to access 20 different folders on the server. When a new accountant is hired, do you have to remember or look up what all those 20 folders are so you can give the accountant the same permissions as the rest of his or her department? Or, suppose that a user who has many different permissions changes departments. Do you have to find each permission that the user has so you can make sure that the user has only the appropriate permissions for his or her new department?

To address such problems, all network operating systems support the concept of *security groups* (or just *groups)*. You first create such a group and then assign all the appropriate users to it so you can administer their permissions more easily. When you grant permission to a folder on the server, you do so by giving the group the network permission. All the members of the group automatically *inherit* those permissions. This inheritance makes maintaining network permissions over time much easier. In fact, you shouldn't try to manage network permissions without using groups this way. You might quickly become overwhelmed trying to keep track of everything, and you're almost certain to make mistakes over time.

Not only can users be members of groups, but groups can be members of other groups. This way, you can build a hierarchy of groups that makes administration even easier. For instance, suppose that you define a group for each department in your company. Half those departments are part of a larger division called Research and Development (R&D) and half are part of Sales, General, and Administration (SG&A). On your network, some folders are specific to each department, some are specific to all of R&D or SG&A, and some can be accessed by every user on the network. In such a situation, you would first create the departmental groups and then create the R&D and SG&A groups. Each departmental group would then become a member in either R&D or SG&A. Finally, you would use the built-in Domain Users group, or another one you created that represents everyone, and then assign R&D and SG&A to that top-level group for every user.

Once you've done this, you can then grant permissions in the most logical way. If a resource is just for a specific department, you assign that departmental group to the resource. If a resource is for R&D or SG&A, you assign those divisions to the resource; then all the individual departmental groups within that division will inherit permission to access the resource. If a resource is for everyone, you would assign the master, top-level group to the resource. Using such hierarchical group levels makes administering permissions even easier, and is practically necessary for larger networks with hundreds of users.

Create Groups

You create groups using the same console as you use for users: the Active Directory Users and Computers. Groups appear in two of the domain's containers: Built-In and Users. The Built-In groups are fixed and cannot be deleted, and cannot be made members of other groups. The Built-In groups have certain important permissions already assigned to them, and other groups you create can be given membership in the Built-In groups. Similarly, if you want to disable a particular Built-In group, you would do so simply by removing all its member groups. Figure 16-9 shows the list of Built-In groups for Windows 2000 Server.

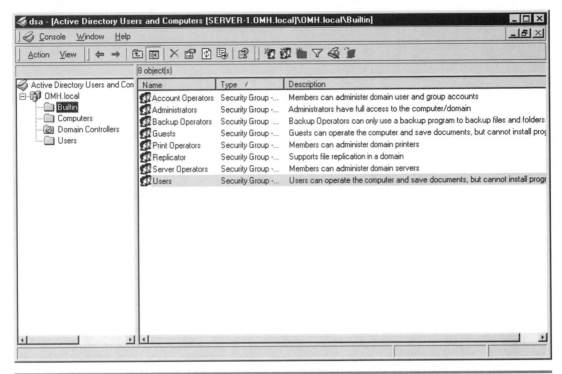

Figure 16-9 Viewing the list of Built-In groups

CAUTION

Be careful changing the membership of the Built-In groups. For most networks, while it's important to understand what these groups are and how they work, you generally want to leave them alone.

Generally, you work only with groups defined in the Users container. Figure 16-10 shows the default groups in the Users container, which you can distinguish from user accounts by both the two-person icon and the Type designation.

To add a new group, first select the Users container in the left pane. Then, open the Action pull-down menu and choose New, then choose Group. You see the Create New Object (Group) dialog box shown in Figure 16-11.

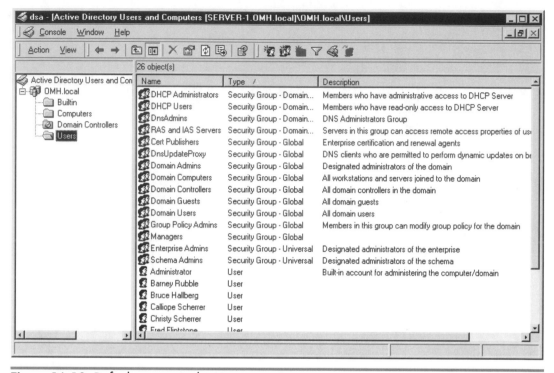

Figure 16-10 Default groups in the Users container

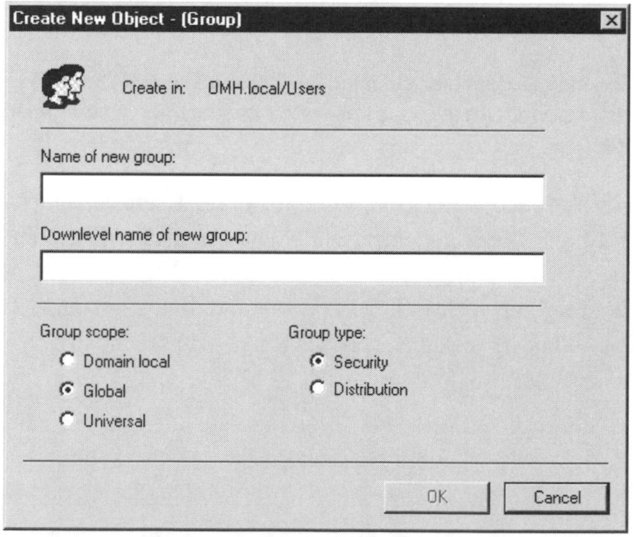

Figure 16-11 The Create New Object (Group) dialog box

First, enter the name of the group in the field provided. You'll see the name you enter echoed in the Downlevel Group field. The Downlevel Group field enables you to specify a different group name for Windows NT computers. However, using different group names is usually not a good idea because it can quickly make your system confusing.

After naming the group, you need to select from the available option buttons in the lower half of the dialog box. Group Scope refers to how widely the group is populated throughout a domain. A *Universal group* exists throughout an organization, even when the organization's network is made up of many individual domains. Universal groups can also contain members from any domain in an organization's network. A *Global group,* on the other hand, can contain members only from the domain in which they exist. However, you can assign Global groups permissions to any domain within the network, even across multiple domains. Finally, *Domain Local groups* exist only within a single domain and can contain members only from that domain.

TIP

Don't worry if you create a group with the wrong scope. You can easily change the group's scope, provided its membership doesn't violate the new scope's rules for membership. To change a domain scope, select the group and open its Properties dialog box (right-click and then choose Properties from the pop-up menu). If the group membership allows the change, you can select a different Group Scope option button.

After you set the group's scope, you can also select whether it will be a Security group or a Distribution group. *Distribution groups* are used only to maintain e-mail distribution lists and have no security impact in Windows 2000 Server. They are used only for e-mail applications such as Microsoft Exchange Server 2000.

Maintain Group Membership

After you complete the Create New Object (Group) dialog box entries and click OK, the program creates the group, but it starts out with no membership. To set the membership for a group, follow these steps:

1. Select the group and open its Properties dialog box (right-click and then choose Properties from the pop-up menu).

2. Click the Members tab. You see the group properties dialog box shown in Figure 16-12.

3. Click the Add button. You see the Select Users, Contacts, Computers, or Groups dialog box shown in Figure 16-13.

4. Scroll through the list to select each member you want to add to the group, then click the Add button to add your selected members to the list of members. The list displays only objects that can be made members of the group.

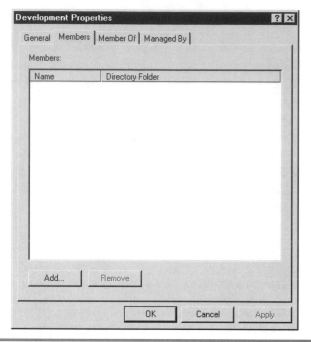

Figure 16-12 The Members tab of the group Properties dialog box

If you want the group to be a member of another group, click the group properties dialog box's Member Of tab, then click its Add button, similar to how you added members to the group.

Progress Check

1. What is the main reason to set up and use security groups?

2. True of false: In Windows 2000, groups cannot be members of other groups.

---

1. It eases the administration of permissions on the network dramatically.
2. False. Windows 2000 allows groups to be members of other groups.

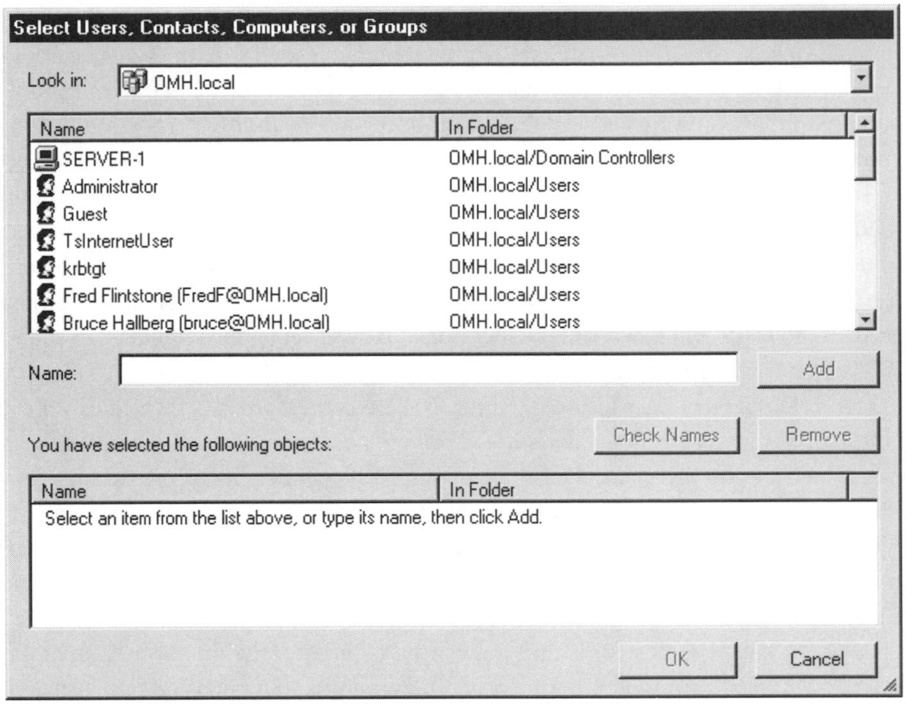

Figure 16-13 The Users, Contacts, Computers, or Groups dialog box

CRITICAL SKILL

16.4 Create and Administer Shares

Drives and folders under Windows 2000 Server are made available to users over the network as shared resources, simply called *shares* in Windows networking parlance. You select a drive or folder, enable it to be shared, and then set the permissions for the share.

Review Share Security

You can set both drives and folders as distinct shared resources (or *shares*), whether they are located on a FAT-formatted drive or on an NTFS-formatted drive. In the case of an NTFS-formatted drive (but not on a FAT-formatted drive), however, you can also set permissions on folders and files within the share that are separate from the permissions on the share itself. Understanding how Windows 2000 Server handles security for shares, folders, and files on NTFS drives is important.

Suppose that you created a share called RESEARCH and you gave the R&D security group read-only access to the share. Within the share, you set the permissions on a folder called PROJECTS to allow full read and write access (called *Change permission*) for the R&D security group. The question is, will the R&D group have read-only permission to that folder or Change permission? The answer is that the group will have read-only permission because when security permissions differ between folders within a share and the share itself, the most restrictive permissions apply. A better way to set up share permissions is to allow everyone Change permission to the share and then control the actual permissions by setting them on the folders within the share itself. This way, you can assign any combination of permissions you want; then the users will receive the permissions that you set on those folders, even though the share is set to Change permission.

Also, remember that users receive permissions based on the groups of which they are members, and these permissions are cumulative. So, if you are a member of the Everyone group who has read-only permission for a particular file, but you're also a member of the Admins group who has Full Control permission for that file, you'll have Full Control permission in practice. This is an important rule: Permissions set on folders and files are always cumulative and take into account permissions set for the user individually as well as any security groups of which the user is a member.

The next thing to remember is that you can set permissions within a share (sometimes called *NTFS permissions*) on both folders and files, and these permissions are also cumulative. So, for instance, you can set read-only permission on a folder for a user, but Change permission for some specific files. The user then has the ability to read, modify, and even delete those files without having that ability with other files in the same folder.

The last thing to remember is that there's a special permission called No Access. *No Access* overrides all other permissions, no matter what. If you set No Access permission for a user on a file or folder, then that's it; the user will have no access to that file or folder. An extremely important corollary to this rule is that No Access permission is also cumulative and overriding. So, if the Everyone security group has Change permission for a file, but you set a particular user to No Access for that file, that user will receive No Access permission. If you set No Access permission for the Everyone group, however, then all members of that group will also receive No Access because it overrides any other permissions they have. Be careful about using No Access with security groups! There are many other fine points to setting and maintaining permissions that go beyond the scope of this book, but you can resolve most permission problems if you remember the rules discussed here:

- When share permissions conflict with file or folder permissions, the *most restrictive* one always wins.

- Aside from the preceding rule, permissions are cumulative, taking into account permissions assigned to users and groups as well as files and folders.

- When a permission conflict occurs, the No Access permission always wins.

Project 16-1 Create Shares

As a network administrator, you will have to frequently create and manage the shares on the network. This project walks you through creating a new share.

Step by Step

1. To create a new share, use either My Computer or Windows Explorer on the server.

2. Right-click the folder or drive you want to share, then choose Sharing from the pop-up menu. You will see the Sharing tab of the folder or drive's Properties dialog box, as shown in Figure 16-14.

3. Click the Share This Folder option button, then assign a share name and, if you like, a comment for the share (users will be able to see the comment you enter). After naming the share, you can select a limit to how many users can simultaneously access the share. (Normally, leave User Limit set to Maximum Allowed.)

The last step you should take is to check the permissions for the share.

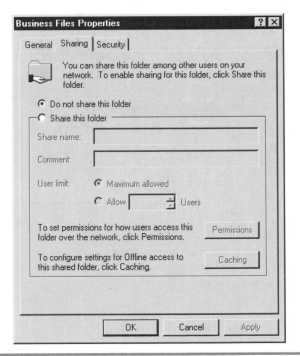

Project
16-1

Create Shares

Figure 16-14 The Sharing tab of a folder's Properties dialog box

(continued)

4. Click the Permissions button, which reveals the Permissions dialog box shown in Figure 16-15. As you can see, the default setting for a share is for the group Everyone to have the fullest possible access to the share. Normally, this setting is what you want. (See the discussion in the preceding section about share permissions for more information about this setting.) Still, if you need to restrict access to the share in some fashion, the Permissions dialog box enables you to accomplish this. Clicking Add brings up the Select Users, Contacts, Computers, or Groups dialog box, from which you can choose those entities and assign them permissions to the share.

5. After adding an entity, you can use the checkboxes in the Permissions window of the Permissions dialog box to set the exact permissions you want.

6. Close all of the active dialog boxes using the OK buttons on each one.

TIP

When you click an entity and some of its Permission dialog box's checkboxes are grayed, this means that the permissions were inherited from a higher level, usually from permissions set on a containing folder somewhere up the directory tree.

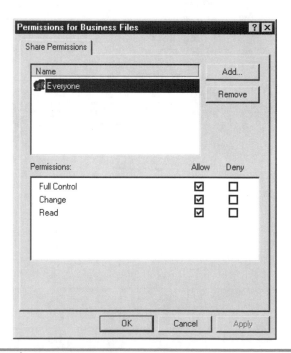

Figure 16-15 Setting a share's permissions

Project Summary

Once a share is created and the share information has propogated through the domain (usually within several minutes), users can browse it through either Network Neighborhood (Windows 9*x* and NT) or My Network Places (Windows 2000). Double-clicking the share will open it, depending on the permissions.

You can hide a share but still keep it available for users who know the share name. To do so, create the share normally, but append the dollar sign ($) to the end of its name. For example, FILES$ might be a share that users cannot see when browsing available network shares.

Map Drives

You can use shares by opening them in Network Neighborhood or My Network Places, and they function just like the folders in My Computer. However, you might frequently want to simulate a connected hard disk on your computer with a share from the network. For example, many applications that store files on the network require that the network folders be accessible as normal drive letters. The process of simulating a disk drive with a network share is called *mapping*, where you create a map (link) between the drive letter you want to use and the actual network share to remain attached to that drive letter.

You can create a drive mapping in many ways. The easiest way is to open Network Neighborhood from the client computer, then locate the share you want to map. Right-click it and choose Map Network Drive. In the dialog box that appears, the name of the domain and share will appear already typed in for you; simply select an appropriate drive letter for the mapping and click OK. From then on, the share will appear to your computer as that drive letter, and users will see this share's letter in My Computer.

To connect to a hidden share, right-click Network Neighborhood (or My Network Places for Windows 2000) and choose Map Network Drive. Choose a drive letter for the mapping, enter in the complete share name (with the appended dollar sign), then click OK. Provided you have permission to access that share, the mapping will otherwise work normally.

You can also map drives using a command-line utility called NET. The *NET command* takes many different forms and can fulfill many different needs, depending on what parameters you give it. To map a drive, you use the NET USE command. Typing **NET USE** by itself and pressing ENTER will list all currently mapped drives. To add a new drive mapping, you would type the following:

NET USE *drive_letter*: *UNC_for_share*

Most network resources in a Windows network use a naming system called the *Universal Naming Convention* (UNC). To supply a UNC, you start with two backslashes, then the name of the server, another backslash, and the name of the share (additional backslashes and names can refer to folders and files within the share). So, if you want to map drive G: to a share called EMPLOYEES located on the server SERVER, the command would be as follows:

NET USE G: \\SERVER\EMPLOYEES

TIP

You can use the NET command from any Windows client for any Windows network. Type **NET** by itself to list all of the different forms of the command. Type **NET** *command* **HELP** to see detailed help on the different NET commands.

CRITICAL SKILL
16.5 Administer Printer Shares

Before setting and working with printers on a network, you need to understand the components involved in network printing and how they interact, as follows:

● A *print job* is a set of binary data sent from a network workstation to a network printer. A print job is the same data as a computer would send to a locally connected printer—it's just redirected to the network for printing.

● The network workstation that sends the print job to the print queue is responsible for formatting the print data properly for the printer. This is done through software installed on the workstation—called a *print driver*—that is specific to each type of printer. Printer drivers are also specific to each operating system that uses them. In other words, a Hewlett-Packard LaserJet 5si driver for a Windows 95 computer is different from an Hewlett-Packard LaserJet 5si driver for a Windows NT Workstation computer. More troublesome, different versions of the same operating system usually use different drivers, so a driver for a Windows 95 computer might not work with a Windows 98 computer and vice versa.

● Print jobs are often sent to the network through a captured printer port. The network client software redirects to the network one of the printer ports on a networked workstation, such as LPT1. The process of redirecting a printer port to a network printer is called *capturing*. Usually, captured ports are persistent and continue through multiple logins until they are turned off.

● Print jobs sent to the network go to a place called a *printer queue*. The print job sits in the queue until the network can service the print job and send it to the printer. Printer queues can hold many jobs from many different users and typically are managed in a first-in, first-out fashion.

● Print jobs are removed from print queues and sent to actual printers by *print servers*. After sending the complete job to the printer, the print server removes the job from the queue. You can accomplish print serving in many different ways. If the printer you are using is connected to a server or workstation on the network, then that server or workstation handles the print server duty. If the printer is directly connected to the network (if it has its own

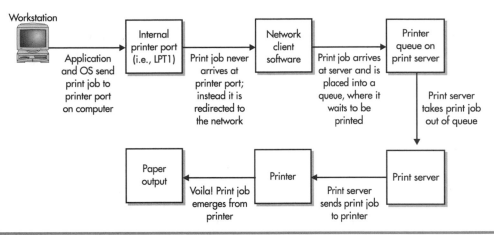

Figure 16-16 Overview of the network printing process

network port), then the printer usually has a built-in print server as part of its network hardware. This built-in print server has the intelligence to log in to the network and to service a particular printer queue.

Print jobs start at the printing application, which sends its printer output to the local operating system. The local operating system uses the printer driver requested by the application to format the actual print job for the printer in question. Then, the local operating system works with the installed network client software to send the formatted print job to the print queue, where the job sits until the printer is available. Then, the print server sends the print job from the queue to the actual printer. Many steps are involved, but once everything is set up, it works smoothly, as you will see in the next section. Figure 16-16 shows an overview of how network printing works.

Project 16-2 Setting Up a Network Printer

This project shows you how to set up a printer connected directly to a Windows 2000 Server that you will make available to network users. In this case, the printer and its Windows 2000 driver are already installed properly, as they would normally be during the installation of Windows 2000 Server. If they are not properly installed, then open the Printers folder and use the Add Printers icon to set up the printer on the server itself.

You can easily set up a printer connected to a server (or workstation) so other network users can access it. However, for networks with more than about 20 users, you're better off either buying printers with network interfaces and built-in print servers or using dedicated print server boxes that interface between a printer and the network. For most laser printers,

(continued)

adding a dedicated network interface and server increases the cost of the printer by about $300. This is money well spent because sending a print job to a printer requires the print server to do a lot of processing. If that print server is also your main file server, its overall performance will decrease significantly while it is printing (and particularly while it services large print jobs). Also, printers with built-in print servers are far easier to relocate on the network. They can go anywhere a network connection exists and where power is available. Once connected to the network at a new location, the printer logs in to the network and starts doing its work immediately.

Step by Step

1. To share a printer connected to a Windows 2000 Server, first open the server's Printers folder. (Open the Start menu, choose Settings, and then choose Printers.) You will see all the installed printers in the Printers folder.

2. Right-click the one you want to share and choose Sharing from the pop-up menu. The Properties dialog box for the printer will appear, with the Sharing tab activated, as shown in Figure 16-17.

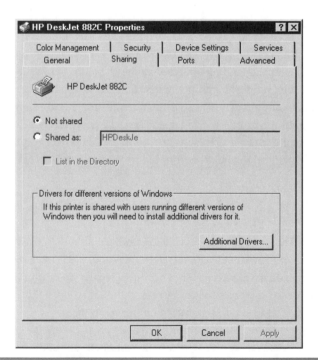

Figure 16-17 Enabling printer sharing

3. Click the Shared As option button and then assign the printer a share name, by which the client computers will recognize the printer. At this point, you can click the OK button because the default permissions for a shared printer are for the Everyone group to be able to print to it. Usually, though, you need to check at least two other available settings, as follows:

- For high-throughput requirements, you might want to use a feature called *printer pooling,* which enables you to set up a number of identical printers, all connected to a single printer queue, that appear to the network as one printer. Users print to the listed printer, and the first available real printer services the job. Using printer pooling, you could have a whole bank of printers appear as one printer to the users and dramatically increase the number of print requests you can handle. Remember, however, that pooled printers must be identical, because they will all use the same print driver. Figure 16-18 shows the tab on which printer pooling is enabled.

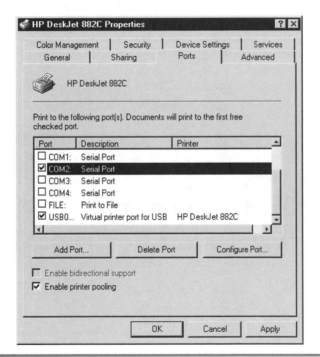

Figure 16-18 Enabling printer pooling

(continued)

16

Administering Windows 2000 Server: The Basics

Project
16-2

Setting Up a Network Printer

- To set the permissions for a shared printer, use the Security tab of the printer's properties dialog box, shown in Figure 16-19. The groups you see assigned in Figure 16-19 are the default assignments for a shared printer, with the Administrators permissions shown. As you can see, three main permissions are assigned to each entity: Print, Manage Printers, and Manage Documents. The Everyone group has permission to print, but not to manage documents in the queue. However, a special group called Creator Owner has permission to manage documents. This means that the user who sent the print job automatically has permission to modify or delete his or her own print job, but not others waiting in the queue.

- Windows 2000 Server can store the appropriate printer drivers for a number of different Windows-based clients that might connect to the server and use its printers. For example, the printer drivers for a particular printer will be different depending on whether the client computer is running Windows 95, Windows 98, Windows NT 4, Windows 2000, or some other version of Windows. When a client computer opens a shared printer on the network, the printer driver is automatically installed for the client computer. You control this setting on the Sharing tab by clicking the Additional Drivers button, which reveals the Additional Drivers dialog box shown in Figure 16-20. To add new drivers, click the appropriate client types that may use the shared printer on the network and then click OK. The program then prompts you for the appropriate disks or CD-ROMs to install those drivers. Then Windows 2000 Server distributes those printer drivers to the client computers when they first use the printer.

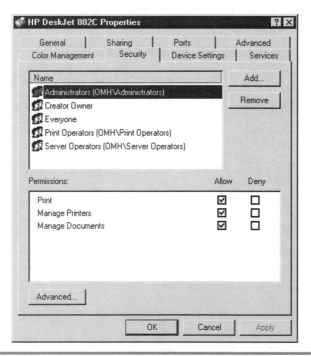

Figure 16-19 Setting a shared printer's permissions

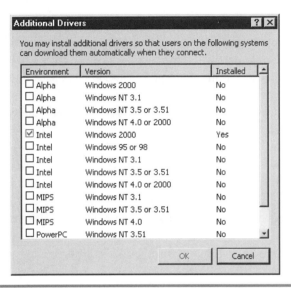

Figure 16-20 Loading additional print drivers for a shared printer

Project Summary

As you can see, setting up networked printers with Windows 2000 Server is a relatively straightforward process that gives you considerable flexibility in how you set up and manage your shared printers. Remember, too, that other printing models are also possible, such as network-connected printers. Consult the documentation that comes with such printers for details on setting them up on your network.

Project
16-2

Setting Up a Network Printer

CRITICAL SKILL
16.6 Work with Windows 2000 Backup

One single task is more important than any other for a network administrator. This task doesn't have to do with making a network secure from hackers, maintaining users, designing new network segments, or solving server or workstation problems. What is it? Making regular and reliable backups of data on the system.

Taking care to make regular and reliable backups is often a thankless job—*until something happens and the backups are needed,* at which point it becomes the most thank*ful* job in the company! And make no mistake about this: Although computers are far more reliable than ever, there are still a myriad of ways in which they can fail and lose or corrupt important data. Remember, there are only two types of network administrators: those who have *had* system crashes and those who *will.* Hardware failures aren't the only culprits, either;

applications or users often make mistakes that lose important data. So having good copies of that data on multiple backup tapes can save the day.

Before delving into the details of how Windows 2000 Server's backup software works, you should review some key terms and concepts important in backups.

Every file and folder object on a server has a number of attribute bits attached to it. Some designate the files as being read-only, as system files, or even as hidden files. One is called *archive* (often referred to as the *archive bit),* which marks whether a file has been backed up. Windows 2000 Server keeps track of files that have been modified. Any time a file is modified on the disk, the archive bit is set to "on." (Such bits are usually referred to as being *set,* which means they are on and are set to the value 1, or as being *clear,* which means they are off and are set to the value 0.) When you back up the system, the backed-up files have the archive bit cleared again. This is how the system knows which files need to be backed up and which ones have been backed up.

Treating the archive bit in different ways results in different types of backups, as follows:

TIP

The following are terms used with Windows 2000 Server backups. Some systems have slightly different names for these types of backups, even though the concepts are always the same. For example, what Microsoft calls a Normal backup, many systems call a Full backup.

- **Normal backups**   Back up everything selected for the backup regardless of whether the Barchive bits are set. All archive bits are set to off as each file is backed up.

- **Copy backups**   Back up everything selected for the backup, regardless of whether the archive bits are set. Copy backups do not change the state of the archive bits, however; they remain untouched. Copy backups are used to make a backup without disturbing a sequence of Normal, Incremental, and Differential backups.

- **Incremental backups**   Back up only those files that have their archive bits set within the selection set. The backup clears the archive bits.

- **Differential backups**   Also back up only those files that have their archive bits set, but the backup leaves the archive bits unchanged.

- **Daily backups**   Are a special type of backup in Windows 2000 Server that is like a Differential backup, except it backs up only files modified on a given day.

Now that you understand the different types of backups available, you can consider different tape rotation schemes that make use of these different types of backups.

The simplest backup scheme is just to run Normal backups every night and rotate tapes. In this model, there are many good ways to rotate tapes. One of the best ways that doesn't consume too many tapes is to label four tapes as "Monday" through "Thursday" and to use them on those days. Then, label four tapes as "Friday 1," "Friday 2," up to "Friday 4," and rotate those each week. Then, make a month-end tape on the last day of the month and keep it forever. This scheme is a good trade-off between using tapes and being able to go back in time to restore files. This scheme will use 20 tapes in a year, at which point you should probably replace the rotating tapes.

TIP

No matter what tape rotation scheme you set up, a good idea is to set up a tape called "Employee Archive." Whenever an employee leaves the company, append his or her files to that tape before you remove those files from the system and keep a list of what employees are on the tape. This gives you a ready reference and quickly available restoration source if a particular person's files are needed at some future time (which happens often).

Another tape rotation scheme involves using the same tapes as listed in the preceding scheme, making full (Normal) backups of the system every Friday night, but then making Incremental backups on Monday through Thursday nights. Because only changed files are backed up during the week, backups during the week happen quickly. The big drawback to this scheme is that if the system crashes on Friday morning, you must restore a lot of tapes to get the system to its most recent backup state. First, you must restore the previous Friday's Normal backup and then restore each of the incremental tapes, in sequence, up to the day when the system crashed. The risk inherent with this scheme is as follows: What do you do if one of those tapes goes bad? Your entire scheme can get messed up if one of the tapes doesn't work. Although bad tapes can be costly in any scheme, they are especially costly in this scheme.

TIP

Although the Backup program included in Windows 2000 Server doesn't offer such a feature, most third-party backup solutions include automatic tape rotation schemes. Such schemes keep track of what tapes you need, how long you've been using them, and what tapes you need in order to restore any given set of files. Using the built-in rotation scheme of any third-party backup software is generally easy, and such schemes usually work well.

One way around the limitations of the preceding scheme is to use Differential backups during the week, instead of Incremental backups. So, you make a Normal backup Friday night and then a Differential on each day of the week. If you had to restore the system after a crash on Friday morning, all you would need to restore is two tapes: one from the previous Friday and the one from Thursday night. This is because Differential backups back up all changed files since the last Normal backup. Monday's Differential backs up the files changed on Monday, Tuesday's Differential backs up the files changed on Monday and Tuesday, and so on.

Ask the Expert

Q: Is there such a thing as too many backups?

A: If you followed the *Department of Justice v. Microsoft* antitrust trial, you were probably astounded at all the old e-mails that the government was able to subpoena from the company. These e-mails were still available because Microsoft had good backup schemes for everything on its network and, apparently, the company never got rid of anything. As demonstrated in the trial, keeping everything isn't necessarily the best idea in the world! I'm sure Microsoft would answer the question posed at the beginning of this section with a resounding "Yes, you can have too many backups!"

Discuss with your legal department setting up a document retention policy and applying it to your e-mail database and backups. Most legal departments are terrified of getting involved in a lawsuit and having "all e-mails relating to such-and-such a matter from June 1993 to September 1999" subpoenaed. If you think about the effort involved in satisfying such a request, you should be terrified, too. For an e-mail system, the task would mean restoring every backup for the time period in question and then searching the e-mail database for all e-mails that fit the criterion, restoring the next tape, and repeating the whole process. If you have hundreds of long-term archival tapes of your e-mail, you're going to be in big trouble trying to fill such a request. Note also that often these sorts of requests are time-limited; you can't take your time in satisfying them.

This is where document retention policies can save you. For example, you might work with the legal department to set up a policy by which you keep only four backup tapes of your e-mail system, two tapes that rotate everyday, and two that rotate every week. So, on Monday you use Daily A, on Tuesday you use Daily B, on Wednesday you overwrite Daily A with Wednesday's data, and so forth. You do the same thing on Fridays with the two weekly tapes. Such a minimal scheme gives you a good chance to restore the e-mail system should something happen, but it doesn't keep hundreds of copies at the same time. Of course, every company will have to come up with its own balance between the security of having more backups versus the risks that might be involved.

TIP

A good idea is to keep a recent set of tapes offsite, in case a fire or some other catastrophe destroys your computer room. I recommend sending the next-to-most-recent full backup of your system offsite and keeping the most recent tape available for use. This is because situations frequently occur when you must quickly restore files from a recent backup, so you always want to have the most recent backups available for this purpose. But you also need to keep a rotating tape offsite that doesn't lose too much data, in case the worst happens.

Use Windows 2000 Server's Backup Software

Windows 2000 Server includes a reliable, easy-to-use backup software program. While it doesn't have all the bells and whistles of some of the third-party backup software programs available (such as ArcServe or Backup Exec), it does a good job and will meet most needs. To access the Backup program, open the Start menu, then choose Programs, Accessories, System Tools, then Backup. When you start the program, you will first see its welcome screen, as shown in Figure 16-21.

Backup does three important things: It backs up files, restores those files, and helps you prepare for a total system rebuild in case of catastrophic failure. The wizards accessed from the Welcome tab work well and enable you to access all the features of the Backup program easily.

To set up a backup, click the Backup Wizard button on the Welcome tab and then click Next once the opening screen of the Backup Wizard appears. You then see the screen shown in Figure 16-22.

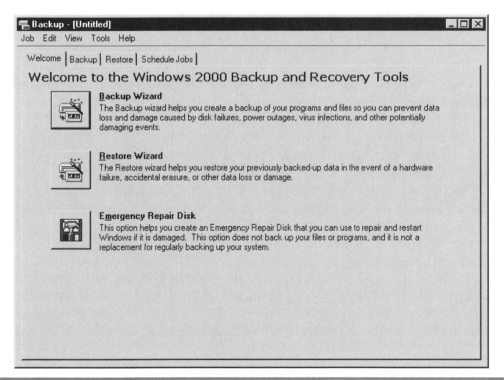

Figure 16-21 Windows 2000 Server's Backup program

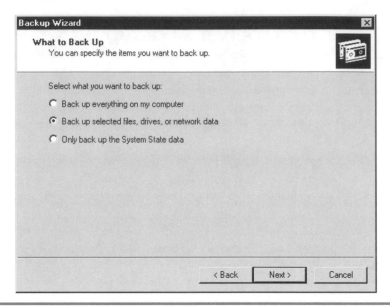

Figure 16-22 Choosing what you want to back up with the Backup Wizard

Choose the appropriate option, such as "Back up selected files, drives, or network data," then click Next to continue. You then have a chance to select what you want to back up with the Items to Back Up screen shown in Figure 16-23.

Use the tree views in the left pane to select the drives, files, or other computer contents you want to back up. You can also select a special category called *System State,* which includes all the information necessary to rebuild a Windows 2000 Server from scratch, such as key system files, registry data, and so forth. (Including System State in most backups is usually a good idea.) After selecting what you want to back up, click Next to continue. You see the Where to Store the Backup dialog box shown in Figure 16-24.

One nice feature of the Backup program is that you can store a backup on any kind of media attached to the computer, including another disk drive, removable media such as tapes, writeable CDs (CD-R or CD-RW), or JAZ or ZIP drives. In the Where to Store the Backup screen, choose the destination type. Then, if you are performing a file-based backup, assign a name to the backup set. After clicking Next another time, you will see a confirmation screen showing all the pertinent details about the backup you are preparing. An important button on

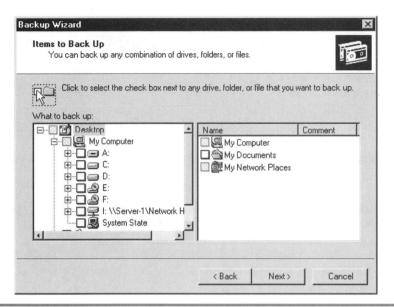

Figure 16-23 Selecting backup material

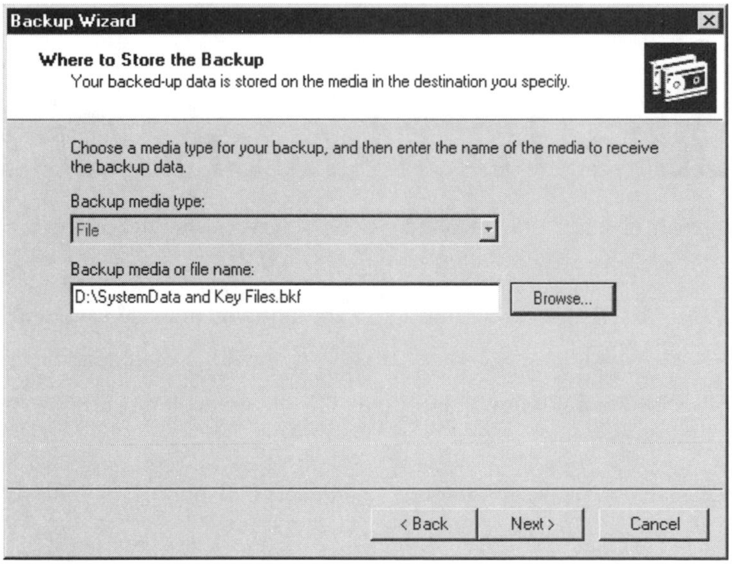

Figure 16-24 Selecting a backup destination

the confirmation screen is labeled Advanced. Clicking the Advanced button takes you through another sequence of dialog boxes in which you can set the following properties:

● Backup type, where you can choose between Normal, Copy, Incremental, Differential, and Daily backup types

● Whether to verify the backup data by having the program read it after it is written and compare its contents to the source contents to ensure that the backup is correct

● Whether to append or overwrite any existing backup data on the media target you chose

● A label for the backup set and media, if you wish to change the default names

● Scheduling information for the backup, which can be used to schedule a backup to take place later, and can also be used to set up automatically recurring backup jobs, which will be managed by the Windows 2000 Server Scheduler service

After completing the Advanced settings, you can click Next on the final Backup Wizard screen either to start the backup or to set it to run at the time that you've scheduled.

Restoring files is easier than backing them up. You can either use the Restore tab or the Restore Wizard. Both methods first prompt you to select either the media or the file you used for the backup from which you want to restore. The methods then enable you to browse the list of backed up files and select the ones that you want to restore. You will have an opportunity to choose whether to overwrite files or to restore the backup to another location on the disk.

✔ *Module 16 Mastery Check*

1. You administer user accounts in Windows 2000 Server using the program called

_____.

2. True or false: To temporarily disable a user account, you must delete it and then re-create it later.

3. True or false: Under a Windows 2000 Active Directory domain, security groups can be members of other groups.

4. You can set security permissions on files and folders only on _____-formatted partitions.

5. If a user has Full Control permission explicitly set on a folder, but they are also a member of a group that has the No Access permission, what permissions do they have in that folder?

6. How can you create a share but make it invisible to browsing on the network, but still usable for those that know its name and who have the proper permissions to the share?

7. Describe what printer pooling does.

8. True or false: You must purchase special backup software to make backups of a Windows 2000 Server.

9. You can perform many network-related tasks using a powerful command-line program called _____.

10. When you set an account to "Account Disabled" status, how long does it take to propagate the change to all of the domain controllers in a large network?

Module 17

Understanding Other Windows 2000 Server Services

One of the strengths of Windows 2000 is that it can do many things and fill many roles. Not only is Windows 2000 Server a powerful and effective fileserver and print server, but it's also extremely capable of performing many other tasks right out of the box.

The preceding two modules showed you how to set up Windows 2000 Server as a basic fileserver and print server, and how to administer Windows 2000 Server on a daily basis. This module overviews other available Windows 2000 services, emphasizing services that come with Windows 2000 Advanced Server. To get the most out of Windows 2000 Server, you need to know what additional services are available, how they work, and what they do. You can find detailed instructions for implementing these services in a dedicated Windows 2000 Server book that discusses the services you are installing in detail.

CRITICAL SKILL
17.1 Explore Dynamic Host Configuration Protocol (DHCP)

If you've been involved with computers for long, you probably remember what it was like to manage TCP/IP addresses manually (and you might still do this now!). You had to visit every computer on the network to set its TCP/IP address manually. You also had to keep track of which computers used which addresses because you had a limited number of addresses with which to work. Plus, as you probably know, when two computers on a network try to use the same TCP/IP address, trouble quickly follows, and you have to spend time sorting out these problems.

DHCP saves the day in such situations. A DHCP server is a computer on the network that keeps track of what TCP/IP addresses are available and parcels them out to computers and other devices that boot up and request a TCP/IP address from the server. With a DHCP server, you needn't worry about address conflicts and you needn't worry about having to renumber the addresses used on computers if your TCP/IP address range ever has to change (as it usually does when you change ISPs for your Internet connection).

TIP

Because TCP/IP is the default protocol for Windows 2000 Server–based networks and because Windows 2000 Server is designed to operate correctly over a TCP/IP-only network, DHCP services are important and are installed with Windows 2000 Server by default. The DHCP services are not enabled by default, however, as it's important never to set up conflicting DHCP servers on a network.

To use DHCP, you must define a scope and other associated TCP/IP settings that the servers give to client computers. A *scope* is simply the range (or ranges) of TCP/IP addresses that the server is allowed to parcel out. Among the associated TCP/IP settings that the server distributes are the addresses for DNS or WINS servers also on the network. When a DHCP server assigns a TCP/IP address to a client computer, the address is said to be *leased* and it remains assigned to that client computer for a set period of time. Leases are usually configured to last for two to seven days (the default setting in Windows 2000 is eight days). During this period, the assigned TCP/IP address is not given out to a different computer.

When a client computer boots up and joins the network, if it is configured to seek a DHCP server, the client computer does so while initializing its TCP/IP protocol stack. Any available DHCP servers respond to the client's request for an address with an available address from the DHCP server's address database. The client computer then uses this address for the duration of its lease.

The administrator can cancel and reassign TCP/IP information when needed. (Usually, he or she will do so after business hours, when the client computers are turned off.) The administrator can then make changes to the DHCP scope information, which is then communicated to the clients when they reconnect to the network. In this way, you can easily make changes to such information as DNS server addresses or even TCP/IP address ranges without having to visit all the computers.

TIP

To access DHCP on a Windows 2000 Server, open the Start menu, then choose Programs | Administrative Tools | DHCP.

Although DHCP is a great tool for managing TCP/IP addresses, you should use it only for client computers not hosting any TCP/IP services that are provided to other computers. For example, you would not want to set up a web server to use DHCP to get a dynamic TCP/IP address because then client computers wishing to connect to the web server will be unable to find the address when it changes. Instead, you should assign fixed addresses to computers that offer TCP/IP-enabled services either to the local network or through the Internet. You can assign these addresses in one of two ways: First, you can simply assign those computers fixed TCP/IP addresses locally and then set up *exclusion ranges* to the scope that the DHCP server manages, which prevents the DHCP server from using or offering those addresses to other computers. Second, you can set up a *reservation* on the DHCP server, which forces the server always to assign the reserved address to a specific computer.

TIP

It's a good idea to use static IP addresses for your network printers. Doing so makes troubleshooting printer connectivity problems easier.

17.2 Investigate Domain Name System (DNS)

DNS is a technology that allows easily remembered names to be mapped to TCP/IP addresses and ports. For instance, when you use a web browser and enter the address **http://www.yahoo.com**, you are using a DNS server to resolve the domain name **www.yahoo.com** to a particular TCP/IP address. Your web browser transparently uses the TCP/IP address to communicate with the server in question. The DNS system makes the Internet much easier to use than it otherwise would be. (Imagine how excited advertisers would be to say, "Visit our web site at http://65.193.55.38!")

NOTE

General DNS information is given in Module 7.

Windows 2000 Server includes a full DNS server. In fact, a DNS server is required for Active Directory to function. If you install the first Active Directory server into a Windows 2000 domain, DNS services are automatically installed; otherwise, you have to select them manually if you want to add them.

You manage the DNS services with the DNS Management Console plug-in, which you access by opening the Start menu and choosing Programs | Administrative Tools | DNS. Figure 17-1 shows the DNS plug-in.

When you set up DNS for an organization, you first establish a root namespace (a virtual location in which domain names are stored), usually using the domain name you have registered for the Internet, such as **omh.com**. You can then create your own subdomains by prepending organizational or geographic units, such as **italy.omh.com** or **accounting.omh.com**. A Windows 2000 Server running DNS services can manage your own domains and subdomains, and you can also set up multiple DNS servers that each manage a portion of the domain namespace. Each DNS server is responsible for storing all the DNS names used for its managed namespace and for communicating any changes to other DNS servers. When you use multiple DNS servers to manage separate portions of your DNS namespace, each DNS server manages a *zone*. Updates between different zones are called *zone transfers*. Windows 2000 DNS services support both full and incremental zone transfers (incremental zone transfers exchange only updated information, which cuts down on network traffic considerably on networks with large DNS namespaces).

Because DNS is integral to Active Directory, it's important for you to establish redundancy for your DNS servers. Microsoft recommends that each domain controller also act as a DNS server, and you must have at least one primary and secondary DNS server for each managed zone. (On small networks, it is possible—and probably desirable because of cost issues—to use only a single DNS server.)

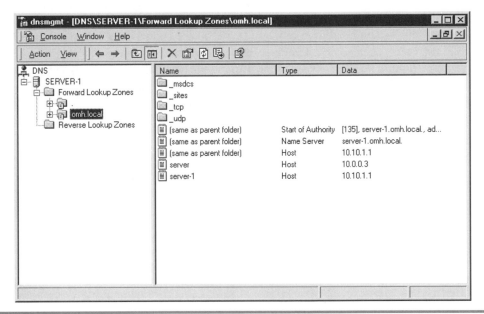

Figure 17-1 The DNS Microsoft Management Console (MMC) plug-in

NOTE

Prior to Windows 2000 Server, Windows-based TCP/IP networks actually used two different naming systems. The first, used with TCP/IP, is DNS. The second, used with NetBIOS and NetBEUI, is Windows Internet Name Service (WINS). With Windows 2000 Server, DNS services also can be configured to provide WINS services to the network for legacy computers. However, migrating to using DNS for network browsing is your best bet if possible.

CRITICAL SKILL
17.3 Compare Remote Access
Service (RAS) and RRAS

RAS (pronounced *razz*) provides a way for you to set up dial-in support to your network, where remote client computers form a remote node connection to the network using some form of dial-up connection. Dial-up connections can be made with modems and telephone lines or ISDN connections. (Of course, both sides of a RAS connection must support the connection type being used.) RAS services enable you to set up a Windows 2000 Server easily to act as a RAS server to the network, and remote users can connect to the server to gain access to the network's resources.

Routing and Remote Access Service (RRAS, pronounced *ar-razz*) is also a remote access technology, but it includes routing capabilities that enable connections to the network over a public network—such as the Internet—using *Virtual Private Network* (VPN) technology. A VPN works by setting up a secure "tunnel" between a client and the RRAS server through which encrypted packets pass. The client computer dials up its normal Internet ISP and then forms a secure VPN connection to the RRAS server over the Internet.

NOTE

VPN technology is discussed in Module 9.

RAS and RRAS are administered through the same tool on Windows 2000 Server. Open the Start menu, then choose Programs | Administrative Tools | Routing and Remote Access to access the MMC plug-in. After the plug-in starts, right-click the server on which you want to enable remote access, then choose Configure and Enable Routing and Remote Access. A helpful wizard guides you through the process and enables you to choose whether to enable only remote access, only routing/remote access, or both. Figure 17-2 shows the Routing and Remote Access plug-in once RRAS has been enabled.

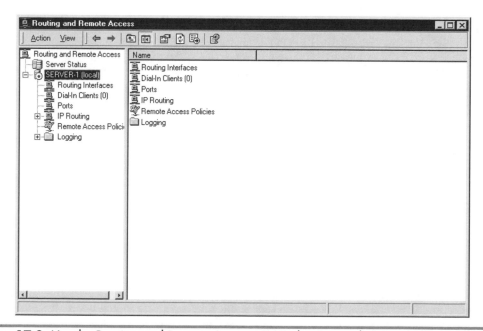

Figure 17-2 Use the Routing and Remote Access MMC plug-in to administer remote access.

Remote access services under Windows 2000 Server are secure and offer considerable flexibility so that you can set them up to work in the way you want. First, you must enable a user to access the network remotely, which you can do by editing the user's Properties dialog box (see Module 16). Then, you can configure RRAS to use a number of control features that enable you to keep remote access secure, including

● Setting times and days when remote access is operational.

● Setting times and days when specific users or groups can use remote access.

● Limiting access to only the RRAS server or to specific services on the network.

● Using callback features, where a remote client dials into the network and logs in. The network then disconnects the connection and dials the user back at a predefined phone number.

● Setting access policies based on remote client computer name or TCP/IP address.

Through the use of RAS and RRAS, you can easily set up Windows 2000 Server to provide important secure access services to remote users, both over dial-up connections and through the Internet.

Progress Check

1. A range of TCP/IP addresses that is managed by a DHCP server is called the _____.

2. If you are setting up a server to handle VPN connections, which would you use: RAS or RRAS?

CRITICAL SKILL
17.4 Explore Internet Information Server (IIS)

Windows 2000 Server includes a set of Internet services that run as part of IIS. IIS includes Web, FTP, SMTP, and NNTP services, each of which can be started or stopped independently. IIS is administered through the Internet Services Manager program found in the Administrative Tools program group. Figure 17-3 shows the Internet Services Manager.

---

1. Scope
2. RRAS

(right margin, vertical) **17** Understanding Other Windows 2000 Server Services

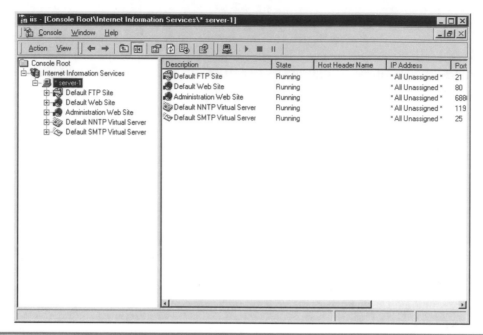

Figure 17-3 The Internet Information Services Manager provides a single place to administer Internet services.

IIS web services provide comprehensive web-hosting software. You can define multiple web sites with IIS, each one administered separately. For each site, you specify the directory in which the site's files can be found, as well as security settings for the site and performance parameters to optimize the performance of the web site.

IIS FTP services enable you to set up an FTP site on a Windows 2000 Server computer. You define the FTP directory, as well as whether directory listings will be shown in UNIX- or MS-DOS-style formats. You can also set security settings to allow or disallow different client computers or client networks access to the FTP server, and specify whether you will permit anonymous FTP logins.

The NNTP server in IIS enables you to set up your own Usenet-style site using the NNTP protocol. Clients can connect to your NNTP server using tools such as Outlook Express or other Usenet news readers.

Finally, the *Simple Mail Transfer Protocol* (SMTP) server allows SMTP connections to be formed between the system running IIS and remote SMTP mail systems. SMTP is the standard protocol for exchanging e-mail over the Internet.

CRITICAL SKILL
17.5 Employ Cluster Services

Windows Cluster Services enables you to combine two or more servers into a *cluster*. You can configure these clusters to fill one of two cluster roles:

● Network load balancing clusters enable you to share TCP/IP-based services—such as a web server—among up to 32 Windows 2000 servers.

● *Server clusters* provide fail-over support in case one of the servers in the cluster fails. The two servers share a common disk array and share access to the array for the various services and applications that each runs. You can perform limited load balancing by running some services on one server and others on the other server. If one server fails, the other one seamlessly takes over its duties. Server clusters also enable you to move services onto one server or another, which is useful when doing upgrades of live, functioning clusters without having to take the cluster off line.

Cluster Services is an invaluable tool when building high-availability, high-performance networks. However, the setup, care, and feeding of clusters are complicated subjects. If you need to deploy clusters, you should carefully read the Microsoft documentation related to their setup and maintenance, and consider purchasing a book dedicated to clustering with Windows 2000.

CRITICAL SKILL
17.6 Discover Windows Terminal Services

The final service discussed in this module, but possibly one of the most powerful, is *Windows Terminal Services* (WTS). WTS enables you to set up a Windows 2000 Server almost as if it were a mainframe—where terminals can connect and all the work is performed on the central computer, which in this case would be a Windows 2000 Server computer. A client computer connects to the Terminal Server using a TCP/IP connection, either over a dial-up or a LAN/WAN connection, and logs in. From then on, the client computer is responsible only for displaying screens and accepting keyboard and mouse input; all work is actually being done

17

Understanding Other Windows 2000 Server Services

on the Terminal Server through the creation of a virtual Windows machine on the server. A *Terminal Server* can create many virtual Windows machines, each one carrying out its own tasks and running its own programs.

When would you use a Terminal Server connection to a network instead of a remote node connection, such as the remote node connections offered via RAS and RRAS? The answer depends on a number of factors, of which the following are possible considerations:

- The remote computer doesn't have adequate resources to run some application or perform some task. By running its programs on the Terminal Server, the remote computer can take advantage of the Terminal Server's resources. For example, suppose that a particular application runs optimally only when it has 2GB of RAM with which to work. In a case such as this, a simple Windows 98 client with 64MB of RAM can connect to the Terminal Server (that has 2–4GB of RAM) and run the application in question. Similarly, some applications might require many processors or direct access to large disk arrays or to some other centrally located resource to which the Terminal Server has access.

- Over low-bandwidth connections, such as 33.6-Kbps modem connections, some applications work far more effectively using a remote control approach rather than a remote node approach. Most remote access connections are low-bandwidth and yet some applications need high-bandwidth requirements to work properly. Because a remote computer connected to a Terminal Server only has to transfer display and input information, the application running on the Terminal Server can run much faster than it could over a remote node connection.

- Some applications and tasks, such as administration of a Windows 2000 Server, cannot be fully performed by another computer even if it has a connection running at LAN speeds. Terminal Services allows a remote computer to run such applications, if the computer has the appropriate permissions. For instance, suppose that your company has a remote network located somewhere in Asia, but the network is not large enough to justify a local administrator. Using Terminal Services, you could connect to that network over the company WAN and perform all necessary administrative tasks, such as configuring hard disks, shares, additional network protocols, and so forth.

Certain applications might require that you use Terminal Services. However, in any case, you might want to consider Terminal Services as an adjunct to your remote access services. If you have many remote users to support, you might find that some users have needs best served by remote node connections and some have needs best served by remote control connections. Running both services on your network will give you considerable additional flexibility in supporting remote users and solving any problems that they might encounter.

TIP

If you implement Terminal Services, make sure that you carefully review Microsoft's license agreement and pricing models, which differ when you use Terminal Services.

Module 17 Mastery Check

1. When a DHCP server assigns a TCP/IP address to a client computer, the address is said to be _____.

2. Active Directory requires which of the services discussed in this module to function properly?

3. To provide remote control administration or remote control applications for a server, you would install _____.

4. Windows 2000 Server can act as an FTP server if you install _____.

5. The service that can provide WINS services in addition to its core service is

   _____.

6. To provide remote node access to a server, you would install _____.

7. A _____ can create many virtual Windows machines, each one carrying out its own tasks and running its own programs.

8. True or false: You should use DHCP only for client computers not hosting any TCP/IP services that are provided to other computers.

9. RRAS includes routing capabilities that enable connections to the network over a public network using _____ technology.

10. Network load balancing clusters enable you to share TCP/IP-based services among up to _____ Windows 2000 servers.

Module 18

Windows .NET Server

This module discusses the upcoming release of Microsoft's Windows .NET Server, one of the biggest server upgrades in the Windows Server line in years. It is expected that .NET Server will be released near the end of 2003.

Because of the importance of .NET Server, individuals learning about networking need to understand it, with a focus on improvements in .NET Server relative to Windows 2000 Server.

CRITICAL SKILL
18.1 Discuss New Features in Microsoft Windows .NET Server

Windows .NET Server is an important upgrade to the Windows 2000 Server family of products, with wide-ranging improvements to security, performance, and server-side features. Microsoft's goal with .NET Server is to make it as good a server operating system as any of the UNIX operating systems, a tall order to be sure. While Windows server families have always compared favorably with UNIX in their ease of use and ease of administration, UNIX has always been far more reliable, and generally performs better on equivalent hardware. Most UNIX servers, for example, run for years without having their performance degrade or having weird errors crop up. Windows servers, on the other hand, generally need to be prophylactically rebooted on a regular basis (such as monthly) to avoid the accumulated errors that can arise from memory leaks and other types of problems.

Microsoft is so confident of the performance, security, and reliability of .NET Server that it is deploying Release Candidate 1 (RC1) to run all of the Microsoft web sites within six weeks of the release of RC1. Certainly, this qualifies as "eating their own dog food," something Microsoft has not always done in the past.

.NET Server Editions

.NET Server will be offered in four different editions, each of which will have its own pricing and its own feature set. These editions are

- **Standard Server** is the most basic version of .NET Server. It has all of the features of the .NET Server family except for the following: cluster service, metadirectory services support, support for Itanium processors, hot-add memory, nonuniform memory access, and various Datacenter Server–specific features.

- **Enterprise Server** is the middle ground of .NET Server offerings. It includes all features of the .NET Server family except the Datacenter Server–specific features. Enterprise Server is analogous to Windows 2000 Advanced Server.

- **Datacenter Server** is the most capable version of .NET Server, oriented toward extremely heavy loads on the most capable server hardware. It includes all features of the .NET Server family except Internet connection sharing and Internet firewall.

- **Web Server** is packaged for focused web-serving tasks. This version is suitable only for acting as a web server, as it is missing many of the features of the rest of the .NET Server family. However, this isn't a bad thing, because if you are putting together a web server using .NET Server, most of the core server's features are superfluous, and removing them lets Microsoft offer Web Server at a much lower price than even Standard Server. Plus, you don't have to worry about managing extraneous features, or any interference they could cause with the job of acting as a web server.

.NET Server New and Improved Features

Microsoft has added a plethora of new features to the .NET Server family relative to the Windows 2000 Server family. This section overviews the key improvements and additions to .NET Server compared with Windows 2000 Server.

Active Directory

Active Directory (AD) has been improved in a variety of ways, including

- AD replication to as many as 5,000 servers (Windows 2000 supported only up to 200 AD servers for replication).

- Faster performance, through improvements to how the Global Catalog works, including cached user passwords for remote users, and more efficient replication between Global Catalog servers.

- New administrative features: Multiple AD objects can now be administered collectively, the Microsoft Management Console tools for AD now support drag and drop and other improvements, and domains can now be renamed.

- There is now a new Forest Trust feature, wherein AD forests can be trusted to each other, and user security information shared between the forests.

Application and Cluster Services

.NET Server includes a host of improvements to its support of applications targeted to it, most notable revolving around the inclusion of Microsoft's .NET framework.

Cluster services (available only in the Enterprise Server and Datacenter Server editions) have been improved to support up to 8 node clusters. Windows 2000 supported only either two nodes (2000 Advanced Server) or four nodes (2000 Datacenter Server). There has been a myriad of improvements to clustering that result in easier administration and better network load-balancing.

File and Print Services

There are probably more Windows servers in use for file and print services than for any of the other roles in which you set up a server. Because of the importance of file and print services, the improvements in this area in .NET Server should be of interest to just about all organizations. These improvements include

- Automated system recovery, in which you can restore a system's operating system, its state, and its hardware configuration in one step. This makes server recovery (such as from a hard disk crash) much easier and faster than before.

- Improvements to disk defragmentation: Disk Defragmenter runs much faster than in Windows 2000, it can defragment the Master File Table (MFT) on line, and it can now be called from a script (so that you can automate defragmentation to occur when the demand on the server is low).

- The CHKDSK program runs twice as fast under .NET Server as in Windows 2000 Server.

- Many new command-line tools for administration of both file and print services: Many administrative tasks are difficult to automate through a graphical user interface, particularly for skilled administrators. The new command-line tools in .NET Server, while perhaps seeming like a step backward, actually offer more powerful choices for system administration.

- Volume Shadow Copies is a new feature in .NET Server. When enabled, the system checkpoints files at times you specify. As files are modified or erased from the system, earlier versions still exist in the shadow copy area of the disk (you define how much disk space to allow for this feature; Microsoft recommends 10 percent). Shadow copies store only differences, and so are very efficient (for instance, each checkpoint does not store a complete copy of the disk's contents, but rather only changes). Users can easily access this feature to recover earlier or deleted versions of their work, rather than ask the IT department to restore from tape. In some organizations, this can save both the user and the network administrator a lot of time, and make recoverable files that might not have been retrievable, even from tape.

- The built-in backup program in .NET Server can now back up open files, by using the shadow copy feature to back up files that are open.

Internet Services

Internet services are becoming important for all servers, not just those that provide web services or other types of Internet services.

Internet Information Services (IIS) 6.0 is included with all versions of .NET Server. Its performance has been radically improved through a new HTTP.SYS program, which now runs in Kernel mode. (Recall that under the Windows NT/2000/XP and now .NET architectures, operating system components run in either User mode, in which the system itself is protected against errors in the component at the expense of performance, or Kernel mode, in which a component has full run of the system, with little or no protection for other running processes. Kernel mode components run much faster than User mode components). The HTTP.SYS program is responsible for responding to HTTP protocol requests made of IIS, and is used extensively for web-serving tasks.

Responding to a raft of security problems in IIS in earlier versions of Windows servers, IIS 6.0 now defaults to a "locked down" state when it is installed. This helps protect an administrator from inadvertently leaving a server more exposed to attack than is strictly necessary for the services that are needed.

IIS 6.0 also has improved architecture, through a variety of measures. First, resources (such as system memory) are now dynamically allocated, which allows many more web sites to be hosted on a single server. Second, new features make IIS more reliable, such as the ability for IIS to monitor the health of its processes; any that are having problems can be restarted automatically without affecting other running processes.

Management and Administration

A number of improvements have been made to the various management tools within .NET Server, as follows:

- Microsoft Management Console is generally improved, now allowing for the selection of multiple objects for manipulation (when appropriate) and an improved graphical interface.

- More than 200 new group policy settings have been added to the system.

- .NET Servers now support "headless server" capabilities, where the server can be installed and managed without an attached monitor, keyboard, or mouse.

- .NET Servers can automatically update themselves through Windows Update. More importantly, there are now Microsoft Software Update Services that let administrators download and test client and server updates before centrally assigning updates to system computers.

- Many management tasks can now be run from the command line. The file C:\WINDOWS\HELP\NTCMDS.CHM documents these tools.

Networking

Networking is really the core of any networked server, and .NET Server includes improvements to its networking features:

- IPv6 capability is built in, along with coexistence support for migration from an IPv4 network to an IPv6 network.

- .NET Server supports use of the Point-to-Point Protocol over Ethernet (PPPoE).

- .NET Servers support network bridging, where separate network segments can be bridged through the server. This feature can be used to bridge two like networks, such as two Ethernet segments, or even to bridge across network types, such as between a dialup ISDN connection and an Ethernet adapter in the same server.

- An Internet connection firewall is built into .NET Server.

Progress Check

1. What are the four editions of Windows .NET Server?

2. Describe what the new Volume Shadow Copy feature does.

CRITICAL SKILL
18.2

Illustrate .NET Server Features

The purpose of the product-specific modules in this book is to familiarize you with the products in question so that you have some appreciation of the product's features and how they work, and will be comfortable approaching them in detail, if and when you need to. In this section, you will see some of the new features of .NET Server, along with representative figures illustrating these features.

NOTE

The figures depicted in this section are based on a prerelease version of .NET Server.

Server Roles

Windows 2000 Server used the Configure Your Server wizard to ease the setup of a server for various duties. Windows .NET Server continues to contain a wizard called Configure Your Server (found in the Administrative Tools menu), but it has been dramatically simplified. Figure 18-1 shows the main working screen of the new wizard.

Each choice shown in the Configure Your Server wizard can be selected in turn, each of which causes all of the software and settings necessary for the selected role to be installed. After a role is installed, you rerun the Configure Your Server wizard to select the next role

---

1. Standard, Enterprise, Datacenter, and Web Server

2. Volume Shadow Copy keeps multiple versions of stored documents on disk volumes on which it has been enabled. Administrators *and* users can easily retrieve stored earlier versions of files, even after files have been deleted.

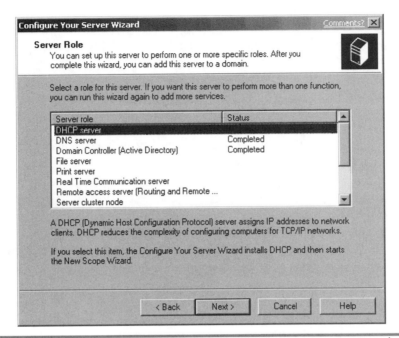

Figure 18-1 The main working screen for the new Configure Your Server wizard

(if any) that you want to install on the server, and in fact the wizard defaults to restarting itself after it completes each installation. The server roles available are

- DHCP server
- DNS server
- Domain Controller (AD)
- File server
- Print server
- Real-Time Communication Server
- Remote access server (routing and remote access)
- Server Cluster Node
- SharePoint Team Services

- Streaming media server (WMS)
- Terminal server
- Web server (IIS)
- WINS server

The really nice thing about the new Configure Your Server wizard is that each role selection will, when selected, prompt you for the choices you need to make to fully configure that role. It makes setting up a .NET Server a snap.

Web Administration

.NET Server includes a new web-driven administration capability that lets you perform many server administrative tasks from the local or a remote computer using a web browser. You can accomplish an amazing array of administration tasks using the web interface. Figure 18-2 shows the main welcome screen for web administration.

The web administration interface requires that IIS be installed, and runs on port 8099 on the server. For instance, if your server is called \\SERVER on your network, then the address for the web administration will be found at http://server:8099.

Volume Shadow Copies

One of the most interesting new features in .NET Server is called Volume Shadow Copies (VSC), and a corresponding feature called Volume Shadow Restore. VSC makes periodic snapshots of changes to documents on monitored volumes. You set the times when it does this, and the amount of disk space to allow for holding VSC images (the default is up to 10 percent of the volume). Then, each time a shadow copy is created, any document changes on the volume are saved. These stored document changes can be accessed by the users using the Volume Shadow Restore feature, which lets a user recover an accidentally deleted file, or revert a file to an earlier version, provided the earlier document was captured by an earlier VSC image. All of this can happen without the user having to ask the administrator to restore files from tape, which is what typically happens without a feature like this.

VSC is somewhat different from NetWare's file salvage feature. Salvage is essentially an undelete capability. However, for many types of document files, NetWare's salvage lets you restore earlier versions, because of the way in which most programs save files (it usually involves a file deletion behind the scenes, so salvage can restore earlier versions through this mechanism). The advantage of VSCs over NetWare's salvage, however, is that it will work with database or other types of files that are modified in place, and also VSC enables .NET's backup program to back up files that are open through the transparent use of VSC images.

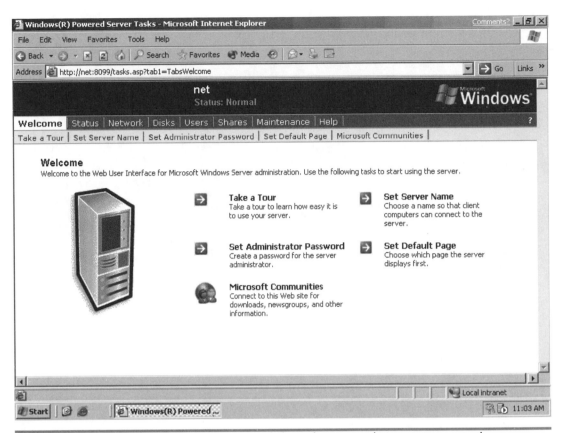

Figure 18-2 Windows .NET Server's new web-based remote administration console

Backup Improvements

The backup program included with most versions of various Windows server products can be run from the command line, and can be scheduled using the scheduler service along with the AT command. However, getting a regularly scheduled backup to work properly with this method always involves some hit and miss while you figure out the proper command-line parameters for both msbackup.exe and the AT command.

The backup program included with .NET Server includes a new scheduling feature that makes scheduling regular backups a snap. Figure 18-3 shows the main screen within backup that lets you set a schedule.

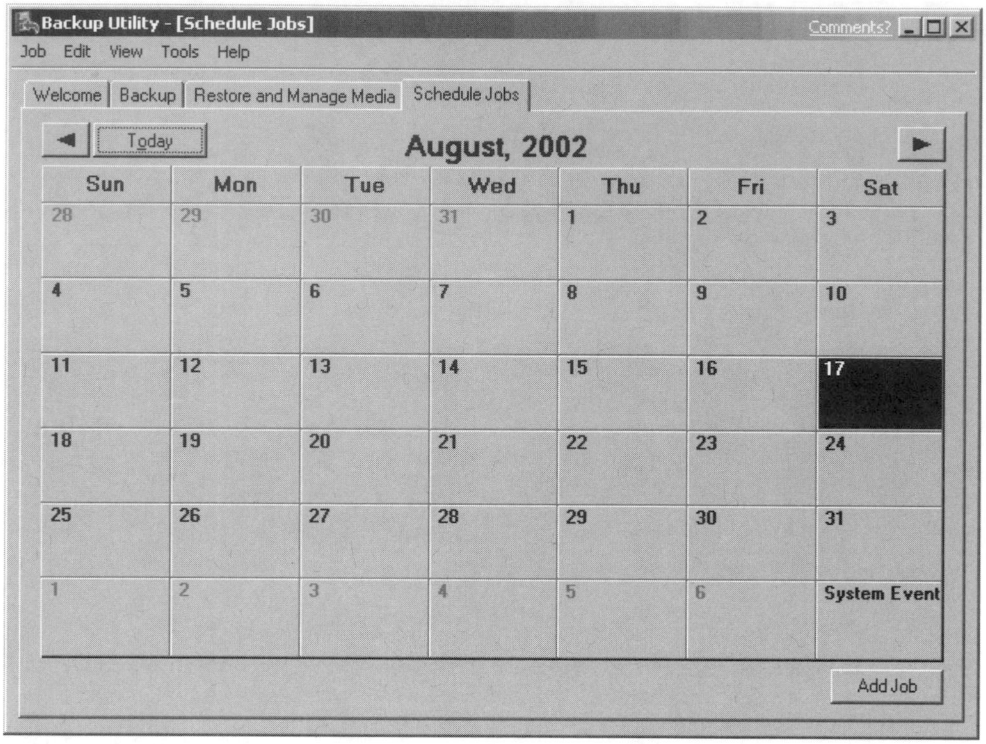

Figure 18-3 The main scheduling screen in .NET Server's backup program

To begin a job schedule, you select a day on which you want the job to start, and click the Add Job button. You are then led through a wizard that lets you define the properties for the backup job, and finally you have an opportunity to set the time and recurring schedule for the job using standard dialog boxes with which you will be familiar.

Another important improvement to the backup program is a feature called Automated System Recovery (ASR). ASR backups are designed to be saved to a single floppy disk that contains key data that can be used to rapidly recover a system from a catastrophic hardware failure. Figure 18-4 shows the initial screen of the ASR wizard.

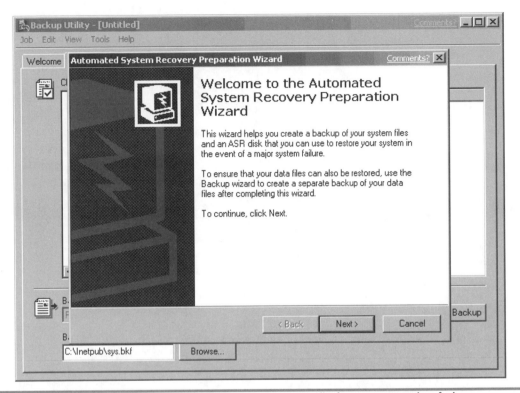

Figure 18-4 The new ASR feature helps you recover rapidly from catastrophic failures.

Internet Connection Firewall

While many organizations that have Internet connections to their network have dedicated firewall devices protecting their entire network, many smaller firms do not. Even firms that have network firewalls can benefit from incorporating firewall services onto their servers as an additional protective measure. Windows .NET Server includes a fairly complete stateful-inspection firewall service that you can use to protect the server, either as a primary defense or as a secondary defense. Figure 18-5 shows two dialog boxes: the left-hand dialog is where

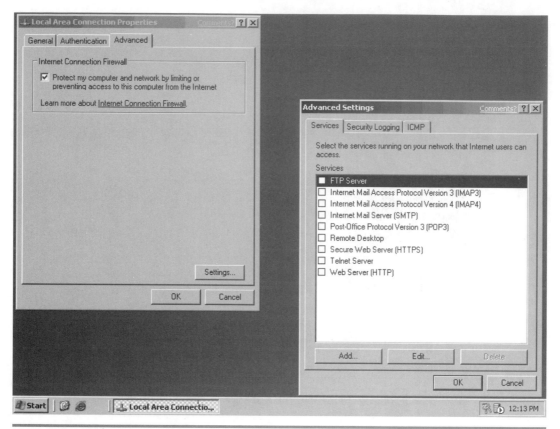

Figure 18-5 When you enable .NET Server's firewall, you can access the Advanced Settings
firewall dialog.

you enable the firewall (it is part of the Properties dialog box for the LAN connection object),
and the right-hand dialog is the first of three in which you define the firewall's settings.

The first of the advanced settings tabs (shown in Figure 18-6) lets you choose which
services on the .NET Server should be allowed to be accessed through its network connection.
The displayed list will depend on what services are installed on the server. New services can
be added using the Add button on the dialog box tab. Each of the predefined services already
includes the IP ports that the service uses, while new services that you add manually let you
set the ports that should be protected (or allowed) for the service.

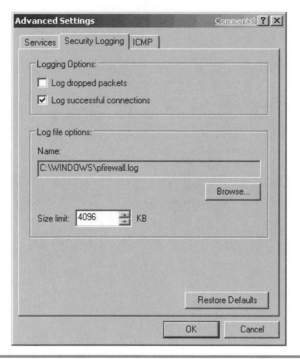

Figure 18-6 The Security Logging tab of the firewall's Advanced Options dialog box

The second tab of the firewall's Advanced Settings dialog box lets you control the logging settings for the firewall. You can select whether to log dropped packets and successful connections (connections that are barred are always logged), the file to be used to store the log, and the size to which the log can grow before old log entries are automatically removed.

The final tab of the firewall's advanced settings dialog box (see Figure 18-7) lets you control how Internet Control Message Protocol (ICMP) packets are handled. ICMP ports are used by utilities such as PING, and are frequent targets for denial-of-service attacks. For each of the types of ICMP traffic, you can select the entry to read more about it in the lower part of the dialog box. Keep in mind that you can enable certain types of ICMP on a temporary basis for troubleshooting purposes, and then turn that traffic type back off when you are done troubleshooting.

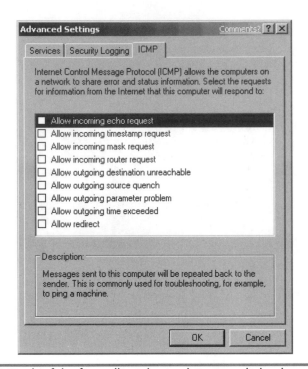

Figure 18-7 The ICMP tab of the firewall's Advanced Options dialog box

IIS Security Lockdown Wizard

One of the big problems with earlier versions of IIS is that their default settings allowed most types of traffic to the server. This often left servers far more exposed to security threats than they should have been. Microsoft has addressed this in .NET Server by making IIS's default configuration fully locked down. Basically, nothing works in IIS until you enable it to work. This is all well and good if you're an Internet security expert, but might be too much to handle if you're not. To address this potential problem, Microsoft includes an IIS Security Lockdown wizard with .NET Server that makes this process very easy. Figure 18-8 shows the initial screen of the Lockdown wizard.

The first choice you make in the Lockdown wizard is which main Internet services to enable and how those services should start when the server is booted. For each of the services (HTTP, FTP, SMTP, and NNTP), you can choose whether their startup is disabled, manual, or automatic. Figure 18-9 shows this screen in the Lockdown wizard.

Next, you can decide which request handlers you want to enable for IIS, as shown in Figure 18-10.

Figure 18-8 The IIS Security Lockdown wizard

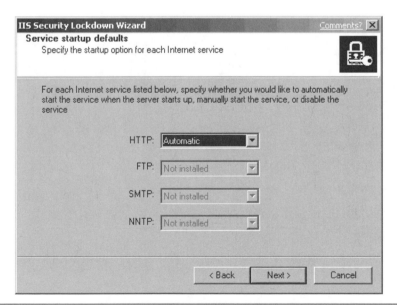

Figure 18-9 The Lockdown wizard's service startup settings

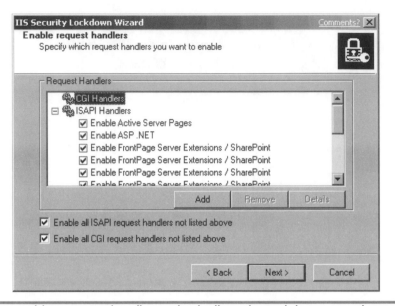

Figure 18-10 Enabling request handlers individually in the Lockdown wizard

✔ Module 18 Mastery Check

1. The four editions of the .NET Server family are called _____,
_____, _____, and _____.

2. If you are setting up a server to host your company's intranet, which edition of .NET Server should you choose and why?

3. In .NET Server, Active Directory can now replicate up to _____ servers, up from the limit of 200 servers in the Windows 2000 Server family.

4. What new feature of .NET Server would you use to prepare to recover your server from a catastrophic failure?

5. What is the name of the new feature of .NET Server that allows users to recover previous versions of their documents?

6. True or false: In .NET Server, Internet Information Services enables all services, but provides a wizard that lets you selectively turn off potential security holes.

7. True or false: Windows .NET Server supports Internet Protocol version 6 (IPv6).

8. To prepare a server to function in different roles, you use the program

   _____.

9. To keep a .NET Server as secure as possible from various network or Internet threats, you would configure its _____.

10. True or false: To schedule automated backups in .NET Server, you must run the msbackup.exe program from the command line and use the AT command for scheduling.

18

Windows .NET Server

Module 19

Installing Linux in a Server Configuration

A key component of Linux's recent success has been the remarkable improvement in installation tools. What once was a mildly frightening process many years back has now become almost trivial. The improvement in the different ways that you can install the software has been even better; CD-ROMs, although they are still the most common choice, are not the only choice. Network installations are part of the default list of options as well, which can be a great convenience when installing a large number of hosts.

TIP

In UNIX (or Linux) parlance, a *host* is any computer on a network, regardless of whether the computer is functioning as a server of some kind or a workstation.

Most default configurations in which Linux gets installed are already capable of creating a server. This is, unfortunately, due to a slightly naïve design decision: A server serves everything—from disk services to printers to mail to news to just about anything. Often, these services are all turned on from the start, depending on the distribution you are using and whether it was installed as a workstation or a server. As you know, the reality of most servers is they are dedicated to performing one or two tasks, and any other installed services simply take up memory and slow performance.

This module discusses the installation process of Red Hat Linux 7 as it pertains to servers. This process requires two things: to differentiate servers from client workstations and to streamline a server's operation based on its dedicated purpose.

TIP

With a variety of Linux distributions available, why does this discussion focus on Red Hat? The answer is simple: Red Hat is both popular and technically sound. Red Hat is friendly to a lot of different types of users and uses and, if you have to install it for the first time, it is also friendly to the user (that the entire distribution is available free from the Internet is also a plus!). As you become more experienced with Linux, you might find other distributions interesting and should look into them. It is, after all, one of the war cries of Linux users everywhere: Freedom of choice is crucial. You should never feel locked into a proprietary system.

CRITICAL SKILL
19.1 Configure Computer Hardware for Linux

Before you get into the actual installation phase, evaluating two things is important:

● What hardware is the system going to run on?

● How should the server be best configured to provide the services you need from it?

Let's start by examining hardware issues.

Hardware

As with any operating system, determining what hardware configurations work before starting an installation process is prudent. Each commercial vendor publishes a Hardware Compatibility List (HCL) and makes the list available on its web site. Be sure you obtain the latest versions of these lists so you are confident that the vendor fully supports the hardware you are using. In general, most popular Intel-based configurations work without difficulty. Red Hat's HCL web page is at **http://www.redhat.com/hardware** and Caldera's HCL is at **http:// www.calderasystems.com/products/openlinux/hardware.html**.

A general suggestion that applies to all operating systems is to avoid bleeding-edge hardware and software configurations. Although these appear impressive, they haven't undergone the maturing process that some of the slightly older hardware has already gone through. For servers, the temptation to use a bleeding-edge configuration usually isn't an issue because a server has no need for the latest and greatest toys, such as fancy video cards. After all, the main goal is to provide a highly available server for the network's users, not to play *Doom*.

Server Design

When a system becomes a server, its stability, availability, and performance become significant issues. These three issues are usually addressed through the purchase of more hardware— which is unfortunate. Paying thousands of dollars extra to get a system capable of achieving all three objectives when the desired level of performance could have been attained from existing hardware with a little tuning is a shame that everyone should make an effort to avoid. With Linux, achieving these objectives without overspending is not hard. Even better, the gains are outstanding!

The most significant design decision that you must make when managing a server configuration is not technical, but administrative. You must design a server *not* to be friendly to casual users. This means no cute multimedia tools, no sound card support, and no fancy web browsers (when possible). In fact, your organization should make a rule that casual use of a server is strictly prohibited. This rule should apply not only to site users, but to site administrators as well.

Another important aspect of designing a server is making sure that it has a good environment. As a systems administrator, you must ensure the physical safety of your servers by keeping them in a separate, physically secure room. The only access to the servers for nonadministrative personnel should be through the network. The server room itself should be well ventilated, cool, and locked. Failing to ensure such a physical environment is a recipe for an accident waiting to happen. Systems that overheat and nosy users who "think" they know how to fix problems can be as great a danger (arguably an even greater danger) to server stability as bad software. Moreover, Linux is particularly vulnerable to hacking at its command prompt.

Once the system is well secured behind locked doors, installing battery backup is also crucial. This backup serves two key purposes. The first purpose is to keep the system running during a power failure so that it can gracefully shut down, thereby avoiding the loss of any files. The second is to ensure that voltage spikes, drops, and various noises don't interfere with the health of your system.

To improve your server situation, you can take the following specific actions:

- Take advantage of the fact that the GUI is uncoupled from the core operating system and avoid starting X Window unless someone needs to sit on the console and run an application. After all, X Window, like any other application, requires memory and CPU time to work, both of which are better off going to the server processes instead.

- Determine what functions you want the server to perform and disable all other functions. Not only are unused functions a waste of memory and CPU time, but they are just another security issue that you need to address.

- Linux, unlike some other operating systems, enables you to choose the features that you want in the kernel. The default kernel you get is already reasonably well tuned, so you shouldn't need to adjust it. If you do need to change a feature or upgrade a kernel, though, be picky about what you add and what you leave out. Make sure that you need a feature before adding it.

Uptime

All this chatter about taking care of servers and making sure that silly things don't cause them to crash stems from a longstanding UNIX philosophy: *Uptime is good. More uptime is better.*

The **uptime** command tells the user how long the system has been running since its last boot, how many users are currently logged in, and how much load the system is experiencing. The latter two statistics are useful measures necessary for daily system health and long-term planning. For example, if server load has been staying consistently high, you should consider a more capable server.

But the all important number is how long the server has been running since its last reboot. Long uptimes are a sign of proper care, maintenance, and, from a practical standpoint, system stability. You often find UNIX administrators boasting about their server's uptimes the way you hear car buffs boast about horsepower. This focus on uptime is also why you hear UNIX administrators cursing at Windows installations that require a reboot for every little change. In contrast, you'll be hard pressed to find any changes to a UNIX system that require a reboot in order to take effect.

Dual-Booting Issues

If you are new to Linux, you might not be ready to commit the use of a complete system for the sake of "test-driving." Because the people who built Linux understand that we live in a heterogeneous world, all distributions of Linux have been designed so that they can be installed on separate partitions of your hard disk, while leaving others alone. Typically, this means that Microsoft Windows can coexist on a computer that also can run Linux.

Because the focus of this module is server installations, this section will not cover the details of building a dual-boot system. Anyone with a little experience in creating partitions on a disk, however, should be able to figure out how to build such a system. If you are having difficulty, you might want to refer to the installation guide that came with your distribution or another one of the many beginners' guides to Linux available on the market.

Some quick hints: If Windows 95 or Windows 98 currently consumes an entire hard disk as drive C:, you can use the **fips** tool to repartition the disk. Simply defragment the partition and then run **fips.exe**. If you are using Windows NT or Windows 2000 and have already allocated the entire disk with data on each partition, you might have to move some of the data around by hand to free a partition.

To repartition a system that has already had Windows 9x, NT, 2000, or XP installed onto it, without having to reformat the disk and rebuild from scratch, you can use a commercially-available software program such as Partition Magic.

Methods of Installation

With the improved connectivity and speed of both local area networks and Internet connections, an increasingly popular option is to perform installations over the network rather than using a local CD-ROM.

In general, you'll find that network installations become important once you decide to deploy Linux over many machines and that you require a fast installation procedure where many systems can install in parallel.

Typically, server installations aren't well suited to being automated because each server usually has a unique task and thus a slightly different configuration. For example, a server dedicated to handling logging information sent to it over the network will have especially large partitions set up for the appropriate logging directories compared to a fileserver that performs no logging of its own.

Because servers are not usually set up using a "one size fits all" approach, the focus in this section is exclusively on the technique for installing a system from a CD-ROM. Of course, after you have gone through the installation process from a CD-ROM once, you will find performing the network-based installations straightforward.

If It Just Won't Work Right . . .

You've gone through the installation procedure . . . twice. This book said it should work. The installation manual said it should work. The Linux guru with whom you spoke last week said it should work.

But it's just not working.

In the immortal words of Douglas Adams, "Don't panic." No operating system installs smoothly 100 percent of the time. (Yes, not even Mac OS!) Hardware doesn't always work as advertised, combinations of hardware conflict with each other, or that CD-ROM that your friend burned for you has CRC errors on it. (Remember: It is legal for your friend to burn you a copy of Linux!) Or, as much as you might hope that it does not, the software has a bug.

With Linux, you have several paths that you can take to get help. If you have purchased your copy from Caldera or Red Hat, you can always call the distribution's tech support lines and talk to a knowledgeable person who is dedicated to working through the problem with you. If you didn't purchase a box set, you can try contacting companies, such as LinuxCare (**http://www.linuxcare.com**), which is a commercial company dedicated to providing help. Last, but certainly not least, is the option of going to other online sources for help. An incredible number of web sites are available to help you get started. They contain not only useful tips and tricks, but also documentation and discussion forums where you can post your questions. Obviously, you want to start with the site dedicated to your distribution—**http://www.redhat.com** for Red Hat Linux and **http://www.caldera.com** for Caldera Linux. (Other distributions have their own sites. Check your distribution for its web site information.)

The following are some recommended online sources for installation help:

- **comp.os.linux.admin** This is a newsgroup, not a web site. You can read it through the Web at **http://www.deja.com**.

- **http://www.linuxdoc.org/** This site is a collective of wonderful information about all sorts of Linux-related topics, including installation guides. Just a warning, though: Not all documents are current. Be sure to check the last time that the document was updated before following the directions. A mix of cookbook-style help guides exist, as well as guides that give more complete explanations of what is happening.

CRITICAL SKILL
19.2 Install Red Hat Linux

This section documents the steps necessary to install Red Hat Linux 6 or 7 on a stand-alone system (both versions have essentially the same installation routine). The section takes a liberal approach to the process, installing all the tools possibly relevant to server operations. Later modules explain each subsystem's purpose and help you determine whether you need to keep it.

You have two ways to start the boot process: You can use a boot floppy disk or the CD-ROM. This installation guide assumes that you will boot off the CD-ROM to start the Red Hat installation procedure. If you have an older machine incapable of booting from the CD-ROM, you need to use a boot disk and start the procedure from there.

TIP

Using the boot disk alters the order of some of the steps during the installation, such as which language to use and whether to use a hard disk or a CD-ROM for installation. Once you get past the initial differences, you will find that the graphical steps are the same.

If your system supports bootable CD-ROMs, they obviously offer the faster approach. If your distribution did not come with a boot disk and you cannot boot from the CD-ROM, you need to create the boot disk. This discussion assumes that you have a working installation of Windows to create the boot disk.

TIP

What if you don't want to use the graphical installer? Don't worry, Red Hat realizes that many people still prefer text-based installation tools and that some people need to use these tools for systems that do not support graphics. If you fall into one of these categories, type **text** at the boot: prompt when starting Linux from either the CD-ROM or floppy disk.

Create a Boot Disk

Once Windows has started and the CD-ROM is in the appropriate drive, open up an MS-DOS Command Prompt window (click Start, then choose Programs | Command Prompt), which gives you a command shell prompt. Switch to the drive where the CD-ROM is located and go into the **dosutils** directory. There you find the **rawrite.exe** program. Simply run the executable and it will prompt you for the source file and destination floppy disk.

The source file is on the same drive and is called **.img**.

Start the Installation

To start the installation process, boot off the CD-ROM. This presents you with a splash screen introducing you to Red Hat 6.1. At the bottom of the screen is a prompt that reads as follows:

```
boot:
```

If you do not press any keys, the prompt automatically times out and begins the installation process. You can press ENTER to start the process immediately.

If you have had some experience with Red Hat installations in the past and you do not want the system to probe your hardware automatically, you can type **expert** at the boot: prompt. For most installations, though, you want to stick with the default. (For Linux, the expert installation really means *expert* and you shouldn't use it without a lot of Linux experience and knowledge.)

NOTE

As the initial part of the operating system loads and autodetects hardware, do not be surprised if it does not detect your SCSI subsystem. SCSI support is activated later in the process.

Choose a Language

The program first displays a menu that asks you which language you want to use to continue the installation process (see Figure 19-1).

The interface works much like any other Windows-style interface. Simply point and click on your selection. When you are ready, click the Next button in the lower-right portion of the screen.

On the left side of the screen is context-sensitive help. If you don't want to see it, you can click the Hide Help button at the lower-left part of the screen.

The Back button in the lower-right of the screen is grayed out at this point because there have been no prior options to select.

Select a Keyboard Type

The next menu enables you to select what kind of keyboard you have. The options are broken into three dialog boxes: The first lists the types of keyboards supported, the second lists available layouts the keyboard can have, and the third enables you to pick available additional variants. The bottommost dialog box is meant for you to type in, thereby enabling you to test whether your keyboard works. You don't have to type anything in the dialog box if you don't want to do so.

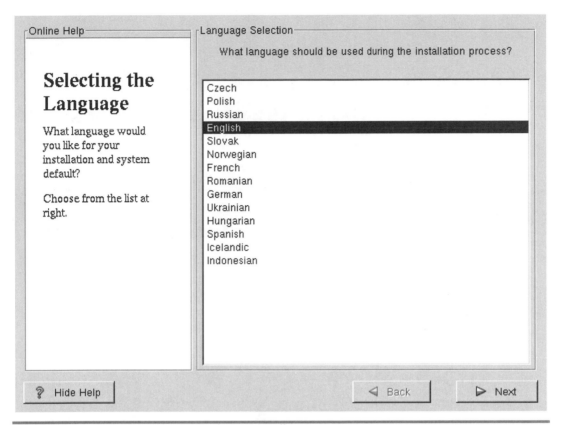

Figure 19-1 Choosing a language during installation

For most administrators, the keyboard type will be one of the Generic options, the layout will be U.S. English, and the variant will be set to None (see Figure 19-2).

TIP

If you ever want to change your keyboard layout or type, you can run the program /usr/sbin/kbdconfig.

When you finish, click Next to continue or select Back to go back to the language selection menu.

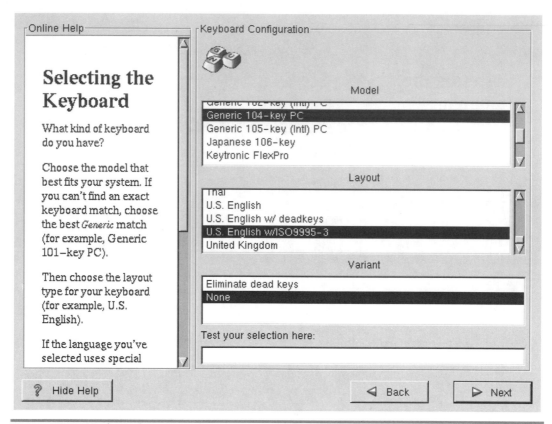

Figure 19-2 Keyboard type installation options

Select a Mouse

You now can select the type of mouse you want to use with the X Window environment (X Window is Linux's graphical user interface). More than likely, the automatic probe of the hardware in the system will have been able to highlight what you already have.

If you need to help Linux detect the mouse, simply select in the displayed directory tree the type of mouse that you have (see Figure 19-3). If you see the name brand of the mouse with a plus sign (+) to the left of it, clicking the plus sign will open a new level of choices for that particular brand. If you have a serial mouse, you also need to select the serial port it is using. You can do so in the lower box in the screen.

If you have a two-button mouse, you want to click Emulate 3 Buttons checkbox at the bottom of the screen. This is because some features of the X Window environment work only with a three-button mouse. By selecting this checkbox, you can click both buttons of a two-button mouse to emulate the middle button.

TIP

If you later change your type of mouse, you can run **/usr/sbin/mouseconfig** to reconfigure your mouse.

Welcome to Red Hat Linux

With the input devices and language selected, you are now ready to begin the actual installation phase of Red Hat Linux. This phase starts with a splash screen that tells you how to register Red Hat Linux if you purchased the boxed version. Once you have read the information about registering, you can simply click Next to continue.

Upgrade or Install?

You next see a screen that enables you to pick how you want to install Red Hat Linux. If you are on an upgrade path, this selection is easy. Simply click Upgrade and then click Next. This leads you through some screens that inform you what the program is upgrading during the process.

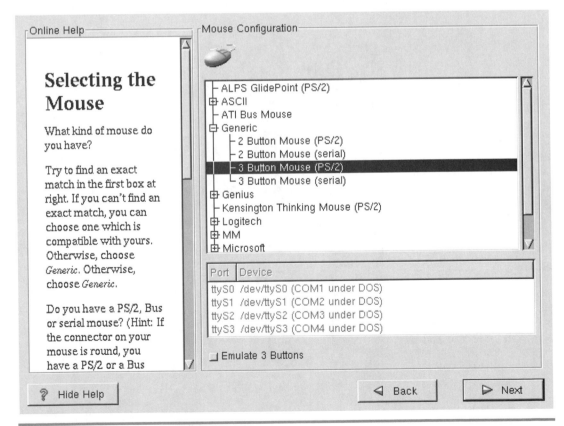

Figure 19-3 Mouse type installation options

For this module, you can assume you're doing a clean installation. This install will wipe out all the existing contents of the disk before freshly installing Red Hat Linux.

Note that the program offers an option to install Linux in a server configuration (see Figure 19-4). This method preselects all the packages for you, as well as a disk partitioning scheme. For this module's example, you want to choose Custom, so you can fine-tune what you install and how you configure it.

Create Partitions for Linux

Because you selected the custom-installation route, you need to create partitions on which Linux can install. If you are used to the Windows installation process, you will find this is a little different from the process by which you partition Windows into separate drives.

In short, each partition is *mounted* at boot time. The mount process makes the contents of that partition available as if it were just another directory on the system. So, for example, the root directory (/) is on the first (*root*) partition. A subdirectory called /usr exists on the root directory, but has nothing in it. You can then mount a separate partition so that going into the /usr directory enables you to see the contents of the newly mounted partition (see Figure 19-5).

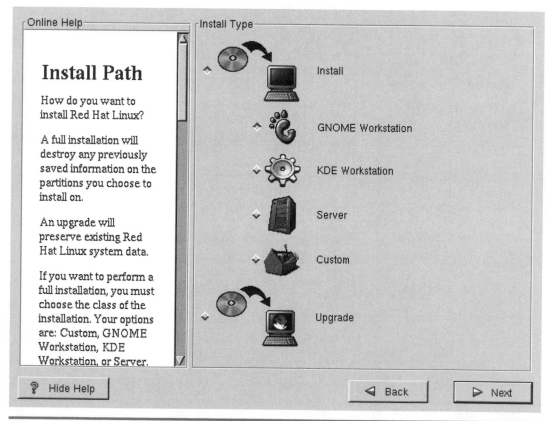

Figure 19-4 The installation method screen

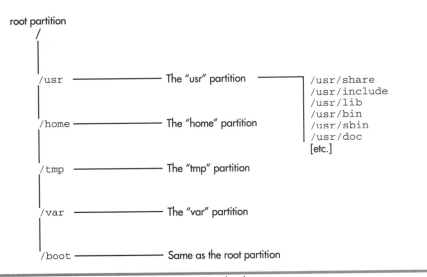

Figure 19-5 How separate partitions exist in a single directory tree

Because all the partitions, when mounted, appear as a unified directory tree rather than separate drives, the installation software does not differentiate between one partition and another. All it cares about is which directory it should place in each file. As a result, the installation process automatically distributes its files across all the mounted partitions, so long as the mounted partitions represent different parts of the directory tree where files are usually placed. Under Linux, the most significant grouping of files happens in the /usr directory, where all of the actual programs reside. (In Windows terms, this directory is similar to Program Files.)

Because you are configuring a server, you must be aware of the additional large grouping of files that will exist over the life of the server. They are the following:

- **/usr** This is where all the program files will reside (this group is similar to C:\ Program Files).

- **/home** This is where everyone's home directory will be (assuming that this server will house these directories). This grouping is useful for keeping users from consuming an entire disk and leaving other critical components, such as log files, without space.

- **/var** This is the final destination for log files. Because outside users (for example, visitors to a web site) can affect log files, partitioning these files is important; it ensures that no one can perform a Denial of Service (DoS) attack by generating so many log entries that the entire disk fills up.

- **/tmp** Temporary files are placed here. Because this directory is designed so that any user can write to it, you need to make sure that users don't abuse this privilege and fill the entire disk by keeping it on a separate partition.

- **Swap** This isn't a user-accessible file system, but it is where the virtual memory file is stored. Although Linux (and other UNIX flavors as well) can use a normal disk file to hold virtual memory the way Windows does, you'll find that keeping the swap storage on its own partition improves performance.

It is a good idea to create multiple partitions on a disk for Linux, rather than a single large partition, which you might be used to doing under Microsoft Windows. As you become more familiar with the hows and whys of partitioning disks under Linux, you might choose to go back to a single large partition. At that point, of course, you will have enough knowledge of both systems to understand why one might work better for you than the other.

Now that you have some background on partitioning under Linux, let's get back to the installation process itself. You should be at a screen that looks like Figure 19-6.

Red Hat developed the Disk Druid partitioning tool as an easy way to create partitions and associate them with the directories to which they will be mounted. When starting Disk Druid, you see all the existing partitions on your disk. Each partition entry shows the following information:

- **Mount Point** This is where the partition is mounted. Initially, this location should not have any entries in it.

- **Device** Linux associates each partition with a separate *device*. For the purpose of installation, you need to know only that under IDE disks, each device begins with /dev/hdXY, where X is

  - **a** for primary chain, primary disk
  - **b** for primary chain, secondary disk
  - **c** for secondary chain, primary disk
  - **d** for secondary chain, secondary disk

Y is the partition number of the disk. For example, /dev/hda1 is the first partition on the primary chain, primary disk. SCSI follows the same basic idea, except that instead of starting with /dev/hd, each partition starts with /dev/sd and follows the format /dev/sdXY, where X is a letter representing a unique physical drive (**a** is for SCSI id 1, **b** is for SCSI id 2, and so on). The Y represents the partition number. Thus, /dev/sdb4 is the fourth partition on the SCSI disk with id 2. The system is a little more complex than that of Windows, but each partition's location is explicit—no more guessing "to what physical device does E: correspond?"

- **Requested** This is the minimum size requested when the partition was defined.

- **Actual**   This is the actual amount of space allocated for that partition.

- **Type**   This is the partition's type. Linux's default type is Linux Native, but Disk Druid also understands many others, including FAT, VFAT, and NTFS.

The second half of the screen shows the drive summaries. Each line represents a single drive and its characteristics. Among the information presented is the following:

- The drive name (without the preceding /dev/)

- The disk geometry in *cylinders/heads/sectors* format

- The total size of the disk

- The amount of disk that has been allocated (partitioned)

- The amount of disk still available for partitioning

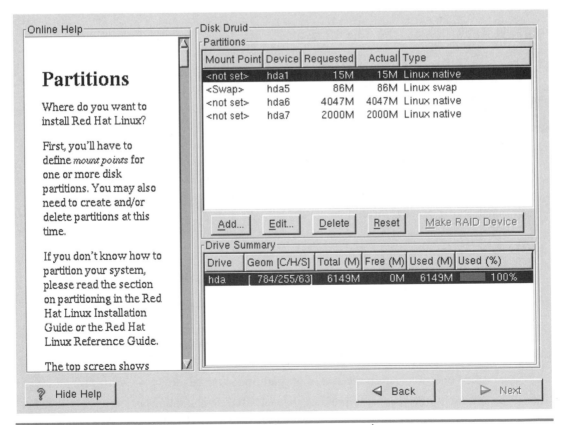

Figure 19-6 The installation screen for the disk partitioning tool

In the middle of the screen are the menu choices that you use to specify what you want to do with Disk Druid. These buttons are as follows:

- **Add** Create a new partition.

- **Edit** Change the parameters on the highlighted partition.

- **Delete** Delete the highlighted partition.

- **Reset** Reset all of the changes back to the original settings.

- **Make RAID Device** Begin the process of setting up a RAID configuration. On any operating system, setting up a RAID configuration is nontrivial and has implications that are not always obvious. This option is beyond the scope of this module.

- **Next** Commit changes to disk.

- **Back** Abort all changes made using Disk Druid and exit the program.

TIP

The program does not commit to disk any changes that you make within Disk Druid until you click the Next button.

Project 19-1 Create Partitions

This project shows you how to create a simple partition scheme for a demo system. The project assumes that you are in the middle of installing RedHat Linux, and are at the point of the installation in which you choose how you will partition the disk. For a production server, you may want to partition disks differently than the way shown here, but for a learning system the approach shown here will work fine.

Step by Step

1. To create a new partition, click the Add button. This brings up a dialog box that should resemble Figure 19-7.

   The elements in the dialog box are as follows:

   - **Mount Point** This is the directory where you want the program to mount this partition automatically at boot time.

   - **Size (Megs)** This is the size of the partition in megabytes.

   - **Grow to fill disk?** By pressing the SPACEBAR to check this box, you are telling Disk Druid that you want to grow this partition later. If you have an especially large disk and you don't know how much space to allocate to what, you might find it handy to size each partition as you need it now and select the Grow to Fill Disk? option.

Thus, as the system gets used and you see which partitions need more space than others, you can easily grow the necessary partitions without repartitioning your disk.

- **Partition Type**   This is the type of partition that will reside on that disk. By default, you want to select Linux Native, except for the swap partition that should be Linux Swap.

- **Allowable Drives**   This specifies the drives on which to create the partition.

2. For the Partition Type setting, choose Linux Swap.

3. In the Size (Megs) field, enter in a value that is twice the size of the installed RAM in the system (if you wish, and the system has plenty of disk space, you can safely go up to four times the size of installed RAM).

4. Click the OK button to save the swap partitions information.

5. Click the Add button again in Disk Druid to add the final partition.

6. In the Add dialog box, enter a forward-slash for the mount point (this means the root directory).

7. For the partition type, choose Linux Native.

8. For the size, either enter in the remaining disk space available, or simply click the Grow to Fill Disk? checkbox to automatically use all available space.

9. Click OK to save the root partition information.

10. In the Disk Druid screen, click the Next button to accept your choices and proceed to format the partitions and continue the installation.

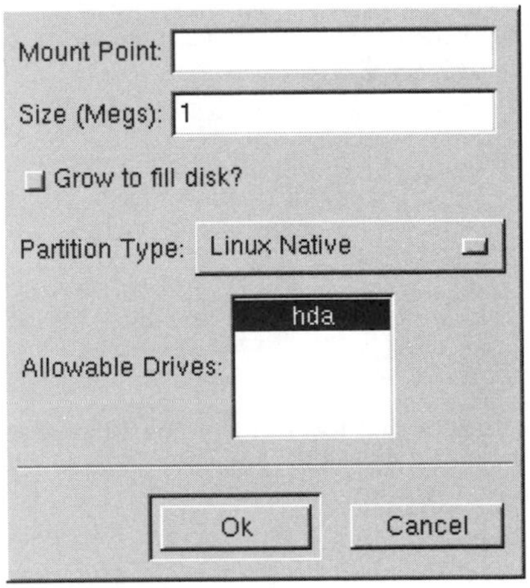

Figure 19-7 The Add Partition dialog box

(continued)

Project Summary

At a minimum, you need to have two partitions: one for holding all the files (mounted as root) and the other for swap space. *Swap space* is usually sized to be double the available RAM if less than 128MB of RAM exists or the exact same amount of RAM if there is more than 128MB. When in doubt, it doesn't hurt to allocate more swap space than these recommendations, within reason.

Other Partition Manipulation Tasks   Once you have gone through the steps of adding a partition and you are comfortable with the variables involved (mount points, sizes, types, devices, and so forth), the actual process of editing and deleting partitions is quite simple. *Editing an entry* means simply changing the same entries that you established when you added the partition. *Deleting an entry* requires only that you confirm that you want to perform the deletion.

Format Partitions

Figure 19-8 shows the screen that lists all the newly created partitions. Because you are wiping the disk of previous installations, you want to select all the partitions to be formatted. (More accurately, Red Hat will be creating a file system on the disk.)

 TIP

If you are using an older drive and you aren't sure about its reliability, click the Check for Bad Blocks While Formatting option, listed directly below all the partitions. This selection causes the formatting process to take significantly longer, but at least you will know for sure whether the disk is reliable.

Progress Check

1. There are two basic types of installation you can run for RedHat Linux. They are _____ and _____.

2. When you boot a Linux system that has multiple partitions, each partition is _____ at boot-time.

---

1. Install and Upgrade
2. Mounted

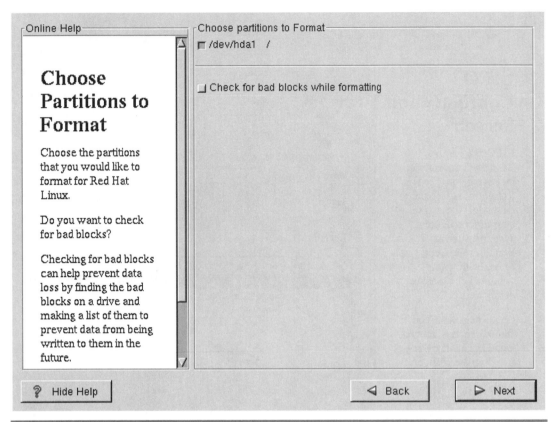

Figure 19-8 The screen for formatting partitions

Install LILO

LILO is the boot manager for Linux. A *boot manager* handles the process of actually starting the load process of an operating system. If you're familiar with Windows NT, you have already dealt with the NT Loader (NTLDR), which presents the menu at boot time, enabling you to select whether you want Windows NT or Windows NT (VGA only). LILO effectively does the same thing, just without flashy menus.

In the Red Hat tool for setting up LILO, three sections of the screen appear (see Figure 19-9). The top of the screen enables you to select whether you want to create a boot disk. For obvious reasons, having a boot disk is a good idea.

The middle block of the screen enables you to select whether you want to set up LILO on the master boot record (MBR) or the first partition on which Linux resides. The MBR is the first thing that the system reads when booting a system. The MBR is essentially the point where the

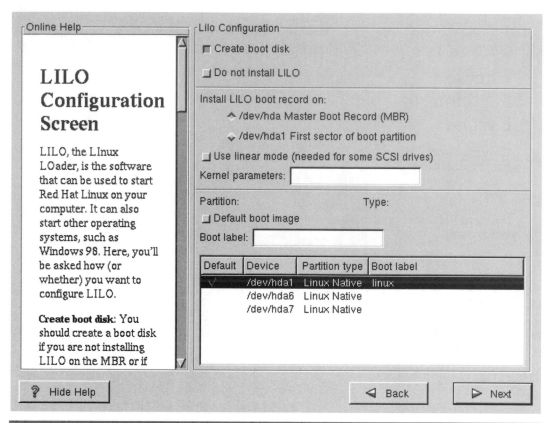

Figure 19-9 The LILO setup screen

built-in hardware tests finish and pass control to the software present within the MBR. If you choose to install LILO in the MBR, LILO loads with a boot: prompt when you turn on your system or reboot it, and enables you to select which operating system to load. In a server configuration, only one choice should exist.

If you are already using another boot loader and prefer it, then you will want to place LILO on the first sector of the root partition. This will allow your preferred boot loader to run first and then pass control to LILO if you decide to start Linux.

Also in the middle block is an option to use linear mode. This option applies only to some SCSI drives or drives that are accessed in Logical Block Addressing (LBA) mode.

The last option in the middle block is a box that enables you to enter kernel parameters to be used at boot time. For most systems, you should not need to place anything in this field. If the documentation for a particular feature or device requires you to pass a parameter in the field, add it. Otherwise, leave the field blank.

Finally, the bottom part of the screen enables you to select which operating systems LILO enables you to select at boot time. On a system configured to support both Windows and Linux, you will see your choices in this block. Because the example system is meant only for Linux, you see only Linux as an available choice.

TIP

The exception is for SMP-based systems, which have two choices. The first choice, linux, is set up to support multiple processors. If this doesn't work out for you, linux-up is also available. This second option uses only one processor, but at least gets you up and running.

Set Up Networking

Red Hat is now ready to configure your network interface cards (see Figure 19-10).

```
┌Online Help──────────────┐  ┌Network Configuration─────────────────────────┐
│                      ▲  │  │ ┌eth0─┐                                        │
│                      │  │  │ └─────┘                                        │
│                         │  │  ☐ Configure using DHCP                        │
│  **Network**            │  │  ☐ Activate on boot                            │
│  **Configuration**      │  │                                                │
│                         │  │  IP Address:  [        ]                        │
│  If you have a network  │  │  Netmask:     [        ]                        │
│  card, you can set up   │  │  Network:     [        ]                        │
│  your networking        │  │  Broadcast:   [        ]                        │
│  information.           │  │                                                │
│  Otherwise, click Next  │  │                                                │
│  to proceed.            │  │  Hostname:    [                    ]            │
│                         │  │                                                │
│  Choose your device     │  │  Gateway:       [        ]                      │
│  type and whether you   │  │  Primary DNS:   [        ]                      │
│  would like to          │  │  Secondary DNS: [        ]                      │
│  configure using        │  │  Ternary DNS:   [        ]                      │
│  DHCP. If you have      │  │                                                │
│  multiple ethernet      │  │                                                │
│  devices, each device   │  │                                                │
│  screen will keep the   │  │                                                │
│  information you have    │  │                                                │
│  given to it. You can   │  │                                                │
│  switch between device  │  │                                                │
│  screens, for example   │  │                                                │
│  eth0 and eth1; the  ▼  │  │                                                │
└─────────────────────────┘  └────────────────────────────────────────────────┘
  ┌ ? Hide Help ┐                      ┌ ◁ Back ┐    ┌ ▷ Next ┐
```

Figure 19-10 Networking setup

19

Installing Linux in a Server Configuration

Each interface card that you have is listed as a tabbed menu on the top of your screen. Ethernet devices are enumerated eth0, eth1, eth2, and so forth. For each interface, you can configure it by either using DHCP or setting the IP address by hand. If you choose to configure by hand, be sure to have the IP address, netmask, network, and broadcast addresses ready. Finally, click the Activate on Boot option if you want the interface to be enabled at boot time.

On the bottom half of the screen, you see the configuration choices for giving the machine a host name, a gateway, and related DNS information. Once you have filled out all these fields, click Next to continue.

Configure the Time Zone

The time zone configuration screen (see Figure 19-11) enables you to select the time zone in which the machine is located. If your system's hardware clock keeps time in Universal Coordinated Time (UTC), be sure to click the UTC button so that Linux can determine the difference between the two and correctly display the local time.

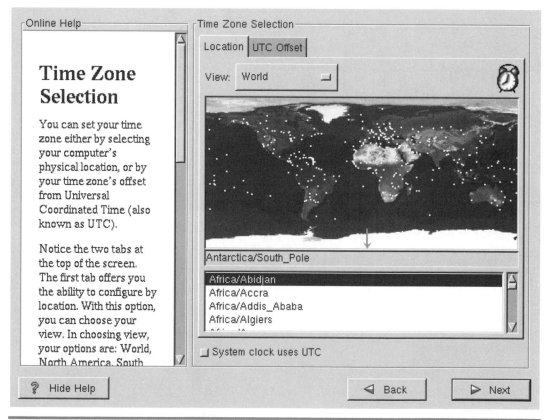

Figure 19-11 Time zone configuration

Create Accounts

The Red Hat Installation tool creates for you one account called *root*. This user account is similar in nature to the Administrator account under Windows NT—the user who is allowed access to this account has full control of the system.

Thus, it is crucial for you to protect this account with a good password. Be sure not to pick dictionary words or names as passwords because they are easy to guess and crack.

To protect root, you must not allow users to log in as the root user over the network. This restriction keeps crackers from being able to guess your root password by using automated login scripts. To allow legitimate users to become the root user, you need to log in as yourself and then use the **su** (*switch user*) command. Thus, setting the root password isn't enough if you intend to perform remote administration; you also need to set up a real user.

Setting up a normal user to do daily work is usually a good idea. By following this practice, you ensure that you don't break configuration files accidentally or other important components while you're just surfing the net or performing nonadministrative tasks. The exception to this rule is certain server configurations that should never have any users except the root user—for example, firewalls.

Project 19-2 Create Initial User Accounts

This project shows you how to create an initial user as you install Linux. Doing so is a good idea, and in fact if you want or need to create multiple user accounts it's easy to do during this part of the installation. This project uses the screen shown in Figure 19-12.

Step by Step

1. In the field for Root Password, enter in a secure, hard-to-guess password for the root user. Remember that the root account owns the entire system and can perform any action, so you need to keep it secure.

2. Confirm your password choice in the Confirm field. If the two passwords you enter don't match *exactly*, you'll see a warning on the screen. (In fact, you'll see such a warning until you finish typing the password in the Confirm password field).

3. For the first user, type their account name in the Account Name field. Remember that account names in Linux, just like everything else, are case-sensitive.

4. Enter an initial password for the new user account in the Password field below the account name, and reenter the password in the Password (confirm) field.

5. Type the full name of the user in the Full Name field.

6. Click Add to create the user account.

(continued)

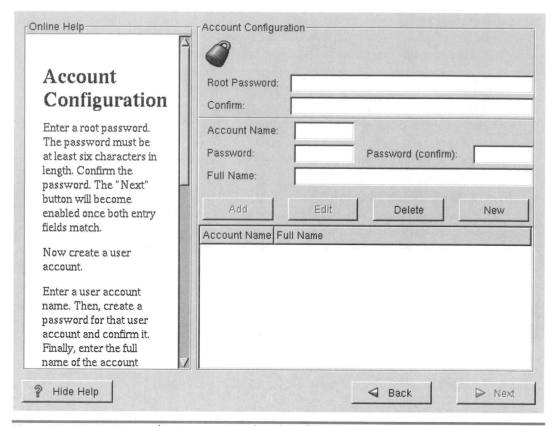

Figure 19-12 Setting up the root password and configuring new users

7. To create additional user accounts, click the New button, and click Add once you have filled out each user's information. You can create as many users as you wish at this stage.

8. When you are finished adding users, click the Next button to continue the installation.

Project Summary

In this project you created a new user, an important step in the Linux installation process. If you make any mistakes while adding new users, you can also delete and edit them.

Configure Authentication

Linux keeps its list of users in the /etc/passwd file. Each system has its own copy of this file, and a user listed in one /etc/passwd cannot log in to another system unless the user has an entry in the other /etc/passwd file. To enable users to log in to any system in a network of computers, Linux uses the Network Information System (NIS) to handle the remote password file issues.

In addition to listing users, the /etc/passwd file contains all the passwords for each user in an encrypted format. For a long time, maintaining such files was acceptable because the process of attacking them to crack passwords was so computationally expensive, it was almost futile to try. Within the last few years, affordable PCs have gained the necessary computational power to present a threat to this type of security, and thus a push to use shadow passwords has come. *Shadow passwords* are a mechanism by which the actual encrypted password entry is not kept in the /etc/passwd file but, rather, in a /etc/shadow file. The /etc/passwd file remains readable by any user in the system, but /etc/shadow is readable by the root user only. This is obviously a good step up in security. Unless you have a specific reason not to do this, be sure to check the Enable Shadow Passwords checkbox (see Figure 19-13).

Another good security trick is to use passwords encrypted with MD5. This algorithm supports longer passwords (256 characters instead of just 8), and because it takes longer to compute the hash, it takes longer for crackers to attack your system.

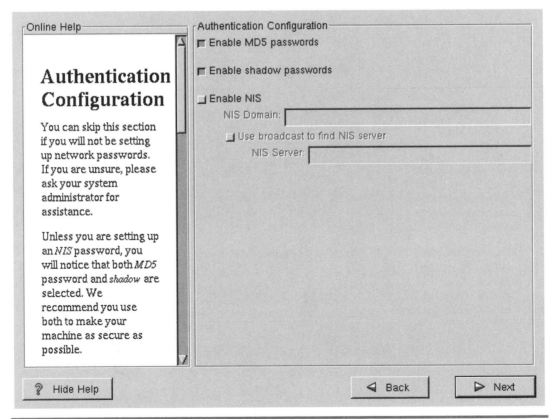

Figure 19-13 The Authentication Configuration menu

If your site has an existing NIS infrastructure, enter the relevant NIS domain and server name in this window. If you don't know these names or you simply want to deal with this part of the configuration later, you can safely ignore these fields.

Once you have selected all the checkboxes necessary and filled out the relevant fields, click Next to continue to the next screen.

Select Package Groups

In the next screen, Selecting Package Groups (see Figure 19-14), you can select the packages to install on the system. Red Hat categorizes these packages into several high-level descriptions. These categories enable you to make a quick selection of what type of packages you want installed and safely ignore the details. You can also select to install all the packages that come with Red Hat—but be warned that such an install can require as much as 1.5GB of software!

Looking at the choices, you see the menu of top-level groups that Red Hat offers. You can simply pick the groups that look interesting, you can pick everything to install all the packages,

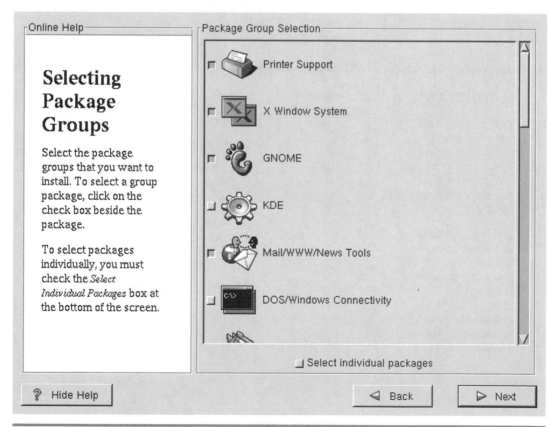

Figure 19-14 Package Group Selection screen

or you can click the Select Individual Packages button at the bottom of the screen. Once you have made your decisions, simply click Next.

If you pick Select Individual Packages, you see a screen that looks similar to Figure 19-15. On the left side of the screen, you see the logical groupings of packages. On the right side of the screen, you see the individual packages that exist in that group. When you click a package, the bottom of the screen shows the name of the package and a brief description. Directly above the description is a button to click if you want to install that package.

If you opted to select individual packages, Red Hat verifies that all the prerequisites necessary for the packages you picked are met. If any are not met, a screen similar to Figure 19-16 shows you any dependency problems with the packages you selected.

If you need to install any packages to allow all your selected packages to work, simply make sure that you select the checkbox Install Packages to Satisfy Dependencies at the bottom of Figure 19-16. Click Next when you finish picking packages.

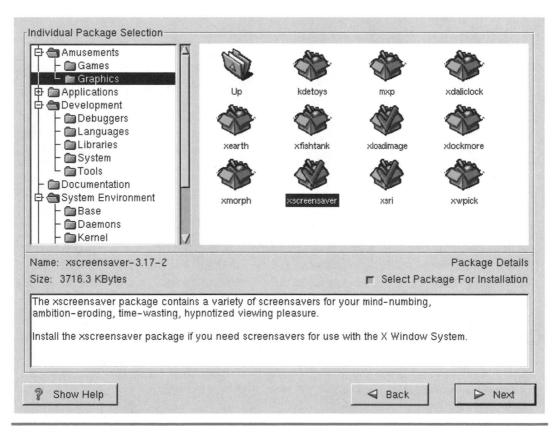

Figure 19-15 Selecting individual packages

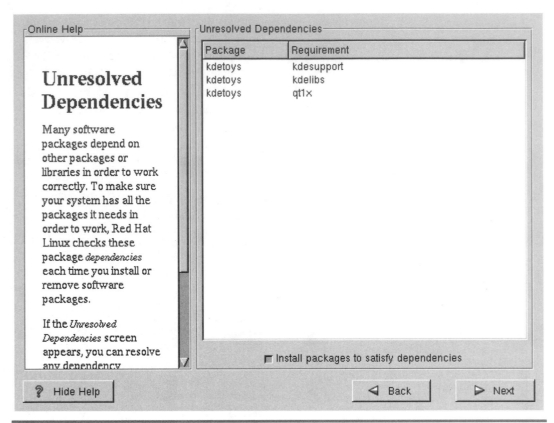

Figure 19-16 Resolving prerequisites for packages

Configure X Window

X Window is the basis for Linux's graphical user interface. It is what communicates with the actual video hardware. Programs such as KDE and GNOME, which you are more likely to have heard about, use X Window as a standard mechanism for communicating with the hardware.

CAUTION

This section describes the last step in configuring Red Hat Linux before the install program commits all the changes that you selected through this process. After this step, the program writes the partitions and installs packages. This step, therefore, is your last chance to abort.

What makes X Window interesting is that it is decoupled from the base operating system. In fact, the version of X that Linux uses—Xfree86—is also available for many other UNIX-based systems, such as those from Sun Microsystems. This means that running a server without ever starting the graphical environment is possible and, as mentioned earlier in this module, doing so is often a good idea. By turning off the GUI, you save memory and system resources that can, instead, be used for the actual server processes.

This doesn't change the fact that many nice administrative tools are available only under X Window, so setting it up is still a good idea.

Red Hat begins by trying to autodetect the type of network card and monitor you have. If you have a brand name monitor and card, you'll likely have the easiest time. If Linux cannot determine the type of video card and monitor, the OS prompts you for the necessary information. If you are prompted for this information, make sure you properly identify the video card installed in your computer, and that you know what chipset it uses (you might want to visit the manufacturer's web site to check). Manually choosing an incorrect driver for a video card will usually force you to redo the installation with the correct information later.

TIP

Before entering the information, you should have the frequency information about your monitor. Trying to send your monitor too high a frequency can cause physical damage. I managed to toast my first color monitor this way, back when monitors were far less robust and X Window configuration tools didn't exist.

Once Red Hat has the necessary information, you see a screen similar to Figure 19-17.

Four choices exist under the description of the hardware configuration: Test the configuration, customize the X configuration, use a graphical login, and skip the X configuration.

The first choice is a button that, when clicked, immediately tests your X Window configuration. This test enables you to verify that the settings work. The second choice is a toggle switch that, when selected, enables you to select the resolution at which X Window will start and the number of colors that it will use. By default, Xconfigurator tries to use the highest resolution with the maximum number of colors available. For some users, this resolution setting is too high and makes fonts hard to read; you might instead want to test with lower resolutions and work your way up.

The third choice, using a graphical login, is just that—you can have X Window automatically start up on boot so that the first login that each user sees is graphical instead of text-based. This choice is often a good one for novice users who have a Linux system at their desk.

The fourth choice is not to configure X Window. You might select this option if you don't need X Window or you want to configure it later. When you finish selecting, click Next to continue.

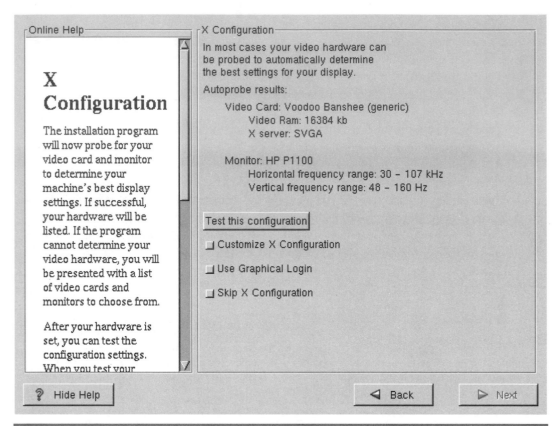

Figure 19-17 The X Window configuration tool, Xconfigurator

Begin the Install

Red Hat now goes through the process of installing all the packages that you selected. Depending on the speed of your hard disk, CD-ROM, and machine, this installation could take from just a few minutes to 10–20 minutes. A status indicator (see Figure 19-18) lets you know how far the process has gotten and how much longer the system expects to take.

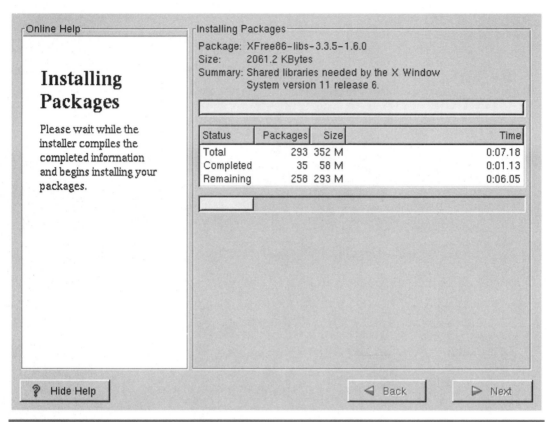

Installing Linux in a Server Configuration

Figure 19-18 The status of the installation

Create the Boot Disk

If you opted to create a boot disk earlier in the installation process, the next screen (see Figure 19-19) prompts you to insert a blank disk. This disk enables you to boot the system in case of a failure, so you can reconfigure any components that are causing problems.

At this point, if you decide you don't want to create a boot disk now, you can click the button Skip Boot Disk Creation to skip the process.

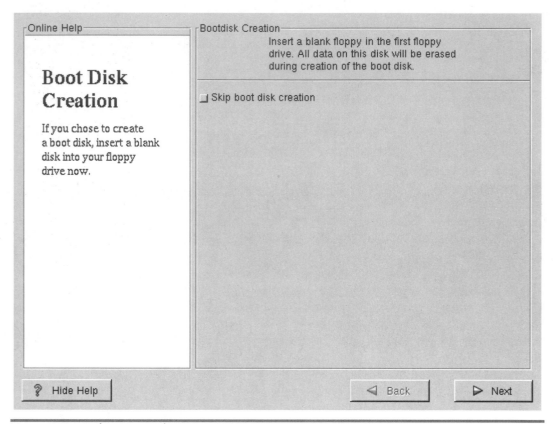

Figure 19-19 The Boot Disk Creation screen

And You're Done!

That's it! The installation process is over. The program prompts you to press a key to reboot the system. As the system reboots, be sure to remove any CD-ROMs or floppy disks you have in your system that are capable of booting before your hard disk.

Module 19 Mastery Check

1. True or false: You can set up a computer to boot to both Windows and Linux.

2. If you need to reconfigure a hard disk that presently has all space devoted to a Windows FAT-formatted partition, you can nondestructively repartition the disk using a Red Hat Linux tool called _____.

3. The easiest way to install Linux on a computer is to install it from

   A. Diskettes

   B. A bootable CD-ROM drive

   C. A network directory

4. When installing Red Hat Linux onto a machine that will be dedicated to its use, you will typically need at least two partitions: one for _____ and the other for_____.

5. The boot manager for Red Hat Linux 7 systems is called _____.

6. True or false: You must design a server *not* to be friendly to casual users.

7. When installing Red Hat Linux 6 or 7, you have two ways to start the boot process: You can use _____ or _____.

8. True or false: Under Linux, the most significant grouping of files happens in the /home directory, where all of the actual programs reside.

9. For each network interface card, you can configure it by either _____ or _____.

10. True or false: Running a server without ever starting the graphical environment is often a good idea.

Module 20

Introduction to Linux Systems Administration

373

Whan Linux first came out in 1991, you either had to be a systems administrator with lots of time or a good hacker to be able to use the system effectively. While this was fine for folks who were willing to spend the time, it wasn't great for the vast majority who saw potential for using Linux, but shied away from the learning curve.

Thankfully, the folks at Red Hat (among other Linux developers) have realized this shortcoming and have gone to great lengths to make Linux not only easy to install, but relatively painless to perform basic administrative duties.

This module provides an overview of some of the basic administrative chores necessary to keep a Linux server running and useful. This module is, of course, by no means a complete guide to systems administration, but it is a start in the right direction. If after reading this module you're interested in learning more about Linux systems administration, take a look at *Linux Administration: A Beginner's Guide* by Steven Shah, McGraw-Hill/Osborne, ISBN: 0-07-213136-5.

TIP

This module makes a few assumptions. Namely, it assumes that you have Red Hat Linux already installed and the graphical user interface (X Window) configured. The module also assumes that you are logging in to the system and running all programs as the user *root*. If you find that your login prompt is in straight text mode, you should log in as *root* and run the program startx in order to get X Window started. If X Window is erroring out, use the Xconfigurator program to set it up correctly.

CAUTION

The root user is almighty under Linux. If you are familiar with Windows NT, you can think of root as being somewhat equivalent to the Administrator account. With root access, you have full control of the system, including the ability to break it. If you are new to Linux, you should definitely take some time to practice on a nonproduction system before trying things out on your system's users.

This module is broken into two distinct sections. The first section deals with Linuxconf, the graphical user interface (GUI) front-end to a great number of systems administration functions. The section steps through using several components of Linuxconf that are commonly used when initially configuring a host.

The second part of the module deals with the command-line interface. While this section isn't about systems administration per se, it is the foundation work for basic system administration tasks. In general, you'll find the section on Linuxconf to be much more geared toward "point here, click there, enter data here, and click on Accept" instructions, whereas the command-line section gets more verbally descriptive and explains the purpose of the commands. The module includes this section because we assume that you are familiar with the high-level features of Linux (such as DNS and its theory of operation) but are not familiar with the details of the UNIX command line.

CRITICAL SKILL
20.1 Use Linuxconf

The Linuxconf tool is the basis for most of the administrative tasks you will need to do. It handles user administration, network administration, disk administration, and so on. What makes Linuxconf especially helpful is that it provides a very consistent interface for Linux administrative tasks. The only downside to Linuxconf is that, like other GUIs, it has limitations. You might find that for more advanced tasks, you will have to use the command-line interface.

You can start Linuxconf by invoking the **linuxconf** command from a terminal window, like so:

```
[root@ford /root]# linuxconf &
```

The ampersand (&) following the command detaches the Linuxconf program itself from the terminal window, thus allowing you to get your prompt back. (This is similar to starting a program from the DOS command prompt in Windows and then getting your C:\> prompt back once the new window opens up.)

The first time that you run the **linuxconf** command, you'll see a window that looks like Figure 20-1.

Take a moment to read through this window's text, as it explains how the user interface works with Linuxconf. If you are already comfortable with graphical user interfaces, understanding this GUI shouldn't be too different for you.

When you're done reading the window's text, simply click the Quit button at the bottom of the window to exit the introduction screen and start Linuxconf for reading. The opening window to Linuxconf will look like Figure 20-2.

The left pane of the window is the hierarchical display of all of the features that Linuxconf offers. Use this tree of features to move around Linuxconf and see its various features. Whenever you click on an item, the corresponding feature will appear on the right side of the window. For example, when you click the User Accounts feature, the User Accounts menu options appear on the right (see Figure 20-3).

When you are done with the User Accounts option (or whatever option is being displayed), be sure to click its Quit button. This exits the menu option, not Linuxconf. To exit Linuxconf altogether, click on the Quit button in the lower-left corner of the window.

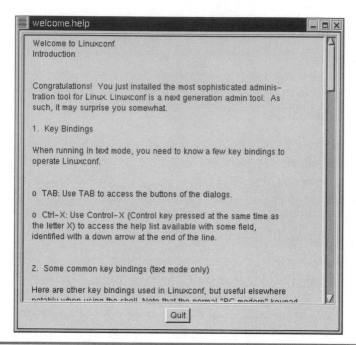

Figure 20-1 Linuxconf's first-time starting window

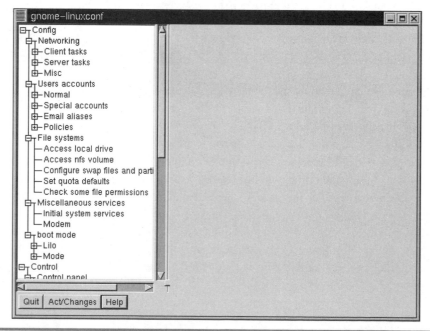

Figure 20-2 Linuxconf's opening window

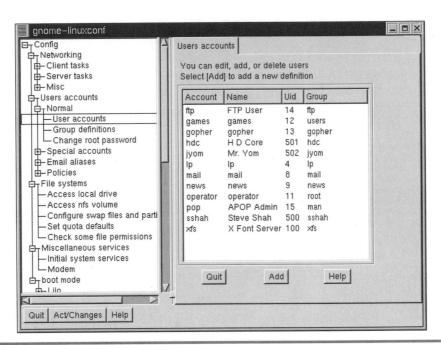

Figure 20-3 The User Accounts menu options

20

Introduction to Linux Systems Administration

Project
20-1

Add Users

CRITICAL SKILL

20.2 Manage Users

To take advantage of the multiuser nature of Linux, you need to be able to add, edit, and remove users from the system. You can perform all of these actions through Linuxconf.

Project 20-1 Add Users

In this project, you will learn how to add users to a Linux system using the Linuxconf program.

Step by Step

1. In the left pane of the Linuxconf window, click Config, then Users Accounts, Normal, and finally User Accounts. This command brings up a window that looks like Figure 20-3.

2. Click the Add button, which appears at the bottom of the list of users. This command brings up four tabbed windows (see Figure 20-4).

(continued)

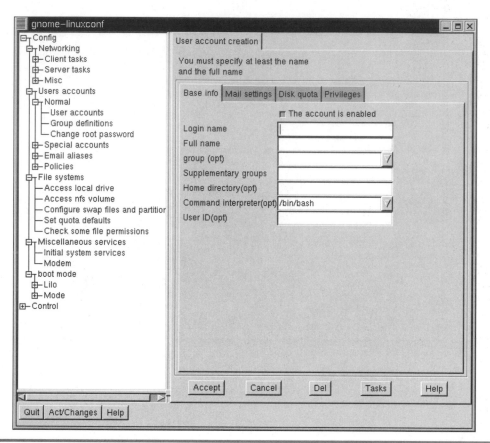

Figure 20-4 Adding a user

3. In the Base Info tabbed window, you must, at a minimum, fill in the login name (of less than eight characters) and the full name of the user. If you aren't sure about the user's home directory, type of shell, and so on, simply leave that information blank, and Linuxconf will determine the correct values for you based on the user's login name.

4. By clicking on the tabs at the top of the window for Mail Settings, Disk Quota, and Privileges, you can control user-specific features. Under Mail Settings, you can enter an e-mail alias and a forwarding address. Under Disk Quota, you can set up the maximum disk space that can be used in that user's home directory. (*Soft limits* are those that the user can exceed temporarily, whereas *hard limits* cannot be exceeded.) Under the Privileges tab is a second-level series of menus that let you fine-tune what services this new user can access.

5. Once you are done, click on the Accept button at the bottom of the window.

6. The program now displays a window prompting you for the new user's password. Enter the user's password here. Once you click OK, the program prompts you again to enter the password. Click on Accept when you are done.

TIP

Picking a good password means not picking a dictionary word (including foreign language words), no matter how bizarre or strange that might seem. Many crackers trying to break into systems use automated programs that take large, multilingual dictionaries and go through each word, one at a time, trying all of them to see if any of them match any passwords. A good technique for picking passwords is to use a phrase and then take the first letter of each word in the phrase. For example, "Snacking on Oatmeal Squares is good for you" translates into SoOSigfy. The phrase is easy to remember, even if the password is horribly cryptic. In fact, its cryptic nature makes SoOSigfy a good password. Another good strategy for picking passwords is to take a word of six letters or more, then substitute two or more letters with numbers. For example, the password le77ers (instead of *letters*) is a pretty good password. Of course, passwords are even better if they're longer.

Project Summary

In this project you added a new user and set the user's password using the guidelines in the previous tip.

Project 20-2 Remove or Edit Users

In this project, you learn how to remove users from a Linux system. For system security reasons, it is a good idea to keep track of who can log in to a system and who cannot. Thus, when a user should have his or her access revoked (for example, if the user is leaving the company, changing departments, and so on), the system's administrator needs to revoke the user's access.

Step by Step

To remove a user, follow these steps:

1. On the left side of the Linuxconf window, click Config, then choose Users Accounts, Normal, then User Accounts. This brings up a window similar to that shown in Figure 20-3.

2. Click on the user you want to remove. This takes you to a screen that looks like the User Account Creation screen shown in Figure 20-4, except that this time the user information is already filled out.

(continued)

20

Introduction to Linux Systems Administration

Project
20-2

Remove or Edit Users

3. Click the Del button at the bottom of the window.

4. The system asks you what to do with that user's data. You can either archive the data, delete the data, or leave it in its place. If you need to be able to get to the user's work files, it is best to leave the data in its place. If you think that the user might come back, archive the data. Otherwise, delete it and reclaim the disk space. Click on the appropriate choice and then click Accept. This brings you back to the user list in step 1—minus, of course, the user you just removed.

If you want to change a user's settings—for example, his or her Full Name entry—you can do so using Linuxconf. To edit a user, follow these steps:

1. On the left side of the Linuxconf window, click Config, then choose Users Accounts, Normal, then User Accounts. This brings up a screen similar to Figure 20-3.

2. Click on the user you want to edit. This takes you to a screen that looks like the User Account Creation screen shown in Figure 20-4, except that this time the user information is already filled out.

3. Change the information that you want to change. Click the Accept button when you are done.

Project Summary

In this project, you learned how to remove users and edit existing user accounts.

Project 20-3   Change Root's Password

As was mentioned earlier, the *root* user is a special user who has a lot of power on the system. Obviously, an account with this much power needs to be protected with a good password. If you think that someone might have gotten the *root* password, or that someone who had the *root* password should no longer have it (for example, a former employee), you should immediately change it. This project shows you how to change the root password on a system.

Step by Step

To change root's password, follow these steps:

1. Click on Config, then choose Users Accounts, Normal, then Change Root Password. This brings up a window similar to that shown in Figure 20-5.

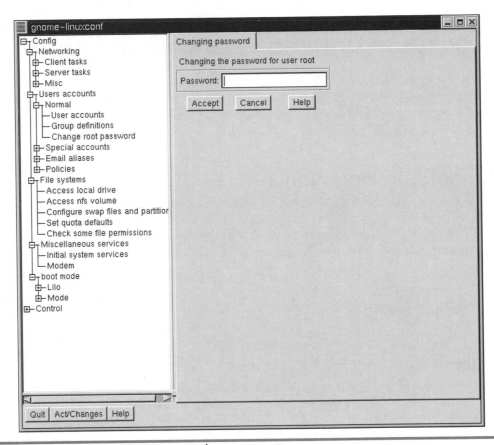

Figure 20-5 Changing root's password

2. Enter root's current password in the Password field. You must enter the current password immediately before specifying a new one as an additional safeguard so that in case you left your screen logged in as root, someone won't be able to walk up to the computer and change the root password on you! Click the Accept button when you are done.

3. Enter root's new password. Follow the suggestion given for the "Adding Users" section to make sure that you select a good root password. Click the Accept button when you're done.

4. The system prompts you again to enter root's new password. This step is to make sure that if you made any typos the first time that you entered the password, you won't be locked out. Click the Accept button when you're done.

Project Summary

In this project, you learned how to change the root user's password. The root password should use a combination of letters, numbers, and symbols.

Configure Common Network Settings

Linux is very much at home in a networked environment. In fact, its design from the onset supports its use on a network. Networks are dynamic and things change—and Linux is easy to change with them. This section explains how to use Linuxconf to change the network configuration in Linux.

Change Your Host Name

Changing the name of your system is quite easy with Linuxconf. Here are the steps to follow:

1. Click on Config, then choose Networking, Client Tasks, then Basic Host Information. This brings you to a window that looks like Figure 20-6.

2. Enter the new host name into the Host Name field and click the Accept button.

   That's all there is to it!

CAUTION

Be careful when changing a Linux machine's host name, IP address, or other IP settings if it runs on a network. Make sure to check with the network administrator before changing these settings.

Change Your IP Address

To change the IP address of your system, follow these steps:

1. Click on Config, then choose Networking, Client Tasks, Basic Host Information, just as you did to change the host name. This will bring you to a window that looks like Figure 20-6.

2. Click on the tab Adapter 1. This brings up the window in Figure 20-7, which displays the configuration information for the first network adaptor on your system. If you want to change the IP address to another adaptor, simply click on the corresponding numbered tab.

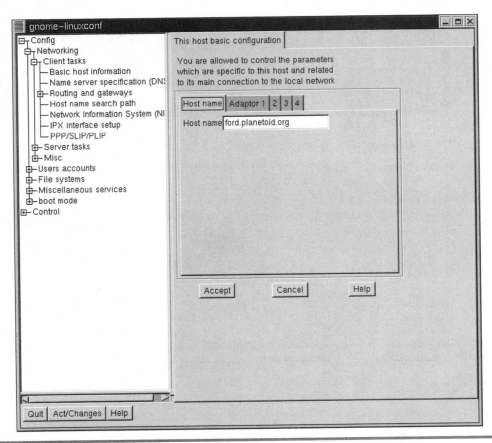

Figure 20-6 Changing your host name

3. Change the relevant settings for the selected adapter. These settings include being able to change the kernel module driver for the adaptor. Immediately above the settings are three buttons that allow you to select whether the settings come from a manual configuration of the device, from DHCP, or from BOOTP.

4. Once you have made all of your selections, click the Accept button to accept the changes.

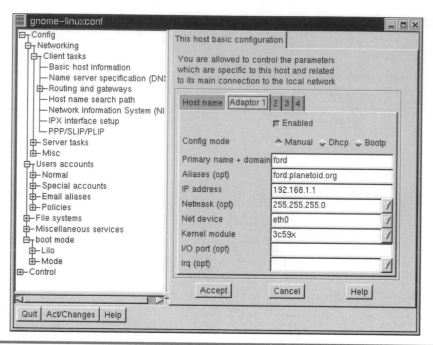

Figure 20-7 Changing the IP address

The /etc/hosts File

The /etc/hosts file contains a list of host names to IP mappings. Most systems use this list so that they can find other machines on the network if DNS ever becomes inaccessible. Typical entries include the host itself, servers for common services (such as the DNS server), and gateway entries.

The steps for adding entries into the /etc/hosts file are as follows:

1. Click on Config, then choose Networking, Misc, then Information About Other Hosts. This brings you to a window that looks like Figure 20-8.

2. Click the Add button.

3. Fill in the form and click the Accept button.

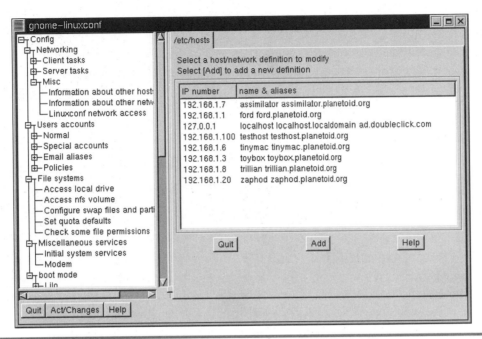

Figure 20-8 Editing the /etc/hosts file via Linuxconf

The steps for editing an entry in the /etc/hosts file are as follows:

1. Click on Config, then choose Networking, Misc, then Information About Other Hosts.

2. Click on the entry that you want to change.

3. Change the relevant settings and click the Accept button to commit the changes.

The steps for removing an entry in the /etc/hosts file are as follows:

1. Click on Config, then choose Networking, Misc, then Information About Other Hosts.

2. Click on the entry that you want to remove.

3. Click the Del button that appears below the settings.

Change DNS Client Configuration

If your system needs to work with a larger network (such as the Internet), it is a good idea to configure your system to point to a DNS server so that it can resolve host names to IP addresses, and vice versa. You can set this information up in Linuxconf by following these steps:

1. Click on Config, then choose Networking, Client Tasks, then Name Server Specification (DNS). This brings you to a window that looks like Figure 20-9.

2. Enter your domain name information in the Default Domain field, and the IP addresses for the DNS servers you want to use in the Nameserver fields.

3. Click the Accept button to commit these changes.

Change Your Default Route

In large networks, it is impossible for a single machine to know how to get to every other machine on the network, especially one as large as the Internet. Thus, when your machine doesn't know where to send a packet, it should have a default route that either does know or

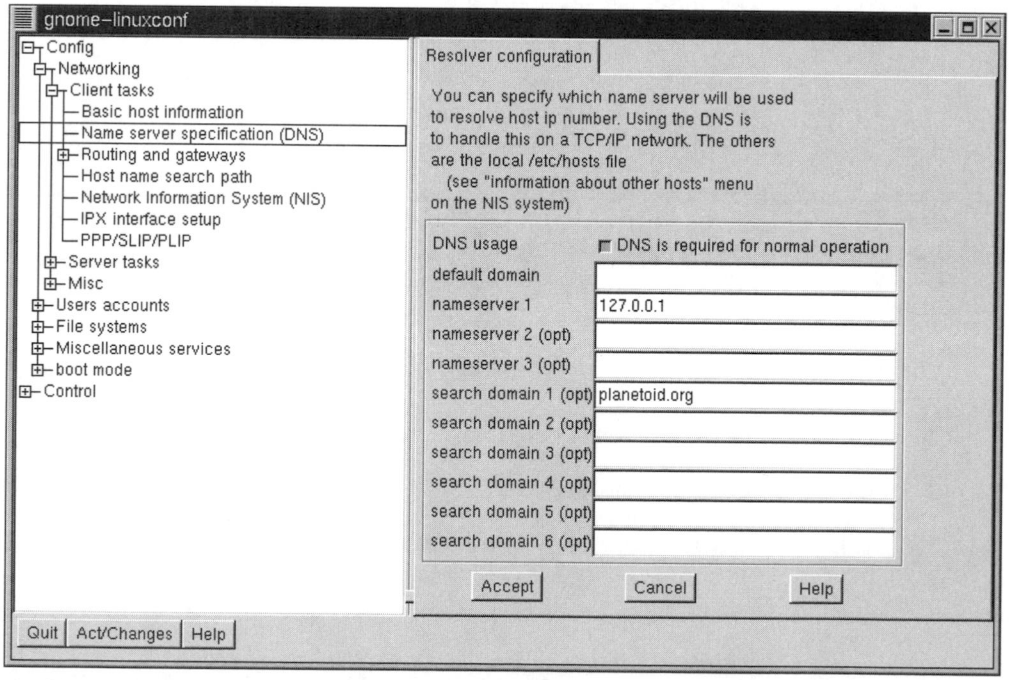

Figure 20-9 Changing the DNS client configuration

20

Introduction to Linux Systems Administration

can find out how to reach the destination machine. Typically, this default is a router of some kind that understands the necessary protocols and can thus learn the locations of the other components of the network.

To set the default route, follow these steps:

1. Click on Config, then choose Networking, Client Tasks, Routing and Gateways, then finally Defaults. This brings you to a window that looks like Figure 20-10.

2. Enter the IP address of your default route in the Default Gateway field. If you don't want to use a default route, you can unselect the Enable Routing checkbox on this page as well.

3. Click the Accept button to commit the changes.

Change How Host Names Are Looked Up

Linux allows you to change the method by which the host name is resolved. This ensures that you do not have to run more advanced services such as DNS and NIS if you don't find it necessary to do so.

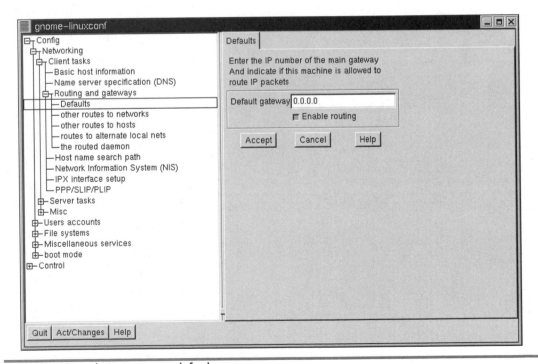

Figure 20-10 Changing your default route

To select the order in which host names are looked up, follow these steps:

1. Click on Config, then choose Networking, Client Tasks, then Host Name Search Path. This brings you to a window that looks like Figure 20-11.

2. Select the order in which you prefer to resolve host names. If you aren't sure, a safe bet is hosts, dns.

3. Click the Accept button to commit your changes.

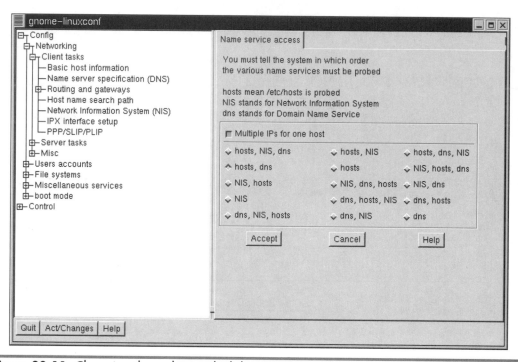

Figure 20-11 Changing the order in which host names are looked up

CRITICAL SKILL
20.4 Manage Client NFS Filesystems with LinuxConf

If your site has an existing UNIX infrastructure, you might want to be able to use Linux as an NFS client to access remote disks. Adding, changing, and removing NFS mounts are easy tasks with Linuxconf.

To add an NFS mount, follow these steps:

1. Click on Config, then choose File Systems, then Access NFS Volume. This brings you a window that looks like Figure 20-12.

2. Click the Add button.

3. Enter the server name, the volume that you are mounting, and the local directory to which you are going to mount the volume. You can, in addition, go through the tabs for this mount and modify the parameters for how the partition will get mounted. However, modify these parameters only if you are familiar with NFS. Don't forget that you must configure the servers to allow your client to mount their volumes.

4. Once you have the information entered, click the Accept button to commit your changes.

To edit a mount point, follow these steps:

1. Click on Config, then choose File Systems, then Access NFS Volume. This brings you to the window shown in Figure 20-12.

2. Click on the mount point that you want to edit.

3. You can change any of the parameters for the mount. When you are done with the changes, you can click the Accept button to commit the changes.

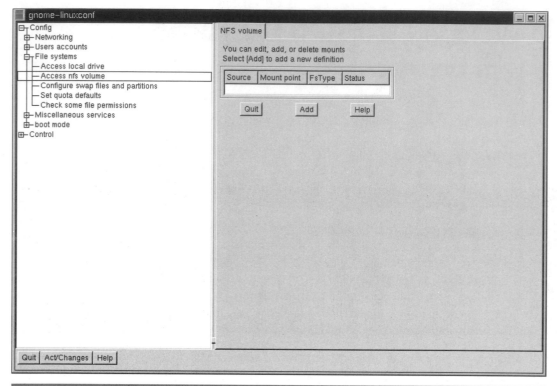

Figure 20-12 Modifying NFS mounts

To remove a mount point, follow these steps:

1. Click on Config, then choose File Systems, then Access NFS Volume. This brings you to the window shown in Figure 20-12.

2. Click on the mount point that you want to remove.

3. Click on the Del button below the configuration information.

TIP

Creating, changing, or removing a mount point does not affect whether the partitions are mounted or unmounted.

Progress Check

1. On a RedHat Linux system, what program allows you to easily administer users of the system?

2. What file do you edit in order to specify a host's name and address on your internal network if DNS is not available?

CRITICAL SKILL
20.5 # Master Linux Command-Line Basics

Historically, the aspect of UNIX that makes it so powerful and flexible has been the options available through the command line. Casual observers of UNIX gurus are often astounded at how a few carefully entered commands can result in powerful actions. Unfortunately, this power comes at the expense of ease of use. For this reason, GUIs have proliferated and have become the *de facto* standard for so many tools.

As you become more experienced, however, you will find that it is difficult for GUIs to present all of the available options to a user, because doing so would make the interface just as complicated as the command-line equivalent. Thus, the GUIs have remained overly simplified, and experienced users have had to resort to the command line.

NOTE

Before you get into a "which interface is better" holy war with someone, remember that both types of interfaces serve a purpose, with each having weaknesses as well as benefits. In the end, the person who chooses to master both will come out ahead.

Before we jump into the nitty gritty of the command-line interface under Linux, you must remember that this section is a far cry from an exhaustive discussion of Linux command-line tools. Instead of trying to cover a lot of tools without any depth, this section covers in detail a smaller handful of tools that are most crucial for day-to-day work.

---

1. Linuxconf
2. /etc/hosts is the file you edit (this file can be found on most Unix systems, not just Linux).

TIP

All of the commands discussed in this section are to be performed in a terminal window. If you are using the GNOME environment, you can open a terminal window by clicking on the picture of a monitor that appears on the control bar at the bottom of the screen. If you are using KDE, you can use the menu in the lower-left corner of your screen; open the Utilities menu and choose Terminal Window. This command displays a prompt that looks something like [root@*hostname* /root]#, where *hostname* is the name of your machine.

Environment Variables

The concept of environment variables is almost the same under Windows NT as it is under UNIX. The only difference is in how you set, view, and remove the variables.

Print Environment Variables

To list all of your environment variables, use the **printenv** command, as in the following example:

```
[root@ford /root]# printenv
```

To show a specific environment variable, specify the variable as a parameter to printenv. For example, to see the environment variable OSTYPE, you would type the following:

```
[root@ford /root]# printenv OSTYPE
```

Set Environment Variables

To set an environment variable, use the following format:

```
[root@ford /root]# variable=value
```

where *variable* is the variable name, and *value* is the value that you want to assign the variable. For example, to set the environment variable FOO with the value BAR, you would type the following:

```
[root@ford /root]# FOO=BAR
```

After setting the value, use the **export** command to finalize it. The format of the **export** command is as follows:

```
[root@ford /root]# export variable
```

where *variable* is the name of the variable. In the example of setting FOO, you would type the following:

```
[root@ford /root]# export FOO
```

TIP

You can combine the steps of setting the environment variable with the **export** command, as follows:
```
[root@ford /root]# export FOO=BAR
```

If the value of the environment variable you want to set has spaces in it, you need to surround the variable with quotation marks. In the preceding example, if you wanted to set FOO to "Welcome to the BAR of FOO," you would type the following:

```
[root@ford /root]# export FOO="Welcome to the BAR of FOO."
```

Clear Environment Variables

To remove an environment variable, use the **unset** command:

```
[root@ford /root]# unset variable
```

where *variable* is the name of the variable you want to remove. For example, to remove the environment variable FOO, you would type the following:

```
[root@ford]# unset FOO
```

Nuances on the Command-Line Itself

One of the difficulties in moving to the command-line interface, especially if you are used to using command-line tools such as Windows' command.com, is dealing with a shell that has a great number of shortcuts that might surprise you if you're not careful. This section reviews the most common of these nuances and explains why they behave the way they do.

Filename Expansion

Under UNIX-based shells such as bash, you expand wildcards seen on the command line *before* passing them as a parameter to the application. This is in sharp contrast to the default mode of operation for DOS-based tools, which often have to perform their own wildcard expansion. This also means that you have to be careful where you use the wildcard characters.

The wildcard characters themselves are identical to those in command.com. The asterisk (*) matches against all filenames, and the question mark (?) matches against single characters. If you need to use these characters as part of another parameter, you can *escape* them by placing a backslash (\) in front of them. This character will cause the shell to interpret a wildcard as just another character.

Environment Variables as Parameters

Although command.com enables you to do the same thing, it isn't very commonly done and thus it's often forgotten: You can use environment variables as parameters on the command line. This means that issuing the parameter $FOO will result in passing the value of the FOO environment variable instead of the string "$FOO."

Multiple Commands

Under the bash shell, it is possible to execute multiple commands on the same line by separating them with a semicolon (;). For example, suppose that you want to execute the following sequence of commands on a single line:

```
[root@ford /root]# ls -l
[root@ford /root]# cat /etc/passwd
```

You could instead type the following:

```
[root@ford /root]# ls -l ;cat /etc/passwd
```

Backticks

How's *this* for wild: You can make the output of one program the parameter of another program. Sound bizarre? Well, it's time to get used to it—this is one of the most creatively used features available in all UNIX shells.

A backtick (`) enables you to embed commands as parameters to other commands. A common instance of the use of this character is to pass a number sitting in a file as a parameter to the **kill** command. A typical instance of this occurs with the DNS server *named*. When this server starts, it writes its process identification number into the file /var/run/named.pid. Thus, the generic way of killing the *named* process is to look at the number in /var/run/named.pid using the **cat** command, and then issue the **kill** command with that value, as in the following example:

```
root@ford /root]# cat /var/run/named.pid
253
[root@ford /root]# kill 253
```

One problem with killing the *named* process this way is that you cannot automate the killing; you are counting on the fact that a human will read the value in /var/run/named.pid so that he or she can kill the number. The second problem isn't so much a problem as it is a nuisance: It takes two steps to stop the DNS server.

Using backticks, however, you can combine the steps into one *and* do so in a way that you can automate. The backticks version would look like the following example:

```
[root@ford /root]# kill `cat /var/run/named.pid`
```

When the bash shell sees this command, it will first run cat /var/run/named.pid and store the result. It will then run the **kill** command and pass the stored result to it—all in one graceful step.

Documentation Tools

Linux comes with two tremendously useful tools for making documentation accessible: man and info. Currently, the two documentation systems have a great deal of overlap between them, as many applications are moving their documentation to the info format. Info is considered superior to man because it allows the documentation to be hyperlinked together in a World Wide Web–like way, without actually having to be written in HTML format. The man format, on the other hand, has been around for decades. Thousands of utilities have only one source of documentation, that being their man pages. Furthermore, many applications continue to release their documentation in man format since many other UNIX-like operating systems such as Sun Solaris default to the man format for their documentation. As a result, both of these documentation systems will be around for a long while to come. Becoming comfortable with both of them is highly advisable.

The Man Command

Man (short for *manual)* pages are documents found online covering the usage of tools and their corresponding configuration files. The format of the **man** command is as follows:

```
[root@ford /root]# man program_name
```

where *program_name* is the name of the program for which you want to read the manual page. Note the following example:

```
[root@ford /root]# man ls
```

While reading about UNIX and UNIX-related sources for information (such as newsgroups), you might find references to commands followed by parenthesized numbers [as in "ls(1)"]. The number represents the *section* of the manual pages, with each section covering various subject areas. The section numbers are handy for some tools, such as printf, that are both commands in the C programming language as well as command-line commands. Thus, two entries would exist for such a command under two different sections.

To refer to a specific section, simply specify the section number as the first parameter and then the command as the second parameter. For example, to get the C programmers' information on printf, you would enter the following:

```
[root@ford /root]# man 3 printf
```

However, to get the command-line information, you would enter the following:

```
[root@ford /root]# man 1 printf
```

By default, the manual page for the lowest section number is printed first.

The section numbers' meanings are as follows:

Section Number	Meaning
1	User tools
2	System calls
3	C library calls
4	Device driver–related information
5	Configuration files
6	Games
7	Packages
8	System tools

The unfortunate side effect of this method of organization is that it can be difficult to use. A graphical interface to this library of documentation has been developed as part of the GNOME project. You will probably find a large icon for this interface, named gnome-help-browser, on your toolbar at the bottom of your screen or as a menu selection on the lower-left corner of your screen. If you don't, you can always start the interface from a terminal window by typing the following command:

```
[root@ford /root]# gnome-help-browser
```

TIP

A handy option to the **man** command is **-k**. With this option, **man** will search the summary information of all the man pages and list which pages have a match along with their section number. For example, the following command will find pages matching the search criteria "printf":

```
[root@ford /root]# man -k printf
```

The Info Command

In addition to man pages, info pages are another common form of documentation. Established as the GNU standard, info is a documentation system that more closely resembles the Web in the sense that documents can be hyperlinked together whereas man pages are single, static documents. Thus, info tends to be easier to read, follow, and find information in.

To read the info documents on a specific tool or application, simply invoke **info** with the parameter specifying the tool's name. For example, to read about emacs, simply type the following:

```
[root@ford /root]# info emacs
```

Usually, you will first want to check if there is a man page. This is because a great deal more information is still available in the man format than in info format. Some man pages will explicitly state that the info pages are more authoritative and should be read instead.

File Listings, Ownerships, and Permissions

Managing files under Linux is different from managing files under Windows NT and especially different from managing files under Windows 95/98. This section discusses the tools necessary to perform basic file management. The order in which the tools are discussed is unusual since the section starts by describing some commands and then steps back to provide some background information. This organization actually makes some of the concepts easier to understand since the text can then refer to the tools, with which you'll already be familiar.

The ls Command for Listing Files

The **ls** command is used to list all of the files in a directory. The command has more than 26 options. The most common of these options are the following:

Option	Description
-l	Long listing. In addition to the filename, show the file size, date/time, permissions, ownership, and group information.
-a	All files. Show all files in the directory, including those that are hidden. Hidden files begin with a period.
-1	Single column listing. List all files in a single column.
-R	Recursive. Recursively list all files and subdirectories.

You can use these options in any combination with one another. See the texinfo page for the complete list of options.

Example: To list all files in a directory with a long listing, type the following:

```
[root@ford /root]# ls -la
```

Example: To list nonhidden files in a directory that start with *A*, type the following:

```
[root@ford /root]# ls A*
```

About Files and Directories

Under Linux (and UNIX in general), you will find that almost everything is abstracted to a file. Linux's developers originally did this to simplify the programmer's job. Thus, instead of having to communicate directly with device drivers, you use special files (which to the application appear as ordinary files) as a bridge instead. To accommodate all of these uses of files, different types of files exist.

Normal Files   Normal files are just that—normal. They contain data or executables, and the operating system makes no assumptions about their contents.

Directories   Directory files are a special instance of normal files in that their contents list the location of other files. Among the files to which directories point might be other directories. From a day-to-day standpoint, it won't matter to you much that directories in Linux (and UNIX) are actually files unless you happen to try to open and read the directory file yourself rather than use existing applications to navigate directories.

Hard Links   Each file in the Linux filesystem gets its own *i-node*. An i-node keeps track of a file's attributes and location on the disk. If you need to be able to refer to a single file using two separate filenames, you can create a *hard link*. The hard link will have the same i-node as the original file and will therefore look and behave just like the original file. With every hard link that is created, a *reference count* is incremented. When a hard link is removed, the reference count is decremented. Until the reference count reaches zero, the file will remain on disk.

  You should note that a hard link cannot exist between two files that are on separate partitions. This is because the hard link refers to the original file by i-node. A file that is referred to by one i-node on one filesystem will refer to another file on another filesystem.

Symbolic Links   Unlike a hard link, which points to a file by its i-node, a symbolic link points to another file by its name. Thus, *symbolic links* (often abbreviated as *symlinks*) can point to files located on other partitions or even on other network drives.

Block Devices   Since all device drivers are accessed through the filesystem, files of type *block device* are used to interface with devices such as disks. The three identifying traits of a block device are that it has a major number, has a minor number, and when viewed using the **ls -l** command, shows the first character of the permissions to be a *b*. Note the following example:

```
[root@ford /root]# ls -l /dev/hda
brw-rw----   1 root      disk       3,   0 May  5  1998 /dev/hda
```

  In this case, the *b* is at the beginning of the file's permissions, the 3 is the major number, and the 0 is the minor number.

  The significance of the major number is that it identifies which device driver the file represents. When the system accesses this file, the minor number is passed to the device driver as a parameter to tell the driver which device it is accessing. (For example, if there are two serial ports, they will share the same device driver and thus the same major number, but each serial port will have a unique minor number.)

Character Devices   Similar to block devices, character devices are special files that allow you to access devices through the filesystem. The obvious difference between block and character devices is that block devices communicate with the actual devices in large blocks whereas character devices work one character at a time. (A hard disk is a block device, but a modem is a character device.) The distinguishing characteristics of a character device are that its permissions start with a *c* and the device has a major and minor number. Note the following example:

```
[root@ford /root]# ls -l /dev/ttyS0
crw-------   1 root      tty        4,  64 May  5  1998 /dev/ttyS0
```

Named Pipes   A named pipe is a special type of file that allows for interprocess communication. Using the **mknod** command (discussed later in the "File Management and Manipulation" section), you can create this special kind of file that one process can open for reading and another process can open for writing, thus allowing the two processes to communicate with one another. Named pipes work especially well when packages refuse to take input from a command-line pipe but you have another program that you need to feed data and you don't have the disk space for a temporary file.

You can tell that a file is a named pipe by the fact that the first character of its file permissions is a *p*, as in the following example:

```
[root@ford /root]# ls -l mypipe
prw-r--r--   1 root      root           0 Jun 16 10:47 mypipe
```

chown: Change Ownership

The **chown** command allows you to change the ownership of a file to someone else. Only the root user can change this ownership. (Normal users may not "give away" or "steal" ownership of a file from another user.) The format of the command is as follows:

```
[root@ford /root]# chown [-R] username filename
```

where *username* is the user's login to which you want to change the ownership and *filename* is the name of the file that will have its ownership changed. The filename may be a directory as well.

The **-R** option applies when the specified filename is a directory name. It tells the command to descend recursively through the directory tree and apply the new ownership not only to the directory itself but to all of the files and subdirectories within it.

chgrp: Change Group

chgrp is another command-line utility that allows you to change the group settings of a file. The command works in much the same way as chown does. The format of the command is as follows:

```
[root@ford /root]# chgrp [-R] groupname filename
```

where *groupname* is the name of the group to which you want to change *filename*. The filename may be a directory as well.

The **-R** option applies when the specified filename is a directory name. As with chown, the option tells the **chgrp** command to descend recursively through the directory tree and apply the new ownership not only to the directory itself but to all of the files and subdirectories within it.

chmod: Change Mode

Permissions are broken into four parts. The first part is the first character of the permissions. If the file is a normal file, then it will have no value and be represented with a hyphen (-). If the file has a special attribute, it will be represented with a letter. The two special files that you are most interested in are directories that are represented with a *d* and symbolic links that are represented with a *l*.

The second, third, and fourth parts are represented in three-character chunks. The first part is the permissions for the owner of the file. The second part is the permissions for the group. Finally, the last part is the permissions for the world. In the context of UNIX, the world is simply all the users in the system, regardless of their group settings.

The letters used to represent permissions are as follows:

Letter	Meaning
R	Read
W	Write
X	Execute

Each permission has a corresponding value. The read attribute is equal to 4, the write attribute is equal to 2, and the execute attribute is equal to 1. When you combine attributes, you add their values.

The reason that these attributes need values is to ensure that you can use the **chmod** command to set them. Although the **chmod** command does have more readable ways to set permissions, it is important that you understand the numbering scheme since it is used for programming. Plus, not everyone uses the naming scheme, and Linux users often assume that if you understand file permissions, you understand the numeric meanings as well.

The most common groups of three and their meanings are as follows:

Permission	Values	Meaning
---	0	No permissions
r--	4	Read only
rw-	6	Read and write
rwx	7	Read, write, and execute
r-x	5	Read and execute
--x	1	Execute only

While other combinations do exist (for example, -wx), they are nonsensical and you are unlikely ever to run across them.

Each of these three-letter chunks is then grouped together three at a time. The first chunk represents the permissions for the owner of the file, the second chunk represents the permissions for the group of the file, and the last chunk represents the permissions for all of the users on the system. The following are some common permissions:

Permission	Numeric Equivalent	Meaning
-rw-------	600	The owner has read and write permissions. You want this setting for most of your files.
-rw-r--r--	644	The owner has read and write permissions. The group and world have read-only permissions. Be sure that you want to let other people read this file.
-rw-rw-rw-	666	Everybody has read and write permissions on a file. This setting is bad. You don't want other people to be able to change your files.
-rwx------	700	The owner has read, write, and execute permissions. You want this setting for programs that you wish to run (such as the file that results from compiling a C or C++ program).
-rwxr-xr-x	755	The owner has read, write, and execute permissions. The rest of the world has read and execute permissions.
-rwxrwxrwx	777	Everyone has read, write, and execute privileges. Like the 666 setting, this is bad. Enabling others to edit your files is a recipe for disaster.
-rwx--x--x	711	The owner has read, write, and execute permissions. The rest of the world has execute-only permissions. This setting is useful for programs that you want to let others run but not copy.

Permission	Numeric Equivalent	Meaning
drwx------	700	This is a directory created with the **mkdir** command. Only the owner can read and write to this directory. Note that all directories must have the executable bit set.
drwxr-xr-x	755	Only the owner can change this directory, but everyone else can view its contents.
drwx--x--x	711	A handy trick is to use this setting when you need to keep a directory world readable, but you don't want people to be able to list the files by running the **ls** command. The setting enables users to read a directory only if they know the filename that they want to retrieve.

File Management and Manipulation

This section provides an overview of the basic command-line tools for managing files and directories. Most of this overview should be familiar if you have used a command-line interface before. Basically, you use the same old functions, just with new commands.

cp: Copy Files

The **cp** command is used to copy files. Like the **ls** command, the **cp** command has a large number of options. See the man page for additional details. By default, this command works silently, displaying status information only if there is an error condition. The following are the most common of these options:

Option	Description
-f	Force copy. Do not ask for verification.
-i	Interactive copy. Before copying files, have the user verify that he or she wants to copy each file.

Example: To copy index.html to index-orig.html, type the following:

```
[root@ford /root]# cp index.html index-orig.html
```

Example: To copy interactively all files ending in .html to the /tmp directory, type the following:

```
[root@ford /root]# cp -i *.html /tmp
```

mv: Move Files

Use the **mv** command to move files from one location to another. The command can move files across partitions as well; however, because that requires a real copy to occur as well, the **move** command can at times take longer.

The following are the most common options to this command:

Option	Description
-f	Force a move.
-I	Move interactively.

Example: To move a file from /usr/src/myprog/bin/* to /usr/bin, type the following:

```
[root@ford /root]# mv /usr/src/myprog/bin/* /usr/bin
```

Example: Although Linux has no explicit rename tool, you can use mv to accomplish this task. To rename /tmp/blah to /tmp/bleck, type the following:

```
[root@ford /root]# mv /tmp/bleck /tmp/blah
```

ln: Link Files

The ln tool allows you to establish one of two types of links: hard links and soft links. (See the "About Directories and Files" section earlier in this module for additional information.) The general format of this tool is as follows:

```
[root@ford /root]# ln original_file new_file
```

The **ln** command has many options, most of which you'll never need to use. The most common option is –**s**, which creates a symbolic link instead of a hard link.

Example: To create a symbolic link so that /usr/bin/myadduser points to /usr/local/bin/myadduser, you would type the following:

```
[root@ford /root]# ln -s /usr/local/bin/myadduser /usr/bin/myadduser
```

find: Find a File

The **find** tool enables you to find files based on a number of criteria. **find**, like the other tools that we have already discussed, has a large number of options that you can read about on its man page. The following is the command's general format:

```
[root@ford /root]# find start_dir [options]
```

where *start_dir* is the directory from which the search should start. Here is a list of the most common options used:

Option	Description
-mount	Do not search filesystems other than the filesystem from which you started.
-atime *n*	Specify that the file was accessed at least *n**24 hours ago.
-ctime *n*	Look only for files changed at least *n**24 hours ago.
-inum *n*	Find a file that has i-node *n*.
-amin *n*	Specify that the file was accessed *n* minutes ago.
-cmin *n*	Look only for files that were changed *n* minutes ago.
-empty	Find empty files.
-mmin *n*	Specify that the file was modified *n* minutes ago.
-mtime *n*	Search only for files modified *n**24 hours ago.
-nouser	Find files whose UID does not correspond to a real use in /etc/passwd.
-nogroup	Look only for files whose GID does not correspond to a real group in /etc/group.
-perm *mode*	Specify that the file's permissions are exactly set to *mode*.
-size *n[bck]*	Search only for files at least *n* blocks/characters/kilobytes big. One block equals 512 bytes.
-print	Print the filenames found.
-exec *cmd*\;	On every file found, execute *cmd*. If you are using the bash shell, be sure to follow every *cmd* with a \; otherwise, the shell will become very confused.
-name *name*	Specify that the filename should be *name*. You can use regular expressions here.

Example: To find all files in /tmp that have not been accessed in at least seven days, type the following:

```
[root@ford /root]# find /tmp -atime 7 -print
```

Example: To find all files in /usr/src whose names are *core* and then remove them, type the following:

```
[root@ford /root]# find /usr/src -name core -exec rm {} \;
```

Example: To find all files in /home with the extension .jpg and that are bigger than 100KB, type the following:

```
[root@ford /root]# find /home -name "*.jpg" -size 100k
```

dd: Convert and Copy a File

The **dd** command reads the contents of a file and sends them to another file. What makes **dd** different from **cp** is that **dd** can perform on-the-fly conversions on the file and can accept data from a device (such as a tape or floppy drive). When **dd** accesses a device, it does not assume anything about the filesystem and instead pulls the data in a raw format. Thus, you can use the data to generate images of disks, even if the disk is of foreign format.

The following are the most common parameters for **dd**:

Option	Description
if=*infile*	Specifies the input file as *infile*.
of=*outfile*	Specifies the output file as *outfile*.
count=*blocks*	Specifies *blocks* as the number of blocks on which dd should operate before quitting.
ibs=*size*	Sets the block size of the input device to be *size*.
obs=*size*	Sets the block size of the output device to be *size*.
seek=*blocks*	Skips *blocks* number of blocks on the output.
skip=*blocks*	Skips *blocks* number of blocks on the input.
swab	Converts big endian input to little endian, or vice versa.

Example: To generate an image of a floppy disk (which is especially useful for foreign file formats), type the following:

```
[root@ford /root]# dd if=/dev/fd0 of=/tmp/floppy_image
```

gzip: Compress a File

In the original distributions of UNIX, a tool to compress a file was appropriately called compress. Unfortunately, an entrepreneur patented the algorithm, hoping to make a great deal of money. Instead of paying out, most sites sought and found gzip, a different compression tool with a patent-free algorithm. Even better, gzip consistently achieves better compression ratios than compress does.

TIP

The gzip tool does not share file formats with either PkZip or WinZip. However, WinZip can decompress gzip files.

TIP

You can usually distinguish files compressed with gzip from those compressed by compress by checking their extensions. Files compressed with gzip typically end in .gz whereas files compressed with compress end in .Z.

The following are the most-used optional parameters to gzip:

Option	Description
-c	Write compressed file to the standard output device (thereby allowing the output to be piped to another program).
-d	Decompress.
-r	Recursively find all files that should be compressed.
-9	Provide the best compression.
-1	Achieve the fastest compression.

See the man page for a complete list. Note that gzip compresses the file "in-place," meaning that after the compression takes place, the original file is removed, leaving only the compressed file.

Example: To compress a file and then decompress it, use the following command:

```
[root@ford /root]# gzip myfile
[root@ford /root]# gzip -d myfile.gz
```

Example: To compress all files ending in .html using the best compression possible, enter the following command:

```
[root@ford /root]# gzip -9 *.html
```

mknod: Make Special Files

As we discussed earlier, Linux accesses all of its devices through files. To create a file that the system understands as an interface to a device, you must specify that the file is of type block or character and has a major and minor number. To create this kind of file with the necessary values, you use the **mknod** command. In addition to creating interfaces to devices, you can use mknod to create named pipes.

The command's format is as follows:

```
[root@ford /root]# mknod name type [major] [minor]
```

where *name* is the name of the file, and *type* is either the character *b* for block device, *c* for character device, or *p* for named pipe. If you choose to create a block or character device, you need to specify the *major* and *minor* number. The only time you will need to create a block or character device is when installing some kind of device driver that requires it. The documentation that comes with your driver should tell you what values to use for the major and minor numbers.

Example: To create a named pipe called /tmp/mypipe, you would type the following:

```
[root@ford /root]# mknod /tmp/mypipe p
```

mkdir: Create a Home Directory

The **mkdir** command in Linux is identical to the one in other flavors of UNIX as well as in MS-DOS. The only option available is **–p**, which creates a parent directory if none exists. For example, if you need to create /tmp/bigdir/subdir/mydir and the only directory that exists is /tmp, using **–p** will automatically create bigdig and subdir along with mydir.

Example: To create a directory called mydir, type the following:

```
[root@ford /root]# mkdir mydir
```

TIP

Under Linux, you cannot abbreviate the **mkdir** command as **md** as you can under DOS.

rmdir: Remove Directory

The **rmdir** command offers no surprises if you are familiar with the DOS version of the command. It simply removes an existing directory. The only command-line parameter available for this command is **–p**, which removes parent directories as well. For example, if the directory /tmp/bigdir/subdit/mydir exists and you want to get rid of all of the directories from bigdir to mydir, you would need to issue only the following command:

```
[root@ford /tmp]# rmdir -p bigdir/subdir/mydir
```

Example: To remove a directory called mydir, type the following:

```
[root@ford /root]# rmdir mydir
```

TIP

Under Linux, you cannot abbreviate the **rmdir** command as **rd** as you can under DOS.

pwd: Show Present Working Directory

It is inevitable that eventually you will sit down in front of an already logged-in workstation and not know where you are located in the directory tree. To get this information, you need the **pwd** command. It has no parameters and its only task is to print the current working directory.

The DOS equivalent is to type **cd** alone; however, under bash, typing **cd** simply takes you back to your home directory.

Example: To get the current working directory, enter the following command:

```
[root@ford src]# pwd
/usr/local/src
```

tar: Tape Archive

If you are familiar with the **pkzip** program, you are used to compression tools not only reducing file size, but also combining multiple files into a single large file. Linux separates this process into two tools. The compression tool is **gzip**.

The **tar** program combines multiple files into a single large file. The reason for separating this program from the compression tool is that **tar** allows you to select which compression tool to use or whether you even want compression. Additionally, **tar** is able to read and write to devices in much the same way that **dd** can, thus making **tar** a good tool for backing up tape devices.

TIP

Although the name of the program includes the word *tape,* you need not read or write to a tape drive when creating archives. In fact, you will rarely use **tar** with a tape drive in your day-to-day work (aside from your backups).

The structure of the **tar** command is as follows:

```
[root@ford /root]# tar [commands and options] filenames
```

The commands and options available to **tar** are as follows:

Options	Descriptions
-c	Create a new archive.
-t	View the contents of an archive.
-x	Extract the contents of an archive.
-f	Specify the name of the file (or device) in which the archive is located.
-v	Be verbose during operations.
-z	Assume that the file is already (or will be) compressed with gzip.

There are many more options that are less commonly used. Refer to the man page for the complete list.

Example: To create an archive called apache.tar containing all the files from /usr/src/apache, type the following:

```
[root@ford src]# tar -cf apache.tar /usr/src/apache
```

Example: To create an archive called apache.tar containing all the files from /usr/src/apache and see the list of files as they are added to the archive, type the following:

```
[root@ford src]# tar -cvf apache.tar /usr/src/apache
```

Example: To create a gzipped compressed archive called apache.tar.gz containing all the files from /usr/src/apache and list the files as they are being added to the archive, type the following:

```
[root@ford src]# tar -cvzf apache.tar.gz /usr/src/apache
```

Example: To extract the contents of a gzipped tar archive called apache.tar.gz and list the files as they are being extracted, type the following:

```
[root@ford /root]# tar -xvzf apache.tar.gz
```

cat: Concatanate Files

The cat program serves a simple purpose: to display the contents of files. While you can do more creative things with it, you will almost always use the program simply to display the contents of text files, much like you would use the type command under DOS. Because you can specify multiple filenames on the command line, it is possible to concatenate files into a single large continuous file. Thus, cat differs from tar in that the resulting file has no control information to show the boundaries of different files.

Example: To display the /etc/passwd file, type the following:

```
[root@ford /root]# cat /etc/passwd
```

Example: To display the /etc/passwd file and the /etc/group file, type the following:

```
[root@ford /root]# cat /etc/passwd /etc/group
```

Example: To concatenate the /etc/passwd file with the /etc/group file into the file /tmp/complete file, type the following:

```
[root@ford /root]# cat /etc/passwd /etc/group > /tmp/complete
```

Example: To concatenate the /etc/passwd file to an existing file called /tmp/orb, type the following:

```
[root@ford /root]# cat /etc/passwd >> /tmp/orb
```

more: Display a File One Screen at a Time

The **more** command works in much the same way as the DOS version of the program. It displays an input file one screen at a time. The input file can come from either more's standard input or a command-line parameter.

Additional command-line parameters exist for this command; however, they are rarely used. See the man page for additional information.

Example: To view the /etc/passwd file one screenful at a time, type the following:

```
[root@ford /root]# more /etc/passwd
```

Example: To view the directory listing generated by the ls command one screenful at a time, type the following:

```
[root@ford /root]# ls | more
```

du: Disk Utilization

You will often need to determine where and by whom disk space is being consumed, especially when you're running low on it! The **du** command allows you to determine the disk utilization on a directory-by-directory basis.

The following are some of the options for **du**:

Options	Description
-c	Produce a grand total at the end of the run.
-h	Print sizes in human-readable format.
-k	Print sizes in kilobytes rather than block sizes. (Hint: Under Linux, one block is equal to 1KB. However, this is not true for all flavors of UNIX.)
-s	Summerize. Print only one output for each argument.

Example: To display in a human-readable format the amount of space each directory in the /home directory is taking up, type the following:

```
[root@ford /root]# du -sh /home/*
```

which: Show the Directory in Which a File Is Located

The **which** command searches your entire path to find the name of the file specified on the command line. If it finds the filename, the tool displays the actual path of the requested file. The purpose of this command is to help you easily find fully qualified paths.

For example: To find out which directory the **ls** command is in, type the following:

```
[root@ford /root]# which ls
```

whereis: Locate the Binary, Source, and Manual Page for a Command

As the description states, this program not only searches your path and displays the name of the program and its absolute directory, but also finds the source file (if available) and the man page for the command (again, if available).

Example: To find out the location of the binary, source, and manual page for the command grep, type the following:

```
[root@ford /root]# whereis grep
```

df: Find Out the Amount of Free Space on a Disk

The **df** program displays the amount of free space on a partition-by-partition basis. The drives/ partitions must be mounted for **df** to retrieve this information. You can also gather NFS information using this command.

The following are some of the parameters that you can use for this tool:

Options	Description
-h	Use a human-readable measurement, other than simply the number of free blocks, to indicate the amount of free space.
-l	List only the mounted filesystems that are local. Do not display any information about network-mounted filesystems.

Additional command-line options are available; however, they are rarely used. You can read about them in the df manual page.

Example: To show the free space for all locally mounted drivers, type the following:

```
[root@ford /root]# df -l
```

Example: To show the free space in a human-readable format for the filesystem on which your current working directory is located, type the following (the trailing period is shorthand that means "current directory, " just as it does under DOS):

```
[root@ford /root]# df -h .
```

Example: To show the free space in a human-readable format for the filesystem on which /tmp is located, type the following:

```
[root@ford /root]# df -h /tmp
```

sync: Synchronize Disks

As most other modern operating systems do, Linux attempts to improve efficiency by maintaining a disk cache. This means, however, that at any given moment not everything you want written to disk has been written to disk.

To schedule the disk cache to be written out to the disk, use the **sync** command. If **sync** detects that writing the cache out to disk has already been scheduled, the tool causes the kernel to flush the cache immediately.

The **sync** command has no command-line parameters.

Example: To ensure that the disk cache has been flushed, type the following:

```
[root@ford /root]# sync ; sync
```

Process Manipulation

Under Linux (and UNIX in general), each running program is composed of at least one process. From the operating system's standpoint, each process is independent of one another, and unless you specifically ask the processes to share resources with each other, they are confined to the memory and CPU allocation assigned to them. Processes that overstep their memory allocation (which could potentially corrupt another running program and make the system unstable) are immediately killed. This method of handing processes has been one of the key reasons that UNIX has been able to sustain its claims to system stability for so long: User applications cannot corrupt other user programs or the operating system.

This section discusses the tools used to list and manipulate processes. This process is very important in a system administrator's day-to-day work since it's always important to keep an eye on what's going on.

ps: List Processes

The **ps** command allows you to list all of the processes in a system, as well as their state, size, name, owner, CPU time, wall clock time, and much more. The command has many command-line parameters, but this section will cover only the most common ones:

Options	Descriptions
-a	Show all processes with a controlling terminal, not just the current user's.
-r	Show only running processes.
-x	Show processes that do not have a controlling terminal.
-u	Show the process owners.
-f	Show which processes are the parents to which other processes.
-l	Produce long format.
-w	Show the process's command-line parameters (up to half a line).
-ww	Show all of a process's command-line parameters, despite length.

The most common parameter used with the **ps** command is **–auxww**, which shows all of the processes (regardless of whether or not they have a controlling terminal), each process's owners, and all of the process's command-line parameters. Let's examine the output of an invocation of **ps –auxww**:

```
USER      PID %CPU %MEM   VSZ  RSS TTY      STAT START   TIME COMMAND
root        1  0.0  0.3  1096  476 ?        S    Jun10   0:04 init
root        2  0.0  0.0     0    0 ?        SW   Jun10   0:00 [kflushd]
root        3  0.0  0.0     0    0 ?        SW   Jun10   0:00 [kpiod]
root        4  0.0  0.0     0    0 ?        SW   Jun10   0:00 [kswapd]
root        5  0.0  0.0     0    0 ?        SW<  Jun10   0:00 [mdrecoveryd]
root      102  0.0  0.2  1068  380 ?        S    Jun10   0:00 /usr/sbin/apmd -p 10 -w 5
bin       253  0.0  0.2  1088  288 ?        S    Jun10   0:00 portmap
root      300  0.0  0.4  1272  548 ?        S    Jun10   0:00 syslogd -m 0
root      311  0.0  0.5  1376  668 ?        S    Jun10   0:00 klogd
daemon    325  0.0  0.2  1112  284 ?        S    Jun10   0:00 /usr/sbin/atd
root      339  0.0  0.4  1284  532 ?        S    Jun10   0:00 crond
root      357  0.0  0.3  1232  508 ?        S    Jun10   0:00 inetd
root      371  0.0  1.1  2528 1424 ?        S    Jun10   0:00 named
root      385  0.0  0.4  1284  516 ?        S    Jun10   0:00 lpd
root      399  0.0  0.8  2384 1116 ?        S    Jun10   0:00 httpd
xfs       429  0.0  0.7  1988  908 ?        S    Jun10   0:00 xfs
root      467  0.0  0.2  1060  384 tty2     S    Jun10   0:00 /sbin/mingetty tty2
root      468  0.0  0.2  1060  384 tty3     S    Jun10   0:00 /sbin/mingetty tty3
root      469  0.0  0.2  1060  384 tty4     S    Jun10   0:00 /sbin/mingetty tty4
root      470  0.0  0.2  1060  384 tty5     S    Jun10   0:00 /sbin/mingetty tty5
root      471  0.0  0.2  1060  384 tty6     S    Jun10   0:00 /sbin/mingetty tty6
root      473  0.0  0.0  1052  116 ?        S    Jun10   0:01 update (bdflush)
root      853  0.0  0.7  1708  940 pts/1    S    Jun10   0:00 bash
root     1199  0.0  0.7  1940 1012 pts/2    S    Jun10   0:00 su
root     1203  0.0  0.7  1700  920 pts/2    S    Jun10   0:00 bash
root     1726  0.0  1.3  2824 1760 ?        S    Jun10   0:00 xterm
root     1728  0.0  0.7  1716  940 pts/8    S    Jun10   0:00 bash
root     1953  0.0  1.3  2832 1780 ?        S    Jun11   0:05 xterm
root     1955  0.0  0.7  1724  972 pts/10   S    Jun11   0:00 bash
```

```
nobody 6436   0.0   0.7   2572   988 ?        S   Jun13  0:00 httpd
nobody 6437   0.0   0.7   2560   972 ?        S   Jun13  0:00 httpd
nobody 6438   0.0   0.7   2560   976 ?        S   Jun13  0:00 httpd
nobody 6439   0.0   0.7   2560   976 ?        S   Jun13  0:00 httpd
nobody 6440   0.0   0.7   2560   976 ?        S   Jun13  0:00 httpd
nobody 6441   0.0   0.7   2560   976 ?        S   Jun13  0:00 httpd
root   16673  0.0   0.6   1936   840 pts/10 S   Jun14  0:00 su -sshah
sshah  16675  0.0   0.8   1960  1112 pts/10 S   Jun14  0:00 -tcsh
root   18243  0.0   0.9   2144  1216 tty1   S   Jun14  0:00 login -- sshah
sshah  18244  0.0   0.8   1940  1080 tty1   S   Jun14  0:00 -tcsh
```

The very first line of the output is the header indicating the meaning of each column. Most of these are self-explanatory:

Heading	Description
USER	The user name of the owner for each process.
PID	The process identification number.
%CPU	Percentage of the CPU taken up by a process. Remember that for a system with multiple processors, this column will add up to greater than 100 percent!
%MEM	Percentage of memory taken up by a process.
VSZ	The amount of virtual memory that a process is taking.
RSS	The amount of actual (resident) memory that a process is taking.
TTY	The controlling terminal for a process. A question mark (?) means that the process is no longer connected to a controlling terminal.
STAT	The process's state. *S* means that the process is sleeping. Remember that all processes that are ready to run (that is, those that are being multitasked while the CPU is momentarily focused on another process) will be asleep. *R* means that the process is actually on the CPU, and *D* is an uninterruptible sleep (usually I/O-related). *T* means that a process is being traced by a debugger or has been stopped. *Z* means that the process has gone zombie. "Going zombie" means one of two things: Either the parent process has not acknowledged the death of its child using the wait system call, or the parent was improperly killed and thus the init process cannot reap the child until the parent is completely killed. A zombied process usually indicates poorly written software. Each process state can have a modifier suffixed to it. These modifiers include W, <, N, and L. *W* means that the process has no resident pages in memory (it has been completely swapped out), < indicates a high-priority process, *N* indicates a low-priority task, and finally, *L* indicates that some pages are locked into memory (which usually signifies the need for real-time functionality).
START	The date that the process was started.
TIME	The amount of time that the process has spent on the CPU.
COMMAND	The name of the process and its command-line parameters.

top: Show an Interactive List of Processes

The top command is an interactive version of ps. Instead of giving a static view of what is going on, this tool refreshes the screen with a list of processes every two or three seconds (the user can adjust the interval). From this list, you can reprioritize or kill processes.

The key problem with the top program is that it is a CPU hog. On a congested system, this program tends to make memory problems worse as users start running top to see what is going on, only to find several other people are running top as well and that they collectively have made the system even slower than before!

By default, top installs with permissions granted to all users. You might find it prudent, depending on your environment, to allow only root to be able to run it. To do this, change the permissions for the top program with the following command:

```
[root@ford /root]# chmod 0700 /usr/bin/top
```

kill: Send a Signal to a Process

For some reason, the **kill** program was horribly named: The program doesn't really kill processes! What it does do is send *signals* to running processes. The operating system by default supplies each process a standard set of *signal handlers* to deal with incoming signals. From a system administrator's standpoint, the most important handler is for signal numbers 9 and 15: kill process and terminate process. (Okay, maybe using *kill* as a name wasn't so inappropriate after all...)

When **kill** is invoked, it requires at least one parameter: the process identification number (PID) as derived from the **ps** command. When passed only the PID number, **kill** will by default send signal 15, terminate process. Sending the terminate process signal is a lot like politely asking a process to stop what it's doing and shut down. Some programs intercept this signal and perform a number of actions so that they can cleanly shut down. Others just stop running in their tracks. Either way, sending the signal isn't a guaranteed method for making a process stop.

The optional parameter is a number prefixed by a dash character (-), where the number represents a signal number. The two signals that system administrators are most interested in are 9 and 1: kill and hang up. The kill signal is the impolite way of making a process stop. Instead of asking a process to stop, the operating system takes it upon itself to kill the process. The only time this signal will fail is when the process is in the middle of a system call (such as a request to open a file), in which case the process will die once it returns from the system call.

The hangup signal is a bit of a throw back to when most users of UNIX connected to the system via VT100 style terminals. When a user's connection would drop in the middle of a session, all of his or her running processes would receive a hangup signal (often called a SIGHUP, or HUP for short). This signal gave the processes an opportunity to perform a clean shutdown or, in the case of some programs designed to keep running in the background, safely ignore the signal.

These days, the HUP signal is used to tell certain server applications to reread their configuration files. Most applications otherwise ignore the signal.

Security Issues of Kill   The capability to terminate a process is obviously a very powerful one. The developers of the **kill** command realized this and made sure that security precautions existed so that users could kill only those processes they had permission to kill. For example, nonroot users could send signals only to their own processes. If a nonroot user attempts to send signals to processes that he or she does not own, the system returns error messages. On the other hand, the root user may send signals to all processes in the system. This means, of course, that when using the **kill** command, the root user needs to exercise great care to ensure that he or she doesn't accidentally kill the wrong process!

Example: To terminate process number 2059, you would type the following:

```
[root@ford /root]# kill 2059
```

Example: To kill process number 593 in an almost guaranteed way, you would type the following:

```
[root@ford /root]# kill -9 593
```

Example: To send the init program (which is always process ID 1) the HUP signal, you would type the following:

```
[root@ford /root]# kill -1 1
```

Miscellaneous Tools

If this entire book were dedicated to the commands available in your Linux system, the tools discussed in this section would each definitely fit into a number of categories that were much more specific. But since this overview is focused on only the most important tools for day-to-day administrative chores, the following varied tools will have to be lumped together as miscellaneous. However, even though this section declines to classify them under their own specific categories, that doesn't mean the tools aren't important!

uname: Show the System Name

The uname program allows you to learn some details about a system. This tool is often helpful when you've managed to log in remotely to a dozen different computers and have lost track of where you are. This tool is also helpful for script writers since it allows them to change the path of a script based on the system information.

The command-line parameters for uname are as follows:

Options	Description
-m	Print the machine hardware type (for example, i686 for Pentium Pro and better architectures).
-n	Print the machine's host name.
-r	Print the operating system's release name.
-s	Print the operating system's name.
-v	Print the operating system's version.
-a	Print all of the preceding information.

It might appear odd that uname prints such things as the operating system name when the user obviously will know that the name is Linux. However, such information is actually quite useful because you can find uname across almost all UNIX-like operating systems. Thus, if you are at an SGI workstation and enter **uname –s**, the tool will return IRIX; if you enter the command at a Sun workstation, uname would return SunOS; and so on. People who work in heterogeneous environments often find it useful to write their scripts such that they behave differently depending on the operating system type, and uname provides a wonderfully consistent way to determine that information.

Example: To get the operating system's name and release type, enter the following:

```
[root@ford /root]# uname -s -r
```

who: Find Out Who Is Logged In

When administering systems that allow people to log in to other people's machines or specially setup servers, you will want to know who is logged in. To generate a report listing the users currently logged in, you can use the **who** command. Simply type the following:

```
[root@ford]# who
```

This command will generate a report similar to the following:

```
sshah     tty1      Jun 14 18:22
root      pts/9     Jun 14 18:29 (:0)
root      pts/11    Jun 14 21:12 (:0)
root      pts/12    Jun 14 23:38 (:0)
```

su: Switch Users

Once you have logged in to the system as one user, you need not log back out and then log in again to assume another identity (for example, if you logged in as yourself and want to become the root user). Simply use the **su** command to switch to another user. This command has only two command-line parameters, both of which are optional.

By default, running **su** without any parameters results in an attempt to become the root user. Linux will prompt you for the root password; if you enter the password correctly, Linux then drops down to a root shell. If you are the root user and want to take the identity of another user, you do not need to enter that user's password.

Example: If you are logged in as yourself and want to switch to the root user, type the following:

```
[sshah@ford ~]$ su
```

Example: If you are logged in as root and want to switch over to user sshah, type the following:

```
[root@ford /root]# su sshah
```

You can use the dash (-) as an optional parameter. This character tells **su** not only to switch identities, but to run the login scripts for that user as well.

Example: If you are logged in as root and want to switch to user sshah with all of his or her login and shell configurations, type the following:

```
[root@ford /root]# su - sshah
```

Module 20 Mastery Check

1. Most Red Hat Linux administrative tasks can be accomplished using a graphical tool called
_____.

2. The most powerful account on a Linux system is called

    A. Administrator

    B. Admin

    C. Root

    D. Supervisor

3. You can manually control the mapping of host names to IP addresses by editing a text file called _____.

4. The _____ command lists your current environment.

5. The _____ command lists files in a directory (like the DOS DIR command).

6. The _____ command (like the DOS TYPE command) displays the contents of a file.

7. The main command to get help on Linux commands is

   A. Help

   B. man

   C. Doc

   D. ? (question mark)

8. The Linux equivalent of the DOS COPY command is _____.

9. The Linux equivalent of the DOS RENAME (REN) command is _____.

10. To see what directory you are in on a Linux system, type _____.

Module 21

Setting Up a Linux Web Server with Apache

421

One of the most popular web server applications is the Apache web server, a free program that runs under a variety of operating systems, including Linux, Windows NT/2000, OS/2, Mac OS X, Solaris, and Netware. The Apache web server, despite being a free open-source program, is a robust, proven platform on which to host a web site. The fact that it is available for free, running on the free UNIX-like operating system Linux, is a huge plus and no doubt helps drive its continuing popularity.

This module discusses the Apache web server and teaches you the basics that you need to understand Apache, download it, find web-based resources to support it, and set up a basic web site on a Red Hat Linux server.

CRITICAL SKILL
21.1 Discuss Apache Web Server

The Apache web server started out as a small development at the National Center for Supercomputing Applications (NCSA) in the early 1990s. Beginning as a very simple UNIX daemon, it was initially programmed by Rob McCool. McCool left NCSA in 1994, and the project began to be extended by a number of different programmers, some of whom added packages (modules) to the core program to enable it to support new web technologies. In those days, the web server was referred to as "a patchy" web server because it kept getting new patches to correct problems or extend functionality. Eventually it came to be called the Apache web server.

Version 1.0 of the Apache web server was released to the public at the end of 1995, and by 1996 was the most popular web server on the Internet. The latest statistics at the time this module was written are for June 2002 (http://www.netcraft.com/survey). These statistics reveal that Apache is being used to host approximately 65 percent (more than 10 million web sites) of the active web sites on the Internet, with Microsoft's IIS a distant second at around 25 percent (more than 4 million web sites).

Apache is presently coordinated through an organization called the Apache Software Foundation, a nonprofit corporation formed in 1999. Their homepage is located at http://www.apache.org.

Apache is unlike most other server applications in that it is not a graphical program (despite the fact that its main purpose is to serve up graphical web pages) and has no graphical installation routine. Instead, Apache runs as a background process on the operating system under which it runs. This background process, called a daemon (pronounced the same as "demon"), is typically called httpd (hypertext transfer protocol daemon). The management of an Apache web server is handled by editing its text-based configuration files, and by stopping and starting the daemon to cause any changes to those configuration files to take effect.

People new to networking are probably used to handling everything on a server through some sort of graphical interface. While this admittedly makes the administration of a server easier, the fact that Apache is text-based and is administered through a command-line interface should not daunt you. It is straightforward to install and administer an Apache web server, and you should have no trouble doing so. In fact, if you followed the Red Hat Linux installation in Module 21 and chose to perform a server installation type, then you already have Apache installed on that computer; you need only to activate it (it is not turned on by default in a Red Hat Server installation).

TIP

This book is designed to familiarize you with important networking concepts, hardware, and software. You might think of it as a "backbone" for learning about the broad field of networking. From this backbone, you will find yourself pursuing some topics in more detail, and one of these topics might be setting up and managing Apache web servers. If this is an area in which you wish to gain greater expertise, you will need to learn more detail than can be covered in this module. Osborne/McGraw-Hill has two books in this area that might interest you:

Apache Server 2.0: A Beginner's Guide, by Kate Wrightson (ISBN: 007219183X)
Apache Server 2.0: The Complete Reference, by Ryan Bloom (ISBN: 0072223448)

CRITICAL SKILL
21.2 Install Apache Web Server

This section demonstrates how you can set up a web site using Apache web server under Red Hat Linux.

The simplest way to install Apache web server under Red Hat Linux is to perform a server installation using the Red Hat Linux installation routine. However, if for some reason you did not install Apache under Linux (for example, if you are using a different distribution of Linux that does not come with Apache, or you performed a workstation Red Hat Linux installation), you can download the latest version and install it manually.

To download the latest version of Apache, use a web browser to go to http://www.apache .org/dist/httpd/. Open the Binaries folder, then open the folder representing the operating system you are using (Linux), and then choose the appropriate package from the list that appears. The packages are organized by (and their names contain) the Apache version, the processor, and the operating system. For example, you might download a file called httpd-2.0.39-i686-pc-linux-gnu.tar.gz (representing version 2.0.39 of Apache for Pentium IV systems running Linux) into a temporary directory on your Linux system, from which you would then install Apache server, as shown next in Project 21-1.

Project 21.1 Install Apache Web Server onto a Linux System

This project will install and test version 2 of the Apache web server onto a Linux system. The project assumes that you have downloaded the version you wish to install (as described in the preceding section). At the end of the installation, you will start Apache and then test it using a web browser.

Step by Step

1. Open a terminal emulation window.

2. To change to the directory that contains the downloaded Apache binary file, Type **cd /directory** and press ENTER.

3. Unzip the gz file using the following command (substitute the actual filename of the file you downloaded after "gunzip"):

   ```
   gunzip filename.tar.gz
   ```

4. Untar the resulting .tar file with the following command (substitute the actual filename found in the directory after performing the gunzip command in step 3. You may use the **ls** command to see its name):

   ```
   tar -xvf filename.tar
   ```

5. The **tar** command in step 4 creates a directory that has the same name as the name and version portion of the tar file. You should change directory (**cd**) to that directory, as follows:

   ```
   cd /httpd-2.0.39
   ```

6. You can now run the Apache configuration script. Enter the following command (it will take only a few seconds to run):

   ```
   ./configure
   ```

7. Now you prepare the binaries by compiling them. This takes two commands, each of which might take several minutes to complete:

   ```
   make
   make install
   ```

8. At this point, Apache is installed but not yet running. To start Apache, execute the following command from any directory:

```
/usr/local/apache/bin/apachectl start
```

There are a number of ways you can test your Apache installation. First, you can use the **ps** command to verify that the daemons are running:

```
ps -e |more
```

The **ps** command will display all running processes. Because the preceding command pipes the output of **ps –e** through more, you might have to press SPACE a number of times to see all of the running processes. In the output, you should see one or more copies of a process called httpd, which is the Apache daemon. You might see many of these; Apache usually starts a number of them, depending on the computer on which you have installed Apache, but this is perfectly normal.

After you've verified that Apache has started, you can also test it using a web browser, such as Netscape. Enter either of the following web addresses:

```
http://127.0.0.1
http://localhost
```

Both of these commands access any running web server on the computer on which they are used. (Remember that the address 127.0.0.1 is always shorthand for the local computer, as is the name localhost.) Apache has a default web page that is installed automatically, and this page should be displayed in Netscape, as shown in Figure 21.1.

You should also be able to access the page from another computer. Assuming that the computer on which you installed Apache has an IP address of 209.200.155.49, the following web address should bring up the page:

```
http://209.220.155.49
```

If you cannot access the page from a remote computer, but can on the local computer, then you should check basic IP connectivity using the **ping** command and typical network troubleshooting techniques.

Project Summary

In this project, you installed and tested Apache web server on your Linux system.

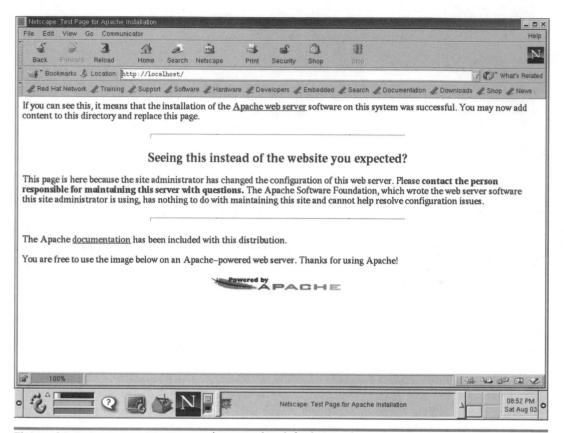

Figure 21-1 Netscape Navigator showing the default Apache web page

CRITICAL SKILL

21.3 Administer Apache Web Server

There are a number of basic administrative tasks that you will need to perform on an Apache server, not the least of which is publishing a web site onto your newly installed Apache web server. This section describes basic administrative tasks.

Stopping and Starting Apache

As you saw in the project that installed Apache onto Red Hat Linux, you use a script file called apachectl to start and stop the server. The apachectl file is located in the /usr/local/apache2/bin directory, and takes three main parameters: start, stop, and restart. For example, the following command will restart the server:

```
/usr/local/apache2/bin/apachectl restart
```

You can also issue the **apachectl** command with no parameters, which will display a brief help screen.

Changing the Apache Configuration

As mentioned earlier in this module, Apache is essentially controlled through text-based configuration files, the main one of which is called httpd.conf. The httpd.conf file is located in the following directory:

```
/usr/local/apache2/conf/
```

The httpd.conf file works through the use of plain-text directives contained in the file, along with the associated settings. For example, the following directive defines where Apache is installed:

```
ServerRoot "/usr/local/apache2"
```

If you wanted to move the Apache installation to a different directory on your Linux computer, you could certainly do so, but you would want to be careful to change the ServerRoot setting before attempting to restart Apache in its new location.

TIP

For any changes to the httpd.conf file to take effect, you must restart Apache using the *./apachectl restart* command.

The httpd.conf file is divided into three main sections, as follows:

- Global environment
- Main server configuration
- Virtual hosts

Each of these sections contains a large number of directives that control how Apache works.

When learning about Apache, you should spend some time studying the contents of the httpd.conf file and reading the extensive comments included in the file. You should also look up the various directives in the online Apache documentation, as the comments in the httpd.conf file should not be considered to be completely informative.

TIP

The online Apache documentation is installed locally onto the computer on which you installed Apache in the /usr/local/apache2/manual/ directory. You can also access it at http://www.apache.org.

Publishing Web Pages

By default (for Apache version 2), the main web site published by Apache is located in the directory /usr/local/apache2/htdocs. If you examine this directory, you will see a number of files called index.html.??, where ?? is equal to the client's language code. Assuming your language code is set to English (en), you can edit the html file index.html.en (for instance, insert your name in one of the existing text strings), save the changes, and then reaccess the web site through Netscape to see that your changes took effect.

Once you are ready to publish a complete web site, you can erase the contents of /usr/local/apache2/htdocs and replace them with the files that make up your own web site. The easiest way to do this is to connect to the computer running Apache by using the ftp program, and then upload the web site's files, either directly to the /usr/local/apache2/htdocs directory, or to a temporary directory on the server's hard disk. Once in the temporary directory, you can move them to the correct location on the server itself using the **mv** or **cp** commands.

TIP

Module 22 covers a number of useful Linux/UNIX commands, such as **mv** and **cp**.

Module 21 Mastery Check

1. The main web site from which you can download Apache, various modules, fixes, and so forth is _____.

2. True or false: The most prevalent web server on the Internet today is Microsoft's Internet Information Server (IIS).

3. When Apache is running and you execute the ps –e command, you will see a number of processes called _____.

4. Apache is controlled primarily through a configuration file called _____.

5. You start, stop, and restart Apache using the command _____.

6. After making changes to Apache's main configuration file, what must you do for the changes to take effect?

7. True or false: Apache runs only under Linux.

8. What actions do you perform to publish web pages to an Apache server?

9. True or false: If you install Red Hat Linux in its "server" configuration, Apache is automatically installed.

10. The program httpd is called a background _____.

Part III

Appendixes

Appendix A

Glossary

10Base-2   Specification for 10 Mbps (baseband) carried over coaxial cable. Also called Thin Ethernet or Thinnet.

10Base-5   Specification for 10 Mbps (baseband) carried over thick coaxial cable. Also called Thick Ethernet or Thicknet.

10Base-Fx   Specification for 10 Mbps (baseband) carried over fiber-optic cable.

10Base-T   Specification for 10 Mbps (baseband) carried over twisted-pair cable.

100Base-Tx   Specification for 100 Mbps (baseband) carried over twisted-pair cable.

802.x   Specification for various types of Ethernet networks.

AAUI   Apple Attachment Unit Interface. A connector for connecting a Macintosh to an Ethernet network.

Access Control List (ACL)   A list of security permissions for a Windows server's files, directories, and other resources. Access Control Lists are also used on other devices, and are essentially lists of who can access what.

Access Rights   The rights that control what a user can and cannot do with a particular network resource.

Account   On a server, the definition for a user of the server's services. A user cannot access a server or a network without a valid account.

Address Resolution Protocol (ARP)   A protocol that resolves a destination's Media Access Control (MAC) address from its Internet Protocol (IP) address.

Administrator   The chief administrator of a network. The administrator generally has permission to perform any task on a network and access any resource, and can assign rights to network users. Sometimes called *supervisor* and *super user*.

AFP   Apple Filing Protocol, a file access protocol for working with files through a network.

Analog   An electrical signal that is multistate and usually has an infinite number of values. For example, a volume knob on a radio is usually an analog adjustment.

ANSI   American National Standards Institute, a private, nonprofit organization that coordinates standards in the United States.

AppleTalk   A set of networking protocols for Macintosh computers.

Application layer   The seventh and highest layer in the OSI networking model. It handles communication between applications across a network. The application layer often performs user authentication on networks.

Archive bit   A bit flag that indicates which files need to be archived (backed up). When a full backup is done, the archive bit is cleared. Any subsequent changes to the file cause the archive bit to be set to on, indicating the need for an archive.

ARCnet   A token-passing network protocol rarely used these days.

ATM   Asynchronous Transfer Mode, a high-speed switched and multiplexed network specification.

Attributes (file)   Characteristics given to files. For example, in DOS files, attributes include Read-Only, System, Hidden, and Archive. Network systems generally add such attributes as Shareable and Delete Inhibit.

AUI   Attachment Unit Interface, which is a box that connects a network cable to a transceiver.

Backbone   A common cable shared by segments of a network. Usually, the backbone portion of a network operates at a higher speed than the individual segments, since it has to carry most of the traffic of all of the connected segments.

Bandwidth   The amount of data that can be carried over a network, usually expressed in mega (million) bits per second, or Mbps. Sometimes bandwidth is also specified in Hertz, as in 10 megahertz (MHz).

Baseband   A network cable that can carry only one signal at a time. See *Broadband*.

Basic rate interface (BRI)   A package of ISDN services that includes two bearer channels at 56 or 64 Kbps each (64 Kbps is common in the U.S.), plus a single data channel that carries 16 Kbps. BRI is sometimes also called 2B + D.

Baud rate   The speed at which an analog signal is carried. Baud rate is analogous to bits per second (bps). Thus 2,400 baud is roughly equivalent to 2,400 bps.

B-Channel   A channel in an ISDN connection that carries (normally) 64 Kbps of data.

Bindery   A database that contains account and security information for Novell networks versions 4 and earlier.

Bit   Short for *binary digit*, a single digit having a value of either 0 or 1.

BNC connector   A bayonet-style connector used in 10-Base2 (Thin) Ethernet networks.

Bottleneck   In a complex system, the part of the system that limits the rate of work for the entire system.

Bridge   A networking device that connects two networks to each other using Layers 1 and 2 of the OSI network model.

Broadband   A network cable that can carry multiple signals at once. See *Baseband*.

Broadcast   A network transmission sent to all nodes of a network or subnetwork.

Browser   An application that interprets and displays data formatted using Hypertext Markup Language (HTML) on the World Wide Web.

Buffer   Memory set aside to cache data between two devices, providing faster access to frequently used data. Operating systems often use buffers to hold frequently used data stored on disks.

Bus   (1) A network topology in which a cable runs from node to node, terminating on each end. (2) A connection backbone used in a computer. Most peripherals connect to this backbone.

Byte   A collection of 8 bits that can represent up to 256 distinct values.

Cache   Memory set aside expressly for holding data frequently accessed from a disk.

Capture   A mechanism that enables a network printer to act like a local printer for a specific computer. Output sent to the computer's printer port is "captured" and redirected to a network printer.

Central Office (CO)   A local switching facility, run by the Regional Bell Operating Company (RBOC), that provides an access point to the RBOC's network.

Challenge Handshake Authentication Protocol (CHAP)   An Internet communication standard for validating encrypted passwords.

Client   A computer on a network that uses data provided by a server.

Client/server   A network design model in which data processing work is divided between a client's processor and a server's processor, letting each perform the jobs to which they are best suited.

CNE   A Certified NetWare Engineer.

Coaxial cable   Cable with a center conductor surrounded by a shield. Common coaxial cable types are RG-58 and RG-8.

Common Gateway Interface (CGI)   A programming standard that connects databases and web browsers.

Concentrator   A network device that connects multiple user devices to a network. Sometimes called a *hub*.

Console A NetWare server's administrative interface.

CSMA/CD Carrier Sense Multiple Access with Collision Detection. A method used with Ethernet networks to manage packets on a segment.

CSU/DSU A Channel Service Unit/Data Service Unit is a hardware device that interfaces between a network's signals and the signals carried over a public network connection, such as a T-1 line.

Customer premises equipment (CPE) Telephone company lingo for interconnection equipment located on a company's premises.

Cyclical redundancy check (CRC) A method to detect errors in transmitted or stored data.

DAT Digital audio tape, a digital tape often used in network backup devices.

Data Communications Equipment (DCE) One end of an RS-232C or other serial connection. DCE and DTE are analogous to "male" and "female" cable connectors, in that both types are needed for a connection. See *Data Terminal Equipment*.

Data Terminal Equipment (DTE) One end of an RS-232C or other serial connection. A DTE device communicates only with a DCE device, and vice versa. See *Data Communications Equipment*.

Datagram On an IP network, a collection of network data along with its associated address and header information. Also called a *packet*.

Data-link layer The second layer of the OSI network model, the data-link layer handles error-free connections between two devices over a common physical connection.

DBMS Database Management System; usually a relational database.

D-channel One of the channels used in all ISDN interfaces; it carries 16 Kbps of data and is used for call setup and other signal control duties. Called the *data channel*, the channel actually carries no user data.

Deadlock   A situation in which two computers or two processes attempt to access a resource simultaneously, and both wait indefinitely for the other one to finish using the resource.

Delayed write   A method used in writing new or changed data to a network server's disks to improve overall performance. Data to be written is temporarily held in memory until the system is not busy (or for a set maximum amount of time), at which time the data is committed to the disk.

Dial-Up Networking (DUN)   A Microsoft term for a dial-up network connection over a modem.

Differential backup   A backup that copies all files with their archive bit set, and does not clear the archive bit when done.

Digital   A signaling method in which all signals are binary (1's and 0's only).

Digital signature   An authentication code embedded in a network message.

Direct cable connection   A serial (RS-232C) connection between two computers. You can also accomplish a direct cable connection between two Ethernet-equipped computers using a crossover RJ45 cable.

Directory   In the tree-shaped structure of a disk's filesystem, a logical container for files.

Disk mirroring   A method, also known as RAID 1, that writes data redundantly to two separate disks.

Domain   (1) On the Internet, a network identified by a name, such as yahoo.com. (2) On Microsoft Windows NT networks, the smallest administrative unit in a network.

Domain Name System (DNS)   An Internet system that resolves domain names to IP addresses.

Drive map   A method that uses a network directory to simulate a local drive letter (such as F: or G:) for a client computer.

DS0   A basic telephone line.

DS1   A digital telephone line used for both voice and data applications. A DS1 carries up to 1.544 Mbps of data, split across 28 separate channels, or carries up to 28 voice channels. Often called a *T-1 line*.

DS3   A digital telephone line that carries up to 44.736 Mbps of data. Often called a *T-3 line*.

Ethernet   A network standard that uses CSMA/CD methods to carry network data over many different types of media at many different speeds.

EtherTalk   An Apple protocol for connecting Macintosh computers to an Ethernet network.

Fast Ethernet   An Ethernet network that runs at 100 Mbps.

FAT   File allocation table. Table used by several operating systems to allocate space for files on physical disks.

Fiber Distributed Data Interface (FDDI)   A fiber-optic LAN that operates at 100 Mbps.

Fileserver   A network server that primarily is responsible for storing, sharing, and retrieving files for network clients.

File Transfer Protocol (FTP)   (1) An Internet protocol for copying files between two computers. (2) A program that uses the FTP protocol to do its job.

Firewall   A network device that protects a network from outside intruders.

Fractional T1   A T-1 telecommunications connection in which only some of the channels are leased for use.

Frame   A Data-Link layer unit of transmission in the OSI network model. Frames can be of variable length.

Frame Relay   A telecommunications server that carries asynchronous data between two points on a WAN. For efficiency, frame relay does not perform error detection and correction, leaving this task up to software on the two connected points.

Full backup   A process where all files on a network drive are copied to tape or other archival media. Each file's archive bit is cleared as part of a full backup.

Full-duplex   A connection in which both ends can transmit and receive simultaneously.

Gateway   A device that connects two networks together at all layers of the OSI network model. An example is an e-mail gateway that transmits e-mail from one network to another.

GB   Short for *gigabyte*, or 1 billion bytes.

Generational Backup   A tape-swapping methodology that gives good restoration granularity without consuming too many tapes. Also called the Grandfather/Father/Son method.

Half-Duplex (Simplex)   A connection in which only one end can transmit at a time.

Handshaking   Negotiating a connection and data transmission between two devices.

Header   Control information carried along with a file or a unit of network data, such as a packet.

HTML   Hypertext Markup Language, a formatting language used to format web pages.

HTTP   Hypertext Transfer Protocol, a network protocol used to retrieve web pages from a web server.

Hub   A network device that connects multiple nodes to a network segment.

IEEE   Institute of Electric and Electronics Engineering. A body that defines standards for electrical devices.

Incremental Backup   A backup method that backs up files that have their archive attribute set and then clears the archive attribute.

Internet   A worldwide public network of services for businesses and consumers.

Intranet   A company-specific network modeled after the Internet.

IPv6   Internet Protocol version 6, which increases the number of IP addresses available dramatically and includes other enhancements to the IP protocol.

IPX   A network protocol used with NetWare networks.

IRQ   Interrupt request line. A hardware switch in a computer that allows a device to signal the processor.

ISA bus   Industry Standard Architecture bus. A computer bus originally developed for the IBM PC-AT.

ISDN   Integrated Services Digital Network. A telecommunications standard for providing digital telephone services to consumers and businesses.

ISO   International Standards Organization. A body that defines many computer standards, including networking standards.

ISP   Internet service provider. A company that provides Internet services directly to businesses and/or consumers.

Java   A programming language, derived from C, that allows automation of Internet web pages.

KB   Kilobyte, or 1,024 bytes. KB represents 1,024 bytes instead of 1000 bytes because 1,024 is the closest binary-driven (powers of 2) number.

Key   A digital password used to sign electronic documents to guarantee their authenticity.

LAN   Local area network. A building-specific network.

LAN Manager   An older Microsoft network operating system.

Leased Line   A dedicated, always-on, telephone connection.

LocalTalk   An Apple networking system for connecting Macintoshes and Apple laser printers together on a low-speed (230-Kbps) network over twisted-pair wire.

Login   The process of providing account and authentication information (such as a password) to a computer or network to gain access to its resources.

Login Script   A set of commands that runs automatically when a user logs in to a computer or network.

MAC   Media Access Control. A sublayer of Layer 2 of the OSI networking model. IEEE 802.x networks divide up Layer 2 into a MAC layer and a logical link control (LLC) layer. The software at the MAC sublayer is unique to every different network media type. In other words, the MAC sublayer software for thin ethernet is different than the software used for twisted pair token ring.

MB   Megabyte, or 1,048,576 bytes.

MCA Bus   Microchannel Architecture bus. A computer bus standard introduced by IBM that was not widely accepted.

MCSE   Microsoft Certified System Engineer. A person who has completed a set of tests given by Microsoft to certify him or her as a networking engineer.

MHz   Megahertz, or 1 million Hertz (signals per second). Roughly equivalent to Mbps (million bits per second).

MIME   Multipurpose Internet Mail Extension. A standard for the attachment of binary data (attachments) to Internet e-mail messages. Also available as S/MIME, which is a secure form of MIME.

Modem   Modulator/demodulator. A device that allows digital signals to travel over an analog telephone line. Each end of the connection requires a modem.

MSAU   Multistation Access Unit. A hub used to connect Token Ring nodes together.

Multiplexing A technique that allows multiple signals to be aggregated onto a single channel.

Multiprocessor A computer, operating system, or application that uses more than one processor to accomplish its work.

Multitasking Running multiple programs simultaneously on a single computer.

NetBEUI NetBIOS Extended User Interface. An enhancement to the NetBIOS protocol.

NetBIOS Network Basic Input/Output System. An older and slower networking protocol originally developed by IBM.

NetWare A network operating system developed by Novell Corporation.

NetWare Core Protocol (NCP) An underlying protocol that manages server and workstation communications on a NetWare network.

NetWare Directory Service (NDS) A directory service for NetWare networks. NDS is also available from Novell as a tool to manage other types of servers, such as Solaris, Windows, and Unix.

Network layer Layer 3 of the OSI networking model. The network layer defines different packet protocols, such as IPX or IP.

Nibble Four bits.

NIC Network interface card. A peripheral card attached to a computer that lets it interface to a network.

NLM NetWare Loadable Module. A special program that runs only on NetWare servers.

Node A computer or device that is a distinct network entity, such as a computer or printer.

NOS Network operating system. An operating system that runs on network servers.

OSI   Open System Interconnection. A reference model that conceptually describes how networks work.

Packet   A collection of data sent as a single entity from one node on a network to another node.

Packet filtering   Examining packets coming into and going out of a network in order to prevent unauthorized traffic and to identify bottlenecks, failing hardware, and other network problems.

Partition   A logical division of a hard disk.

Patch Cable   A cable that connects between a patch panel and a network hub, or from a wall jack to a computer.

PCI   Peripheral Component Interconnect. A very fast bus introduced by Intel Corporation to allow high-speed communications between peripherals and the computer in which they are installed.

Peer-to-Peer Network   A network that spreads shareable resources among all of the client computers on the network. A peer-to-peer network has no central network servers.

Physical Layer   Layer 1 of the OSI networking model. The physical layer defines the specifications for the physical wiring of a network.

Point-to-Point Protocol (PPP)   An IP-specific protocol that enables remote nodes to connect to a network over telephone connections.

Post Office Protocol (POP)   A communications protocol for the exchange of e-mail over the Internet.

Presentation Layer   Layer 6 of the OSI networking model. The presentation layer "presents" network data to the system, and may include compression/decompression or encryption/decryption functions.

Primary Rate Interface (PRI)   An aggregation of ISDN B channels plus one D channel that provides 1.544 Mbps of network bandwidth through the telephone network.

Print Job   A unit of printing from a client computer to a network printer.

Print Queue   A place on a network server that accepts and accumulates user print jobs and then sends them to the network printer in sequence.

Print Server   A computer or dedicated device on a network that accepts jobs from print queues and sends them to the individual printers.

Protocol   A syntax for communication over a network.

RAID   Redundant array of inexpensive disks. A variety of methods that allow high-speed fail-safe arrays of disks to be used in concert.

Registry   A database used on Microsoft Windows operating systems that stores computer and user settings.

Remote Access (Node and Control)   The process of accessing a network from a remote computer, usually over a telephone line or sometimes through the Internet. Remote node access makes the remote computer a node on the network. Remote control access lets the remote computer "take control" of a computer that is already a local node on a network.

Remote Access Service (RAS)   A Windows NT service that provides remote node access to remote computers.

Repeater   A device that extends the distance that a network segment can be run.

Requestor   Special networking software that runs on a client computer that interfaces between the computer's operating system and the network operating system. Requestors are specific to each different type of NOS.

Ring Topology   An electrical arrangement of nodes on a network in a ring configuration.

RJ-45   A snap-in connector used with some kinds of network media, similar to modular telephone connectors (called RJ-11) used in homes, but larger.

Router   A device that routes network traffic from one network to another.

Routing Information Protocol (RIP)   A protocol that allows routers to communicate with each other to discover the best route between networks.

SCSI   Small Computer Systems Interface. A high-speed interface used primarily to interface hard disks to network servers.

Segment   An individual part of a network that connects two or more computers together.

Server   A computer on a network that provides some kind of network service to client computers.

Session Layer   Layer 5 of the OSI networking model. The session layer controls a persistent connection between two network devices or programs.

Share   A Windows NT or Unix shared directory, available for use over a network provided the user has permission.

SNMP   Simple Network Management Protocol. A protocol that enables special management software to manage network devices.

SMTP   Simple Mail Transfer Protocol. An Internet standard for the exchange of e-mail between systems on the Internet.

SPX   Sequenced Packet Exchange. A NetWare protocol used in concert with IPX.

Star Topology   A network arrangement in which individual cables connect a central hub to the nodes that it services.

Switch   An Ethernet device that switches traffic between two or more network segments.

TB   Terabyte, or 1 trillion bytes.

Token   An electrical signal circulated around Token Ring networks. Only the computer that "has the token" can transmit on the Token Ring network.

Token Ring   A network designed by IBM that uses a ring topology and circulates a token to manage traffic on the network.

Transceiver   A device that connects a computer to a network cable. Often transceivers are built into NIC cards.

Transmission Control Protocol/Internet Protocol (TCP/IP)   A standard network protocol used on the Internet and on many private networks.

Transport Layer   Layer 4 of the OSI networking model. The transport layer coordinates the packet exchange between network nodes. Examples of transport layer protocols are TCP and SPX.

Twisted Pair   Cable that uses small-gauge wires twisted together within a common sheath to carry network or telephone signals. Twisted-pair cable comes in unshielded (UTP) and shielded (STP) varieties.

UPS   Uninterruptible power supply. A battery-driven power supply that allows a server to continue operating when a building's power supply is cut off.

URL   Uniform Resource Locator. An address that allows a resource on the Internet to be located and accessed.

Virtual Private Network (VPN)   A secure, virtual network connection formed over a public network, such as the Internet.

Wiring Closet   A closet or room that brings together all of the cables needed for a building's network. Some buildings have separate wiring closets on each floor of the building, or for each 100 meters of horizontal distance.

Workstation   A generic computer client on a network. Sometimes also a high-powered computer used for engineering purposes.

Appendix B

Answers to Mastery Checks

Module 2: Laying the Foundation

1. **Hexadecimal refers to the base-___ numbering system.**

   Base-16

2. **Octal refers to the base-___ numbering system.**

   Base-8

3. **In the binary system, a single digit is called a _____. Eight of these strung together is called a _____.**

   A single digit is a *bit* (short for *binary digit*). Eight bits is a *byte*.

4. **What is the value of a number written as 1010 in each of the following numbering systems (express the answers in decimal—Base 10—notation)?**

   A. Decimal _____

   B. Binary _____

   C. Octal _____

   D. Hexadecimal _____

   A. 1,010.00; **B.** 10; **C.** 520; **D.** 4112

5. **What does the abbreviation Mbps mean? How is that different from MBps?**

   Mbps is millions (mega) of bits per second, while MBps is millions (mega) of bytes per second. 1 MBps is roughly eight times faster than 1 Mbps.

6. **Which is faster, 100 KHz or 0.1 Mbps?**

   100 KHz is 100,000 cycles per second. 0.1 Mbps is 100,000 bits per second. These two values are equal.

7. **Each position in the base-10 numbering system is a power of 10. What does each position in the hexadecimal numbering system represent?**

   Powers of 16

8. **If you needed to transfer 562,000 bytes over a connection running at 56Kbps, how long would the transfer take?**

   Multiply 562,000 bytes by 8 to get the number of bits, or 4,496,000. Then, divide the total number of bits to be transferred by the bits per second, in this case 56,000, to yield approximately 80 seconds. (When you use this method, you will usually only approximate the actual time, because error checking, which consumes part of the bandwidth, sporadic slow-downs, or collisions in the connection can't easily be estimated.)

9. **True or false: Numbering systems can be created using any base that one wishes.**

   True

10. Four bits together is called a _____.

Nibble

Module 3: Understanding Networking

1. The lowest level of the OSI Model is called the _____ layer. It describes how which of the following things work?

A. Keyboards and mice

B. Disk drives

C. Network cable

D. Network routers

   C. Physical layer; **C** (Network Cable) is defined at the physical layer.

2. The two main types of relationships between computers on a network are called _____ and _____.

Client/server and peer-to-peer

3. The OSI Model is divided into ____ layers. It was developed by the _____ in 1983.

Seven layers, created by the ISO (International Standards Organization)

4. Which of the following are advantages of client/server network systems relative to peer-to-peer network systems?

A. They are more secure.

B. They cost less.

C. It is harder to back up the stored data.

D. They provide centralized management of a network's resources.

   A and **D** are the correct answers.

5. Which of the following distinguishes a server-class computer from a standard desktop computer?

A. Faster processor

B. Faster graphics rendering

C. Faster disk drives

D. Redundancy, such as in the power supplies or cooling fans

   A, **C**, and **D** are the correct answers.

6. **Client/server network systems should not be confused with client/server _____ systems.**

    Client/server networks should not be confused with client/server database systems.

7. **A connection between a LAN and the Internet *requires* which of the following hardware?**

    A. Firewall

    B. Router

    C. CSU/DSU

    D. Server computer

    B and **C** are the correct answers.

8. **Cat-3 network cable supports __Base-T networks, while Cat5 network cable supports ___Base-T networks.**

    Cat3 supports 10Base-T, while Cat5 supports 100Base-T.

9. **What is the main difference between a hub and a switch?**

    On a hub, all of the connected nodes share one logical network connection and are said to be on the same collision domain. On a switch, each connection is always point-to-point with no interference for nodes not part of any given connection.

10. **True or false: One can change the technology at any particular OSI network layer without affecting the higher layers in any way.**

    True. This means that one can continue to run IP (Layer 3) over a variety of Layer 2 technologies, such as Ethernet, ArcNET, Token Ring, and so forth, with no changes required to IP itself.

Module 4: Understanding Network Cabling

1. **What are the three main network topologies?**

    Bus, star, and ring

2. **What is an inherent advantage that Token Ring has over Ethernet?**

    It is impossible to have data collisions on a Token Ring network, and therefore they behave predictably as the load on them increases.

3. **When cabling a new network, what type of cable should you choose to run in most cases?**

    Category 5e cable is the wisest choice.

4. **You would choose fiber-optic cable when you need to _____.**

    Span distances greater than twisted pair or coaxial cable can handle, such as connecting together buildings that are more than 100 meters apart.

5. **BNC connectors are used with what type of Ethernet network cable?**

   10Base-2 Thin Ethernet

6. **What is the modular connector used with 100Base-T networks called?**

   RJ-45

7. **From the name 100Base-T, you can know which of the following statements are true?**

   A. It is for a broadband network.

   B. It uses twisted-pair cable.

   C. It operates at 0.1 Gbps.

   D. It uses BNC connectors.

   B and **C** are true. The 'Base' in the name refers to *baseband* and not *broadband* and it uses RJ-45 connectors. (**C** is true because 0.1 Gbps is the same as 100 Mbps.)

8. **You need to understand the 5-4-3 rule for what type of network? What does the 5-4-3 rule mean?**

   Thin Ethernet (10Base-2) networks use the 5-4-3 rule. It means five segments, four repeaters, three populated segments.

9. **True or false: A Token Ring network is logically and physically arranged in a ring configuration.**

   False. Logically it is a ring, but physically it is wired in a star configuration.

10. **True or false: 1000Base-T networks require fiber optic cable.**

    False; the 'T' refers to twisted pair, and one big benefit of the 1000Base-T standard is that it allows 1 Gbps bandwidth over Category 5 twisted pair cable.

Module 5: Network Hardware

1. **Two main types of firewalls exist, those that use _____ and those that use _____.**

   Network-based and application-based

2. **A gateway is used to make a connection where which layers of the OSI Model are dissimilar?**

   Gateways can connect two systems where *any* of the layers of the OSI Model are dissimilar.

3. **True or false: Repeaters examine packets passing between the two networks that they connect and decide whether or not to pass them along based on their destination address.**

   False. The description in the question applies to routers, not repeaters.

4. **Which of the following statements about hubs are true?**

   A. Each node connected to a hub is on its own private collision domain.

   B. Hubs can typically automatically sense a node's connection speed and adjust accordingly.

   C. Hubs are only available within stackable 24-port configurations.

   D. A hub is also called an Intelligent LAN Concentrator.

   B and **D** are true.

5. **True or false: Hubs are always physically wired in a ring configuration.**

   False. Hubs are always physically wired in a star configuration.

6. **If a network is designed with a backbone that runs at a faster speed than the hubs, the backbone typically runs at ____ times the speed of the hubs.**

   Ten

7. **The Internet predominantly uses what type of device to form its various connections?**

   Routers are used extensively to form the Internet's connections.

8. **True or false: A firewall's sole job is to enforce network security policies that you create.**

   True

9. **True or false: A router becomes a node on the network to which it connects.**

   True

10. **Indicate which of the following protocols are able to be routed through a router: Appletalk, NetBIOS, NetBEUI, TCP/IP, and IPX/SPX.**

    Appletalk, NetBIOS, and NetBEUI are not routable, while TCP/IP and IPX/SPX are routable.

Module 6: Making Network Connections

1. **DS1 and DS3 connections are more commonly called _____ and _____.**

   T-1 and T-3

2. **True or false: The theoretical maximum speed of POTS when analog lines are at each end of the connection is 64 Kbps.**

   False. The maximum theoretical analog POTS data speed using modems is 33 Kbps.

3. **True or false: An ISDN BRI connection typically uses three data channels and one bearer channel.**

   False. A BRI connection is almost always 2B + D or 2 bearer channels plus 1 data channel.

4. **True or false: An ISDN PRI connection operates at speeds similar to DS1/T-1.**

True

5. **True or false: WAN links are usually much less expensive than LAN links.**

False. WAN links are usually much more expensive than LAN links.

6. **To keep transmitted data secure over a public network, you can use _____ technology.**

VPN, short for Virtual Private Network

7. **Two main types of connection types are switched and _____.**

Dedicated

8. **POTS is an acronym that stands for _____.**

Plain Old Telephone Service

9. **The most common form of xDSL is _____.**

Asymmetric DSL (ADSL)

10. **Data transfer needs tend to be either synchronous or _____.**

Asynchronous

Module 7: Understanding Network Protocols

1. **What are the following protocols used for?**

A. SMTP

B. DHCP

C. DNS

D. TCP/IP

SMTP is used for e-mail transmission, DHCP is used for allocating TCP/IP addresses dynamically, DNS is used for converting URL names into their corresponding TCP/IP address, and TCP/IP is used to carry data over a network.

2. **TCP/IP addresses are composed of _____ parts, called _____.**

Four parts, called octets; also correct is two parts, called the netid and the hostid.

3. **To take a range of TCP/IP addresses, such as a Class C, and subdivide it, you use _____.**

Subnetting

4. **Which of the following protocols are routable, assuming an appropriate router is in place?**

   A. TCP/IP

   B. IPX/SPX

   C. NetBIOS

   D. NetBEUI

   A and **B** are routable.

5. **FTP stands for both _____ and _____.**

   File Transfer Protocol and File Transfer Program

6. **A single computer that uses TCP/IP internally routes incoming data to the appropriate service or program through the use of _____.**

   TCP/IP ports

7. **DNS stands for _____.**

   Domain Name System

8. **Web pages are transmitted using a protocol called _____, which stands for _____.**

   HTTP, Hypertext Transfer Protocol

9. **Every TCP/IP address always has a corresponding _____ that indicates which part of the address is the netid, and which is the hostid.**

   Subnet mask

10. **A TCP/IP address range that fixes the first two octets and leaves the remaining two octets open for the user to allocate is called a Class ___ address.**

   Class B

Module 8: Exploring Directory Services

1. **As a user of a network, a directory service on a network is primarily useful for _____.**

   Finding network resources

2. **As a network administrator, a directory service on a network is primarily useful for _____.**

   Centrally administering network resources

3. **True or false: Windows NT domains are full directory services.**

   False. While NT domains have some of the properties of a directory service, they are not considered a full directory service.

4. **True or false: Novell's eDirectory directory service can be used to manage Windows NT and Windows 2000 servers, as well as Linux and Solaris servers.**

   True

5. **LDAP stands for _____.**

   Lightweight Directory Access Protocol

6. **The LDAP protocol is based on the _____ directory service.**

   The X.500 directory service

7. **Which of the following are benefits of the LDAP directory service relative to the X.500 directory service?**

   A. LDAP has many more features than X.500.

   B. LDAP enjoys broad support by other directory services that are often compatible with LDAP.

   C. LDAP is simpler and easier to implement than X.500

   B and **C** are the correct answers.

8. **True or false: It is often a good idea to run directory services on multiple servers, so that redundancy exists.**

   True

9. **Microsoft's Active Directory handles redundancy using a _____ approach.**

   Multimaster

10. **Microsoft's Windows NT domains handle redundancy using a _____ approach.**

    Primary/slave (also called Primary/backup)

Module 9: Connections from Afar: Remote Network Access

1. **True or false: It is often easy to find one good remote access solution that will meet the needs of all the users needing remote access.**

   False. Typically different types of remote users will need different remote access solutions.

2. **True or false: Client/server applications are typically more amenable than monolithic applications to being used over a remote access connection.**

   True. Client/server applications are often less bandwidth-intensive than their monolithic counterparts.

3. **The three things that most remote users need are _____, _____, and _____.**

   Access to e-mail, access to files, and access to a LAN-connected application

4. **When you are connecting to the Internet using a dialup line, you are typically using a remote_____ type of connection.**

   Node

5. **When you are remotely controlling a computer program running at a distant site, you are typically using a remote_____ type of connection.**

   Control

6. **Name two situations in which remote control connections are best (compared to remote node connections).**

   1) An application requires high-bandwidth access to the LAN. 2) The administrator needs to centrally manage all aspects of the application and, therefore, needs all of it to run on the LAN.

7. **Name four reasons you should consider using an ISP for dialup access, having users access the LAN through the company's high-speed Internet connection.**

   1) No need to support any modems yourself, directly. 2) No long-distance tolls for connections. 3) The remote users can take advantage of a high-speed connection between the Internet and the LAN. For example, if the remote user has a DSL or cable modem connection to the Internet, they will also have a high-speed connection to the company LAN through the company's high-speed Internet link. 4) Better global services through large ISPs.

8. **VPNs work by taking advantage of an existing network connection (usually over the Internet) and then creating an encrypted _____ through which the data packets pass.**

   Tunnel

9. **True or false: IPSec is limited to only TCP/IP traffic, while PPP and L2TP can both handle a variety of different network protocols in addition to TCP/IP.**

   True. PPP and L2TP can both handle NetBEUI, IPX/SPX, and AppleTalk in addition to TCP/IP.

10. **You can set up a simple (but functional) VPN service using _____ software included with _____operating system.**

   The Routing and Remote Access Service (RRAS) included with Windows NT (SP3 or greater) or Windows 2000.

Module 10: Securing Your Network

1. **Which is the more common threat for which you need to plan network security: internal or external?**

   Internal threats are typically much more common than external threats.

2. **What steps should you take with a network operating system's default Guest and Administrator accounts?**

   Disable any Guest accounts and rename the Administrator account to something less obvious. Also, create a backup administrative account.

3. **True or false: The strictest security settings you can set in your network are always the best for overall security.**

   False. Security settings that are too strict can cause users to bypass the security (for example, by writing their passwords down), leaving your network less secure.

4. **An attack that makes part or all of a network unusable is called a _____.**

   Denial of Service attack (DoS)

5. **True or false: To protect against computer viruses, you only need to run antivirus software on your network's desktop computers.**

   False. The most important places to run antivirus software are on any e-mail servers, network fileservers, and if possible, the network's firewall or router.

6. **True or false: It is better to keep any web servers you maintain for use by the outside world outside your demilitarized zone.**

   False. Public web servers should be *inside* the DMZ, which is immediately outside the network's security firewall.

7. **In typical file access permissions, what is the difference between change rights and full-control rights?**

   Full-control rights allow the user to grant rights to others.

8. **True or false: A good security program can make virtually any network completely secure.**

   False. No network is ever completely secure.

9. **When an outside person tries to learn a user's account name and password by, for example, posing as a network support person on the telephone, the practice is called _____.**

   Social engineering

10. **A device or computer that sits between two networks and enforces a security policy between those two networks is called a _____.**

Firewall

Module 11: Network Disaster Recovery

1. **What is meant by the term "backup rotation granularity"?**

The time points available for a backup rotation scheme as you try to go back further in time. For example, in a G-F-S scheme, you can restore from any day of the week for the preceding week, or for any Friday for the preceding three weeks, or for any month ending earlier than a month prior.

2. **True or false: If a network's servers are running fine, backups are unnecessary.**

False. Backups are *always* important.

3. **Name five concerns that a disaster recovery plan should address.**

A disaster recovery plan should address communication issues, off-site storage, types of disasters, detailed recovery plans, and key equipment.

4. **How many times are DLT tapes rated to be able to be used?**

One million times (and with a 30-year shelf life)

5. **What is the most common backup rotation scheme called?**

Grandfather-father-son

6. **For a network server that employs _____, backup tapes are actually the second level of defense against hardware failure.**

RAID disk drives configured to provide some redundancy.

7. **A backup that backs up all files with the archive bit set, but leaves the archive bit unchanged is called a _____ backup.**

Differential. If the backup clears the archive bit, it's called an *incremental backup*.

8. **True or false: High-end databases can have their files backed up just like the files of any other application.**

False. Such applications almost always need to have their files backed up and restored using procedures described in detail by the database maker.

9. **There are two newer tape technologies that are successors to DLT and that have higher capacities. They are called _____ and _____.**

Super DLT (SDLT) and Ultrium

10. **True or false: One of the most important topics to address in a disaster recovery plan is communications.**

True. In fact, without an effective communications plan, a disaster recovery plan is incomplete and will be inadequate to address a real disaster.

Module 12: Purchasing and Managing Server Hardware

1. **True or false: All servers benefit from having multiple processors installed.**

False. Many servers receive absolutely no benefit from more than one processor. For instance, some servers (and some server-based applications) cannot make use of more than one processor.

2. **Describe what the following RAID levels do:**

A. RAID 0

B. RAID 1

C. RAID 5

RAID 0 stripes data across multiple disk drives. RAID 1 mirrors data between two disk drives. RAID 5 stripes data across multiple disk drives, but also stripes redundancy data that can protect data in the event of a drive failure.

3. **Name three things that server state monitoring can track.**

Any three of the following items: proper fan operation; system voltage; memory errors, even if corrected by ECC memory; disk errors, even if corrected automatically; in-case temperature; operating system hangs; computer case opening.

4. **Which type of RAM offers a greater degree of safety from data loss: parity or ECC?**

ECC (Error Checking and Correcting) memory offers the greatest degree of safety.

5. **Which of the following disk technologies offers the highest performance?**

A. Ultra160 SCSI

B. Ultra2 SCSI

C. EIDE

D. Wide-SCSI

A is the correct answer. Ultra160 SCSI is the fastest within the list.

6. **Generally speaking, how much improvement in server processor performance does doubling the number of processors in a server gain?**

   A. 25 percent

   B. 50 percent

   C. 100 percent

   D. 200 percent

   B is the correct answer. Generally, a doubling of processors yields a 50 percent improvement in overall speed. This result is highly variable and depends on the server application, however.

7. **Which of the following methods is the best way to determine how many processors you need in a server for a given task?**

   A. Use one processor for every 250 users

   B. Keep adding processors until the processor utilization drops to 15 percent for each processor while load is placed on the server

   C. Ask the vendor of the main server application or other users of the same application about their experience with the application and how their server is configured

   D. For a 10MHz network, use one processor, for 100MHz, use two processors, and for 1GHz, use four processors

   C is the best choice in almost all cases. Actual experience is always the best guide for making decisions such as this.

8. **In a server computer, what does a "bus" do?**

   A computer bus (whether in a server or workstation) acts as a central transfer mechanism for all data in a computer. While sometimes there are multiple busses in a computer, there is generally only one main "highway" through which all data on a system passes.

9. **True or false: For a server, the best type of RAM to use is parity RAM.**

   False. ECC memory is the best, followed by parity RAM.

10. **True or false: For most servers, you're fine using IDE-based disk subsystems.**

    False. Most server functions benefit greatly from SCSI-based disk subsystems.

Module 13: Purchasing and Managing Client Computers

1. **Generally speaking, computer capabilities double every ____ to ____ months.**

   18 to 24 months

2. **True or false: You are better off running the wrong desktop computer platform than running two desktop computer platforms.**

   True, if possible in a given environment.

3. **Generally, Macs make sense in companies that have a strong _____ or _____ bent.**

   Graphical or publishing bent

4. **True or false: The purchase price of a computer represents the main portion of its lifetime cost.**

   False. The purchase price of a computer represents a small portion of its lifetime cost.

5. **True or false: The most important consideration when purchasing a desktop computer is getting the lowest price.**

   False. The most important consideration is getting a computer that meets the needs to which it will be put. Price should never drive the selection of a computer.

6. **True or false: If a computer uses the best components available, you are assured of a highly capable and reliable computer.**

   False. Even the best components need to be set up to work harmoniously and reliably together.

7. **Serviceability is the assessment of the ease of _____ a computer system.**

   Working on or servicing

8. **True or false: When you install a network workstation, you should choose to install all of the available networking software for the operating system in question.**

   False. Installing superfluous networking software (such as protocols that aren't in use on the network) only unnecessarily complicates the computer's environment, and will typically reduce performance and increase problems.

9. **The general average useful life of most desktop computers is around ____ to _____ years.**

   It's a very general rule of thumb, but typically three to four years.

10. **TCO is an abbreviation standing for _____.**

    Total cost of ownership

Module 14: Designing a Network

1. **The most important task when designing a network is _____.**

   Assessing needs

2. Most networks are built

A. All at once

B. Slowly, piece by piece, over time

    B is the correct answer.

3. When designing a network from scratch, you should estimate how the needs will change over (choose all correct answers):

A. One year

B. Three years

C. Five years

D. Ten years

    A, **B**, and **C** are the correct answers. (It never hurts to also estimate for D if you have enough information to do so!)

4. True or false: When designing a network, you should assess how critical the data stored on the network will be for the company, and how the use of the network will impact the company's ability to accomplish its goals.

    True

5. An accounting system designed around _____ needs a different network design than one using a _____ design.

    Client/server; monolithic

6. Know the number of _____ in the company as well as the company's total number of users.

    Number of users in each department or functional area

7. True or false: Dynamic Host Configuration Protocol (DHCP) is a network service that requires such little overhead that you can easily host it on a server that does other jobs.

    True

8. True or false: For most new networks, you almost certainly will decide to use one of the flavors of Ethernet.

    True

9. True or false: When choosing servers for PC-centric networks, the decision is usually between Novell NetWare 5 and Windows 2000 Server.

    True

B

Answers to Mastery Checks

10. To achieve maximum speed for a network for minimal incremental cost, you should always consider designing the backbone to run at _____ times the speed of the individual node connections.

Ten times

Module 15: Installing and Setting Up Windows 2000 Server

1. Which of the following are valid Windows 2000 Server configurations?

A. Member server

B. Domain Controller

C. Domain partner

D. Stand-alone server

E. Primary Domain Controller

A, **B**, and **D** (E is incorrect because Primary Domain Controllers only existed under Windows NT Server 4).

2. In what general circumstances does Microsoft recommend choosing either Per Seat client licensing or Per Server client licensing?

When using one server in a network, choose Per Server. When you expect to have more than one server, choose Per Seat.

3. True or false: All Windows 2000 Server's file and folder security features are available on the FAT32 file system.

False. Most file and folder security features require NTFS.

4. Name the three different server versions of Windows 2000 Server.

Windows 2000 Standard Server, Windows 2000 Advanced Server, and Windows 2000 Datacenter Server

5. Prior to setting up a new server, you should spend 1–2 weeks performing a

_____.

Server hardware burn-in testing process

6. True or false: You can install Windows 2000 Server as an in-place upgrade to Netware 5 or Netware 6.

False. Only Windows NT 3.51 or 4.0 can be upgraded directly to Windows 2000 Server.

7. **True or false: The Administrator account is a temporary account used only for the initial setup of Windows 2000 Server.**

   False. The Administrator account is needed for day-to-day administration on the server.

8. **Prior to installing Windows 2000 Server as an in-place upgrade from Windows NT, you should first perform both a _____ and _____.**

   Server survey and at least one pre-upgrade backup

9. **How much available disk space do you need to install Windows 2000 Server?**

   About 1 GB

10. **What is the name of the resource that lets you know whether a computer is compatible with Windows 2000 Server?**

    The Hardware Compatibility List (HCL) found at http://www.microsoft.com/hcl

Module 16: Administering Windows 2000 Server: The Basics

1. **You administer user accounts in Windows 2000 Server using the program called _____.**

   Active Directory Users and Computers

2. **True or false: To temporarily disable a user account, you must delete it and then re-create it later.**

   False. Instead, use the Disable Account feature.

3. **True or false: Under a Windows 2000 Active Directory domain, security groups can be members of other groups.**

   True

4. **You can set security permissions on files and folders only on _____-formatted partitions.**

   NTFS

5. **If a user has Full Control permission explicitly set on a folder, but they are also a member of a group that has the No Access permission, what permissions do they have in that folder?**

   They have No Access. The No Access permission always wins over other permissions, even if the other permissions are explicit and the No Access permission is inherited.

6. **How can you create a share but make it invisible to browsing on the network, but still usable for those that know its name and who have the proper permissions to the share?**

   Create the share name with a dollar sign ($) appended to the name, such as the name SHARE$.

7. **Describe what printer pooling does.**

Printer pooling lets you designate multiple identical printers to service a single print queue; each printer alternates in servicing each job that is sent to the single printer queue.

8. **True or false: You must purchase special backup software to make backups of a Windows 2000 Server.**

While many network administrators use third-party backup programs such as Arcserve or Backup Exec, Windows 2000 Server includes a program called Backup that is adequate for straightforward backup needs.

9. **You can perform many network-related tasks using a powerful command-line program called _____.**

The NET command (type NET HELP for basic instruction).

10. **When you set an account to "Account Disabled" status, how long does it take to propagate the change to all of the domain controllers in a large network?**

Because the Account Disabled status is a high-priority change, all domain controllers are immediately informed of this setting, and the change takes place instantly.

Module 17: Understanding Other Windows 2000 Server Services

1. **When a DHCP server assigns a TCP/IP address to a client computer, the address is said to be _____.**

Leased

2. **Active Directory requires which of the services discussed in this module to function properly?**

DNS is required for Active Directory.

3. **To provide remote control administration or remote control applications for a server, you would install _____.**

Windows Terminal Services

4. **Windows 2000 Server can act as an FTP server if you install _____.**

Internet Information Server (IIS)

5. **The service that can provide WINS services in addition to its core service is _____.**

DNS can provide WINS services.

6. **To provide remote node access to a server, you would install _____.**

Remote Access Service (RAS)

7. A _____ can create many virtual Windows machines, each one carrying out its own tasks and running its own programs.

Terminal Server

8. True or false: You should use DHCP only for client computers not hosting any TCP/IP services that are provided to other computers.

True

9. RRAS includes routing capabilities that enable connections to the network over a public network using _____ technology.

Virtual Private Network (VPN)

10. Network load balancing clusters enable you to share TCP/IP-based services among up to __ Windows 2000 servers.

32

Module 18: Windows .NET Server

1. The four editions of the .NET Server family are called _____, _____, _____, and _____.

Standard, Enterprise, Datacenter, and Web

2. If you are setting up a server to host your company's intranet, which edition of .NET Server should you choose and why?

You would choose the Web edition. By using a focused edition, your costs will be lower and the server will perform its dedicated function more effectively.

3. In .NET Server, Active Directory can now replicate up to _____ servers, up from the limit of 200 servers in the Windows 2000 Server family.

.NET Server's AD can replicate up to 5,000 AD servers.

4. What new feature of .NET Server would you use to prepare to recover your server from a catastrophic failure?

Automated System Recovery (ASR), part of the backup program.

5. What is the name of the new feature of .NET Server that allows users to recover previous versions of their documents?

Volume Shadow Restore is the feature used by users to recover their previous versions, while Volume Shadow Copy is the feature that runs on the server and creates the shadow copy images from which Volume Shadow Restore operates.

6. **True or false: In .NET Server, Internet Information Services enables all services, but provides a wizard that lets you selectively turn off potential security holes.**

   False. IIS's default settings is to *disable* all services, and the Lockdown wizard lets you selectively turn on potential security holes.

7. **True or false: Windows .NET Server supports Internet Protocol version 6 (IPv6).**

   True

8. **To prepare a server to function in different roles, you use the program _____.**

   You use the Configure Your Server wizard.

9. **To keep a .NET Server as secure as possible from various network or Internet threats, you would configure its _____.**

   Internet connection firewall

10. **True or false: To schedule automated backups in .NET Server, you must run the msbackup.exe program from the command line and use the AT command for scheduling.**

    False. The backup program in .NET Server now has a built-in graphical scheduling feature.

Module 19: Installing Linux in a Server Configuration

1. **True or false: You can set up a computer to boot to both Windows and Linux.**

   True

2. **If you need to reconfigure a hard disk that presently has all space devoted to a Windows FAT-formatted partition, you can nondestructively repartition the disk using a Red Hat Linux tool called _____.**

   fips

3. **The easiest way to install Linux on a computer is to install it from**

   A. Diskettes

   B. A bootable CD-ROM drive

   C. A network directory

      B is correct.

4. **When installing Red Hat Linux onto a machine that will be dedicated to its use, you will typically need at least two partitions: one for _____ and the other for _____.**

   Holding all the files, swap space

5. **The boot manager for Red Hat Linux 7 systems is called _____.**

   LILO

6. **True or false: You must design a server *not* to be friendly to casual users.**

   True

7. **When installing Red Hat Linux 6 or 7, you have two ways to start the boot process: You can use _____ or _____.**

   A boot floppy disk or the CD-ROM

8. **True or false: Under Linux, the most significant grouping of files happens in the /home directory, where all of the actual programs reside.**

   False (/usr is correct)

9. **For each network interface card, you can configure it by either _____ or _____.**

   Using DHCP or setting the IP address by hand

10. **True or false: Running a server without ever starting the graphical environment is often a good idea.**

    True

Module 20: Introduction to Linux Systems Administration

1. **Most Red Hat Linux administrative tasks can be accomplished using a graphical tool called _____.**

   Linuxconf

2. **The most powerful account on a Linux system is called**

   A. Administrator

   B. Admin

   C. Root

   D. Supervisor

   C is correct.

3. **You can manually control the mapping of host names to IP addresses by editing a text file called _____.**

   /etc/hosts

4. **The _____ command lists your current environment.**

   printenv

5. The _____ command lists files in a directory (like the DOS DIR command).

ls

6. The _____ command (like the DOS TYPE command) displays the contents of a file.

cat (the answer "more" is also correct, but pauses for every screen)

7. The main command to get help on Linux commands is

A. Help

B. man

C. Doc

D. ? (question mark)

   B is correct.

8. The Linux equivalent of the DOS COPY command is _____.

cp (stands for copy)

9. The Linux equivalent of the DOS RENAME (REN) command is _____.

mv (stands for move)

10. To see what directory you are in on a Linux system, type _____.

pwd (stands for print working directory)

Module 21: Setting Up a Linux Web Server with Apache

1. The main web site from which you can download Apache, various modules, fixes, and so forth is

_____.

http://www.apache.org

2. True or false: The most prevalent web server on the Internet today is Microsoft's Internet Information Server (IIS).

False. As of mid-2002, Apache runs more web sites than all other web servers combined.

3. When Apache is running and you execute the ps –e command, you will see a number of processes called _____.

httpd

4. Apache is controlled primarily through a configuration file called _____.

httpd.conf, located by default in the /usr/local/apache2/conf/ directory

5. **You start, stop, and restart Apache using the command _____.**

   /usr/local/apache2/bin/apachectl start | stop | restart

6. **After making changes to Apache's main configuration file, what must you do for the changes to take effect?**

   Restart Apache using the command /usr/local/apache2/bin/apachectl restart

7. **True or false: Apache runs only under Linux.**

   False. Apache runs under many operating systems, including Linux, Windows NT/2000, OS/2, Mac OS X, Netware, and Solaris.

8. **What actions do you perform to publish web pages to an Apache server?**

   Place the pages that compose the web site into the folder /usr/local/apache2/htdocs. You do this either by using ftp to place the files there, or by using some other file-copying mechanism in Linux (such as the cp and mv commands, or through a Linux graphical file manager) to place the files in that directory. It is a good idea to restart the Apache server after you have updated the web files, although this isn't strictly necessary.

9. **True or false: If you install Red Hat Linux in its "server" configuration, Apache is automatically installed.**

   True

10. **The program httpd is called a background _____.**

    Daemon (pronounced just like "demon")

Index

INTERNATIONAL CONTACT INFORMATION

AUSTRALIA
McGraw-Hill Book Company Australia Pty. Ltd.
TEL +61-2-9900-1800
FAX +61-2-9878-8881
http://www.mcgraw-hill.com.au
books-it_sydney@mcgraw-hill.com

CANADA
McGraw-Hill Ryerson Ltd.
TEL +905-430-5000
FAX +905-430-5020
http://www.mcgraw-hill.ca

**GREECE, MIDDLE EAST, & AFRICA
(Excluding South Africa)**
McGraw-Hill Hellas
TEL +30-1-656-0990-3-4
FAX +30-1-654-5525

MEXICO (Also serving Latin America)
McGraw-Hill Interamericana Editores S.A. de C.V.
TEL +525-117-1583
FAX +525-117-1589
http://www.mcgraw-hill.com.mx
fernando_castellanos@mcgraw-hill.com

SINGAPORE (Serving Asia)
McGraw-Hill Book Company
TEL +65-863-1580
FAX +65-862-3354
http://www.mcgraw-hill.com.sg
mghasia@mcgraw-hill.com

SOUTH AFRICA
McGraw-Hill South Africa
TEL +27-11-622-7512
FAX +27-11-622-9045
robyn_swanepoel@mcgraw-hill.com

SPAIN
McGraw-Hill/Interamericana de España, S.A.U.
TEL +34-91-180-3000
FAX +34-91-372-8513
http://www.mcgraw-hill.es
professional@mcgraw-hill.es

**UNITED KINGDOM, NORTHERN,
EASTERN, & CENTRAL EUROPE**
McGraw-Hill Education Europe
TEL +44-1-628-502500
FAX +44-1-628-770224
http://www.mcgraw-hill.co.uk
computing_neurope@mcgraw-hill.com

ALL OTHER INQUIRIES Contact:
Osborne/McGraw-Hill
TEL +1-510-549-6600
FAX +1-510-883-7600
http://www.osborne.com
omg_international@mcgraw-hill.com